To Wayne

James H. Keeffe

"Happy Birthday!!"

Two Gold Coins and a Prayer

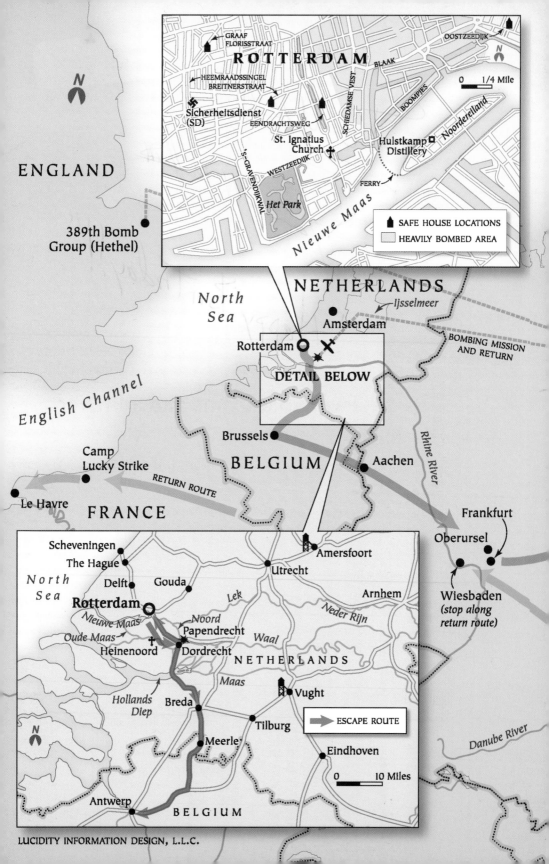

Rotterdam Detail (Inset, Top)

N

GRAAF FLORISSTRAAT

ROTTERDAM

BLAAK

OOSTZEEDIJK

HEEMRAADSSINGEL
BREITNERSTRAAT

SCHIEDAMSE VEST

BOOMPJES

0   1/4 Mile

Sicherheitsdienst
(SD)

EENDRACHTSWEG

St. Ignatius
Church ✝

Hulstkamp
Distillery ☐ Noordereiland

'S-GRAVENDIJKWAL

WESTZEEDIJK

FERRY

Het Park

Nieuwe Maas

■ SAFE HOUSE LOCATIONS
☐ HEAVILY BOMBED AREA

Main Map

N

ENGLAND

389th Bomb
Group (Hethel)

*North
Sea*

NETHERLANDS

Ijsselmeer

Amsterdam

Rotterdam ◎

✕

DETAIL BELOW

BOMBING MISSION
AND RETURN

English Channel

Camp
Lucky Strike

Brussels

BELGIUM

Aachen

Rhine River

RETURN ROUTE

Le Havre

FRANCE

Frankfurt

Oberursel

Wiesbaden
*(stop along
return route)*

Escape Route Detail (Inset, Bottom)

Scheveningen

The Hague

*North
Sea*

Delft

Gouda

Amersfoort

Utrecht

Arnhem

Rotterdam ◎

Nieuwe Maas

Noord
Papendrecht

Lek

Neder Rijn

Oude Maas

Heinenoord ✝

Dordrecht

Waal

NETHERLANDS

*Hollands
Diep*

Breda

Maas

Vught

N

Tilburg

Meerle

Eindhoven

Danube River

ESCAPE ROUTE

0   10 Miles

Antwerp

BELGIUM

LUCIDITY INFORMATION DESIGN, L.L.C.

Lt. Keeffe's Wartime Odyssey

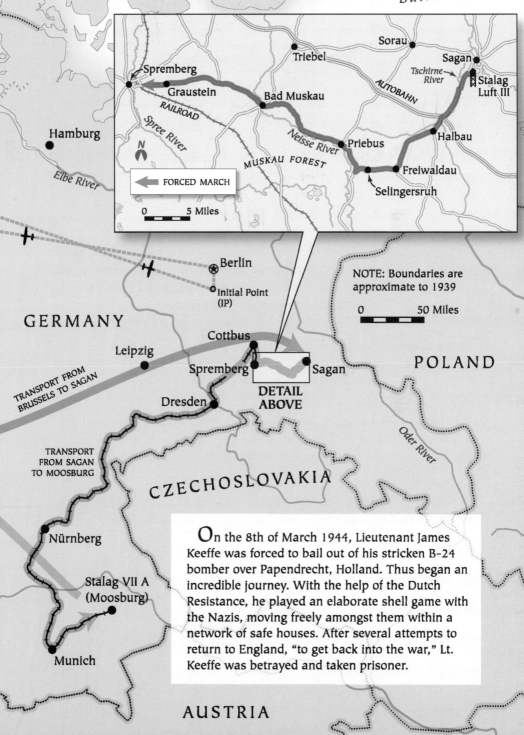

Baltic Sea

Detail (inset map):
Sorau
Triebel
Sagan
Spremberg
Tschirne River
Stalag Luft III
Graustein
Bad Muskau
AUTOBAHN
RAILROAD
Spree River
Neisse River
Priebus
Halbau
Hamburg
N
MUSKAU FOREST
Freiwaldau
FORCED MARCH
Selingersruh
0   5 Miles

Elbe River

Berlin
Initial Point (IP)

NOTE: Boundaries are approximate to 1939

0   50 Miles

GERMANY

Cottbus

Leipzig

Spremberg
Sagan
POLAND

TRANSPORT FROM BRUSSELS TO SAGAN

DETAIL ABOVE

Dresden

Oder River

TRANSPORT FROM SAGAN TO MOOSBURG

CZECHOSLOVAKIA

Nürnberg

Stalag VII A (Moosburg)

On the 8th of March 1944, Lieutenant James Keeffe was forced to bail out of his stricken B-24 bomber over Papendrecht, Holland. Thus began an incredible journey. With the help of the Dutch Resistance, he played an elaborate shell game with the Nazis, moving freely amongst them within a network of safe houses. After several attempts to return to England, "to get back into the war," Lt. Keeffe was betrayed and taken prisoner.

Munich

AUSTRIA

Praise for
Two Gold Coins and a Prayer

"This book stands as a solid, proven first person account of the widespread courage of those forced under the boot heel of Nazi Germany, from the oppressed northern European citizenry to the imprisoned Allied [airmen]."
— Dennis D. Bailey, *The US Review of Books*

"[One of] the rare, precious memoirs that are well-researched, historically correct, and honestly portray the wartime experiences of men who accomplished great things all the while retaining the foibles which plague all human beings."
— James R. Lankford, National Historian, 14th Armored Division

"As I read of your father's joys and ordeals, it was as though I were there with him. The documentation and illustrations are excellent!"
— Sgt. John Rhodes, Operation Clerk, 389th Bomb Group

"This was far and away one of the best 8th Air Force evasion and POW accounts that has ever been written…I give it my highest recommendation."
— Mark Copeland, *8th Air Force News* Historian and Editor

"This book is a must read for anyone with an interest in the plight of downed airmen during World War II."
— Meg Godlewski, *General Aviation News*

"Your documentation, letters, photos and notes add greatly to the story. These things gave me a feeling of intimacy with your father's experiences that I do not ever recall feeling after reading another book."
— Robert Tinnell, Physics teacher, Salem, Ore.

Two Gold Coins and a Prayer

THE EPIC JOURNEY
OF A WORLD WAR II BOMBER PILOT, EVADER,
AND POW

James H. Keeffe III

As told to him by his father, Lt. Col. James H. Keeffe Jr., USAF (Ret.)

Appell Publishing
Fall City, Washington

APPELL PUBLISHING
PO Box 1209
Fall City, Washington 98024

www.AppellPublishing.com

Appell Publishing is an imprint of Doofstom Mandenmaker, LLC.

Library of Congress Control Number: 2010926511

ISBN-13: 978-0-9843600-0-0
ISBN-10: 0-9843600-0-X

First Edition 2010
Second Printing June 2011

Map by Robert Cronan, Lucidity Information Design
Book and Cover Design by Jeanie James, Shorebird Media

The text of this book was printed on recycled paper comprised of 100% post-consumer waste.

PRINTED IN THE UNITED STATES OF AMERICA
2 3 4 5 6 7 8 9 10

Dedication

This book is dedicated to my father, Lt. Col. James H. Keeffe Jr., USAF (Ret), and all the other USAAF airmen and fellow Kriegies who fought and won the air war in the European Theater of Operations during World War II. Dad, you have always been my hero.

I also dedicate this book to the memory of those in the Dutch Resistance who at great risk to themselves and their families, sheltered, fed, and extended their hands in friendship to my father and countless other Allied airmen who ended up on the ground in occupied Holland.

Sancta Maria, Mater Dei, ora pro nobis peccatoribus,
nunc, et in hora mortis nostrae. Amen.

The Hail Mary

You haven't seen a tree until you've seen its shadow from the sky.

Amelia Earhart

Table of Contents

Introduction

This is now, and that was then.

It was the 8th of March 1944. Our choices were few and timing was "immediate." Over the large Dutch inland sea, the Ijsselmeer, with two engines out and all fuel gauges reading empty the options were:

1. Fly west as far across the North Sea as possible, then 'ditch' our B-24 'Liberator' four-engine heavy bomber and hope for pick-up by a British rescue boat.

2. Find and land on a German airfield in Holland, evacuate the crew, burn-up the plane and surrender to Luftwaffe personnel.

3. Crash-land on a Dutch farm, take care of the wounded and then disperse.

4. Turn south, put the lowering plane in a tight circle on auto-pilot over farm land, bail-out the crew and, once on the ground, either assemble or disperse as warranted.

Quickly we chose and set in motion option "4." After parachuting, once on the ground at about 4:40 in the afternoon I hid in a shed behind a house on Noordhoek, near the small town of Papendrecht. And thus began my four-and-a-half-month odyssey in Nederland.

In the darkness of that first evening, agents of the local Resistance took charge of and spirited me to the city of Dordrecht, and later to Rotterdam—by bicycle, of course! (For obvious reasons it is much safer to hide strangers in large towns or cities, and the larger the better.)

By now the Dutch had suffered through almost four long years of always worsening occupation. Ever harsher penalties were being meted out, often being enforced in summary fashion. Hide Jews in your home or business, and, upon their discovery, immediately be set out on the street in the clothes you happened to be wearing. The situation worsened further with the implementation of

"Nacht und Nebel Erlass" and the Nazi policy of *"Schrecklichkeit."* Aid or hide a downed Allied flyer and the policy of *"An der wand!"* (Against the wall!— Bang!) could be, and often was, carried out immediately.

And of course there were multiple German police agencies to carry out these many frightful policies. Among others were the Gestapo (Geheime Staats Polizei), the SD (Sicherheits Dienst), the GFP (Geheime Feld Polizei), the Feld Gendarmerie and the impressed local police. Finally, and in many ways the worst of all, were the traitorous Dutch NSBers (Nationaal Socialisch Beweging [Movement]) with their "Landwacht" armbands and virtually unlimited power.

Despite all of this, at great personal and familial risk, throughout the war hundreds of Allied airmen were helped, sheltered, hidden, transported, cared for, and passed on. In my case I was sheltered in seven homes in Nederland and one in Belgium. As you read through these multifaceted pages I urge you to keep in mind the ever present life and death risks these good people chanced, on even a daily basis, and the ominous dread which was their constant companion.

For me, all of this and more became life's greatest adventure.

James H. Keeffe Jr.
Lt. Col., USAF (Ret)

ii

Foreword

"There I was standing on the ground in enemy occupied Holland. I had just bailed out of my crippled heavy bomber and had no idea what had happened to my crew. I was hungry. I'd had only two hours of sleep in the past thirty-six hours. My face was smeared with mud and blood. And I was just four days away from my 21st birthday."

So begins the incredible saga of Jim Keeffe. The words were the basis for his unique "there I was story," often told later to his fellow prisoners of war as readily as they told their stories to him. Now six decades later, those same perceptive words set the stage for an extraordinary tale of an American B-24 bomber pilot that symbolizes the experiences of thousands of America's best young men who traversed the angry skies during the ominous days of WWII. Keeffe's fate, blown by the winds of war, was predicated on his bravery, intelligence, wits, determination and instinct to survive. And, as he quickly found out, having a sense of humor helped from his early days as a new recruit until his final joyous liberation at Stalag VIIA in Moosburg, Germany, in April of 1945.

The moment the reader joins Keeffe during early flight training, that reader is hooked. Flying vicariously at the side of the exuberant young airman, the reader first experiences the thrill of flight in the nighttime California desert. As the brash pilots, with their plane lights turned off, fly low to the ground straight towards the terrorized drivers below, the fun-seeking trainees appear to not have a care in the world. But soon after they have earned their pilot's wings those same rollicking boys find themselves abruptly thrown into the dangerous flak-riddled skies in the European Theatre of Operations. The brutality of war is immediate as their own personal dramas play out.

A seasoned pilot with the 389th Bomb Group, Keeffe felt that spark of electricity that went through the young crews when a mission briefing map indicated they were to fly into the heart of the Third Reich. His mission to "Big B" (Berlin) launches his odyssey through war-torn Europe, first as an evader in occupied Holland helped by the Underground and then as a prisoner of war in Stalag Luft III.

This excellent first-hand account, told in stunningly rich detail, is one of the most realistic memoirs I have read. *Two Gold Coins and a Prayer* reveals the selfless sacrifice of the Dutch, subjugated by Nazi rule, and is a tribute to the heroism of every member of the Resistance who provided a safe haven, no matter how temporary, to any allied flier.

We are all richer for having read the story of Jim Keeffe and the vast cast of characters he encountered during his wartime days as he and his fellow fliers gained the wisdom that only adversity can teach. This engaging tale is at times poignant, hilarious, hard-hitting and inspired. Hollywood couldn't come up with such a story—even if it tried.

Marilyn Jeffers Walton
Author of *Rhapsody in Junk—A Daughter's Return to Germany*

Preface

"When are you going to write a book, Dad?"

I was probably ten years old when I first asked my dad this question. At that time we were living in Ellensburg, Washington. He was a United States Air Force Major, teaching ROTC on campus at Central Washington State College.

As kids, my father told us stories about being a B-24 bomber pilot and a prisoner of war during World War II. In 1963 the WWII thriller, *The Great Escape,* starring Steve McQueen, came to Ellensburg. Dad had some German artifacts from the war, and he helped put together a display in the window of the Liberty Theater to promote the screening of the movie. Along side the large movie poster was his red Nazi flag with a big black swastika in the middle, a German military helmet, and some other items. I thought it was really cool, especially since MY dad was in the same German prisoner-of-war camp named Stalag Luft III that was depicted in the movie.

Years went by. In 1978, Dad took a trip to Europe to "visit some people I met during the war." By that time, as a Lieutenant Colonel, he had been retired from the Air Force for twelve years. When he came home from his trip to Europe, we asked that same question. "When are you going to write a book?"

His answer was always the same. "Oh, I'll get around to it sometime."

In 1995, Dad helped to organize a POW (prisoner-of-war) reunion in Poland at the site of Stalag Luft III. He, along with more than three hundred forty ex-POWs, their wives, and grown children, traveled to Poland and wandered throughout the old camp, which was by then overgrown with pine trees.

Again, when he came home, we posed the question. "Come on, Dad! When are you going to write your story? You're not getting any younger, and we need and want, to know what happened to you during the war." Once again it was, "Well, maybe sometime."

Fast forward to the year 2002. My youngest brother, Brian, was working at Microsoft Studios, in Redmond, Washington. He was learning how to run the state-of-the-art sound recording equipment and was encouraged to practice on the gear whenever he could to hone his skills. That presented the perfect opportunity. If Dad wasn't going to write his story, at least we could record him telling it. Thus began a wonderful couple of years going with my dad to the studio in the evening every week or so and listening to him recount the story of his years during the war.

Session after session, hour after hour, Dad and I sat in a sound-proof room wearing headphones and speaking into a microphone, while Brian, on the other side of a window, laid down the audio tracks. I'd ask a question and Dad would launch into an answer as if he were back in time re-living the experience. His memory for detail was phenomenal. Two years sped by, and finally we were finished. We ended up with nearly thirty-five hours of edited audio that were burned onto a dozen CDs. Now we had our dad's story. It wasn't a book, mind you, but at least we had it recorded.

During that time, we also started driving to the Boeing Museum of Flight, just south of Seattle, the last week of June. That's when the Collings Foundation flew in with their B-17 and B-24 four-engine heavy bombers. Every year the Collings Foundation, a wonderful organization that has preserved many vintage WWII aircraft, has their "Wings of Freedom" tour, where they fly the bombers to cities around the country. We took Dad down to the bombers and wandered all through them. As we climbed up into and walked through the B-24, he pointed out the various places that related to his story. "This is where Sergeant Miller, our left waist gunner, was killed." "Those are oxygen bottles we had to use when we flew above a certain elevation." "There's where Sergeant Hughes passed out on the bomb bay door." "This is the camera hatch I bailed out of." Listening to my dad describe battle scenes and operational details of the bomber, I knew I wasn't satisfied with having his story sitting on a handful of audio CDs. Since he wasn't going to write the book—I would.

I bought a transcription pedal, plugged it into my PC, and began to transcribe all the audio files into Word files. As I worked my way through the hours of audio CDs, the people, places, and adventures in his story began to come alive for me. There were stories of bombing missions, air battles, getting shot down, or "shot up" as my dad would say. There were stories of brave Dutch Resistance and Underground people who risked their lives for him; tales of betrayal, fear, excitement, misery and death, and stories of other airmen who shared the experience of battle, prison, and liberation.

After many months of transcribing and rewriting what was initially an interview into a readable story, I began to realize the book had taken on an entirely new dimension and purpose. One day it became clear—I wanted to write not just my dad's WWII story, but I needed to tell the story of the brave men and women he met along the way. Not only fellow airmen, but also ordinary civilians who lived extraordinarily brave and dangerous lives under Nazi occupation—a tyrannical police state of suspicion and fear, where disappearance and death were right around the corner. I hope and pray I have done their memories justice.

So, button up your high-altitude, electrically-heated flight suit. Climb into the copilot's seat. Cinch down your combat helmet and seat harness. Adjust your oxygen mask and make sure your throat mike works. Turn the page, hang on, and fly right into the thick of it!

James H. Keeffe III
Son of James H. Keeffe Jr.

Big 'B'

Falling Behind

"What the hell's going on? Give me power, Jim!" Mac shouted. He was flying formation from the right seat.

I quickly scanned all the instruments and could see that the number three engine manifold pressure was coming down. The cylinder head temperature of number three was dropping too. RPM was lagging, but not a lot.

We were on our element lead's left wing when suddenly they pulled ahead of us, and we began dropping down and falling behind. There was no fire and no smoke, yet we'd definitely lost power in our number three, and the RPM continued to drop slowly.

Even though I throttled up the other three engines, we kept losing altitude and falling farther behind the other airplanes. With my helmet on, I hadn't heard any difference in the roar of the engines—no banging or farting to give us a clue, but now it was as if a switch had been turned off. Within seconds, it was clear that we wouldn't be able to rejoin the formation.

"We've lost number three, Mac," I said.

"Do we need to feather the propeller?" he asked.

"Yeah," I said. "If the RPM drops too low, we might not be able to later. And it will act as a terrible drag as it loses power and spins down."

"All right, do it!" he said.

I reached up and hit the feathering button for number three. Then I turned my head and looked across Mac out the right-side cockpit window. The propeller was indeed feathering, its leading edge turning into the air stream and causing the wind-milling to stop.

When we lost the number three engine, we had just turned north at the IP (Initial Point)[1] onto our bomb run. Our mission target was the Vereinigte Kugellagerfabriken AG (VFK) ball and roller bearing factory in Erkner on the southern outskirts of Berlin. Our bombardment group, the 389th, was the last Group of the last Wing of the last Division of the whole damn 8th Air Force. This was 8th Air Force Mission 252.

It was Wednesday, the 8th of March 1944. On the 6th of March, the 389th had carried out its first full strike on Berlin,[2] the heart of the enemy. On the 7th, there had been no 2nd Air Division missions, and we'd been told that evening that there would be no mission the next day either because of bad weather over Germany.

Since we were scrubbed for the 8th, I stayed up late playing cards and ping pong and got to bed around 11:30 p.m. Then, lo and behold, we were awakened at 2 a.m. We could always tell how bad and how long a mission would be according to the time they woke us up. If they didn't come until 6 a.m., the chances were it was a "No Ball" mission close to the coast. Well, here it was 2 a.m., which probably meant that our destination was "Big B" (Berlin).

After only a couple of hours of sleep, I was groggy and I actually put on two different socks. Mac and I finished dressing and went down to the mess hall. Stevens, our navigator, and Moulton, our bombardier, showed up shortly thereafter. Breakfast was pretty grim because we knew we were flying out and would probably get shot at. I didn't eat much.

In the briefing room, we found out that the mission was indeed Berlin—a "maximum effort" with the 2nd Air Division providing two hundred and nine B-24s, together with four hundred and fourteen B-17s from the 1st and 3rd Air Divisions; a total of six hundred and twenty-three 4-engine heavy bombers.[3] For the 389th Bombardment Group, this meant all four squadrons would form up every combat-ready aircraft. Several bombers were down for various maintenance issues, leaving twenty-seven available for the mission.

An elaborate plan was in place to get all the bombers off the ground and formed up. The main runway had a perimeter taxiway all the way around that fed airplanes to the takeoff direction of the main runway from both sides, and each airplane taxied at a designated time on the clock. Two squadrons taxied on one side of the main runway, and two taxied on the other side. For a mission like this one, after taxiing to the main runway, the crew of each airplane shut down all engines so the fuel trucks could come in and top off the tanks. Then the ground crew defrosted the wings and tail.

Our takeoff was pretty hairy, and if a swath of trees hadn't been cut down through Hethel Wood beyond the end of the runway, I wouldn't be here to tell you about it. We were so heavily loaded that after we were airborne, we sank below the height of the trees until we picked up enough speed to climb higher.

The 389th formed up over the north coast of East Anglia, the eastern bulge of England, where we were joined by two other groups forming the 2nd Combat Bombardment Wing. Then our wing formed up with the other two wings of the 2nd Air Division. Soon, all three divisions of the 8th Air Force were assembled, and we flew in formation east across the English Channel. As England fell away behind us, our gunners loaded belts of ammunition into the link trays of their .50 caliber machine guns, slapped down the cover plates, pulled the slide handles back twice to chamber the first round, and test fired their guns over the water.

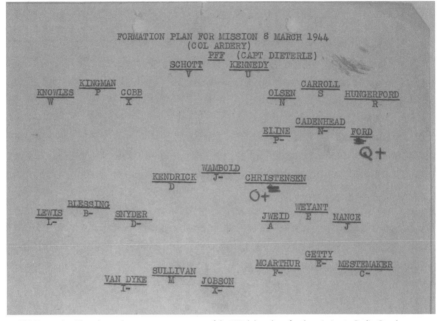

This Formation Plan shows the group arrangement of the 389th bombers for the mission to Berlin. Bombers are arranged in elements of three and are represented by the pilot's last name and individual aircraft letter. (Courtesy of Kelsey McMillan, 389th Bomb Group Historian)

On the way to Berlin, we didn't see any flak or German fighter aircraft because they were focused on the lead of the bomber stream, which was far ahead of us. We just flew formation at the back end of the whole 8th Air Force—all the way across Germany.

We were the number two airplane in an element of three, flying on the left wing of the element leader, a little below his wing. This is why Mac, as aircraft commander, was flying in the right seat. Normally, we bombed as a section, comprising two squadrons of nine airplanes each. One section, together with the second section, formed the thirty-six airplanes of the 389th Bombardment Group.

We were flying a brand new B-24J with a nose turret requiring a gunner, so we had borrowed a turret gunner from another crew. I felt sorry for this poor guy because this was his first mission and because he was with a strange crew. He brought our crew count to eleven.

As we headed to the IP, we were in our assigned positions. Our pilot "Mac" was Lieutenant James B. McArthur. I was, at that time, Lieutenant James H. Keeffe, Jr., flying copilot. Down behind me on the flight deck was Sergeant Raymond C. Hall, radio operator. Above Hall was Sergeant William "Bill" D. Hughes, flight engineer and top turret gunner who was rotating his turret scanning the skies for enemy fighters. Below the cockpit, up in the nose, were three crewmen; Lieutenant Raymond H. Moulton "Moose", bombardier, Lieutenant Donald M. Stevens, navigator, and Sergeant Hugh W. Smith, the borrowed nose turret gunner.

Back in the waist of the airplane was Sergeant John B. "JB" Allen, the ball turret gunner, already closed up in his turret, which had been lowered down outside through the bottom of the airplane. The waist gunners were Sergeant Kenneth J. Miller on the left side and Sergeant Clyde Baker on the right. Behind them, manning the tail turret twin .50's was Sergeant Karl F. Turlay. As required on all missions, we were under strict radio silence—absolutely no chit chatting on the radio and minimal conversation over the intercom.

When we reached the IP, five to eight minutes from the target, we turned north onto the bomb run and began to encounter flak. We tightened up the formation in order to get the most concentrated bomb pattern possible on the ground. Mac was concentrating on the formation flying, working the throttles when he needed to. Whenever he took his hands off the throttles, I jiggled them a little more to even out the manifold pressure. Our altitude was 24,000 feet. We were racing toward the target.

Cutting the Corner

It was perfectly clear over Germany, no clouds in the sky above or below us. The ground was covered with snow. Looking out over the nose of the airplane, I could see smoke coming up from Berlin several miles ahead, but it hadn't reached our altitude yet. It looked like the target was getting quite a pounding from all the groups in front of us.

As soon as we started entering the flak boxes, those three-dimensional areas of space into which the German flak crews shot their guns, Stevens quit the nose and, carrying an oxygen walk-around bottle, came up to the flight deck.

"What do you want?" I asked him.

"I can't function any longer," he said to me with fear in his voice.

"For God's sake, Stevens, we're on the bomb run. Sit down, shut up and don't bother us!"

A few seconds later, we began to fall away from the formation.

Over the intercom the bombardier asked, "What the hell's going on? Why are we dropping back?"

"We've lost number three," I told him.

Mac and I spoke quickly and decided to 'cut the corner.' We were headed north on the bomb run, and we'd have to make a 90-degree turn to the left to head west back to England after dropping our load.

"I'm going to cut across and re-join the formation," Mac said.

We knew that after "bombs away" the leader would lose altitude, and the entire formation would follow. This was done in order to pick up speed and pick up stragglers, which we had just become. More importantly, it was done to avoid those flak boxes which the Germans were prone to fire into.

When we turned a few degrees left, Moulton, the bombardier, called up again.

"What are we going to do?" he asked.

"Moose, pick out a big 'target of opportunity,' a factory. Make sure it's not a school or a hospital," I said.

"I've got a big building that I'm sure is a factory," Moulton replied a few seconds later.

"OK, let that be it," I said.

By this time Mac and I had pretty well stabilized the airplane on the three remaining engines.

"I'm putting the airplane on auto pilot, Moose. Take over!"

"I'm ready to take over," he replied.

I put the plane on auto pilot, and Moulton took over the flying of the airplane. For precision bombing it was critical that the bombardier take control. Using his bomb sight, Moulton made slight adjustments, moving the airplane left and right to get the target within his eye piece. As soon as the cross hairs were over the target, he pushed the button on the bomb release cable and called out, "Bombs away!" We were carrying a full load of general purpose bombs and all eight thousand pounds fell on the target.

The rest of the group had already dropped their bombs ahead of us on the main target, the Erkner bearing factory. They had made their left turn to the west and had descended to about 17,000 feet to pick up stragglers. After we dropped our bombs, we picked up speed in our descent and were able to catch up to the group. The group leader did a great job of holding down the speed so we cripples could be gathered back into the formation.

The best place for a cripple was in the diamond slot within an element of three airplanes. The normal flight formation was an inverted "V" of three airplanes: the leader, a right wing and a left wing. The cripple was supposed to come up behind and below the leader forming a diamond. That's what we did. We climbed into the diamond slot within our flight.

It was quite easy to tell the different bombardment groups from each other because five-foot white circles with black letters were painted on the tail and on the wings of each airplane. For the 389th Bomb Group, the letter "C" was superimposed on those white circles. Of the other two bomb groups in our wing, the 453rd was Circle-J, and the 445th was Circle-F. Mac could easily make out the Circle-C in white and black on our group's tails, and he continued on the cut to re-form with them, despite the fact that we had only three engines.

389th Bomb Group, 566th Bomb Squadron B-24, piloted by Lt. Frank Lewis, releasing bombs over Berlin. Extensive battle damage during the mission caused this aircraft to be grounded upon return to England where it was salvaged for parts. (Courtesy of Paul Wilson, author of The Sky Scorpions)

As we flew back across Germany heading west toward England, we had no opposition. However, several minutes after leaving the Berlin target area, I noticed a single B-24 wandering around all by itself outside of our group. It was keeping up with us, more or less, and closer inspection indicated that the airplane had a feathered propeller. The B-24 flew a little higher than us, then a little lower. It was from another group. I couldn't make out its tail markings, but it wasn't Circle-C.

I called Moulton. "Stevens has crapped out on us," I said. "Take over the navigation of the plane and plot us a course back home."

A short time later, a shout came over the intercom from one of the gunners. "Two German fighters coming in high from the rear at about five o'clock!" I looked around, trying to find the fighters. Finally I could see them, but I also noticed that the wandering lone B-24 was no longer out there to the north.

Then came a shout from one of the gunners. "My God! That B-24 is right below us, and he's coming up under us!"

Within a couple of seconds, the crippled bomber pulled up in front of us! When the pilot saw the two German fighters, he crammed his way into our diamond position! He had dropped down under us and then pulled up right in front of us. The prop wash from his three good engines really rattled our airplane, instantly pitching us up onto our right wing with the dead number three engine. Flung onto one wing like that, we dropped down and away from the formation.

"Help me, Jim!" Mac shouted.

Falling right wing low, the nose came down below the horizon, and it took both of us struggling with the wheel, pulling it back and to the left, to bring the right wing back up and straighten the airplane out to stop the roll. We were losing altitude quickly.

As we fought to bring the right wing up, one of the gunners—I think it was Turlay—called out, "Here come those two fighters!"

All hell broke loose. The airplane shook as our gunners began to shoot their single and twin .50 caliber machine guns. Coming in from dead astern, the two German fighters, Fw-190s, split up. From five o'clock and seven o'clock, they both opened up with their 20mm cannons and .30 caliber machine guns.

I could hear the roar of our .50s, and could hear bullets from the two enemy fighters hitting our airplane. Somebody called out, "I got him! I got him!"

Looking instinctively out of the left cockpit window, I could see one smoking fighter dropping down and away. "There's one going down on the left," I called to Mac.

Somebody else called out over the intercom, "There goes one down on the right side!" Mac looked out his right window and saw the other enemy fighter trailing smoke. Incredibly, both German fighters had been hit, and both were trailing smoke! We never saw them again.

By this time all our gunners had stopped shooting. The last word over the intercom, before it went dead, was from one of the gunners. "Number two engine's smoking!"

Pressing my throat mike, I called back to Sgt. Turlay who was manning the tail guns. "Karl, what's going on back there?" No response. "Anybody hear me back there?" Nothing. A piece of radio gear must have been hit and damaged.

We were losing more power and altitude. I saw from the engine instruments that we had lost another engine. The number two engine manifold pressure was coming down, and the cylinder head temperature was dropping quickly. I pointed this out to Mac and then feathered number two. We re-trimmed the airplane and increased power to the remaining two engines.

By now our forward speed had decayed, and our group was pulling away from us. It was "Good luck chaps, hope you make it back to England." The group didn't wait for cripples because the integrity of the group—not the individual airplane—is primary.

I quickly took stock of our situation: we had the airplane under control; we had nailed both the German fighters, at least as far as their ability to attack us was concerned; we were alone due to that S.O.B. who had forced his way into our slot in the diamond formation; and, the rest of the group was slowly pulling away and disappearing ahead of us.

"What the Hell is Going on Back There?"

With two engines out, we were losing more speed, dropping in altitude and burning more fuel than if all four engines had been running. After the fighter attack stopped, we were around 14,000 feet and descending slowly.

Stevens, scared to death, cringed behind me on the floor of the cockpit. After we got the number two engine feathered and decided we could still fly the airplane, and after I made sure there were no more fighters around, I turned around and beckoned for Stevens to come up to me. Unhooking my oxygen mask, I shouted at him, "Go to the back of the airplane! Find out what's going on and come back and report to me! I need to know what the situation is back there, and make sure somebody is in the tail turret because that's where the attack will come from if we're attacked again!"

Stevens turned around and dropped down into the bomb bay area on his way to the back, but he never returned.

With the intercom system out, the only way to communicate was to shout over the air rush and the roar of the engines. After several minutes, turning around again, I signaled for Sgt. Hughes to come up to the cockpit. By this time, he had come down out of the top turret, unhooked himself from his oxygen and electrical systems, and was busy checking the fuel, transferring fuel, and trying to find out how much damage had been done to the airplane.

"We're low on fuel, Lt. Keeffe!" he shouted to me.

"Go to the back end and find out what the hell is going on back there! Make sure the tail turret is manned and find out where Lt. Stevens went!" I shouted back at him.

He left—and didn't come back either.

In front of the pilot's windscreen, half way down the nose to the front of the airplane, was the astrodome, a bubble of plastic where the navigator hung his sextant in order to take shots on either the sun or the stars for navigating. Up popped Moulton's head in the astrodome, and he looked back at Mac and me and began to give us course corrections by signaling with one, two, or three fingers, and then either left or right…two degrees left, one degree right, and so on.

Moulton continued in this fashion signaling us course corrections along a westerly direction toward Holland. Several minutes passed; neither Stevens nor Hughes had come back to report. We were nearing the Dutch/German border.

Turning to McArthur, I shouted, "Mac, we've got to know what's going on in the back end, and I don't know what the hell's happened to Stevens and Hughes. I'll go to the back and, rest assured, I'll return and give you a report!"

Mac nodded as I unhooked the electrical connection to my heated suit, unplugged the oxygen mask hose and intercom cable to my helmet, unhooked my seat belt and climbed up out of the seat wearing my back-pack parachute. Turning around, I dropped down to the flight deck. Before stepping down through the well to the bomb bay, I noticed Sgt. Hall sitting at the radio desk behind the copilot's seat. He was fidgeting and scared to death.

As I stepped down into the bomb bay, I immediately saw Hughes passed out and lying on the port side front bomb bay door. I knew that Hughes had the poorest oxygen tolerance of any of the crew. We had a rule with him: he had to be on oxygen from 5,000 feet up and on oxygen until we went through 5,000 feet on the way down. He had forgotten, in the heat of trying to get everything taken care of and following my instructions, to re-hook his mask and take a walk-around bottle with him.

I was instantly alarmed because I knew how flimsy this type of bomb bay door was. Consolidated Aircraft had designed these doors to roll up the sides of the airplane so there wouldn't be any drag when they were opened. However, there was a problem. Never put weight on these doors! Everybody had been thoroughly instructed never to put weight on them because doing so could pull the rollers out of the tracks on either side.

Well, here was Sgt. Hughes sprawled on the forward port bomb bay door with his harness on but no parachute chest-pack. If that bomb bay door had been forced open, it would have torn off in the wind and he would have gone out with no parachute.

I grabbed his harness and pulled him back off the roll-up door onto the narrow catwalk and then back up onto the lower deck near the nose wheel. The catwalk, about ten inches wide, was the main keel of the airplane and ran fore to aft through the bomb bay. The bottoms of the bomb racks were attached to it.

After putting Hughes' mask back on his face, I plugged in a walk-around bottle to his oxygen hose and slapped his cheeks. Finally he came to.

"Bill, did you get to the back end?"

"Gee, I don't know, Lieutenant., I don't know."

"Fine. You get back in the turret, stay on oxygen, and don't come off it again."

That's exactly what he did.

I turned back around and went through the bomb bay along the catwalk, squeezing myself between the bomb racks. How I did that with a back pack parachute on I'll never know. When I reached the back of the bomb bay, I climbed up the short three-foot-metal ladder leading to the little door in the bulkhead that separated the bomb bay from the waist. Opening the door, I stepped into the waist and started walking around the ball turret, which I noticed was raised up into the waist. Then I saw what had happened to the rest of the crew.

The first thing I noticed was the ball turret gunner, Sgt. John B. Allen, standing in the lower level of the waist, right by the waist windows. Allen was on my left side. On my right side looking aft, the tail gunner, Turlay, was down on the floor working on another gunner. He was putting a tourniquet on the gunner's left arm because the left hand and wrist were blown off. The gunner was Sgt. Miller.

Sgt. Baker, the other waist gunner, was rolling around on the floor in pain. I looked around and shouted at Sgt. Turlay above the air rush and engine noise, "Where's Lt. Stevens?"

Still working on Miller, Turlay nodded over his shoulder gesturing off to the starboard corner of the forward part of the waist. Over in the corner, up against the bulkhead leading into the bomb bay, was a heap of something I presumed was just a pile of parachutes, bags, flak jackets, and other items belonging to the waist gunners. I went over to it.

Lifting a flak vest I saw, cowering underneath in the fetal position, Lt. Stevens. He had taken all the flak vests from the rear, laid one or two of them down on the floor and then pulled the others around and over him. He was completely covered with all the gunners' flak vests! I ripped the vests off the top of him and exploded! I called him every name in the book; then I started kicking him. "Get your ass up to the front of the airplane," I screamed. "I never want to see your stinking face again. You're a bloody coward!"

I kicked Stevens all the way to the door of the bomb bay and out through it. He had on his Mae West and his parachute harness, but his canopy pack was in the front of the airplane, up on the flight deck. What a cowardly, selfish thing for him to do, taking everyone's flak vests when the possibility of being attacked again was extremely high.

Seeing him under those vests made my blood boil! My heart was pounding, and my fists were clenched tight when I turned back to the scene in the waist.[4]

By this time, Turlay had pretty well gotten the tourniquet finished on Miller's arm. Miller hadn't been wearing a flak vest so he'd been spattered in the face and in the chest area with metal fragments. His left hand had been severed just above the wrist. I never saw it. He didn't seem to be bleeding much, and I turned my attention to see what other problems we had.

I looked at Miller's waist-mounted .50 caliber machine gun and quickly identified the fact that it had taken a direct hit right where the belt feed went into the breach of the gun. It was all mangled and the cover plate had been waffled up. I couldn't believe steel could be bent like that.

"Karl, you've got to get back to your guns. Is your turret OK?" I asked.

"Yes it is, Lieutenant" he replied.

"Well, you'd better get back in that turret right now because if we get attacked again, it's going to come from the rear."

He went back and climbed into the tail turret. I tried to see if there was any life in Miller. I felt the skin on his face, and it was cold. I lifted up his eye lids. His eyes weren't moving and were glazed over. I thought he was dead.

Allen was still standing there.

"J. B., why are you out of the ball?" I said. "Get back into your turret."

"It's no good, Lieutenant. I can't use it."

"Why can't you use it?"

"Because—come here and I'll show you."

We went over to the open ball turret hatch, and he pointed down inside to the bullet-proof glass front-piece of the turret. It had taken a direct hit, probably by a 20mm shell, which had starred the glass completely so that he couldn't see through it when looking through his gun sight. It was obvious he couldn't aim his guns to shoot anything.

"Take over this starboard waist gun," I told him, pointing to Baker's .50 caliber machine gun. "Let's see if it's still working."

To test the gun, I grabbed the two handles and pulled the trigger, firing off a few rounds. The gun nearly whipped out of my hands, putting three or four rounds through our vertical stabilizer on the right side of the airplane! It was working just fine.

"OK, take over this gun and watch for attacking fighters."

I then knelt down and talked to Sgt. Baker.

"Where are you hit, Clyde?"

"In both my legs," he said, gritting his teeth.

"Are you in pain?"

"Oh yes! It's awful, terrible."

He had on long underwear under a blue "bunny" electric suit. Over this he was wearing a flying suit, and he had electric slippers attached to the bottom of the legs of the bunny suit. Over these slippers, of course, he was wearing heavy wool socks and heavy, clumsy winter flying boots.

I pulled off my electric gloves and let them dangle by the electric cords that attached them to my jacket sleeves. Keeping my nylon glove liners on because it was well below zero in the waist, I unzipped his boots. There was blood in them, but it was sort of caked. We had instructions regarding the wounded. If they were bleeding, we were to stop the bleeding somehow with pressure, with a tourniquet or whatever. But if they weren't bleeding, it was best to leave them alone until they got back to base because we didn't have the equipment to adequately help them. The plane, which was cold as a freezing wind tunnel, was not the best place to treat a patient.

Baker wasn't bleeding directly any longer, so I merely zipped his boots back up to retain his body warmth. His electric suit was still plugged in, so he would stay warm.

Taking a quick assessment, I ran down the list: Turlay was back in the tail turret; Allen had taken over the one good waist gun; Miller was probably already dead, and Baker was in pain.

To take care of Baker's pain, I grabbed a first-aid kit off the inside wall, broke its seal and opened it up to get the morphine syrette that was supposed to be inside. When I opened up the syrette box, what I found inside, instead of the morphine, was a pebble! I quickly removed the second first-aid kit from its location, opened it up and could tell immediately there was nothing in the syrette box.

"Dammit! What the hell's going on?" I was furious! Someone had stolen the morphine, probably before the hospital crew stocked the airplane for the mission.

There were two other first-aid kits in the nose, so I hurried back through the bomb bay and crawled on my hands and knees past the nose wheel to the nose turret and bombardier's area. Moulton was standing up with his head in the astrodome, and Smith was at his pair of .50 caliber guns in the nose turret.

I found and opened the two first-aid kits, and each had the little box with a morphine syrette. However, they were both frozen as hard as rocks instead of being soft and squishy like toothpaste. Wondering what to do, I decided to thaw them by putting them in my mouth. I crawled back past the nose wheel, into and through the bomb bay, squeezed between the bomb racks, and climbed back up through the short bulkhead doorway into the waist.

After one syrette became soft enough, I punched a hole through the metal cover of the tube with the needle, screwed the needle onto the tube and jabbed it down through the clothing layers into Baker's upper leg muscle. I guess I expected it to work instantly. I waited about three or four minutes, knowing that McArthur was up in the cockpit flying the airplane, still waiting for me to return to tell him what was going on.

"Can you feel anything? Is that helping?" I asked Baker a few minutes later.

"No, sir," he moaned. "I'm in terrible pain."

What I didn't know then, but found out later, was that he'd been shot with 7.92mm bullets through both legs in almost the same place—just above the ankle between the bone and the Achilles tendon.

Because I wasn't seeing any results from the first morphine syrette, I decided to use the other one I had in my mouth. It was now pliable, so I punched a hole in it, screwed the needle on and jammed it into his other thigh.

"You stay here," I said to Allen. "Watch both sides and use the gun if necessary. I've got to get back to the nose."

After taking one last quick look around the waist, I went forward, climbed back into my seat in the cockpit and told Mac what was going on. We had long since crossed the Dutch border and were heading toward the North Sea.

"We'll Never Make it Back"

When I got to the cockpit, the flight engineer, Sgt. Hughes, was bouncing off the walls. "The fuel's all gone! The engines are going to quit!" he shouted.

On the cockpit aft bulkhead of the B-24 were vertical glass tubes, which physically showed how much fuel was in the gas tanks. I looked at them. They were both virtually empty.

"We're not going to make it to England for sure," I told Mac. "We're not even going to make it to the North Sea, and that's not a smart place to go down into anyway." B-24's didn't ditch very well. They tore apart because the bomb bay doors came off and allowed water to flood in, usually causing the airplane to break in two. Also, survival in the water would have been less than five minutes because we didn't have "poopy suits," water survival suits, and the North Sea is very cold.

We decided to turn south over the Ijsselmeer (formerly the Zuiderzee—or Southern Sea) and try to find a German airfield. The plan was to land on the airfield and get everyone out of the airplane. In the nose and in the waist were magnesium flare pots, about the size of a one-pound coffee can. They were put there intentionally to burn up the airplane so it wouldn't fall into enemy hands. It was impossible to put out the fire once the pots started burning. We were going to evacuate the crew and then get both the magnesium pots going to burn up the airplane, but we didn't find any German airfields. They were all camouflaged.

"The fuel's gone, you gotta do something! We don't have any time left," Hughes continued to shout.

By now, we were down to about 6,000 feet. We didn't want to crash land the B-24, which is what we would have done had we been over the United States. But here in Holland, all we could see were lots of small pastures and farm land parcels, all surrounded by little three-foot-wide canals. The Dutch word for this type of canal is *sloot*, and the Dutch actually used boats in them. These canals would tear the airplane apart if we attempted to land in a field, so our only option was to bail out.

"I'll get them started here in the front end, out the bomb bay," I said to Mac. "Then I'll go to the back and get those guys out. I'll pull on the rudder cable so you'll feel it in your feet to let you know that we're gone in the back end."

"OK," he replied, "I'll make a 360-degree turn, and we can all get together on the ground."

By now, Moulton and Smith had come up from the nose to the flight deck. Stevens was already there along with the radio operator, Hall, and the flight engineer, Hughes. I told Hughes to open the bomb bay doors, which he did by flipping a switch under the flight deck, just inside the passageway leading to the nose.

I shouted to Sgt. Smith, who was closest to the bomb bay doors. "It's been nice knowing you, Sgt. Smith. Jump!" Out he went and immediately disappeared from view. I found out later that he injured his back due to the strong wind over the ground that day—post-frontal wind from the northwest.

The next nearest person was Stevens, our great navigator.

"Get your ass out there and jump!" I shouted to him.

He went out onto the ten inch wide catwalk and just stood there with the bomb bay doors open beneath him. The roar of the engines and the noise of the air-rush in and around the bomb bay were deafening. Stevens stood there for a few seconds, then turned around and came back. "I'm not going!" he shouted.

"Oh, yes you are!" I pushed him back out onto the catwalk where he wrapped both arms around a bomb rack. I followed him onto the catwalk and pulled one of his arms off the bomb rack. When I reached for his other arm, he put his first arm back around the bomb rack. We ended up struggling. After a few seconds I realized we weren't getting anywhere, so I changed tactics and looked down and out of the bomb bay and gasped. As he glanced down to see what I was gasping at, I put my foot up onto his abdomen area and heaved. Out and down he went, facing upward with both arms akimbo, screaming.

"Ray, keep these guys bailing out and I'll go to the back end!" I yelled to Moulton.

As I went to the back end, Moulton got Hughes out and then bailed out himself. At first Hall wouldn't jump. Mac had to yell at him before he'd jump, but finally he did.

In the back end, I got Turlay out of the tail turret and had Allen open up the camera hatch door. I re-examined Miller and felt for a pulse. Nothing. He was stone cold. I opened his eyes, and they stayed open. There was nothing that could be done, so I left him.

Kneeling down next to Baker, I got close to his ear. "Clyde, can you hear me?" After a few seconds, he kind of gave a half-assed nod of his head. "Put your hand on your D-ring. We're going to have to throw you out." He nodded and did nothing. I took his hand and put it on the D-ring on the chest pack some-one had put on him, but it fell away. He was on cloud nine. Then I remembered that I'd given him not one morphine syrette, but two! I was surprised he was even conscious.

Crewman opening the camera hatch located in the tail end of the B-24. View is looking forward past the two waist gunners toward the bomb bay. The crewmen are wearing oxygen masks and electrically heated flying suits. The rail system, leading from the ammunition box by the right waist gunner and past the camera hatch, carries the machine gun belts for the tail turret .50 caliber machine guns. (Lt. Col. Keeffe collection)

I looked around. The gunners had intercom cables that were about ten feet long, plugged into radio jack boxes on either side of the waist. These cables gave them about ten feet to move around in while wearing their ear-phones and their throat-mikes. I ripped one of these cables loose and tied one end of the cable around Baker's D-ring and the other end onto a gun mount that was bolted to the floor of the airplane.

Turlay and I dragged Baker back a few feet to the open camera hatch, which was in the bottom of the airplane near the tail gunner's position. It was about two and a half feet wide and three feet long.

With Baker lying next to the open hatch, I told Turlay to go look out his rear turret and let me know if Baker's parachute opened. "See you later Clyde," I said to Baker as I patted him on the cheek, "I hope you have a safe trip down and everything works out." Grabbing his harness, I dragged him over the camera hatch and let go. He fell through and was immediately snatched away by the wind.

The com-cord attached to Baker's D-ring and the gun mount went taught, and then slackened. "I saw his parachute open!" Turlay shouted as he came back the few steps to the open hatch.

That left just the three of us at about 5,000 feet of altitude.

"OK, one of you go ahead and jump," I said.

"You go, Karl."

"No, you go, J. B."

"No, you go Karl, and I'll follow you."

"No, you go J. B."

"Hey, we don't have time for this crap," I finally shouted, "I'll go!"

Then I showed them, high over the waist window, one of a group of cables.

"Here's the rudder cable. Whoever is last out, pull on this three times to let Lt. McArthur know that the back end is empty, and promise me you'll follow me out."

They both nodded.

I knelt down facing the rear and put my hands on the far end of the camera hatch opening. I said a little Hail Mary prayer, brought my hands together, and out I went. I turned over once and had a last look at the airplane. It was right above me, flying away. I turned over again and never saw the airplane after that.

Once out of the plane, all the noise was gone—the roaring engines, the vibration, the air rush noise. It was absolutely quiet. This was really very strange because the body falls at about one hundred and twenty-five miles an hour, and you'd think there'd be a lot of noise.

I had neglected to fasten the chin strap of my helmet, so it blew off. I paid no attention to it because I was turning over very slowly. The earth would go by; then the sky would show up; then the earth would go by again.

Absolutely peaceful and calm. It was wonderful.

I had complete use of my faculties. I looked at my D-ring to make sure it was there and put my hand on it. I looked at my gloved hands and realized that I had put my electric flying gloves back on before I jumped.

Then I looked at my feet. I'd heard that sometimes your boots would come off, but mine didn't. They were brown rubber and very nice good boots.

We'd been told that the Germans frequently shot at airmen in parachutes, not only from the ground, but sadly from some of the fighter planes. Slowly, slowly I turned over and over and intentionally delayed opening my parachute. I had decided long ago that if I ever had to bail out, I wouldn't open my parachute until I was close to the ground.

Every time the earth went by it seemed to spread out. I began to see features. I could see roads and I could see telephone poles. I turned over again and I could see the wires between the telephone poles,

"This is close enough," I thought, and I gave about a two-inch yank on my D-ring.

The D-ring was made of quarter-inch steel and had a cable that went through a cable-housing over the shoulder. There were three pins attached to this flexible cable, which came out of the back of the parachute, permitting rubber bungee cords to open the pack. The Army Air Force had a rule that if someone parachuted out of an airplane and hung onto the D-ring, he could keep it as a souvenir. Here I was coming down over Holland thinking about a souvenir.

I gave another little yank, but nothing happened. I looked down with my mind reeling and saw the ground racing up toward me,

"You stupid jerk," I said to myself, "all you did was take out the slack!"

Then I really yanked hard and wide, and when I looked at my hand, the D-ring was gone. I had flung the D-ring away!

Immediately the blissful quiet was replaced with a loud hissing *Shwur wur wur wur wur wur wur wur wur*!

The first thing that came out of the parachute back-pack was a small parachute, probably only a foot and a half in diameter, with wire springs that forced it open. We called this the pilot chute. Once it opened, air resistance pulled the main canopy out. Next, the risers, which had been placed back and forth under rubber bands, came out making the shwurring noise.

A few seconds later there was a tremendous *thunk*! as the main chute opened with a snap, and my one hundred and twenty mile an hour fall braked instantly to about twenty miles an hour. Fortunately, my harness was tight enough so I didn't sustain any injury to the groin. But the force of the canopy opening while I was still in a slow roll caused me to swing immediately sideways and up above the horizon.[5]

"My God," I thought, "this thing's going to collapse!"

I started running sideways in the air, which caused me to swing back down over a river, a huge river.

"Oh no, I can't swim!" I thought, even though I could swim, and I had on a Mae West.

Immediately after my parachute snapped open, the peaceful silence of falling through the air exploded into a ruckus of noise. I could hear sirens coming up from the ground below, as well as different kinds of weapon fire. *Poom! Poom! Poom! Drrrrrrrrrrrt! Drrrrrrrrrrt! Drrrrrrrrr!*

I continued with the running motion as I swung up above the horizon and then back down across the river and across the dike road. The roof of a house swung by just feet beneath me and then I plowed sideways right into a bare apple tree.

From our mission briefing, I knew a heavy rain storm and a front had come through the area the previous day. The front had already moved east of Berlin, but the ground in Holland was still very wet and soggy. There was no grass under the apple trees, just loose dirt that had turned to mud, and I fell out of the tree face first into the mud.

Earlier that day over Berlin, I had picked up a little piece of flak that had hit me just above my left eye. I had bled a little bit, but the blood had dried. When I crashed down through the tree and went face first into the mud, the cut above my eye opened back up.

The sirens and weapons fire became much louder now that I was on the ground. Machine guns and heavier guns, antiaircraft guns, were shooting at our dying airplane. Soon, I heard vehicles roaring along the dike road up above where I was.

I stood up, wiped the mud off my face and noticed a group of people standing between two houses: women, children, and old people. One man broke away from the little crowd and walked out to me. He was wearing an overcoat and a fedora hat.

There I was, standing on the ground in enemy-occupied Holland. I had just bailed out of my crippled heavy bomber and had no idea what had happened to my crew. I was hungry. I'd had only two hours of sleep in the past thirty-six hours. My face was smeared with mud and blood. And I was just four days away from my 21st birthday.

End Notes
'Big B'

1. The Initial Point (IP) is where the bomber stream begins its final approach to the target. The distance could be anywhere from eight to twenty miles. At the IP, after each element and section tightens itself up, the pilot of each aircraft transfers control of his bomber to the bombardier who maintains a straight heading all the way to the target. At this point there is no deviation from the heading no matter what is happening, whether it be German fighter attacks or flak bursts.

2. *Sky Scorpions,* pg. 94

3. *The Mighty Eighth War Diary,* pg. 196

4. Lt. Stevens would have been court-martialed had we made it back to base. I would have brought charges against him for "cowardice in the face of the enemy," and for "failure to carry out a legitimate order in a combat situation." There would have been two boards that he would have had to meet. The first one, probably, would have been an FEB, Flying Evaluation Board. That board would have yanked his wings—no more navigator. The second board would have been a court-martial, and I'm sure he would have been found guilty. He probably would have lost his commission as a second lieutenant.

5. After the war, I described my bail-out experience to several long-time parachutists, and they all figured I had opened my parachute at about 300 feet.

How It All Began

The Aviation Bug is Born

I was born the 12th of March 1923, in Sioux City, Iowa, the third of six children and the oldest boy. When I was almost ten years of age, my father took on a project that eventually led me to acquire a love for flying that directed and shaped my life. He was a civil engineer who had been in the bridge building business for the State of Nebraska, but had decided to go into business for himself. At the peak of his career he owned a construction company and a brick company. He also invented and patented a truss-less arch for airplane hangars so that the tail, as well as the body of a plane, could be brought into the hangars. He named this business "The Keeffe Dome Company."

There was a fellow in Sioux City by the name of Hanford who owned a milk processing and ice cream factory. Hanford also owned the airport that later became the Sioux City Airport. My dad built two truss-less arch hangers for the Hanford Airport. As a result, Art Hanford and Dad became very good friends, and Art arranged for Dad to take flying lessons.

My dad took me for my first ride in an airplane. My younger brother, Bob, came along as well. We flew in a bi-plane, the Waco-D, which had an open front cockpit for the passenger, or passengers, and a rear cockpit for the pilot. Bob was nine years old, and I was ten. I remember turning around in the front cockpit and looking back at Dad. He had on a leather helmet and goggles, and he was wearing a big grin. I don't think he did any acrobatics with us because this was our first ride. But that first ride was all it took. When I stood on firm ground again, I knew I'd been bitten by the aviation bug.

In the late 1920s, all kinds of aviation records were being broken. For instance, Lindbergh flew solo across the Atlantic, and a pilot by the name of Wiley Post, with his navigator, Harold Gatty, was the first to circumnavigate the earth in an airplane. Upon their return, Post and Gatty toured all around the United States in a Lockheed high-wing monoplane. Wiley Post was minus one eye and wore a black patch over it. This is a little difficult for a pilot because having only one eye changes depth perception capability.

I met Wiley Post and Harold Gatty when they visited the Hanford Airport. I met Post again when he toured with a comedian by the name of Will Rogers, a very funny man. One of Will Rogers' favorite targets was congressmen. He regaled audiences with his fictitious book, which he supposedly titled *Simple Science for United States Senators*. He loved to poke fun at politicians. Wiley Post and Will Rogers were on their way to Alaska where Post outfitted his airplane with floats. He landed on a lake somewhere and, when trying to take off, hit a submerged log, causing the airplane to crash. Both Post and Rogers died.

As a kid, I was always around an airport. All through my teen years I loved to build model airplanes, both gliders and rubber band-powered models. At that time, there were no such things as gas-powered models like today.

In 1940, I was seventeen years old and war was fast approaching. The Japanese had already expanded into Manchuria and China and were taking over Indochina. Adolf Hitler had been proclaimed *Fürher und Reichskanzler* (Leader and National Chancellor) of Germany, and the Nazi party was dominant. The German military was also spreading out, as Benito Mussolini, the Italian dictator, had done, into Africa from Italy. First, Hitler sent his army westward and invaded the Rhineland in early 1936 (which had been taken away from them after WWI). A couple of years later Hitler, welcomed by the Austrian Nazis, went into and annexed Austria—virtually without firing a shot. Next, the Germans took over Czechoslovakia, and on the 1st of September 1939, they invaded and very quickly conquered Poland. Britain and France said, "Enough's enough." War was declared against Germany.

In the United States, most people were either anti-war or strongly neutralist. However, the federal government foresaw a lot of things, one being the fact that the American military was too small. It had shrunk to being almost non-existant after World War I. The air arm, the Army Air Corps, was pathetically small.

Although the American people wanted to remain neutral, as did many politicians, the federal government instituted several programs, one of which was unveiled by President Roosevelt on the 27th of December 1938. It was called CPT, "Civilian Pilot Training." Any qualified boy who was eighteen years of age and passed the physical and mental exams could take CPT.

The CPT program had several levels. The first license a pilot earned was called a Student Pilot License, the next level was a Private Pilot License, and above that level was a Commercial Pilot license. There were several other levels including Instrument Pilot, Instructor Pilot, multi-engine rating, seaplane rating, and so on and so forth.

While I was in high school, our family moved from Sioux City, Iowa, to Salt Lake City, Utah, and then out to Seattle, Washington, where we finally settled. I was in the National Guard when it became activated in 1941. I missed going into active duty because I was two-and-a-half months short of my eighteenth birthday. During 1941, while the rest of my National Guard unit was on active duty, I finished up another year at Seattle University. In the summer of 1941, I entered the CPT training program held on-campus. In the evenings I went to Seattle U for the ground school. During the day I learned to fly.

To become a private pilot at that time, one had to have thirty-five hours flying time total. (Later that was increased to forty hours.) Of those thirty-five hours, about twenty-five hours were dual instruction—student with instructor. One of the first important milestones was soloing.

The flying program was conducted on a grassy field just outside the town of Issaquah, twenty miles east of Seattle. This flying field was set up by the Witters Flying Agency, which had originally been located at Boeing Field. Witters had to vacate Boeing Field because traffic was increasing there, so they relocated to the more rural part of the county and leased a cow pasture where they set up operations.

I think I soloed at seven hours, though normally the dual time prior to soloing was eight hours. The airplane I flew was the Piper Cub two-seater, which was a high-wing monoplane called the J3F. It was a very nice little plane.

I received my private pilot's license at the end of the summer of 1941, at the age of eighteen. Up to this point, all my flying time, including training, had been during daylight hours only.

Off to Alaska and the Yukon Territory

By June of '42, the Japanese had bombed Pearl Harbor and my National Guard unit had been sent off to Southeast Asia. My dad found me a job with a construction company up on the Alaskan-Canadian Highway, which was being built in anticipation of war. Eventually, it would stretch fifteen hundred miles, connecting Dawson Creek, British Colombia, to Fairbanks, Alaska.

I went by chartered yacht, a beautiful boat called the "Cadrew," up the Inland Passage to Skagway, Alaska. From there, I went up the funicular railroad through White Pass to the upper plateau, changed trains and traveled through Carcross to White Horse. White Horse, in June, was a dingy, crummy place.

The air was thick with the biggest mosquitoes I'd ever seen. It was necessary to wear light gloves and a hat called a fedora. The brim of the fedora had mosquito netting attached to it which I tucked in around my neck.

The construction company, the E. W. Elliot Construction Company out of Seattle, was there to build the base camp and the quarters for that portion of the Alcan Highway. The company had contracted with a restaurant in town to provide meals for its employees. We dubbed the restaurant "The Greasy Spoon."

The locals, several of whom were married to Indian women, ran carnal houses out of their homes; in other words, they were peddling their wives' bodies to the men on the labor crew. I was not very impressed with either the place or my job as a time keeper in the payroll office.

Up above on a plateau outside the miserable town of White Horse was an airfield. Every day the weather was good, which was most of the time, American airplanes flew into the White Horse airfield for refueling and then continued farther up into Alaska. The Japanese had occupied a couple of islands in the Aleutian chain, Attu and Kiska, and were preparing for an invasion into the massive Alaskan interior.

There was another kid up there in White Horse, and he and I palled around together. One day we went into town, which had only gravel or mud streets (I don't think there were any sidewalks), to have lunch. After eating, we came outside the restaurant, and discovered a 1922 Model T Ford Phaeton Sedan parked right out front. It was brand new! I couldn't believe it!

Jim Keeffe, age 19, sitting in a 1922 Model T Ford Phaeton Sedan outside a restaurant in White Horse, Yukon Territory. (Lt. Col. Keeffe collection)

I climbed into the Model T and had my friend take a picture of me. About that time, the owner of the car came out, and I spoke with him.

"I hope you don't mind. I was having my friend take a picture."

"Oh no, it's OK young fella," he replied.

"Would you mind telling me where in the world you got this car?" I asked him.

"Well, I've had it blocked up in a shed for the last fifteen to twenty years. I struck it rich one time, and I went down to the States and saw these new-fangled things, these cars, and I bought three of 'em and had 'em shipped up here. I put two of 'em up on blocks and drove one until it crumped. Then I drove another one until it crumped, and this is the third one, which I think will last me until I die." Well, this Phaeton Sedan was in mint condition. It was beautiful!

Frequently, when flights of airplanes came in, I would run and jump into a company truck and drive up onto the plateau. Watching these planes really triggered my desire to get into flying. At the airfield were small twin engine bombers like the B-25 Mitchell. But more importantly there were P-39 fighters with tricycle landing gear, the first Army Air Corps airplanes with a tricycle landing gear (a wheel under each wing and one under the nose). There were also cargo airplanes carrying troops and equipment. .

P-39 fighters parked on the flight line at the airfield outside of White Horse. (Lt. Col. Keeffe collection)

I became restless. I wanted to fly, and I finally decided to quit my job and go back to the States When I got back to Seattle, I joked with my dad. "I'm sorry, Dad, for quitting the nice job you got me. It was a cushy job except for the bugs and mosquitoes and the lousy food."

"I Want to Join the Navy"

Returning home to Seattle, I told my dad and mom that I wanted to join the Navy and become a pilot. My folks and I talked it over. "Well you're nineteen," they said. "We're already at war, and the Navy's better than the infantry, so go ahead and do it."

I went to the Exchange Building in Seattle on a Monday, Tuesday, and Wednesday in early July 1942 and took all of the Navy tests, which included physical and psychological exams and interviews. During this time, I began to form some opinions about the Navy. I didn't like the way the Navy officers treated the sailors and the corpsmen who were conducting the physical tests.

On Wednesday afternoon, after completing all those tests, I was taken in to see the guy in charge of the place. He was sitting at his LSD, which is navy terminology for "Large Steel Desk." He had both of his arms stretched out in front of him resting on the desk with his fists touching each other. The objective of this exercise was to display the three solid stripes on the end of each of his sleeves.

I knew enough of Army and Navy ranks to know he was a full Commander. However, one of the stripes was brand new, which indicated he had recently been promoted. Additionally, I could tell if a Navy officer was a line officer (an officer who is trained in combat command) because there would be a star on the right sleeve above the three rank stripes. That star stood for line officer operations. This guy didn't have a star on his sleeve.

"He's a retread," I thought.

Mentally I made up a name for him, "Commander Blimp," because he was on the chubby side. The chair in front of his desk was very low to the ground, which made me appear rather insignificant and made him look bigger.

He went through the results of my tests. "You did pretty well on this, and you did pretty well on that," he said. Finally he shuffled the papers together and added, "But don't let this all go to your head because you'll never be a Regular Navy Officer."

I didn't know what a Regular Navy Officer was and, at the age of nineteen, I couldn't have cared less. It rather upset me the way he was talking to me, remember, I had already formed my opinion about the way the officers were treating the sailors.

"You come on down Saturday morning to the Federal Building on 1st Avenue in Seattle," he finally said. The Navy personnel examined a group of people all week long, and those who passed the tests were sent to the Federal Building on the following Saturday morning to be sworn in. The Navy always had newspaper people there to take pictures and, of course, anyone who was anybody was joining the Navy Air Program.

After finishing with Commander Blimp, I went home, and Mom and Dad asked me what I thought. "You know, I don't think I like the way the Navy treats sailors, and I don't like being talked down to," I told them.

That evening, I pulled out my aviation magazines and compared the new tricycle-geared P-39 Air Cobra to the Navy F4F. The P-39 had a 37mm cannon that fired through the propeller hub and had its engine behind the pilot. It was the U.S. Army Air Forces' number one fighter. On the F4F, the pilot had to use a hand crank to bring the gear up, and it took something like one hundred and thirty-eight turns to bring the landing gear up after takeoff. I also compared the B-25 to the TBD, Torpedo Bomber Douglas. "I wonder if I'm being smart joining the Navy," I thought to myself. "Their airplanes aren't as good as the Army's, and I sure don't like the way they treat their people."

The next day, just for the heck of it, I went downtown to the Orpheum Building, to the Army Air Forces Aviation Cadet testing group. I walked into their suite, which was about halfway up inside the building.

It was a beautiful summer day. The windows were open, a breeze was wafting through the place, and there were some Army officers in brown riding boots, pink riding pants, shirts with no neckties, and open collars. Some of them even had their sleeves rolled up, all very relaxed. I couldn't help but think, "Boy, what a difference between this and the Navy."

A young lieutenant came up to me and asked, "May I help you, sir?"

"No, I'm just kind of snooping around, thanks. If you don't mind, I'd like to look over some of your material."

"Please help yourself, and if you have any questions, I'll be happy to answer them for you," he said.

I looked at the material, but I was also taking the measure of the place. I liked how the officers were treating the enlisted men, some sergeants who were there. I finally asked the officer if I could take the tests.

"Sure," he told me.

Well, to make a long story short, in one day I did with the Army what had taken me three days to do with the Navy.

I took their physical tests and I distinctly remember one of them. There was a vertical board with a small hole in it on a table along with a wand that looked like an ice pick (actually, it was an electrode). The hole in the vertical board had a piece of electrified metal surrounding it. I was supposed to put the ice pick probe in the hole without touching the sides. Five or six of us were taking the test at the time, so there was a lot of sparking going on; *click, click, click*. This test was to see if I had control over my hand movements. There were several tests like that.

I was given a physical examination and then a written examination. When I finished up, I was shown in to see an Army captain who was sitting behind his desk with his shirt collar open and his sleeves rolled up. "Cool!" I thought.

"Well young man, you did very well on your tests, and we would be honored to have you as an Aviation Cadet in the Army Air Forces."

"I have to tell you one thing," I said. "I've already taken the Navy tests, and I've passed everything."

He was a smart captain, so he asked, "Were you sworn in?"

"No, sir, I wasn't sworn in. They're going to swear me in the day after tomorrow, Saturday."

"You're a very lucky man," he said to me. "You have two choices. You can either join the Navy Air, as they need pilots too, or you can join the Army Air and believe me, you're the type of person we're looking for. So, here is what I suggest. Why don't you go home, talk it over with your parents and make a decision, but please understand we'd be very happy to have you."

I went home and talked with Mom and Dad that night and made my decision. The next morning, I went back to the Orpheum Building and was sworn into the United States Army Air Forces. I did not go to the Federal Building; in fact, I forgot about them until Saturday morning.

The Shortest Navy Career Ever

I must have stayed out rather late that Friday night because I was still in bed late Saturday morning when my mother came upstairs. She woke me up to tell me I had a phone call.

"Jim, there's a Navy officer on the phone," she said as she came into my bedroom, "and he doesn't sound very happy."

"A Navy officer?"

"Yes. He asked for Mr. Keeffe, so I asked if he wanted Jim senior or Jim junior. He fumbled around a bit and asked for Jim junior."

It was just after noon, and I suddenly remembered that I was supposed to have been at the Federal Building at 10 a.m. that morning to be sworn in.

I went downstairs and picked up the telephone and said, "This is Jim Keeffe Jr. speaking."

The voice on the other end was Commander Blimp.

"Mr. Keeffe, where were you this morning!"

"Well sir, I've been home in bed," I told him.

"Young man, this is a hell of a way to start your career in the Navy. You were supposed to be down here to be sworn in, and you were AWOL!"

"Well sir, I beg your pardon. I was not AWOL because I don't belong to you. I was not sworn in. Besides, Commander, I've already joined the Army Air Forces."

"You what?" he boomed.

"I joined the Army Air Forces yesterday, and I was sworn in."

Bang! The telephone was slammed down. That was my Navy career. I had the shortest Navy career of anybody I know.

Pilot Training Begins

I was sworn in as a sergeant in the Army Reserve. In early August, I received a telegram instructing me to report to Aviation Cadet Flying Training in Santa Ana, California.

I said goodbye to my family and to Pat Eisen, my girlfriend. My mother and my sister, Peggy, took me to the King Street Train Station where I boarded a train with a one-way ticket. I rode the train down to Santa Ana, California, and was bused out to the Army Air Forces West Coast Flying Training Command base.

The base was expanding tremendously. The military was constructing a lot of barracks, but, additionally, they had a lot of tents. The tents were shaped like pyramids and normally held eight cots for eight men. The other new recruits and I were housed in these tents until we were assigned to a training squadron. We went through all the tests again, and we also went through very thorough physical examinations. After the physicals, we took a battery of tests that were called "Stanine Tests." Upon completion, we were rated for one of three air crew positions: pilot, navigator, or bombardier. I ended up with a nine on all of my stanine tests and came away with a pilot rating.

Cadet Keeffe at Aviation Cadet Training in Santa Ana, California, 1942. (Lt. Col. Keeffe collection)

My group of new recruits was assigned to class 43-E, which meant we would graduate the following year (1943) in the fifth class (E being the fifth letter of the alphabet). I moved into a barracks where a group of us, who'd been

CPT pilot-trained, was pulled out and taken to an interview with a captain.

"We're very sorry," he said. "You men aren't supposed to be here. This 43-E class is for flying sergeants only, and you're going to become officers. There was a foul up in your orders. We're going to send you home, and you can come back when you're called next time."

We didn't like this at all.

"Sir," I said, "we've already said our goodbyes. We're already here, we're already pilots, and we've had CPT training. We want to continue."

"You can't stay for pilot training," he replied, "But I can continue you in either navigator or bombardier training."

"No, thank you," I said. "We don't want to be bombardiers or navigators. We want to be pilots. That's what we already are."

We were moved around for three or four days until the captain finally agreed.

"OK, you can stay and go through pilot training, but now we have to hold you until the next class because your class is already through the pre-flight training."

So we were reassigned to 43-F. We went through ground school, which concluded at the beginning of December. Ground school was comprised of many different classes: we had code class, where I quickly learned Morse code; we had aircraft recognition class; we had engineering classes, aerodynamics classes, and so on and so forth. We also did some shooting with .45 caliber semi-automatic pistols and Thompson sub-machine guns.

Finally, we received assignments to Primary Training bases.

Primary Training, Tulare

Pilot training at that time consisted of four programs: Pre-flight at Santa Ana, which I finished in December, then Primary, Basic, and Advanced.

Primary schools were all run by civilians. I was assigned to Tex Rankin's School of Aeronautics located at Tulare, California. Tex Rankin was one of the famous pilots from the 1920s and 1930s.

Tulare was north of Bakersfield and south of Fresno and Stockton. We traveled by bus north from Santa Ana, through Bakersfield, up to Tulare and on out to the base. It was the 8th of December 1942. It was a beautiful little base. The flying field itself consisted of a 1/4 mile square grass field. The airplanes were bi-planes—Boeing PT-17s. We called them the Kaydets, and they were wonderful.

When we arrived at the base the bus stopped outside the gate. We got out with our suitcases and the upper classmen grabbed us.

The three pilot training phases, Primary, Basic, and Advanced, were each nine weeks long. Because these classes overlapped, the people in the 43-E class (the class we were originally assigned to) were already partway through the Primary class. With our arrival, they became upper classmen. They gave us hell, just the way they had been given hell four and a half weeks earlier. They made us run everywhere we went, forcing us to leave our bags outside for several hours the day we arrived.

Soon after we arrived we met our instructors. Five of us aviation cadets were assigned to one instructor. My instructor's name was Charlie Hahn. He was a middle-aged man who had been a pilot for a zillion years. I don't know how many flying hours he had, but he probably had more hours flying airplanes than he had driving cars. Charlie Hahn was a very kindly fellow; he had us, his five students, to his home for Christmas Day.

L to R: Cadets Keeffe, Johnson, Kirksmith, Instructor C. E. Hahn. (Lt. Col. Keeffe collection)

The routine for half of us in Primary class was ground training in the morning and flying training in the afternoon. The other half of the class did their ground school in the afternoon and their flying in the morning. For several days we did both our flying and ground school, and then the San Joaquin fog set in, which was typical in December and January. For about three and a half weeks there was no flying.

Fortunately, we had been able to see the base before the fog set in, so we were familiar with all the buildings and the quarters. They were all single-story and there were no tents. The fog was so thick that when we fell out in the morning for formation, the guy taking roll would drop down and get below the fog to count legs! The fog finally broke in the beginning of January; then they flew the pants off us. I soloed at about six hours.

During the foggy days, we had ground school morning and afternoon. When the flying started back up again, we flew both morning and afternoon. Cadets were eliminated at a ferocious rate. My recollection is that about eighty percent of our class there at Tulare washed out.

The entire training was conducted by civilian instructors, but the check pilots were Army officers. Their airplanes were called Maytags, for "washing machines." Anyone put up for a ride in a Maytag faced the possibility of being eliminated. I had my ride in the Maytag and had no problem.

Flight training was quite interesting. Because of the location of the plane's center of gravity, the pilot always flew from the rear seat, even when flying alone. Therefore, we cadets trained from the back seat while the check pilot or the instructor rode in the front seat. Each cadet had a helmet with two little right-angle pipes and a rubber hose called a Goss-port. The instructor in front communicated with the cadet in the back through a funnel-shaped mouthpiece attached to this rubber hose, which was attached to the Goss-port in the back seat. There were no radios in the planes. The instructor could talk to the cadet, but the cadet couldn't talk to the instructor; instead, the instructor would turn around and get facial expressions from the cadet.

At the time I got to Tulare I already had 40 hours of flying. While there, I was mischievous and practiced aerobatics quite a bit. The PT-17 was a beautiful acrobatic airplane. The only things I did that were out of line I did during the last seven to ten days of flying. One of the other cadets and I chased cows, which I'm sure the farmers didn't appreciate. We'd locate a small herd, get down below the ridge line and then come right up over the ridge line aimed at the cows, all pretty low to the ground. Boy would they scatter!

One day, about two thirds of the way through training, I was up on a training flight.

"Mr. Keeffe, do me a snap roll to the left," said Mr. Hahn. (Cadets were called "Mister," and an officer was "Sir.")

It was easier to do a snap roll to the left rather than to the right, because the torque of the engine and the turning propeller were trying to roll the plane that way anyhow.

I did a snap roll, but instead of doing a single snap roll, I did a snap and a half, and we wound up upside down.

Upside down, Mr. Hahn turned around and looked at me. He grabbed his speaking tube and said, "Roll out."

So I half rolled out, up-righting us.

He then turned around and said, "Did you do that on purpose?"

"Yes," I nodded, with a smile on my face.

"Do it again to the right."

I did a snap and a half to the right and wound up upside down again.

"Roll out."

I rolled out.

"Have you been practicing?" he asked.

"Yes, sir," I nodded.

"Do you realize if my seatbelt hadn't been fastened I might have fallen out of the airplane when you stopped us upside down?"

"Yes, sir," I nodded.

"OK, Mr. Keeffe, let's go back to the barn."

He told me later that I was one of the best cadets he'd ever had. That was Charlie Hahn.

Taking off and landing were rather interesting at Tulare. We could take off in any one of eight different directions depending upon the wind. The flight personnel set what we called the "T," a pivotal "T," on the ground to show us the direction of the traffic. Early mornings in the valley were dead calm and cool, but inevitably the wind would come up at about 8:30. One day we would take off, for example to the north, and then the wind would come up and the "T" might be changed about 45 degrees, or maybe even 90 degrees, to another direction. When the wind came up, instructors were sent up to collect all the students and herd them back to the home base.

One time when we were in the air the wind changed and the instructors rounded everybody up except one cadet they couldn't locate. The wind was blowing pretty hard, but everybody else got on the ground safely. Finally, at the end of the flying period, which was about an hour or an hour and a half long, here came this lone PT-17 with yellow wings and blue fuselage. He was coming in with the normal pattern for the direction he had taken off in. In other words, he came in trying to land to the north, but he now had a very strong cross wind that kept blowing him off course.

He made three approaches. Each time he was drifting too much, but he was smart enough to come in with power and go around and try it again. The flight personnel were shooting flares at him trying to get his attention to look at the wind "T," and also the wind sock, which would show him that the direction of traffic had changed. He never got it. He finally came in again, the third time, the last time.

The cross wind was so strong that his forward speed was very slow, about twenty or thirty miles an hour. We were all standing out there watching him. I could see his ailerons moving up and down and his rudder going back and forth, and I knew he was going to do a snap roll. I watched his control surfaces and knew exactly what he was doing. He was pushing in the left rudder and, at the same time, moving the stick off to the right. He was setting himself up for just what happened. He did a snap roll! He was in close to the ground and the snap brought his nose up, flipped the plane, and he pranged on the ground.

Fortunately, because it was a bi-plane, the upper wing protected him. Just as he went into this snap roll, he ran the power clear to full to go around again. He went around all right, pivoting on the vertical stabilizer! He broke the rudder off, and his airplane spun around upside down about one and a half times, bending the propeller. Finally the engine seized, and he stopped. Then he did another dumb thing; upside down and scared to death, he undid his seat belt and fell out and broke his neck. He lived, but that was it for his military flying career.

About the end of January we finished up. We were now the upper classmen, and we gave the incoming class hell for four and a half weeks. Finally, it was time to move on to Basic.

Basic Training, Lemoore

We didn't have far to go, just up the valley from Tulare a few miles to Lemoore. Lemoore Army Air Base was a military base with all military officers and all military instructors. We arrived by bus and were taken into the theater for a welcoming address by the Training Group commander.

"You cadets are here to learn to fly military airplanes. You are going to be military pilots. We don't give a damn what you do with these airplanes as long as you don't crash them and as long as we don't get too many complaints from the farmers around here. Go fly, because very shortly you are going to be in a war situation."

Lemoore was wonderful. We went from the open cockpit bi-plane into the Vultee BT-13 and BT-15. "BT" stands for Basic Trainer. Essentially, these two were the same airplane, although the BT-13 was more expensive. This plane was made entirely of metal except for the control surfaces, which were all fabric. The BT-15, however, had a fuselage after-section made from plywood. There was a lot of trouble with this airplane. In fact, we were restricted from doing snap rolls in them because the torque would twist the structure and bring it out of alignment. We did a lot of flying, and we were checked out for night flying. This was the first night flying we'd done. We also started formation flying and instrument flying, neither of which we had done before.

My instructor pilot was a first lieutenant by the name of Theodore J. Gaines.

Lt. Gaines was a Greek-American who lived nearby, and he and I remained friends even after the war. He was a very good instrument pilot.

Cadet Keeffe flying the BT-13 trainer. Instructor Lt. Theodore Gaines, Lemoore Army Air Base. (Lt. Col. Keeffe collection)

Lemoore had a main field along with three auxiliary fields while Tulare had only one satellite field. Normally, we went to the auxiliary fields, which were away from the home base, to do our flying training and then came back at the end of an hour.

The seating was reversed at Lemoore; the pilot sat in the front seat, and anyone else who went along, including the instructor, rode in the back seat. Center of gravity wasn't as big a problem as in the bi-plane.

Our squadron commander, Captain N. F. Bundgard, was a wild man. On the BT-13 and BT-15, just in front of the front cockpit wind screen and canopy, was a radio mast that was about three feet high with a wire going back to the vertical stabilizer for the radio, and a lead coming into the cockpit. In flying formation Bundgard would get down under three airplanes. Deftly working the stick, he'd come up and touch his radio aerial mast on a wheel of one airplane, drop down again, slide over, and come up and touch a wheel of the next plane, then, move up to the front airplane and do the same thing, and then drop behind. He didn't seem worried at all about the spinning propellers of both airplanes! This guy had guts and was crazy.

One evening, Capt. Bundgard drove with me out to the auxiliary field where we hopped into an airplane and went flying. It was dark by the time we headed back to the field to land. The San Joaquin Valley at night was pitch black except for along U.S. 99, which was well to the east of us. The farms had neither fences nor fence posts, and the roads went along section lines, or quarter sections, straight as arrows. This particular night, down below us, we saw a vehicle traveling along a road.

The BT-13 had radios, which the PT-17 did not have, so we could talk between the two cockpits with an open microphone. I was in front and he was in back.

Squadron Commander Capt. Bundgard, Lemoore Army Air Base. (Lt. Col. Keeffe collection)

"Keeffe, let's have some fun," said Captain Bundgard, "I've got the airplane!"

He peeled off and switched off the airplane's lights. On the right wing was a green light, on the left wing was a red light, and on the tail, a white light, just like on ships. Bundgard dropped down in front of the oncoming car, which had its headlights on, and put the main wheels of our plane onto the asphalt road ahead of the car. He had already changed the prop pitch into low pitch, high RPM.

"Keeffe, when I tell you, turn on the landing lights."

I could see the car coming toward us.

"What the hell's he going to do?" I wondered.

We got closer and closer to the car, and it seemed that we were going to crash head-on.

"Turn on the landing lights!" he shouted.

As I turned on the landing lights, he pulled right up over the car and turned to the left.

"Turn out the lights!" he shouted.

The engine exhaust from the cylinders was collected in a manifold that funneled into one pipe out the right side of the engine. At full power, a blue flame about three feet long came out of the pipe. In a left hand bank, no one would be able to see this from the ground.

Well, the car went bouncing off the road out into the fields and came to a stop.

"Look at that crazy driver out there in the boondocks," Bundgard said. "How'd you like that, Keeffe?"

"That was kind of fun," I told him.

"Fine, let's go do it again!" he said.

After terrorizing a few more motorists, he laughed and said we should "head back to the barn" to see if anybody had called up.

Fun and games!

At Lemoore, the only things I found exciting were night flying and getting used to the engine exhaust blue flame that came back almost to the cockpit. However, a couple of things happened to me there that I was very lucky to survive.

After being briefed in the flight briefing room, standard practice was to run and get my parachute, run to my assigned airplane, get into it quickly, strap up, and crank the engines up. Then I'd hurry and taxi out, trying to beat everybody else, so I could get airborne and not wind up in a queue waiting for takeoff. The flight line was a patch instead of a runway, so three, four, or five of us could be side by side checking our mags (magnetos) prior to taking off.

One day, I was one of the early birds with three or four other guys. We were all parked with our brakes set at the edge of the patch, checking the engines and the mags, and getting ready to go. Two or three of us advanced our throttles and took off separately but almost side by side. I was quickly airborne, but instead of gradually climbing to altitude like normal, I went straight up. All of this happened very fast.

I noticed the other pilots were still well below me and climbing gradually. Seeing them made me realize that something was wrong with my plane. At the same time, I realized that my stick force was building up tremendously. My airplane was at way too steep a climb angle. I pushed the stick forward to bring the nose down so that I wouldn't go into a stall, but the nose wouldn't come down. One of the pre-flight checks the ground crew did was to set the elevator trim tabs for takeoff position. Doing so caused the nose of the plane to rise slightly upward during takeoff. To set the trim tabs they had to roll a big open wheel that had a cable going across it. Rolling the wheel one way made the cable move the trim tabs up, and rolling the wheel the other way made the trim tabs go down. How far up or down the trim tabs were set was controlled by how far one way or the other the wheel was rolled. It took all of my strength to hold the stick forward and, at the same time, reset the trim tabs to nose down. I rolled and rolled and rolled that wheel. Finally, I got the pressure off the stick. The plane was right on the verge of a stall. But it didn't stall, and I was able to climb out in a normal fashion.

It was then that I figured out what had happened; somebody had gotten into the airplane and intentionally rolled the trim all the way around, which put the nose in a full up position upon take off. There was an indicator on the trim wheel, but whoever set the trim had ignored it. If those other airplanes hadn't been beside me and lower than I was, I probably would have stalled and crashed and burned right there. Seeing those airplanes saved my life.

I had another close call at Lemoore, this time while landing. The normal way we approached the field for landing was for the planes to come in from either side to form a final approach stream. On one occasion, I came nose on with a guy coming from the other direction. My recollection is he was in the sun. I was looking into the sun, but fortunately, at the last moment, I saw him. I pulled up, and he turned. That was a lousy final approach method; we almost crashed head-on.

Along about the 1st of April we finished up Basic Training. That was a happy time at Lemoore.

Squadron 11 photo at the beginning of Basic Training, Lemoore Army Air Base. Cadet Keeffe is far right in the first row and best friend Benny Kendall is in the back row sixth from the left. (Lt. Col. Keeffe collection)

Advanced Training, Yuma

Buses took us from the middle of the San Joaquin Valley in central California across the state to Yuma, Arizona. We arrived at Yuma Army Air Field the first week in April, and we graduated there on the 21st of June 1943. It was hot when we got there, and it was a hell of a lot hotter in June when we left. I'm glad we didn't have to spend the summer there.

Yuma had board sidewalks and dirt roads. It was the only base where I never went into town. At Lemoore and Tulare, we'd gone into town occasionally, but I had no desire to go into Yuma, Arizona. The base was out in virtually desert conditions. My recollection is that there were no trees on the base. The cadet barracks were not at all what we'd had at Lemoore or at Rankin. Rankin had the best cadet quarters. Lemoore's were a step down but still good. Yuma's were tar paper shacks and rather miserable, the absolute minimum.

We flew three types of airplanes, one of which was the AT-17; "AT" stands for Advanced Trainer. This airplane was the Cessna twin-engine Bobcat. It had retractable landing gear, two engines, two propellers, and radio equipment. The AT-17 was designed as a small civilian passenger airplane. It could seat up to six people behind the two pilots. The Advanced Trainer military version had no seats in the back end.

At each step, from Primary to Basic and Basic to Advanced, the airplanes had more and more gadgets. At Yuma, for the first time, we cadets began flying with each other. In the twin engine airplanes we had to have a pilot and a copilot.

Gunnery training. Cadet Keeffe is second from the right. (Lt. Col. Keeffe collection)

The second airplane we flew at Yuma was the AT-6, Advanced Trainer 6. It was a fine single-engine airplane equipped with one .30 caliber machine gun. We used this airplane for aerial gunnery and ground attack gunnery. We got the feel for flying and firing and, for the first time, experienced the noise and minor vibration of a gun working on an airplane. Because we were learning aerial gunnery, we also did skeet shooting with pump shot guns at the base shooting range. The range had a couple of towers that flipped out the skeet so we could practice.

The third type of airplane we flew was a really fine twin-engine airplane, the Curtiss AT-9. It was all metal, twin-engine, accommodated two pilots and was considered pretty hot. I really loved this airplane, but some of the cadets were afraid of it and didn't like it.

I came to realize something about myself during Advanced Training. I had always considered myself an average or normal pilot. In Advanced, flying with other cadets in my flight, I quickly learned that some of them were certainly not as good a pilot as I was. Some of the mistakes they made were things like flying the airplanes literally into the ground or making very bad landings.

Cadet Keeffe in a twin-engine Curtiss AT-9 trainer, Yuma Army Air Field, Arizona.
(Lt. Col. Keeffe collection)

Yuma, Arizona, was hotter than Hades. The AT-17s were fabric covered monoplanes, and because of the intense heat the glue that held the frame and the wings together would leak out onto the ground. This was a potential safety problem and the officials were quite concerned.

Our usual wakeup time at each of the bases, Tulare, Lemoore and Yuma, was around 6:30 a.m. About an hour before this, the ground crew would start up the engines, test them, and check out all fifty, sixty, or seventy airplanes, depending upon how many were going to fly that day. So we woke up every morning to horrendous engine noise. This was especially true at Yuma because there were two engines on most of the airplanes.

One afternoon, my flight assembled outside on the grounds for our daily flight assignments. It was a typically hot day and most of us were perspiring profusely as we stood at attention. There were also a half dozen officers, mostly second lieutenants, in our flight, but they didn't have to stand in formation with us. They were able to wait in the shade or go inside a building.

Standing in the heat not only makes you sweaty, but you can get pretty tired and lethargic. Sure enough, a couple of the men started yawning. This didn't go over well at all with the flight leader, who got so angry that he made us stand at attention in that searing hot air for over two hours as punishment. A couple of the second lieutenants who were lazing around in the shade decided to get into the act and walked around us making smart remarks. There's always a smart-ass or two in every group. This sort of thing is crap and does nothing for leadership.

Punishment formation. Cadets standing at attention in the searing heat. Cadet Keeffe at near end of middle row with Cadet Kendall in front of him. Yuma Army Air Field, Arizona. (Lt. Col. Keeffe collection)

I remember very clearly standing at attention in the scorching heat at the end of one of the rows of cadets. A good friend of mine, Benny Kendall, was at attention directly in front me, and I watched the sweat begin to soak the back of his flying suit, right below the neck line. As the minutes dragged by, the wet stain on his flying suit got bigger and bigger, and I could feel my own sweat begin to drip down my sides. Well into the second hour under the sun, the back of Benny's flying suit was completely soaked through. Every time I stole a glance at him, I felt more sweat drip down my sides. A couple of cadets locked their knees while at attention, effectively cutting off the circulation to their lower legs, and they keeled over backwards in a faint. It was a long, hot, sweaty two hours.

The base commander was an iron-ass and was pretty tough on the enlisted men. One of the sergeants, who worked on the airplanes down on the line, had had a couple of run-ins with the commander. This sergeant was a retread from WW I and had been an officer at that time. After the run-ins with the base commander, he received a commission that made him senior to the base commander. Within two days the base commander was transferred to North Africa. (By this time, June of 1943, the war had already taken the United States into North Africa.)

We cadets never had anything to do with the senior officers, and we had very little to do with the ground crew. Normally, the ground crew did all of their checking of the airplanes while we were being briefed for the day in our flight rooms. By the time we went out to the airplanes, the ground crew would be finished, and they'd stand around while we started the engines. Then they'd go inside and take it easy playing cards and the like.

As it had been at Tulare and Lemoore, the schedule here at Yuma was arranged so that two training days were collapsed into one day. One half of the class flew in the morning while the other half of the class did ground school. Then in the afternoon, the morning fliers became the ground school people, and the morning ground school people became the fliers. The only time there was trouble with this arrangement was during night flying training—there couldn't be flying all night long.

In Primary we had no night flying or instrument training. In Basic we started instrument training and night flying and were checked out solo in night flying. In Advanced we did ordinary flying, acrobatics, instrument flying, night flying, and cross-country flying. We actually flew two or three short cross-country flights in Basic, but in Advanced our flights were much longer.

When I started out at Santa Ana in the Pre-Flight class of 43-F, I was in one room with eight or nine other cadets, and all of our last names started with "K." The roster started out with Kaville, Walter I.; next was Keeffe, James H., Kendall, Ben N.; then another Kendall, and a couple of Kennedys. Kaville was washed out in Primary. He just wasn't very coordinated. He became a trumpet player in an Army band.

Cadet Benny Kendall, Yuma Army Air Field, Arizona. (Lt. Col. Keeffe collection)

Benny Kendall and I went all the way through training together, and later through B-24 Transition. He was a cigarette smoker. At Lemoore Basic

Training, in the cadet barracks, we were in double bunks. I always preferred the upper bunk and he preferred the lower bunk, so we got along fine except for his cigarette smoking. The first thing he did in the morning when we were awakened was to lie in bed and smoke a cigarette. That was pretty horrible, me being a non-smoker.

Benny and I flew often together in the AT-17. During one of our flights, I asked him to go to the back for some reason, so he got out of his seat up in the cockpit and went to the back. I pushed the nose down, and he floated up off the floor. As long as I had the nose going down faster than he was falling, he floated around in the air. As soon as I leveled off and began to bring the nose up, gravity took over and he collapsed onto the floor. Then when I gave it more throttle, and roared upward in a climb, poor old Benny couldn't even stand up. I gave him a hard time for about half an hour. He couldn't get back to the cockpit because he was either up in the air floating, or I had him squashed on the floor. You do crazy things.

Back when we were at Basic, we identified what types of planes we preferred flying: cargo, heavy bombers, attack bombers, multi-engine fighters, or single engine fighters. I chose light bombardment, which means twin-engine, small crew airplanes, or twin-engine fighters. This was the type of training base Yuma was. Luke Field, up near Phoenix, was a single-engine fighter training base. They flew only the AT-6. Another base in Arizona was for the P-38 fighters. I wish I'd gone there.

Graduation

We graduated from cadet training and were commissioned on the 22nd of June 1943. Before the graduation ceremony that morning, we suited up in our Army officer uniforms and walked over to a very rough building that was the base theater. Only a few families came because not much traveling was done during the war; traveling was expensive and gas was rationed.

The Training Group commander gave a speech. We were each given a little box with two gold second lieutenant bars inside, and we put the bars on each other. We were also given silver wings, which we put on each other. For those who had family members there, the wife, mother, or father did the honor of pinning on the wings and bars.

I remember part of the Training Group Commander's speech very clearly.

Young officers, you are no longer misters. You are no longer cadets.
You are now officers. You are second lieutenants. You will be addressed

as "Lieutenant" from now on. You will be saluted by the enlisted men, and you will return their salutes. You will spread to the four winds when you walk out of this building and go to your different assignments, and home on leave. Let me leave you with one thing. When you walk out of this theater, leave the base, go into town, and head to where ever you are going, people are going to be watching you because you are young, healthy, handsome Army officers now. They can tell you are a second lieutenant by looking at the rank on your shoulder or on your collar. But they are not going to know whether you've been a second lieutenant for two hours, two days, two weeks, two months or two years. How you carry yourself, how you deal with people is going to determine what their impression is of you as an Army officer. We hope, we expect, that you will carry yourselves the way you have been trained and the way you have performed thus far as aviation cadets.

Lieutenant Keeffe's commissioning cards awarded 22 June, 1943. (Lt. Col. Keeffe collection)

When the Training Group Commander was finished, he saluted us all and we returned his salute. Then we left the theater. Lined up outside were two or three hundred enlisted men waiting for us. Tradition had it that when an enlisted man salutes a newly commissioned officer for the first time, the new officer gives the man a dollar. So the airmen were all lined up out there to collect some dollars. When we left the building, we were very excited, and there was quite a bit of saluting and dollar exchanging.

That same day, I received my orders to go home for two weeks leave and then report to Kirtland Army Air Field in New Mexico as a pilot of the twin-engine AT-11. The AT-11 was used to train bombardiers and navigators. I was given what was really a pretty fine assignment. I was to be one of the pilots flying bombardier and navigator cadets while they trained in bombing and navigation.

It didn't take long at all for me to get home to Seattle. When I arrived at my parents' home, they and my girlfriend couldn't believe the changes in me. At twenty years old, I was probably in the best physical condition I'd ever been in. I was lean and maybe mean, and I could arm wrestle any of my friends and take them down right then and there.

Orders Changed to B-24 Transition Training

My orders were changed while I was at home on leave. In 10 days, I was to report to my new assignment, which was B-24 Transition Training at Davis-Monthan Army Air Field in Tucson, Arizona. I wasn't going to be a fighter pilot or a light bomber pilot after all. I was going into heavy bomber training. Needless to say, I wasn't very happy. To make matters worse, I had to report there the 2nd of July, so I wasn't going to be home for the 4th of July celebration.

After arriving at Davis-Monthan, I was assigned a room in the BOQ—Bachelor Officers' Quarters—and guess who was there? Benny Kendall, the guy I'd gone all the way through training with. He and I shared a room during our training at Davis-Monthan.

The same day I arrived on base, I went down to the flight line and climbed into a monster of an airplane, a well-used B-24 heavy bomber, and sat down in one of the cockpit seats. I couldn't believe how many instruments and gadgets there were, and I didn't like it at all. But a job is a job, so I started the training. Benny and I trained in parallel for a while.

Like the P-39 fighter, the B-24 had tricycle landing gear, which was another change. I'd never flown with this type of landing gear before; the B-24 would be my first. The airplanes we had flown in Primary, Basic, and Advanced were tail-draggers (a wheel under each wing and one under the tail).

We were all heading toward becoming aircraft commanders, or first pilots, and our training was preparing us for this. Benny and I flew and trained as a pair; he and I were student-pilot officers, and we had an instructor-pilot officer and maybe one crew chief. First, Kendall or I would strap into the pilot's seat and fly for an hour with the instructor pilot. Then the other one of us would fly for an hour with the same instructor pilot and the same crew chief. About a week or two into training, I came down with a cold and was sick for four or five days and couldn't fly.

At about the same time, the base suddenly received orders to take the low-flying-time officers and send them to other bases as copilots. Bomber losses were increasing in Europe, and the powers that be were shuffling men and crews all over the place to fill the needs of the growing air war. The normal training program had been interrupted suddenly because of these heavy bomber losses in Europe. That's why I had been pulled out of my assignment to Kirtland and sent to Davis-Monthan. And here at Davis-Monthan, it happened again.

Lt. James McArthur "Mac" in B-24D pilot seat. (Lt. Col. Keeffe collection)

I fell into the low-flying-time group because I had been sick for a few days. This was enough to separate Kendall and me. Benny Kendall continued on and became an aircraft commander.[1] The men in the low-flying group, which included me, were sent off to different bases to be trained as copilots.

About the middle or latter part of August of 1943, I was assigned to go to Blythe, California. Believe me, Blythe was almost the end of creation, worse than Yuma.

The Jimmy McArthur Crew

Blythe Army Air Base is on the Colorado River along the main highway from Phoenix, Arizona, to Los Angeles. This was another tar-paper-shack base, black tar paper in the hot California sun. I arrived there and was immediately assigned to a B-24 bomber crew—the Jimmy McArthur crew. Lt. McArthur already had a navigator, a bombardier, two waist gunners, a radio operator, a flight engineer/top turret gunner, a tail gunner, and a ball turret gunner. That made nine people including McArthur, and I made the tenth and final crewman.

The training style was similar to that at Davis-Monthan, in that we flew as pilot and copilot with an instructor pilot overseeing us. Parts of two crews were flown together; first pilot and copilot of crew A would fly in the flight seats and then they would switch with first pilot and copilot of crew B.

On one training flight, McArthur and I were going to take the second part of the full training period so we weren't in the pilot seats for takeoff. We were behind the seats on the flight deck, and I was looking out the small window on the port side behind the pilot's seat during takeoff. We weren't strapped in because there was no place to strap into.

Lt. James Keeffe in B-24D copilot seat during training flight, Blythe Army Air Base, California..
(Lt. Col. Keeffe collection)

At the rear of the flight deck in the B-24 was a hatch (door) in the top of the airplane that opened downward, and it was somebody's responsibility to see that it was closed and latched before takeoff. The flight engineer/top turret gunners loved to climb out the hatch and sit on top of the fuselage just behind the cockpit while the airplane was taxiing in or taxiing out. When they got back inside, they were supposed to close and latch the hatch door. On this particular training day, somebody had closed the hatch but hadn't latched it. On takeoff, with all the shimmying and shaking, the hatch opened and swung down. I was looking out the window when the U-shaped handle on the thing hit me very hard on the left side of my neck. I saw a huge flash of stars and heard a crunch. The pain that I felt gave me an uneasy feeling that this was going to cause me grief for a very long time. And so it did.

The crew was rather interesting. Lt. James B. McArthur, from Chicago, Illinois, was a good pilot. If he had been a weak pilot, we wouldn't have gotten along very well. He was also a nice guy although we were never close friends. Lt. Raymond "Moose" H. Moulton, the bombardier, was from Charlton Depot, Massachusetts. He was also a very nice guy, and we became relatively close.

The Jimmy McArthur crew. Back row L to R: Lts. Stevens, McArthur, Keeffe, Moulton, Sgt. Hughes. Front row L to R: Sgts. Allen, France, Hall, Turlay, Bassimer. Blythe Army Air Base. (Lt. Col. Keeffe collection)

The ball turret gunner was Sgt. John "JB" B. Allen from Providence, Rhode Island. Sgt. Karl "Butch" F. Turlay, the tail turret gunner, was from Homewood, Illinois. Both Allen and Turlay were great guys, and we got along quite well. Turlay had worked in a foundry for a while before he joined the Army Air Corps. The two waist gunners were Sgt. Frank N. France and Sgt. Raymond C. Bassimer. Sgt. William "Bill" Hughes hailed from Arcadia, Kansas, and was our engineer and top turret gunner. The radio operator was Sgt. Raymond C. Hall, from Buffalo, New York. Lt. Donald M. Stevens, the navigator, was from Florence, Kentucky. Right from square one I didn't like him and my initial impression didn't change over time.

The gunners had been through gunnery school; the navigator and bombardier had been through their schools; the radio operator had been through his school, and we pilots had been through pilot training. Now at Bythe, we all came together to learn how to become a ten-man crew. We did formation flying, bombing practice, navigation, cross-country flying, and so on and so forth. Once we flew cross-country to El Paso, Texas, to go through automatic-pilot training.

There were a couple of different types of training units at Blythe. An Operational Training Unit, or OTU, was made up of crewmen who were trained as a group and then sent overseas as a group along with their airplanes. Then there was an RTU, Replacement Training Unit, which, as the name implies, sent their crewmen, either individually or as an entire crew, to replace lost crews. In fact, I would say probably seventy percent of the people sent overseas were replacement crews, rather than new groups. Our crew wound up being sent overseas as a replacement crew.

B-24 flying cross-country during training at Blythe Army Air Base. (Lt. Col. Keeffe collection)

Every day at 5 p.m. a sand storm blew through Blythe and the surrounding area. There'd be sand everywhere! I'd go back to my quarters after dinner and find sand on our dressers, on top of our clothes, everywhere. My bed always had sand on it. No matter how hard I tried to keep my mouth closed while outside, I invariably had that gritty sand in my teeth.

On Saturdays, we had tough physical training. Normally we'd run three miles and do a lot of tough calisthenics, shower up by noon, eat lunch and then have the rest of Saturday and Sunday off. We were to be back on base at 3 p.m. on Sunday for Retreat Parade and the taking down of the flag. This was one way of making sure everyone was back on Sunday.

One hot afternoon, Mac and I were lying in our underwear in our room when Lt. Stevens came to the door; he had just come back from Pasadena. Both Mac and I had standup lockers for our clothing and there was a small mirror on the inside of each locker door. As soon as Stevens walked into the room, I turned my back to him, but I could still see him in one the mirrors.

He stood there primping in front of a mirror, bragging to McArthur.

"Mac, I was just up in Pasadena last night, and I met a girl who thinks I'm God!"

"Stevens, just take the damn mirror and get out of here, please," I said, as I turned around.

Normally on a training flight, the bombardier and the navigator worked in the nose, but when they weren't working, they'd come up and sit on the floor of the flight deck. In the B-24, on the bulkhead wall at the rear of the flight deck compartment, were two brackets that held relief tubes. These were plastic cones, four to six inches long, which funneled into rubber hoses, which vented outside of the airplane. They were called relief tubes and were for relieving our bladders. When the pee vented outside into the air stream, it broke up into tiny little droplets and no one would worry about it.

On one flight, we'd been at high altitude. I think we'd been practicing bombing from 22,000 feet, and we were finished and on our way back to base. I looked at the altimeter, which read 8,000 feet, then got up, took off my oxygen mask and helmet, and told McArthur I was going to go take a leak. He looked at me as I stood up out of the cockpit seat and nodded. I stepped down onto the flight deck and saw Moulton, the bombardier, sitting on the floor. By the time I stepped down and crossed the flight deck, just a few short steps, I was anoxic, but I didn't realize it.[2]

I picked up a relief tube hooked to the side next to where Moulton was sitting and peed into it. I said something to Moulton and then climbed back into the cockpit and sat back in my seat. After putting on my helmet and oxygen mask, I looked at the altimeter which now read about 14,000 feet.

"Jimmy, how come you climbed back up?" I asked.

"I haven't climbed back up. We've been descending all the time."

"No, we were at 8,000 feet when I got up to go pee."

"No we weren't," he laughed. "We were at 18,000. You must have misread the gage."

Boy had I!

It turned out that after the bomb runs, Moulton and Stevens had come out of the nose and up onto the flight deck to sit because it was very cold in the nose. The flight deck wasn't much warmer, but it also wasn't nearly as drafty as the nose. Stevens forgot something and went back down through the hole, past the nose wheel, and up into the front end to get whatever it was he was after. He left his oxygen mask hooked into an oxygen hose back up on the flight deck, so on his way to the nose he used a walk-around oxygen bottle. When he got back up to the flight deck, he picked up his oxygen mask and saw that it had frozen urine all over the inside of it. Of course he raised hell!

"Moulton, did you do this!?" he yelled.

"Not me, I've been sleeping."

Then Stevens brought his mask up and showed it to McArthur and me, and we both said that we hadn't done it, and we didn't know who had.

We landed and, in the heat of the desert, the urine began to liquefy again. Stevens came up and complained bitterly to McArthur.

"Some SOB did this, and I want to know who it is. I'll bring charges against him!"

"For God's sake Stevens," I said, "quit bitching. Just take the damn thing to Personnel Equipment and get a new one."

He went off mumbling to Personnel Equipment and came back later with the same mask and a little box.

"They don't have any more masks," he moaned. "They just gave me a cleaning kit."

Shortly after this, Moulton came over to me.

"Jim, come on over here. I couldn't believe what you were doing. You did it on purpose. You had to have!"

"No, I didn't. I thought I was using the relief tube."

"I couldn't believe it, you came right past me," Moulton said, "and then you turned around and picked up Steven's mask and took out your dinky and filled it up."

We both had a great laugh, but I really did think I was peeing into the pee tube!

There were four very bad crashes during my time at Blythe. I never found out why the planes crashed, but it had to be either from pilot error or from mechanical problems. The B-24 did poorly in crash landings and in water landings. It had a high-performance wing, but the wing didn't provide much lift during landing. The keel of the B-24 was ten inches wide by four inches high and ran down the length of the bomb bay. B-24s that got into trouble during a landing on dry ground, or while ditching in the water, often broke in two because of the weak keel.

The B-17, on the other hand, did well in both crash landings and water landings because of the location and capability of the wing. It was a high-lift wing, which allowed the B-17 to drift down smoothly as compared to the B-24.

A lot of the airmen at Blythe had their wives in tow, living in the town's shacks. After a crash, the poor wives of the dead and injured would gather at the Officers' Club, which we ended up calling the "Weeping Wives Club."

Just before we finished up at Blythe, we were each given a form which certified that we had received all the training indicated on the form. Well, we had only received maybe twenty-five percent of what was indicated and when I complained, I was told to just sign it! I didn't like that at all. We had to be certified for all the training whether we'd had it or not. We called it "square filling."

Finally, in late October of 1943, our crew got orders to go to Topeka, Kansas, to another airbase. The weather was turning cold although there was no snow on the ground in Kansas yet. We went there as a crew to be outfitted with all our clothing, including flying clothing, kit bags, winter flying clothing, sheep skin boots, and helmets. I stuffed all my new supplies into a parachute bag, along with a Colt .45 semi-automatic pistol that was issued to me.

About a week later, a few brand new B-17s straight from the factory flew to the airbase and landed. They were piloted by members of Ferry Command.[3] Our crew hopped aboard a couple of the new B-17s and began the journey to England as an official replacement crew.

To England

Our crew split up when we boarded the two B-17s at Topeka, Kansas. We didn't come together again as a crew until we arrived in England. McArthur, Stevens, and three sergeants went on one B-17. Ray Moulton and I and three of the other gunners went on the other B-17.

First stop was LaGuardia Field in New York where we over-nighted. Moulton and I, and a couple of other officers we met there, took a bus into New York City to Gallagher's Steak House for dinner. It was a great dinner and toward the end we all put our money together, and I ended up being the one to pay the bill. In my head I tried to figure out a ten percent tip and added that to the amount I handed to the waiter.

As I turned away and headed to the door with Moulton, the waiter ran up to me (he had quickly counted the money I had just given him) and sneered in a loud and sarcastic voice, "Are you sure you young officers can spare this?"

This made me angry. "Well, let me see it," I replied.

He opened his palm.

"Here, let me count it," I said. After he dumped the tip money into my hand, I counted it. "This is more than ten percent of the bill. That's enough." I told him.

"This is New York!" he retorted.

"Fine, New York. If you can't use it, I certainly can," I said as I closed my hand on the money. Then I walked out of Gallagher's Steak House leaving New York standing there with his mouth hanging wide open.

The next morning we took off in the same B-17 and flew to Bangor, Maine, spent the night there, and then it was on to Goose Bay, Labrador.

Goose Bay was covered with snow, and the runway and taxiways were mostly covered in ice. After we spent a couple of days there, we headed east over the Atlantic Ocean to what was supposed to be Prestwick, on the west coast of Scotland. After flying all night, the Ferry Command crew became confused when they spotted some green land below us through the clouds. We saw a large body of water which I'm sure they thought was the Irish Sea, because right after that, down through the clouds, we could see land again. The pilot dropped down below the clouds and saw some bombers on an airfield below us. Thinking this was Scotland, and the correct airfield, the pilot went in and landed.

Well it wasn't Scotland, it was Northern Ireland! The body of water we had flown across was a huge lake, and we had landed at an airfield called Nutts Corner. The crew felt rather sheepish because they were supposed to deliver the B-17 to Scotland, and here we were in Ireland.

We left the Ferry Command crew there at Nutts Corner. Late that afternoon, we were put aboard a bus and taken to the port city of Belfast. Just after dark we boarded a "packet," or ferry boat. There were no autos or trucks on this packet; it was strictly for people, for mail, and for packages. The trip aboard this packet was an all-night affair, taking us eastward across the Irish Sea toward England.

After passing the Isle of Man, we crossed the mouth of Morecambe Bay in the early hours. Around 6 a.m. we cruised into the port town of Heysham. As the packet pulled up to the dock, an interesting thing happened. Down on the dock were a couple of roustabouts—longshoremen—and these guys were obviously having an argument. It was fairly quiet once the engines of the ship were shut down, so we could hear these fellows down below us.

"I'm going to thump you!" one of them yelled.

"No, I'm going to thump you!" roared the other one.

They were circling each other with their fists up, hollering that they were going to thump each other. Quite a few Americans were aboard the packet along with some Irish and English, and the Americans started to laugh about this thumping business.

Nobody hit anybody, but the roustabouts were circling and yelling. When the two heard the laughter of the Americans, they both stopped and looked up at the railing. In the dim port lighting, they could see that we were in U.S. uniforms and they called up, "You damn Yanks, why don't you go back to where you came from!"

That was our arrival in England—Thanksgiving Day of 1943.

End Notes
How It All Began

1. Sadly, Benny Kendall was killed during a bombing mission to destroy a German airfield at Udine, in northeastern Italy, on 1 January 1944. He flew with the 449th Bombardment Group, 718th Bomb Squadron. MACR-2711.

2. Anoxia is a condition brought on by a lack of oxygen in the blood, and therefore the brain. The higher the altitude, the lower the atmospheric pressure, which means less oxygen gets into the system under normal breathing. The same amount of oxygen is present in the air, but the pressure to push it through the sacs in the lungs into the blood stream is less. Pilots, as well as high-altitude mountain climbers, need to breathe pressurized oxygen to stave off the effects of anoxia. The symptoms of anoxia can range from light-headedness, dizziness and confusion to unconsciousness.

3. Ferry Command was created by the R.A.F, the British Royal Air Force. Its function was the transporting of new aircraft from factories to bases of operations. Many Ferry Command pilots were civilian pilots, both men and women, who freed up Military pilots to fly combat

Missions

England and Into Combat

A British Army bus was waiting near the dock, and a group of about twenty of us grabbed our gear and hopped aboard. We were driven for quite a distance southeast to a town called Stone, where a reception center had been built. The town was rather primitive, just a bunch of huts and mud. Stone was quite a bit north in England, and it was close to December. The weather was cold, damp, and miserable and the ground was wet and muddy.

We arrived at Stone after dark and after the evening meal. The bus dropped us off at the dining hall. It had already been cleaned up, and the kitchen was shut down; they'd already had their Thanksgiving turkey dinner. The mess sergeant wasn't happy about having a bus load of officers and sergeants show up so late. To make a long story short, our Thanksgiving dinner in 1943 consisted of sliced bread and cold cuts of turkey and ham.

Stone was not a pleasant place and, thank God, we weren't there very long, maybe three or four days. During one of those days the balance of our crew showed up: Lt. McArthur, the aircraft commander, and Sgt. Hughes, the engineer. That was it, no navigator and no waist gunners!

"What happened to Stevens and the gunners?" I asked McArthur.

"We lost Stevens on the way over due to VD," he said with distaste. "He contracted gonorrhea, probably in California during one of his forays into Los Angeles. They pulled him off the crew at Goose Bay, Labrador, and put him in a hospital. Bassimer got sick in New York and called his mother. Somehow she pulled some strings and was able to get him off the crew."

Then Mac described his trip. "On the way over, our B-17 stopped first at

LaGuardia Field in New York Harbor where we spent the night. The next morning they flew us up to Westover, Massachusetts, to the airbase there. Then we flew from Westover up to Presque Isle, over-nighted there and then flew up to Goose Bay. When we got there, they had considerable snow and the runway and taxiways were covered with ice. We stayed overnight and flew on into England the next day. Sgt. France had been sick since we left Presque Isle and just before boarding the bus for Stone, he was pulled from the crew." Now we were a crew of three officers instead of four, and four sergeants instead of six.

After a few miserable days at Stone—rainy, cold, soggy, and muddy—we were once again put on a bus and driven for several hours to Cheddington, an airbase in central England, not too far north and a little west of London.

Located at Cheddington was a B-24 United Kingdom Orientation Program. The B-24s were sent here, and the new crews flew with instructor crews. The new crews became familiar with the weather, which was always horrible, and with the English radio systems for voice as well as the radio beacons we'd be using. Because we were a new crew, we went through all the flights with the instructor crews. We also had to do some transition flying because we hadn't flown for almost a month.

Cheddington had been occupied by the Royal Air Force, but now the U.S. permanent party, which had taken over the base, inhabited a good part of it including the Officers Quarters and the Officers Club. As for us combat crews, officers and sergeants, we were put into a Quonset hut in what had been the Royal Air Force sergeants' area.

Inside the hut were a lot of steel cots. In the middle was a little pot-belly wood stove in a three-foot-square sandbox. It took a while, but we were finally able to get a fire going in the little stove. Each steel cot had three cushions instead of a mattress. The English called these mattress sections "biscuits." The pillow was made out of a round biscuit, like a long piston, and it was as hard as a bloody rock. There were four or five woolen blankets that had not been refined. If you rubbed your hand over the blankets it became oily from the lanolin of the sheep. Trying to make a bed and sleep in it with those damn biscuits was nearly impossible; we didn't have the know-how. The things would separate during the night with the result that our rear ends became pretty cold.

We officers weren't permitted to go to the base Officers Club even though we were combat personnel. We and our sergeants had to eat in what they called the Sergeants Mess. Believe me, it was a mess. The food was so bad we had a difficult time eating it. In fact, some of the crew eventually got so hungry they broke into the kitchen to get cans of food and loaves of bread.

Two other crews we had trained with at Blythe shared the Quonset hut with us. The aircraft commander for one of these crews was Miles Snyder. He was quite a cowboy even though he was from Massachusetts. Several wires hung from the ceiling in the Quonset hut, and each one had a light bulb dangling from it. These were the only lights. There were no chairs or desks or clothing lockers. When Miles wanted to go to bed one night, he asked someone to turn out the lights. No one did, so he took out his .45 and began shooting at the lights. Well, of course the .45 slugs penetrated the metal of the Quonset hut, but he did put out one of the lights.

Cheddington was down in a valley. The living quarters were on the side of a hill leading up from the valley, and halfway up this hill toward the ridge line was a canal for ferrying commerce. There were canals all over England. They were used as a cheap way to ferry commercial goods around. The road went up the hill, and at the top was a beautiful old stone church that was used every Sunday. Halfway up this road, just prior to crossing the canal, was a pub that catered to the people who worked the canal boats up and down this narrow canal.

One day we took a truck ride from Cheddington to another similar base for B-17s, Bovingdon, where we bought clothing. I bought a foot locker, some shoes, and some English-made U.S. uniform parts. It seemed that everywhere we went we were in the dark, in the mud, and in the rain. When we stepped off a truck or a bus, it was into the mud, and when we got back onto the truck or the bus, it was out of the mud. England in the winter time is bleak, cold, damp, and dreary.

We picked up two new waist gunners while at Cheddington: Sgt. Kenneth Miller and Sgt. Clyde Baker. They were both part of the permanent party at Cheddington, and both were becoming sick and tired of doing nothing. They climbed out of a nice, comfortable assignment into what for the ten of us would become the frying pan. With the addition of Miller and Baker, we were at full strength with six sergeants, but we were still minus a navigator.

For entertainment while at Cheddington, we were taken to several dances put on by the townsfolk for the morale of the workers. Many of the local young ladies had been drafted as farm workers and were also trained to operate anti-aircraft guns. We went to a town called Luton for a couple of these dances.

I also went into London several times and was very fortunate the first time I was there. I wound up in the west end of London where there are a lot of theaters, hotels and historical sites. At the Regent Palace Hotel, I met a very nice young lady whose name was Betty Price. I was told the hotel was full and there was no room for me. I guess I looked pretty sad because this young lady took care of me. Somehow she pulled some strings and was able to get me a room. Thereafter, whenever I had the opportunity, I walked to the train station from Cheddington Base and trained into London. I developed a very nice relationship with this young lady.

Just after the first of the year, the beginning of 1944, we finally got our assignments. McArthur's crew and Miles Snyder's crew were both assigned to a permanent base at Hethel, a small village six miles southwest of Norwich, in East Anglia, which is a hundred miles from London to the north, northeast.

Neither Snyder's crew nor our crew had any idea that the air war would be over for them and for us in three short months. Snyder would sit out the remainder of the war in neutral Switzerland after landing his B-24 at Dubendorf Airfield. We would be forced to bail out of our crippled bomber over occupied Holland into an unknown and bleak future.[1]

The 389th Bomb Group, Hethel Airfield, Station 114, East Anglia

The train ride from London to Hethel took a couple of hours. When we arrived at the base, Station 114, both our crew and Snyder's crew were assigned to the same squadron, the 566th Bombardment Squadron (Heavy), which was part of the 389th Bombardment Group (Heavy). On the base at Hethel were three other squadrons, the 564th, the 565th, and the 567th.

Hethel airfield had three runways crisscrossing each other. The hanger area and the administration area were together, and the four squadrons' airplane parking areas, called hardstands, were spread out all the way around the airfield. Surrounding the three runways was a taxiway with all the hardstands, like cul-de-sacs, positioned on the outside of it. This is where the individual bombers were located. Each of the four squadrons had an area along the peripheral taxiway.

Out in the boondocks, to the north of the airfield, was the bomb dump. This is where, stacked up out in the open, the bombs were stored without fuses and without tail fins. The tail fins, the fuses, the .50 caliber ammunition, in fact all ammunition, were kept in a separate building. Everything was dispersed at Hethel to minimize damage in case of German air attacks. Each of the squadron billeting areas was in a different section of what was called Hethel Wood.

The U.S. 8th Air Force consisted of three air divisions. The B-17's of the 1st Division were the first of the bombers sent over to England. These bombers had a white triangle on the tail with the letter "A," "B," "C," or "D." The 2nd Division, all B-24s, had a white circle on the tail, and the 3rd Division, comprised mostly of B-24s, but also some B-17 groups, had a white square. Painted on the side of each airplane, using letters, was squadron information and individual airplane information. These identification markings were changed from time to time.

The 389th Bombardment Group belonged to the 2nd Combat Wing of the 2nd Division of the 8th Air Force Bomber Command. On our tail and on our wings, we had a large white circle with a black "C." The white circle was the identifier for the 2nd Air Division, and the "C" designated the 389th Bomb Group.[2]

It didn't take long for us to be assigned to our quarters. There was a war going on and we were now in it. We flew two or three familiarization flights shortly after we arrived, and then the crew was scheduled for its first combat mission.

I didn't go on our first combat mission because one of the older more experienced combat pilots flew in the copilot seat to check out Jimmy McArthur and the balance of the crew. Thus the crew always had one more combat mission than I had.

Mission #1 "Big Week"

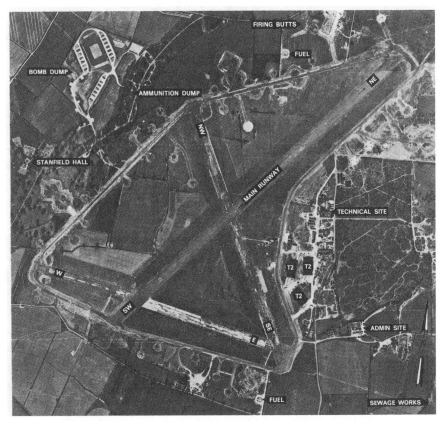

Hethel Air Field, Station 114, East Anglia, England. (Annotations added by Roger Freeman, author of Airfields of The Mighty Eighth, Then and Now *– reprinted with permission)*

My first mission was on the 21st of February 1944. It was a raid in which the 8th Air Force bombers hit several air bases in Germany during what came to be called "Big Week." The 8th Air Force in England, commanded by Major General Jimmy Doolittle, and the 15th Air Force out of Italy, had decided that the backbone of the German aviation manufacturing industry and the German Air Force, the Luftwaffe, needed to be broken. Throughout the entire week of the 20th through the 25th of February, raids were aimed at airfields and aircraft production factories in Germany, and they were rather successful.

Our particular airplane and the squadron we were in, the 566th, bombed an airfield at a town called Diepholz, located in west central Germany. This was a target of opportunity because the weather kept the group from hitting the primary targets around Brunswick.

On this first mission, 8th Air Force Mission 228, Mac was flying formation from the right seat and I was flying in the left seat. For the first time I saw flak.[3] I found flak bursts to be rather interesting. They looked more or less like vertical elongated columns with blackish-gray smoke at the base coming out in two puffs to the side. Each burst had this configuration, and we quickly learned a few things: if you can see the flak burst, it's not going to damage you because it has already done its work elsewhere; if you can hear it exploding, it's getting too close; if you can hear it rattling around in the airplane, it's really too close!

We encountered our first German fighter planes that day. We didn't have the protection of our own fighters because, as of yet, our fighters didn't have the distance capability to go this far inland. The German fighters, Me-109s and Fw-190s, flew out ahead of us, then turned and came in toward us. I watched as they queued up for their attack. They rolled over onto their backs and fired at us from upside down while going through our formation. They fired from this position because their planes were heavily-armored on the bottom; the engine was in front of the pilot with armor plating underneath it and the pilot's seat.

As I watched, unusual looking little reddish-orange balls came streaking towards us, one behind the other, and then zipped past down the outside of our airplane in the blink of an eye. They seemed to me to be about as large as basketballs with black speckles in the middle.

"What in the world are those?" I thought. All of a sudden it dawned on me that they were explosive 20mm cannon shells from the fighters! Later on, I learned that only about a sixth of the shells in a machine gun stream are visible. In between the visible shells, whether they are incendiary, tracer, or explosive, are many armor piercing and solid ball shells. What is invisible to the eye is the murderous hail of lead and armor piercing tungsten. [4]

After their first pass, I watched eight to ten German fighters roll back upright, peel off to the left and climb up parallel with our formation. They accelerated ahead of us and reformed to make another run. As they made their second run at us, I began to see those orange balls popping, headed our way. Instinctively, I ducked and dropped way down in my seat and put my head down. I didn't think about it, I just did this in order to protect myself.

Out of the corner of his eye, McArthur caught me ducking down and shouted at me, "Keeffe, are you hit?"

Sheepishly, I sat up in my seat. "No, I'm not hit. It was just automatic."

Then I thought to myself, "Well, you boob, the skin of the airplane is only about 1/16th of an inch of aluminum, and ducking isn't going to help anything."

In front of our faces was the wind screen that was made out of an inch-and-a-half thick bullet-proof laminated glass. I had seen attempts to penetrate bullet-proof glass and knew it could not be penetrated, even with 20mm or 37mm rounds. Before shells could get through that glass, the glass would probably tear out of its frame.

There wasn't much to that first mission. I don't even remember dropping the bombs. I just remember the German fighters queuing up, and I remember wondering what in the world those orange balls were. It was a pretty simple mission. Other than ducking that one time, I don't remember anything frightening about it at all. I don't think our airplane was even hit. But our second mission was completely different.

Anatomy of an 8th Air Force Bomber Mission

Forming up was quite exciting. Everything was done like clock work. Putting up a thousand bombers from air bases all over east England was absolutely staggering. On that first mission of ours, I doubt there were more than three or four hundred bombers, but eventually the 8th Air Force was putting upwards of a thousand bombers in the air for a mission.

When Squadron Command got a set of mission orders, an orderly was sent around to the air crews' quarters to wake us all up in the middle of the night. The first thing we did was look at our wrist watches to see what time it was. The later we were awakened, the easier, or at least the shorter, a mission was likely to be. The earlier they woke us up, the longer, and probably the more dangerous, the mission because we would be over enemy territory longer. That first mission we were awakened at 5 a.m.

Here is how a typical mission unfolded. We'd be told the night before if we were being scheduled for a mission the next day. Therefore, if the corporal woke us during the night, we knew our scheduled mission was actually going to happen. We'd get dressed in our flying clothes and go down to the dining hall. The food, I hate to say, was pretty grim: scrambled powdered eggs mixed with water, and a lot of Brussels sprouts, which were probably not the smartest things for an air crew to eat because they produced a lot of gas. We really didn't feel like eating anyway if we were going to go up and get shot at. After breakfast we'd go to the briefing room. Many of us at Hethel had somehow acquired bicycles, and we'd ride them to the briefing.

The night before the mission, as soon as Group Command received a mission alert notice from 8th Air Force Bomber Command Headquarters down near London, the airplanes were prepared. This meant that each plane, presuming that it was mechanically signed-off for flying, had to be completely fueled up. Then the armorers would bring out the ammunition, a hell of a lot of .50 caliber ammunition—over five thousand rounds per airplane.

Each airplane was assigned particular types of bombs depending on what the planners wanted to accomplish. There were high-explosives bombs, delayed-action bombs, armor-piercing bombs, and fragmentation bombs for use against airplanes parked outside German factories, for instance, or against personnel. There were incendiary bombs made up of three-foot-long by two-inch-square sticks of incendiary, bundled together and capped by a nose casing at one end of the bundle and a tail casing at the other end. This type of bomb had an aneroid fuse which could be set to operate at any particular altitude, plus or minus five hundred to a thousand feet. When the bomb was dropped, somehow or other the aneroid fuse caused the thing to come undone or explode, and the incendiary sticks separated and somehow ignited. The flames could not be put out because they were burning magnesium. There were also leaflet bombs, again with aneroid fuses, and the armorers set them to open at various altitudes—5,000, 10,000, and sometimes 20,000 feet depending upon how large a scatter area the mission planners wanted covered with propaganda leaflets.

The ground crew took care of everything: checking the batteries, the radios, the lights, and so forth. The hospital crew took out and installed four first aid packets on each airplane. The first aid packets snapped into receptacles inside the bomber, two in the front end and two in the back end. They were about the size of half a loaf of bread and had canvas covers with zippers that were sealed at the hospital for security.

In the meantime, having gotten up, dressed and eaten, the crews pedaled their bicycles down to the briefing room in a windowless building. The officers sat in the front and the sergeants in the back. Up on the stage was a large curtain-covered screen that displayed a map of Europe.

After everybody got seated, the mission commander would come in and everyone would be called to attention.

"Be seated, gentlemen," he'd say to us, and then he'd walk to the front.

Military police would secure the building, close the door into the briefing room and stand guard inside and outside the room. The curtain was then drawn back, uncovering the map of Europe.

With pins and colored string, the route for the mission was laid out on the wall map. All speculation as to the target was now over. A board listed all the airplane numbers and showed, for each of the four squadrons, which airplane each crew was assigned to fly. The board also identified the group leader and the group alternate leader.

Crewmen of the 389th Bomb Group gather in the mission briefing building and listen intently as the Operations Officer describes the details of a mission. The huge wall map shows the mission target and flight routes. (Courtesy of Kelsey McMillan, 389th Bomb Group historian)

Then came the briefing. The operations people covered the airplanes and the operation, and the mission commander described the mission.

> "We'll form up at our usual area over East Anglia. We will then follow the such and such group climbing to altitude outbound across the English Channel. The gunners will test fire their guns over the North Sea. We will be on alert from ten minutes before hitting the Dutch coast and on into the target. We'll make this turn and that turn. Here on this latter turn, the IP, is the beginning of the bomb run. I want tight formation all the way from the IP to the target, because we want a good cluster, a good pattern. We don't want to have to come back here tomorrow again. Now here is the route home, and the first to land will be the cripples, or any airplanes with wounded aboard. We'll have fighter protection as far as the east Dutch border, but not beyond that."[5]

Next, the Intelligence Officer headed to the front of the room and described where the German fighters were located and where the anti-aircraft guns were located. We then had specialized briefings: the gunners left for another part of the building to be briefed by the gunnery sergeants and the armorers; the navigators went to pick up their prepared navigation kits; the bombardiers gathered together and talked about bomb settings and about who would do what and when; and the pilots talked together about such things as flying the formation, emergency procedures, and where to land in case of emergencies.

Then we all walked over to an attached building to pick up our gear: parachutes, helmets, and oxygen masks. We had already dressed for flying before coming to the briefing, and we had our .45 pistols with us.

At some bases the commanders proclaimed, "On a mission nobody carries a gun, because if you end up on the ground and the Germans see you with a gun, they'll probably shoot first and ask questions later." Other base commanders, like ours, let their men take guns if they wanted to. Still other base commanders required everyone to carry a gun. It all depended on who the group commander was.

Normally, about the time we were getting all our gear together, the chaplain came around to say some prayers and distribute Holy Communion to anyone who wanted it. Our chaplain was a real salty character, a Catholic priest named Father Gerald Beck. He was late-middle aged and tough as nails. In fact, he was the first one in the group to earn a five-mission Air Medal. For every five combat missions, an airman was eligible for the Air Medal. Father Beck, affectionately known as "Pappy Beck," beat everybody in the number of these Air Medals because he flew on just about every mission. Eventually the group CO found out the chaplain was going on all the missions and declared, "No more combat missions for you! We need you here on the ground."

Once all the briefings were finished and we'd gotten all our gear, we went outside as a crew and climbed aboard a truck along with two or three other crews to ride out to the hardstands and the airplanes. When our crew unloaded from the truck, we put our gear down in ten piles right next to our airplane. (Later, on our last mission, there were eleven piles due to a nose gunner who'd been added to our crew.) Each guy then checked out his particular place in the plane and ran through his particular check list, both outside and inside the aircraft.

The gunners walked over to a shack near the hardstand to get the barrels for their .50 caliber machine guns, which they were supposed to have cleaned, oiled, and stored after the last mission. They'd attach the barrels and then set the ammo belts into the receivers of the machine guns.

The ground crew had already hung the bombs in the bomb racks during the night. These men worked in all kinds of weather, and they put in a tremendous effort to get our airplanes loaded and ready to go.

Each bomb always had two fuses. The nose fuse worked off a little propeller that turned so many turns and then fell off, thus arming the nose fuse. The tail fuse was either an impact fuse or a delayed-action fuse. There were also delayed-action nose fuses. Inside this type of fuse was a safety wire that went to a place on the bomb rack. These fuses also had pins in them. The bombardier got his position on the airplane prepared and then pulled all the pins out of the bombs. The bombs were still safe until they fell away from the airplane; the wires through the safety points stayed on the bomb rack, and the bombs falling away from the nose wires and the tail wires activated the fuses.

389th Bomb Group B-24 bombers parked in their hardstands. In the spring of 1944, the circle 'C' on the tail fins was replaced with a white vertical bar on black. 'HP' on the rear fuselage shows these aircraft belong to the 567th Bomb Squadron. (Courtesy of Paul Wilson, author of The Sky Scorpions)

The flight engineer checked other things. He made sure the windshield was clean, and he'd perform an F.O.L. (fuel, oil, and lubricant) check, which included the hydraulic and electrical systems. Finally he set up the top turret area which he would man once we were on our way over the English Channel. Everyone had things to do.

Finally, the pilot-in-command, later called the aircraft commander, called us all out of the airplane to stand by our personal equipment piles. He gave a short briefing and asked if there were any questions. When he was finished, we grabbed our gear, and climbed up into the airplane and went to our positions.

Once seated in the cockpit, McArthur and I would run through another check list before starting up the engines.

"Brakes?"

"On."

"Superchargers?"

"Off."

"Cowl flaps?"

"Open."

"Wing flaps?"

"Up."

The list was quite extensive but Mac and I never hurried or skipped any steps; each one was vital. More than once an airplane failed to take off, resulting in a horrific accident and the loss of an entire crew because some item in a check list had been ignored.

Everything was done by the clock. We all had to be in the airplane at a particular time. Then came a start engine time when we were to check the engines, the radios and all critical equipment. The radio was to be on receive-only, which was known as "radio silence." No transmissions whatsoever were permitted because the Germans listened in constantly on all radio channels, trying to pick up any information they could.

B24s line up on the taxiway heading toward the takeoff runway.
(Photo supplied by Brian Wickham, courtesy of Bill Jangl and Norman Nutt of the 44th Bomb Group)

On the clock again we checked our taxi time. Then we taxied and got behind the airplane scheduled ahead of us, and we'd be followed by the one scheduled behind us. All the airplanes from the four squadrons did this. Two squadrons taxied up one side of the airfield, and the other two squadrons taxied up the other side, with both lines converging at the takeoff runway. If the mission wasn't too far and fuel was not a problem, we waited for takeoff time with the engines running. If it was a long mission, we'd all get into position ready for takeoff, nose to tail, and then shut down. The fuel trucks would then come and top off the fuel tanks. Sometimes the ground crew would also de-ice the airplanes by spraying some kind of alcohol-based liquid on the propellers and on the leading edges of the wings and tail.

At takeoff time, commands were given from the tower with flare pistols called Very pistols. If the engines had been shut down and the tanks filled up, they would fire a Very shot in orange, which meant "start your engines." Then they fired a green shot, which meant "start your takeoff." Normally, an airplane went down the runway every thirty seconds, and it took about a minute and a half to two minutes of run to get airborne. The rule was, if you had trouble on takeoff, you were to pull off to the side because the mission had to keep going. One after another, the airplanes took off.

Finally, when it was our time to take off, Mac ran up the engines and watched the RPMs. I set the wing flaps to twenty degrees and checked to make sure the auxiliary hydraulic pump was ON and the auxiliary power unit was OFF. Then I switched the cowl flaps to TRAIL and continued on down the takeoff list.

As Mac eased the throttles forward, the airplane picked up speed and started down the runway. I'd call out the forward ground speed to Mac because he had to concentrate on keeping the airplane going straight down the runway and getting it into the air. Seventy miles per hour was a critical forward air speed because, at that speed, you were committed to take off.

As the airplane lifted off the runway and gained altitude, I applied the brakes to stop the wheels from spinning and then retracted the wheels. Next, I set the superchargers and throttles for CLIMB, fiddled with the RPMs, brought the wing flaps to UP, and switched the booster and auxiliary hydraulic pumps to OFF. McArthur would keep his attention on flying and maneuvering the airplane once we spotted the assembly plane, the formating leader.[6]

389th Bomb Group assembly (formating) plane, the "Green Dragon."
(Courtesy of Paul Wilson, author of The Sky Scorpions)

Each of the bomber groups had a wildly-painted B-24 called the assembly plane that was used as a formating leader. These were normally old, worn out airplanes that were no longer satisfactory for combat. They were the first ones off, and they didn't carry bombs, so they were relatively light. The entire length of the fuselage of the formating B-24 for the 389th Bomb Group was painted with wide alternating green and yellow stripes. The reason for the wild painting was so that we knew it was our group forming and not somebody else's group.

The assembly plane would take off first and climb into a racetrack pattern at an assigned altitude, say 5,000 feet, at an assigned assembly area, located by homing in on our designated Buncher beacon and dialing in a particular radio compass course. The second airplane off was the leader of the mission. Normally its pilot was a colonel or a lieutenant colonel, somebody from the group headquarters or one of the squadron commanders. Then the rest of the airplanes would take off, one right after the other, and locate the assembly plane and follow it around in the racetrack pattern.

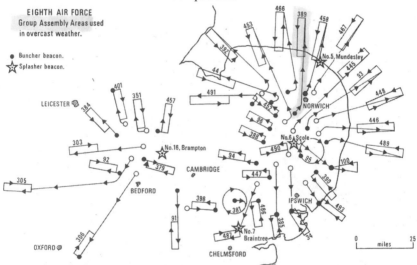

Diagram showing the group assembly areas of the 8th Air Force in East Anglia.
The 389th Bomb Group's assembly area is due north of Norwich. In a "maximum effort" mission,
this was how 800 to 1,000 bombers would assemble prior to heading across the English Channel to the Continent.
(Courtesy of Roger Freeman's Mighty Eighth War Diary)

First we'd form up into threes, and then into three threes, which made up one squadron. Therefore, one squadron was made up of nine airplanes. Thirty-six airplanes, or four squadrons, made up a group. Each group was assigned to one air base. If our mission orders from 8th Air Force Bomber Command required a "maximum effort," this meant that our entire group of thirty-six planes, or however many were flight worthy, had to be sent on that mission. Normally there were, in addition to a thirty-six plane maximum, three or four spares to go along in case any one of the thirty-six had to abort the mission. If a crew had to abort the mission, they had to fly out over the North Sea and drop their bombs unarmed into the water before they could go back and land at the base. It was strictly forbidden to return to base with a bomb load.

Once we were formed up, the leader, on a particular minute of the clock, left the racetrack pattern with his group of thirty-six airplanes and joined up with a second group of thirty-six planes. Then these two groups joined up with a third group of thirty-six planes. These three groups, one hundred and eight airplanes, formed a wing. While flying in formation, a group normally flew in two sections; two squadrons of a group made up Section One, and the other two squadrons made up Section Two. Therefore, a squadron was made up of nine airplanes; two squadrons were a section; two sections formed a group; three groups were a wing; three wings made up a division; and finally, the three divisions made up the 8th Air Force Bomber Command. And that's how a bombing mission rapidly got up to nearly a thousand airplanes.

Halfway across the North Sea, the gunners would test their guns, and our crew would talk to each other by way of intercom. Nobody used the radio, neither airplane to airplane, nor commander to the other airplanes; strict radio silence. If one of the airplanes had to abort—drop its bombs and go back to base and land—the number one spare airplane took its place. Any pilot who aborted had better have a very good reason. If only one spare was needed, the other two or three turned around halfway across the North Sea, dropped their bombs in the water and made their way back to base.

All this time we'd be slowly climbing to our final cruising altitude. Once we reached cruise altitude it was sit-and-wait time until what we called "coast in." Whether the mission would take us across the coast of Holland, Belgium, or France, once we crossed the coast, everyone would be on hyper alert.

Normally, the B-17s of the 1st and 3rd Divisions took off from their air bases about forty-five minutes ahead of us. They usually got to the target first with us right behind them. After the bombing run, we'd pass the B-17 formations on the way home and be on the ground debriefing by the time they landed back at their bases. The B-24 was about fifteen mph faster than the B-17; however, the B-17 could fly higher. The highest they ever bombed from was upwards of 32,000 feet. B-24s could go faster and farther due to better fuel consumption as well as fuel carrying capacity.

Another difference between the two heavy bombers was the engines. The B-17 had a rather poor engine: a single-row, nine cylinder Wright engine, the R-1820, which had a lot of trouble with oil. The B-24, on the other hand, had a much better engine: a Pratt and Whitney R-1830 twin-row, with seven cylinders to the row, making a total of fourteen cylinders.

Smoke markers are clearly visible in this photo of an element of the 389th Bomb Group right at the moment of "bombs away!" The group lead bombardier releases his bomb load which include smoke markers. Seeing the smoke, signals the other bombardiers to immediately release their bombs allowing for maximum concentration on the target. (Courtesy of Mark Brotherton collection)

Flying at altitude was not a walk in the park. The bombers weren't pressurized and, because of all of the open areas, were quite drafty inside. The waist windows were open, and the turrets and the bomb bays leaked air. The sound of the four engines was so loud we had to shout to be heard. The temperature got down to -50 to -55 degrees centigrade, which was very, very cold. The waist gunners particularly, and occasionally the ball turret gunners, suffered from frostbite and severe freezing of fingers and parts of their faces.

We all had electric flying suits. The gunners wore what we called the "bunny suit." It was a one-piece blue suit with a zipper and an electric cord that could be plugged into an electric control box. We could adjust the amount of heat, just like an electric blanket. However, the darn suit had hot spots. For example, if I had my arms bent, the elbow would be cool and the bend in the arm would be hot because there were more wires there than under the elbow.

The bunny suit also had electrically-heated slippers and electrically-heated leather gloves. We normally wore fine nylon gloves inside the leather gloves. The heated gloves were big and bulky but sufficiently flexible so the gunners could use them. The same held true for the pilots and the bombardier.

Each of the side-mounted .50 caliber machine guns in the waist of the airplane had two handles, one for each hand, so the trigger could be operated with either index finger. Some of the gunners used both fingers. Each gun had a charging handle. If there was a jam, the gunner merely reached up with his right hand and pulled the charging handle, which kicked out the bad shell and put in a new one. This could all be done without taking off the heated gloves. If a gunner took off his gloves, he risked freezing his skin to the metal of his guns. He only did that once.

My flying suit was a brand new type F-2 with slippers and special flying boots. These boots were different from the fur-lined boots, which were too big and too clumsy. The F-2 had electric pants and an electric jacket which I wore over green gabardine wool pants and jacket. If we came down in enemy territory, I could take this suit apart, throw away the electric pants and electric jacket, and have a very nice escape suit with black suspenders. We could not have operated those bomber streams without electric flying clothes.

The return trip to England after our first mission to the German fighter base at Diepholz was in formation and typical for an uneventful mission. Over the North Sea we began our letdown, remaining in group and squadron formation all the way. Even when coming in over the base, we followed a procedure. The sections broke into elements of three airplanes formed in a triangle, and we came across the flying field as a whole string of elements. The inside pilot started his turn, the leader started his turn, and then the other wing man did his turn followed by the next three. We flew in a racetrack pattern around the field, dropping lower all the time. Then we made the final 180-degree turn and came on in and landed.

After rolling out on landing, we taxied onto the taxiway back to our hard-stand. Once in the hardstand, I pushed down on the left brake pedal, powered up the right engines and spun the airplane around so it was pointed back toward the taxiway. Then we ran through a pre-shut-down checklist. Everything about flying the airplane was done with checklists. It was a very smart way to operate.

We then shut down the airplane. There were no wounded and there were no holes in the airplane. The ground crew met us at our hardstand to find out what the mission had been like. The gunners took the barrels out of their machine guns, cleaned them and took them over to the nearby storage shed. Very quickly the armorers came and collected any unfired ammunition, and if any bombs hadn't dropped, they also took care of those. It only took five to ten minutes to shut everything down and get our stuff together.

We all climbed into the back of a waiting truck and the driver drove our crew to debriefing. Debriefing was held in a room, usually the mess hall, where a lot of tables were set up with a debriefing officer sitting at each one of them. Each debriefing officer had a form and pads of paper and each crew went to a separate table for debriefing. One of the first things we did when we entered the room was to go to a table with large shot glasses on it. Anyone who wanted a shot of good Scotch whisky had one, or a cup of coffee or milk. I was kind of lucky because I had learned to like good Scotch whisky, and McArthur didn't drink, so I normally got two scotches.

A bomber crew in debriefing after a mission. (Courtesy of Kelsey McMillan, 389th Bomb Group historian)

When we sat down with the debriefing officers, we answered all sorts of questions.

"Did you see any airplanes hit or go down?"

"What was the enemy fighter response?"

"What was the flak like?"

"Did you see anything unusual?"

All individuals on the airplane were supposed to have made notes so they could identify where an airplane had gone down, how many parachutes had been seen, what the enemy fighter attack had been like, what the flak had been like and where it was located. All this information was debriefed.

After that, we stowed our parachutes, helmets, and oxygen masks in our lockers. Then we got on our bicycles and headed back to our huts where we either took a shower and went to sleep, or just flopped down and went to sleep.

Essentially, this is what an uneventful mission was like.

They Stopped Counting at Three Hundred Holes

Three days after our first mission, Big Week was in full motion, and we received orders for our second mission, 8th Air Force Mission 233. That mission, on the 24th of February, consisted of all three bomb divisions.

Once formation was completed, and the bomber stream began its flight across the channel, the three divisions split up, each to a separate target destination. The 1st Air Division, with two hundred sixty-six B-17s, set course for its main target, the ball bearing factories at Schweinfurt, Germany. The 3rd Air Division, consisting of three hundred four B-17s, headed toward its target, Rostock, Germany. Our division, the 2nd Air Division, which was all B-24s, was sent to destroy a major fighter factory. The target was the Messerschmitt

8,000 Tons on Reich in 36 Hours

Target: Germany

These are the German aircraft centers struck by the U.S. and British air forces in the heaviest 36 hours of aerial assault the enemy has yet felt.

2,000 U.S. Planes Out Again; Nazi Fighter Output Is Cut 30 Pct.

Two Day Raids of 1,000 Bombers Each Follow Devastating RAF Blows At Stuttgart and Leipzig

Two thousand American warplanes struck again at the German aircraft industry yesterday in the fourth major Allied assault on the Reich in 36 hours.

Switching their main attack from the Nazi fighter factories, whose production was slashed more than 30 per cent by the heaviest daylight raid of the war Sunday, the Fortresses and Liberators pounded airdromes, plane depots and two plants.

The attack carried the total tonnage dropped in the four raids to about 8,000, far and away the heaviest battering of the war.

Yesterday's assault, with nearly as many aircraft in the air as the 1,000 bombers and 1,000 fighters which Sunday ripped the heart out of the Germans' capacity to build fighter planes, cost 15 bombers and five fighters, it was announced officially. U.S. fighters destroyed 33 enemy planes, but there was no immediate announcement of aircraft destroyed by the bombers.

The attacks yesterday comprised the 12th day of operations this month for the heavies of the U.S. Strategic Air Force in Europe, equaling the previous high mark for any full month's operations.

The second great daylight blow was struck in the wake of the RAF's second straight major night effort—an attack Sunday night in "very great strength" on Stuttgart, in southwestern Germany.

Marauder medium bombers of the Ninth Air Force and RAF medium and light bombers meanwhile contributed to the strain on the Luftwaffe with their second straight day of attacks on targets in France and the Low Countries, all without loss.

Bombed yesterday were two air-frame-component factories in Brunswick, which were badly damaged on Sunday; targets at industrial Hanover, and large aircraft parks and other military installations near the Netherlands border, including Bramsche, Lingen, Vechte, Quakenbruck, Diepholz and Ahlhorn.

The military paper, Stars and Stripes, Vol.1 No. 93, Tuesday, Feb. 22, 1944, highlights a series of bombing missions during the first two days of what became known as "Big Week." (Lt. Col. Keeffe collection) aircraft fighter factory outside the town of Gotha, located in the eastern part of central Germany. It was to be a maximum effort. By that point, almost all of the missions were maximum efforts.[7]

Our group, the 389th, led the wing and the division that day. The 389th was divided into a lead section of fifteen airplanes and a second section of fifteen airplanes. (We had a total of thirty combat-ready bombers available for the mission.) Our squadron, the 566th, was in the second section. My recollection is that we flew this mission at 14,500 feet. Normally, we were supposed to get up to around 22,000 feet for the B-24, but this time we were given orders to fly at an intermediate altitude because this put us above small flak and gave us a better bombing pattern for maximum damage to the aircraft factory and the fighter field right next to it.

After forming up over East Anglia and gaining altitude over the channel, we flew across into Germany and then turned southeast. We weren't intercepted by fighters on the way to the target and, because the mission planners had tried to route us around the flak, we didn't encounter much of that either. The skies over Germany were perfectly clear, and there was probably four to six inches of snow on the ground. After a short time, we made a left turn and headed due east, setting ourselves up for the approach to the IP, which was five to eight minutes away from the target.

Something happened in the lead airplane of the lead section. Somewhere between the point where we made our left turn heading east and the IP itself, the lead navigator made a mistake. There was a town between these two points called Eisenach. The lead navigator thought he was coming up on Gotha, but in fact he was coming up on Eisenach. He set the bombardier up on what turned out to be a truck factory, not the aircraft factory. The lead fifteen airplanes, the first section of two squadrons, bombed that truck factory at Eisenach. The lead of the second section, our fifteen airplanes, realized the first section was making a mistake, so after the first section dropped their bombs and turned off, we kept on going.

Radio silence was broken and the number two lead, second section, called the first section. "You bombed the wrong target. We're going on." So we continued on, and now we were the lead for the balance of the 2nd Division following us.

I was amazed at the beauty of the day as we approached the target, perfectly blue skies and a picturesque snowy landscape below. I could see everything down there. One thing I noticed as we came in on our bomb run from the IP was countless airplanes taking off. Many of the German airfields, like English airfields, didn't have runways. The fighters used grass fields. I could see these multiple individual fighters taking off far below us, and they were blowing snow out behind them as they took off, just like a boat leaves a wake behind it. They weren't taking off in single file like on a runway, they were taking off in multiples spread out over the snow covered fields.

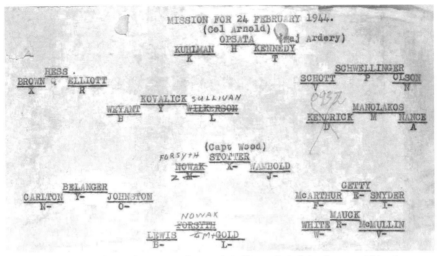

Mission formation sheet for 24 February 1944. The target is the Messerschmitt fighter factory and fighter base near Gotha, Germany. (Courtesy of Kelsey McMillan, 389th Bomb Group historian)

The aircraft factory was located just outside the town of Gotha. On the ground was a very large square that was divided diagonally into two triangles. The factory and the factory airfield were situated on one triangle, and a fighter base was situated on the other triangle. But that day fighters were coming up from both airfields. They had been alerted by the mistaken bombing at Eisenach just five or ten minutes earlier.

We had a good bomb run. The lead bomber's marker bombs fell away, and all the other bombardiers released on them. After dropping our bombs, we turned off back to the west, but within about three minutes, the manure hit the fan and all hell broke loose.

The German fighters I had seen taking off just minutes earlier came up fast. The Germans were flying several kinds of fighters: single-engine fighters, twin-engine fighters, even twin-engine big fighters. They made head-on passes at us and then set themselves up into a circle pattern that moved along with our bomber stream. As they came on nose into us, they fired and then continued in their circle and attacked again. It became pretty grim, and airplanes began to go down.

We were lucky because, as a new crew, we were put inside the formation and positioned on the left wing of our element leader. You didn't want to be on the outside of a formation; you didn't want to be at the tail end (the last airplane in a formation was known as a "tail-end Charlie"); and you didn't want to be the leader. As bombers on the periphery began to go down, the German fighters worked their way into the center of the formation. Almost immediately I saw a B-24 that was flying above and to the left of us veer off and go into a spin.[8]

Gotha Messerschmitt fighter factory and base. The German Luftwaffe fighter base is above the diagonal road, and the factory complex is below. Left: Reconnaissance photo prior to the mission. Right: Photo from one of the bombers taken during the bomb run. Little dots in the snow are German fighter aircraft; single-engine FW-190s and ME-109s, twin-engine ME-210s and JU-88s. (USAF archive photo)

At one point during the attack, I looked out the cockpit window on my left—Mac was flying formation from the right seat—and I saw another B-24 in trouble and on fire. This airplane was the element lead to our left, only a few hundred feet away, flying level with us. Flames were pouring out of the airplane's windows and out of the fuselage where the bomb bays had blown open. I glanced back along the waist but couldn't see through the waist windows. Normally I could see right through the fuselage because the waist windows were at the same location on both sides of the fuselage.

I couldn't see through because of the mass of red and yellow flames. Standing at the waist window facing outward was a gunner. I remember very clearly that he had both his hands up over his face as he stood there in the flames. Then he fell, or jumped, through the window and fell away with his clothes on fire. About the same time, the airplane began to nose downward a few degrees, and I saw the nose wheel doors open and the nose wheel pop out. The bail-out procedure for the navigator and the bombardier, who were in the nose of the airplane, was to throw the nose wheel up over center, which took a fair amount of effort. This caused the nose wheel to drop out on its own. The wheel would not lock down, but at least the doors would open. This was where the two men were supposed to bail out.

Either the bombardier or the navigator came out head first on the front of the nose wheel. The wind, of course, virtually glued him to the nose wheel. He struggled unsuccessfully, so he went back in and turned around and came out feet first. This all happened in a very short period of time, just seconds, and then *blewy*! The airplane exploded, and the tail broke off. Our airplane was making its own terrific noise. The noise of the engines running, Sgt. Hughes firing his machine guns in the top turret right behind the cockpit, and the air rush—everything together created a huge roar. I watched this B-24 explode, but I couldn't hear it, nor could I smell it.[9]

B-24 bomber hit by flak - entire waist section on fire. Notice fuel bladder beginning to bulge out of left wing and damage to the fuselage near the tail. This airplane exploded seconds after photo was taken.
(USAF archive photo)

When an airplane blew up while flying at a hundred and fifty or sixty miles an hour, the speed of the debris slowed down very rapidly. I saw it explode, and then it was gone. It was behind us, all in a matter of seconds; ten young men dying in an exploding inferno, masked by the roar of our own engines, and all this happening while our own airplane was under attack.

After I watched the B-24 explode, I turned and looked out the right side cockpit window and was amazed to see a German Fw-190 fighter arc down to our level, parallel to us and heading in our direction. He was very close-in to us; under a hundred feet. He came down with very little speed, and he was on fire too! He pulled the nose of his fighter up slightly, which decayed his speed even more, so that we were flying side by side. I barely had time to wonder what he was up to when he popped his canopy, which spun away behind us, and then he made a very big mistake.

He stood up in the cockpit on the pilot's seat of the airplane and pulled his rip cord. Out came his parachute, which blossomed out behind him and opened in the flames. The shock of the parachute opening was enough to yank him right out of his fighter.

Instantly, all happening in milliseconds, the German fighter pilot went right back through the burning parachute canopy, like through a hoop of fire. I continued to look out the window and watched him plummet down. His shroud lines were twisting together up above him, and little flickers of flaming parachute were breaking off. The poor guy undoubtedly had not been wounded during his attacks on our airplanes, and yet he was falling from close to 14,000 feet in a failed attempt to bail out of his burning fighter. It was going to take him a minute plus to go down, and then there'd be a big thud, and that would be the end of it. What a way to go.

B-24 bomber exploding after being hit by flak.[10] (Courtesy of USAF Museum)

B-24 hit by a rocket from a German ME-262 jet fighter.[11] (Courtesy of USAF Museum)

After the lead section had released their bombs on the wrong target, they made large "S-ing" maneuvers back and forth waiting for us to catch up to them, which we finally did, but not until after the 389th lost one more airplane. When our section caught up with the first section, and we all applied power, I watched as a B-24 to the left of us began to drop behind. German fighters pounced in for the kill and, even though many of the tail gunners of our formation opened up on the fighters to try to protect the B-24, the outcome was inevitable. Its number two engine was hit and exploded, and the airplane fell away.[12]

That was the last we saw of the German fighters. The entire attack lasted only about five to seven minutes, but it seemed like an eternity. We remained on high alert during our return flight with the gunners at their stations all the way across the channel.

B-24 N+ 42-40619, Lt. Carlton crew. One of four bombers from the 567th Bomb Squadron, 389th Bomb Group, shot down during the Gotha mission. Three crewmen were killed (KIA) and the remaining seven were captured and taken prisoner. (Courtesy of Paul Wilson, author of The Sky Scorpions)

When we got back to England and landed at the base, we taxied in and shut down the airplane at our hardstand and gathered up our gear. Next we wrote down the condition of the airplane, how the plane had flown, and any problems it had so that the ground crew could fix them. During this time both my hands began to shake. I felt very embarrassed about this, so I put them in my pockets or put them behind my back and held them. They shook for the rest of the day.

By the time the ground crew was finished, they'd counted over three hundred holes in our airplane! Not a single member of our crew, despite those three hundred holes, was injured. There were only nine of us that day because we didn't have a nose gunner or a navigator. Not one of us had been hit, not one scratch!

A truck came to pick us up, and we climbed into it and went to debriefing.

Heading into the building, we each had our shot of Scotch whisky. I had a couple of extra ones to try to steady my hands. It was a rather grim debriefing as I sat at the desk with the rest of our crew, giving our accounts of what we'd seen. We expected to see all the crews there, but seven full crews were missing. One airplane from our squadron, piloted by Lt. Nowak, had gone down. One had been lost from the 565th. But the 567th squadron had taken the brunt of the attack and had lost four airplanes.

I think our mission eventually got credited with forty-three German fighters shot down out of the one hundred and fifty to two hundred German fighters sent up. Our own Sgt. Hughes got credit for destroying an Me-110.[13]

When we were through, Colonel Arnold, the group commander, got up on stage and apologized to all of the crews for having screwed up the mission by bombing the wrong target. "Those of you in the last section, the second section, take off. Do anything you want, you all have leave for five days," he said.

I went to my quarters and cleaned up and rested for a short while. Then I hopped on a train and went to London for two or three days. That second mission had been pretty grim.

"My God," I thought, "if we're going to lose seven airplanes from our group every time, the possibility of finishing twenty-five missions is very small."[14]

Years later, I looked at some strike photos of the Gotha mission that had been taken by two or three airplanes in the group during the bombing and immediately following it. A USAAF "reccie (reconnaissance) plane" had gone in before the mission and taken pre-strike photos. Right after the mission another reccie plane flew over the target and post-strike photos had been taken to assess the damage. The strike photos were pretty spectacular in that I could see the massive black smoke billowing up from the burning factories and aircraft.

Thirty-one airmen from our bomb group alone were KIA (killed-in-action) on that Gotha mission. Forty-one airmen became prisoners-of-war, and one evaded capture and eventually returned to England.[15] Total 8th Air Force losses for the 24th of February 1944, for all three bomber divisions, were 33 B-24s and 16 B-17s, with over 500 casualties, of whom 484 were listed as MIA.[16]

Scrubbed Missions, Near Misses and "No-balls"

After I came back from London, we received orders to go on a couple of other missions. Each time, however, we formed up in the air with a full load of bombs and ammunition, only to have the mission cancelled, or "scrubbed" as we called it, because of weather or other conditions.

Since we were a new crew, we didn't have our own airplane so we normally got what was available. We could end up flying a different airplane for each mission. For example, the airplane we had for the Gotha mission was a B-24D, which had a glass nose and no turret. Only the men who'd been around for quite a while had their own ground crew and their own airplane. If we'd received our own, I would have wanted to name it *Little Joe* as a sort of spoof, because the B-24 certainly wasn't little.

During a mission briefing we'd find out which airplane we were assigned to for that mission. The names of the pilots for each crew would be listed in chalk on a huge blackboard. Next to each pilot's name would be the aircraft number he was assigned to and the hardstand number where that plane was located.

On one mission scrubbed over the English Channel because of bad weather, we had a near catastrophe after we formed up. Either our group of thirty-six airplanes was out of position, or a group of B-17s was out of position. Our group was in a left turn and a group of B-17s was in a right turn, and we flew right through each other. None of the aircraft collided! I couldn't believe it. Mac again was flying formation, and we were both frozen in our seats. The groups just flew right through each other with no collisions.

Midair collisions did happen frequently, though. It was bad enough if we lost one airplane crashing on takeoff. But when we had midairs, and these midairs included more than two airplanes, it got pretty grim rapidly.

One type of bombing mission had a secret code name called "No-balls." We had just begun to learn that the Germans had buzz bomb sites[17] all located near the English Channel coast of France and Belgium. These buzz bombs were aimed principally at London. We began to bomb these sites and these were easy missions. We were only over the coastline for maybe five minutes, just long enough to bomb the "No-ball" site, but we got the same credit for these missions as for missions that penetrated deeper into the occupied countries and Germany.

On the 4th of March we formed up to go to Berlin, but the weather was bad where we were formating, and it was also bad over the continent. By the time we were halfway across the English Channel, the weather had deteriorated to the point that the mission was cancelled and we were called back. A few groups didn't get the message and went on and bombed Berlin anyway.

Our airplane had a near disaster during takeoff for that scrubbed mission. Shortly after I arrived at Hethel, I'd noticed that a long section of trees had been cleared out of the woods at the end of the main runway. I asked somebody why the trees had been cleared and was told that sometimes fully loaded airplanes needed a little more room to gain altitude upon takeoff.

Well, that cleared section of woods saved us the day of that scrubbed mission. As we gathered speed going down the runway, McArthur began to pull back on the wheel to raise the airplane. It began to ascend, but not quickly enough. The end of the runway was fast approaching us. The airplane slowly rose up about eighteen feet into the air and then, unbelievably, it began to settle and drift downward.

McArthur shouted for more power, and I gave him all we had. He pulled back as hard as he could on the wheel to get lift, but as we passed the end of the runway, the airplane drifted down below the tops of the trees. Thank God for that cleared section of woods! Ever so slowly, the airplane gained altitude again. We lifted above the tree line and continued upwards to rendezvous with the assembly plane. If those trees hadn't been removed, we would surely have crashed and exploded.

When we got back to the airfield after the mission was aborted, I spoke with a few mechanics about what had happened. They told me the wings had probably iced-up, dampening the ability of the wings to generate lift. Other crews weren't always so lucky, both at our base and other 8th Air Force bases. Many dozens of young men lost their lives to accidents such as the one we almost had.

The Long Haul to Southern France

The big lead-up for the 8th Air Force in England was to get a large enough group of American bombers together during daylight to bomb Berlin. The English were already bombing Berlin at night with single airplanes. To prepare us for such a long-distance mission, we received orders (mission #248) on the 5th of March to go on a very long mission from Hethel, clear down to an area called Landes De Bussac on the Spanish border of France. The Germans had a pilot training airfield there named Pau. Our mission planners knew that it was essential to destroy not only as many of Germany's airplanes, airfields, parts factories, and oil supplies as possible, but it was just as important, if not more so, to destroy the one part of the equation that could not be replaced—the pilots.

Although the weather the past few days had resulted in aborted missions, it finally cleared up on the 5th. This was our longest mission. It took about eight and a half hours to fly down to southern France and back. At the time we didn't know that this mission was also designed to prepare us for Berlin. This third mission was, as far as combat missions go, a piece of cake. We flew all the way down without any opposition, dropped our bombs on the flying field, messed up the training of their pilots and then flew back to England.

Our "Replacement" Navigator

After two or three missions, our Squadron Commander, Lt. Colonel Thomas Conroy, called McArthur, me, and Moulton into his office.

"You men look like a good crew. I'm going to make you a lead, but we have to fill out your crew first. Before you came here you got two replacement waist gunners down at Cheddington. Now you're minus a navigator, so I'll put in a requisition to the Combat Crew Replacement Center for one."

During this time, we were suffering high combat losses that resulted in our crew being chosen to move out of the open-bay barracks we called Quonset huts, into one of the more permanent, single-storied buildings. The rooms in our new quarters were quite small. Mac and I shared one room, and Moulton was in another. When we got a navigator, he would bunk with Moulton. Our room had a desk, a chair, a table, two small vertical lockers, and a small stove for heating the room. We also had a double-deck bunk bed.

A day or so after Lt. Colonel Conroy sent for a navigator, I was in our quarters and decided to go to the operations section. I climbed on my bicycle and left the quarters area, which was in Hethel Wood, and headed for the main part of the base. It was cold and rainy so I was wearing winter clothing.

I pedaled through the woods and out onto the perimeter road of the base. Coming toward me was a large Dodge 6x6 truck, all buttoned up. It had a canvas cover over the back and a canvas drop-cover over the open end at the back. The truck was traveling fairly fast and splashing muddy water up from the puddles. The road was only about a lane and a half wide, so I got over as far to the right as I could, but the driver didn't slow down. I cursed at him with rather strong language as he roared passed me.

Sitting next to him I could see a head, and the head had a face, and the face was grinning. I couldn't mistake him. It was Donald M. Stevens, the navigator that McArthur had lost on the way over to England. He'd been taken off the crew at Presque Isle, Maine, to get treated for gonorrhea! Lo and behold, here he was, sitting in this truck grinning at me. I'm sure he didn't recognize me, but he was laughing because his driver was splashing water all over this guy on a bicycle.

I turned right around and rode back down the muddy road in the same direction the truck was heading. He was going much faster than I was and I soon lost sight of him. When I got back to our quarters, I dropped the bicycle outside and ran through the front door and into my room. McArthur was lying in his bunk. He looked up as I came flying through the door.

"Jimmy, guess who I just saw?"

"Not Stevens!" he said.

"Yep! Donald M. Stevens. He was in a truck being driven by some GI."

McArthur groaned, "What the hell are we going to do?"

"Do you want him?" I asked.

"No!" he shot back.

"Well, let's go to Colonel Conroy and find out what's going on."

The two of us grabbed our bikes and went back out into the mud and ped-aled to the Orderly Room of the 566th Squadron.

The Colonel was at his desk and, after saluting, McArthur spoke to him. "Colonel Conroy, have you gotten a name? It's been several days now since you requisitioned a navigator. Do you have a name?"

"Yeah, I have it here somewhere," he replied as he shuffled through some papers. "Here it is. It'll be a Lt. Donald M. Stevens."

"We don't want that guy," Mac and I both blurted out. "We got rid of him in the States due to VD and we don't want him!"

"Well, you're going to have to put up with him for a mission or two. I'll requisition another navigator, and when that one comes in, I'll put Stevens with a different crew and give you the new navigator."

Shortly after that, Stevens showed up at the 566th Orderly Room and was assigned to Moulton's room. He flew on a practice run and then on one of our scrubbed missions. Four days later, the 8th of March, was his first mission, which he would have gotten credit for had we returned to England. The 8th of March was my fourth mission and the crew's fifth, and for all of us—our last mission. We were being sent to bomb Berlin.

If we had made it back to our base from that Berlin mission, I would have brought charges against one member of our crew for his cowardly conduct and for his failure to carry out a direct order. But we didn't return to England that day. In fact it would be many, many years before I stepped upon the English shore again.

End Notes
Missions

1. Holland is used primarily throughout the story to refer to the Netherlands.

2. Aircraft markings were periodically changed in order to confuse the Germans. In the spring of 1944 the 389th Bomb Group's circle "C" was replaced with a white vertical bar on a painted black tail.

3. Flak is short for **Fliegerabwehrkanone**, which translated literally means "flyer defence canon," and is German for anti-aircraft gun. There were heavy and light Flak batteries manned by 6 to 10 men (and boys as the Germans began to run low on manpower). The most common heavy Flak weapon was the 88mm. These guns fired time-fused high-explosive shells that could reach an altitude of 35,000 ft., well within the range of our heavy bomber formations.

4. There are many different types of shells, both cannon as well as .50 caliber. For instance, we had rounds of .50 caliber shells that were armor piercing and made of high grade steel inside of a copper jacket, the copper being for the rifling of the barrel. We also had rounds of .50 caliber explosive shells. These explosives shells apparently had a little powder train and exploded after a flight of "x" seconds. Then there were incendiary shells. These shells ignited in flight and remained flaming after they hit and stuck into something. Then we had a fourth kind called tracers. A tracer had a bright tail fire coming from the slug so the gunners could see where their stream of fire was going. I believe cannons had the same types of shells as mentioned above. On the bombers we didn't have 20mm guns because they were too big. The .50 caliber was a big gun, but the 20mm and 37mm guns were much larger. I'm sure they had armor piercing, tracer, explosive, and incendiary shells.

    The armorers made up the machine gun belts. They had a machine with some kind of a trough, and they laid out the bullets in this trough. The types of bullets they put into a machine gun belt depended upon the type of mission. For example, they might want every tenth round to be an incendiary shell, and maybe every other round to be an explosive shell, and every twentieth round to be a tracer. The armorers could tell one type of shell from another type by looking at the color on the first 1/4- to 1/2-inch of the bullet part of the shell. The bullets had been dipped in colored fluid, and my recollection is that a normal round had no paint, an armor piercing bullet was painted black, and an incendiary bullet was painted red. Normally, at the tail end of the machine gun belts in fighter aircraft, they'd have five or ten rounds of white tracer to tell the fighter pilot he was out of ammunition.

5. At this stage of the air war, fighter protection didn't extend much beyond this range because the fighters did not yet have drop tanks—extra fuel tanks mounted under the wings that could be dropped when empty.

6. "Formating" was what we called forming up, or assembling, in our designated airspace, in our designated positions.

7. *The Mighty Eighth, War Diary*, pg.186, 187, author Roger Freeman.

8. Lt. White crew, tail marking W- aircraft serial number 42-100338 (MACR-2943) crashed near Lichtenfels.

9. Lt. Belanger, tail marking Y- aircraft serial number 42-73504 (MACR-2941) crashed at Gotha.

10. This photo shows the B-24 flown by Lt. Col. Clarence Lokker, commander of the 781st BS, 465th BG, exploding after being hit by flak over Blechhammer, DL, on the 20th of November 1944. Amazingly, four crewmen were able to escape the flaming explosion and parachute to the ground to become POWs. Information found at http://www.samoloty.ow.pl/str208a.htm.

11. This B-24 was cut in half by a rocket fired from a German ME-262, the first jet fighter used in aerial combat. The B-24 was piloted by Lt. Robert L. Mains of the 714th BS, 448th BG, and was shot down on the 4th of April 1945. Photo credited to Lt. Col. (Ret.) Harold Dorfman, lead navigator of the 448th BG.

12. Lt. Nowak, tail marking M-aircraft serial number 42-109828 (MACR-2927) crashed at Brotterode.

13. I didn't know Sgt. Hughes was credited for a kill that day until many years later when I saw a list on a web site dedicated to the 389th Bomb Group. This web site is designed and maintained by the official 389th Bombardment Group historian, Kelsey McMillan. For more information, visit the web site at: http://www.389thbombgroup.com.

14. During that time of the war, a crew could go back to the states after flying 25 missions.

15. KIA and MIA numbers for the 389th Bomb Group were compiled by Chris Gregg, whose grandfather, Lt. Harry Gregg, was a bombardier with the 567th/389th. Chris' web site is http://www.389thbg.net.

16. Loss statistics for the three divisions sourced from *The Mighty Eighth, War Diary*, pg.187, author Roger Freeman.

17. In 1941, the Germans developed a jet-powered flying bomb and designated it the V-1. It got its nickname "Buzz bomb" from its distinctive buzzing sound, due to the pulsing nature of the jet engine.

Lt. Keeffe in free-fall, bailing out over Papendrecht, Holland. Drawing by Lt. Jimmy Blackstock, POW in Center Compound, Stalag Luft III. (Lt. Col. Keeffe collection)

Evasion

The Death of a Heavy Bomber

From the desk of C.P. Vanderplank in the Executive Offices of Life Magazine, Time & Life Building, Rockefeller Center, New York 20

August 6, 1945

Dear Mrs. Keeffe:

I am attaching a copy of a letter that came to us from a LIFE subscriber in Holland -- a doctor who helped your son when he had to bail out of his crippled bomber last March.

It is really an amazing story, and although you have probably heard it in more detail from your son by now, I am glad to carry out Dr. Lemoine's wishes and send it to you, along with a copy of the map he drew on his original letter.

While I was able to find out through the War Department that your son was evacuated to the United States, I was not able to obtain his present address. I am sending this to you.

We join Dr. Lemoine in the hope that the end to this story is a happy one -- and that he will soon hear from your son himself.

Sincerely,

C. P. Vanderplank[1]

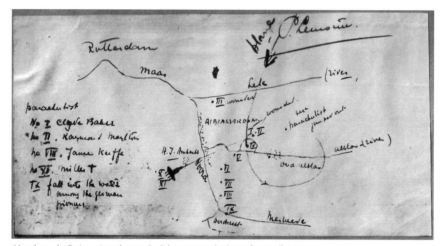

Map drawn by Dr. Lemoine who watched the crewmen bail out of Lt. Keeffe's B-24. He sent this map, along with the letter below to C.P. Vanderplank of Life Magazine, who forwarded it on to Lt. Keeffe's parents after the war. (Lt. Col. Keeffe collection)

                    Cortgene 25
                    Alblasserdam, Netherlands
                    11-6-45

Dear Sirs:

Here follows a little story of one of your four engine bombers.

On the 8th of March, 1944, American four engine bombers started in the morning from Great Yartmouth in England for Germany. In groups of 35 they passed the Dutch coast near Egmond on Sea at 12:15. Over Osnabruck they reached the south and east of Berlin, turned on, and on retreat sent their bombs on a German factory in Berlin. It was 14:45. One of them which you follow now was on a height of 23,000 feet over Berlin and had just loosed his bombs when the third engine was shot out by ground flak.

The plane lost altitude and again over Osnabruck at 15,000 feet the second engine was shot out by ground flak. They were a prey to German airplanes.

From the eleven (crew) the first pilot Miller (address unknown) was killed (above Osnabruck) and later two wounded a.o. Clyde Baker. He was shot through his both Achilles tendons. With their two outside engines they must lose more altitude, but escaped the German airplanes.

Over the southern sea they threw overboard all
their ammunition radios, flag, m.p.'s etc. to rise -
but then the bomber began to swing; they could not
find their bearings, deviated to the south and above
the Alblasserwaard (look at the map) they had no
more gas (petrol). Then the eldest man of the crew
took the navigation while the other nine left the
ship by parachute. The first they set out was the
wounded Clyde Baker, who had had a morphium injec-
tion (above Osnabruch) by James Keeffe.

Just on my daily trip in Oud Alblos, it was
16:15, I saw them in the air and following on my
motorcycle I reached two men: Clyde Baker, radio
operator, born 24/1/1920, address Hazelrowe 1704,
Warren, Ohio (number of the metal place around his
neck, 35283254 T42), and Raymond Moylton, gunner, 22
years, address Charlton Depot, Mass., who had broken
his ankle by (the fall) falling.

Baker, who at first didn't know where he was,
gave me, after a shake of hands, his pistol, packet
marker II (with French, Belgium and Dutch money,
compass and maps), his flying cap, with receivers ANB - H - l and wrist watch. I told him that
the Germans will come directly. At that time - for
me - it was very dangerous to do so and he promised
me - upon his honor - to say nothing to the Germans.
I promised him to send back after the war his wrist
watch (while he gave me his packet marker II for my
medical assistance). 20 minutes later the Germans
came and they were furious. It was impossible, they
said, a soldier had no arms!! No compass, etc., but
-- they did not! After many cries they asked me to
inquire. And then, as I said, "You don't have a
pistol, do you," they said, scarcely smiling, "No"!
(Moylton had also given me all he had.) Under great
protestation of the Germans (in Germany they could
walk or they were killed or lynched as the German
soldiers said). I sent them with a luxury motorcar
to the German hospital in Dordrecht. "You would
never do this for us," said the Germans scornfully
to me, swinging their pistols. I never heard anything more of these boys.

At the same time another man of the crew, who
opened his parachute when he was at an altitude of
nearly 100 meters, stood in no time, unwounded and
perfectly on the ground. He quickly rolled up his
parachute, hid it in a small ditch and crept in a
rabbit hutch. There he was found in the evening by
a little boy, who told his father, who warned one
of the illegal workers (underground men). This boy,
named R. Vet, took the American into his house; and
under the eyes of the German soldiers and water
pioneers (they patrolled all the day and night
over every 50 meters), set him over the river, the
"Noord," in the same night, with great danger for
life, and conducted him to Dordrecht. The following day I met here James H. Keefe (address J. H.
Keefe, 3237 Hunter Boulevard, Seattle, Wash.) who
told me the story of this four-engine bomber. The
bomber fell down in Hendrik-Soo-Ambacht, after nine
parachutists had left it. The eldest man survived
the unfortunate landing, was wounded and was taken
prisoner by the Germans.

J. H. Keefe cycled on the 10th of March under
armed escort (illegal worker) with R. Vet to
Rotterdam and later to Den Haag where he was taken
over to the English Secret Service, which could arrange for him to get home. We also heard nothing of
him.

Will you be so kind to send this story to the
family of these three men, who risked their lives
for our liberation.

Probably they will send us a letter about the
end of this story, which we all hope will be that
they are safe and alive. Tell James Keefe that
afterwards Mr. R. Vet was taken prisoner by the
Germans for illegal work in Rotterdam. He was sent
to concentration camps in Amersfoort (Holland),
condemned to death, he uncomprehensibly became par-
doned, was sent to Vught (Holland) in September '44
and later to Oranienburg in Germany and then to the
south of Germany, Nov. 1944, after which we never
had a sign of him. I was also unfortunate, for in
April '45 I was set in prison in Rotterdam the last
three and a half weeks of war.

Excuse my bad English and three cheers for the
Americans (and the death of the Japs).

Dr. P. J. G. H. Lemoine

(Author's note: All letters, correspondence and diary entries included in this book are printed exactly as they were originally written, including mistakes.)

Near where Dr. Lemoine was watching the ten of us parachute out of the stricken B-24 as it circled lower and lower, was the town of Hendrik-Ido-Ambacht. A major road, Vrouwgelenweg (Mrs. Gelen's Way), headed south out of this town. Perpendicular to this road was a stand of very high poplar trees that served as a wind break for a brick house built right on the side of the road. Occupying this house was a Dutch doctor, who happened to be a member of the *Nationaal-Socialistische Beweging* (National-Socialist Movement), or simply put, he was an NSBer—a Dutch Nazi. His neighbors didn't like him one bit, and they loved to tell the story of the day the American bomber almost crashed into the despised NSBer's house.

The people living near where our airplane flew over came out of their houses to watch, because all the local German anti-aircraft and machine guns were making quite a racket shooting at it. The anxious people on the ground watched as the stricken plane descended, like a wounded bird, in a slow, agonizing circle. One after another, little white canopies appeared in the sky behind the plane, seemingly from nowhere. The people could see a frightened crewman suspended under each one.

The NSB doctor also heard all of the commotion and came out to watch what was going on. He had gone upstairs and was standing on the balcony at the back of his house, facing the tall row of poplar trees. The bomber circled and came back. Then it headed straight for his house.

The airplane descended right down the tall row of poplars, heading almost directly toward the doctor. The tops of the trees exploded into a spray of shattered branches and wood fragments. Pieces of the skin on the bottom of the bomber tore off, and still it came closer. The friction of the bomber tearing through the treetops slowed its forward speed and, fortunately for the doctor, pitched the nose of the airplane up, causing the right wing to just miss striking the second floor balcony as it passed over the side of the house. Then the airplane stalled and plopped down across Vrouwgelenweg, skidding on its belly through a field where it ground to a stop with very little damage. When the airplane hit the field, one engine tore off and gouged a deep furrow in the dirt, but the other three engines stayed on the wings. There was no fire or explosion because there was no fuel left to burn.

Just before the airplane plowed into the row of poplars, the doctor, think-ing it was going to hit his house and him, froze in fear, and wet and soiled his pants. Unfortunately for him, his neighbors witnessed these reactions. To the shame and humiliation of the Dutch Nazi, the tale spread throughout the local community.

Most of the shooting stopped after the airplane came to rest in the field, and some of the local Dutch farmers ran up to the airplane and climbed inside. They found Sgt. Miller in the waist, dead. They scrounged around quickly and took some artifacts from the airplane.[2]

Then the Germans showed up, and the farmers ran away from them and the airplane. They wanted nothing to do with the Germans. If they were caught prowling around, they could find themselves in serious trouble. The Germans posted soldiers around the airplane to keep it under guard, but the farmers knew there was a body in the back end of the airplane, and they had noticed that the left hand was gone. A few of them went into town and started the process of requesting the body from the Germans. Initially, the Germans weren't going to let them have it.

The Germans were always angry with locals who helped injured Allied airmen. "You help these American airmen," they were known to complain, "but you would never help a German Luftwaffe crew member!"

At first the German authorities put up resistance when the locals asked for Miller's body in order to bury it. The Burgermaster of Hendrik-Ido-Ambacht contacted a Mr. C. Bax, the local undertaker, to retrieve the body. When Bax couldn't get any satisfaction from the local German authorities, he contacted a higher German headquarters in the town of Dordrecht up the river. There, he finally got permission from the German officer in charge to take the body for burial.

The townspeople took Miller's body to the Hendrik-Ido-Ambacht town cemetery, an old cemetery surrounded by a tall stone wall. They conducted a burial ceremony that was attended by several hundred people. This really an-gered the local Dutch Nazis, and that night some men stole into the cemetery, stomped on all the flowers and tore out the cross the townspeople had placed on the grave. The next day the people replaced the flowers with more than before. That night the Dutch Nazi thugs climbed over the cemetery wall again and tore them all up. Subsequently, the people brought even more flowers, and that night those got all smashed up, too. After three days of this, the local higher ranking NSBers told the men who were smashing up the flowers to stop it because they were making the organization look like a bunch of fools.

After the war, Mr. Bax wrote a very nice letter to Sgt. Miller's mother, de-scribing to her the burial of her son.

This road is the Vrouwgelenweg and through the trees can be seen the NSB doctor's house. Lt. Keeffe's descending B-24 plowed through the tops of the poplar trees leading to the back of the house, from right to left, passed over the side of the house and over the road where it plopped down in a field on the other side. The photo was taken in 1959 and shows Anton Sanders and family, whom you will soon meet. (Lt. Col. Keeffe collection)

Mr. C. Bax
Vrouw Geelenweg 3a
H.I.Ambacht
Holland

H. I. Ambacht
September, 1945

Dear Madame:

    I had planned for a long time to send you the news of the funeral of your son, Kenneth Miller. I presume that you would be very much interested in hearing of the circumstances under which he was buried. I'll be able to do this or to tell you this better than anybody else in as much as I am the undertaker and directed the funeral. Therefore, I will take this opportunity to tell you about it in detail.

    On March 8, 1944, at 5 P.M., an airplane flew or passed very low over our village apparently trying to make a forced landing. The airplane came lower

and lower and finally touched the ground. The direction in which the plane was going brought it before
a clearing between a house and nursery which was
surrounded by tall trees and I have seen for myself
how the left wing of the plane touched the trees and
shirred off several trees that were 25 centimeters
thick (about a foot thick) and finally about 50 yards
further fell to the ground. Soon we discovered that
the only person in the plane had lost his life.

On March 9, I received an order from the Burgo-
master (same as a Mayor) of our village to pick up
the body and take it to the cemetery. In accordance
with his order, I took a casket and went to the
place where the body was laying. When I arrived
there with the constable we were asked by the Nazis
if we had permission to transport the body. We could
not show authority and we were obliged to leave the
body where it was for the time being. The constable
went with one Nazi to telephone a commander in the
city of Dordrecht and from him we received permission to transport the body. Then I proceeded to
put the body into the casket. I had a good chance
to look at the face of the victim and his face did
not show that he had suffered at all. His right arm,
however, was seriously injured and his hand was cut
off by the wrist. I presume that this caused severe
bleeding which was the cause of his death. Then
we inhabitants of the village showed great interest which was aggravating to the Nazis. The funeral
took place on March 10 and even though the hour of
the funeral was not previously announced there were
a great number of people waiting at the cemetery to
be witnesses to this sorrowful ceremony. We placed
the casket on the brier and walked toward the grave
followed by about 500 people. Your son, madam, had
a very honorable funeral and the interest shown by
so many people should not be considered as caused by
curiosity but by a great sympathy for this allied
pilot who gave his life for our cause. When we
arrived at the grave the casket was placed above
it and during reverent silence was lowered. Among
those present was the Burgo-master, the town secretary and a minister of the Dutch Reformed Church.
After the casket was lowered the Burgo-master spoke

a few words after which the minister said a few
words and closed with a final prayer in the English
language. After this I said the following: "Dear
Friends, there is not a relative present to request
me to say a few words at this time; nevertheless I
will take it upon myself to speak for the unknown
mother and say a word of thanks to the Burgo-master
and the Rev. Roskott in appreciation for the words
they spoke at this occasion. Also I want to thank
all those present at the funeral of our deceased
friend".

In deep sorrow the people left the cemetery.

Madam, perhaps this writing will open a wound which
was partially healed, still I thought it my duty to
tell you about these details so that you may know
that our simple village people have paid the last
honor to an unknown friend who lost his life in the
battle for the good cause.

Respectfully,
C. Bax

It took about a week, but eventually the Germans hauled our B-24 away. First
they stripped all the weapons and ammunition, the radios, the Norden bombsight, and other useful equipment out of the airplane. Then they brought in large
flat-bed trucks and a crane, and after removing the wings and sectioning the
fuselage, they lifted the large pieces of the bomber onto the trucks and hauled
them away. Before they left, a couple of the German soldiers took one of the
bulletproof windshield pieces, stood it up against a stump and shot at it with
different weapons, but they weren't able to penetrate the glass.

Don't Loiter with Multiple People!

We had instructions to always hide our parachutes and Mae Wests. Well, my
canopy was strung all over the top of the apple tree I had slammed into, and
there was no way anyone was going to get that parachute out of that tree, short
of taking a half hour to do it. I probably would have had to cut it up. "To hell
with it!" I said to myself.

Scrambling out of my harness, I unhooked my Mae West and threw it on
the ground. The man wearing the fedora came up to me, and I shouted at him
asking if he was a Dutchman.[3] I found out after the war that he thought I had

said, *"Ich bin ein Deutschman!"* (I am a German!) He had come out to see an American, and all of a sudden he became confused because he was faced with the possibility that I was German.

We had also been told, "If you get safely on the ground, get rid of your gun. If the Germans see you with a gun, they will probably shoot first and ask questions later."

I took my .45 out of my pocket and, wanting to get rid of it, I thought I'd give it to the man wearing the fedora; he could give it to somebody in the Underground. But to make sure he didn't use it on me, I took the clip out of the gun and put it in my pocket. As soon as he saw me take my gun out, his hands shot up.

After he calmed down, the Dutchman took my gun by the muzzle with the handle of the gun hanging down. I could tell he'd never handled a gun before. I finished getting out of my harness, and then I hurried away from that tree. Because there were fences on both sides of this long narrow yard, the natural thing to do was to head up toward the houses to the left and the group of people standing there. Additionally, in my pockets I had a money packet and a small survival packet. These were issued to each crewman at the beginning of the mission.

When I reached the small group of people, I took the survival packet out of my pocket. It was in a rubberized envelope about four-inches wide by five-inches long and a quarter inch thick. In my nervousness and excitement I ripped it open, and everything spilled onto the ground: compass, safety pins, fish hooks, needles, even a very fine silk map. The people and I picked everything up, and I tried to stuff it all back into the packet and back into my pocket. Nobody spoke English, and they were all chattering and pointing at me because my face was covered with mud and blood.

"Jim, you're doing this the wrong way," I thought. "You're not supposed to go to a group of people. You've got to get away from these people and go hide!"

I reached out and took my pistol back from the man who was still holding it by the muzzle, and I put the clip back in it. Looking around, I wondered where I could go or what I could do.

My first decision was that I had to get away from these people. I ran across the back yard of the house toward a tall board fence. With the adrenaline really pumping, I climbed up onto the fence. All I saw ahead of me was a sea of fences. The lots were narrow, about forty to fifty feet wide, but very long, and each one had a house on the left end of it up against the dike road. I dropped down into the next yard, ran across it and climbed up the next board fence. From the top of this fence I looked back and noticed that all the people had disappeared. Later, I learned that the Germans would shoot anybody on the spot who helped an airman in any way. The Germans had a term, "*An der Wand*!" (Against the wall!) *Bang*! So the locals had scattered quickly and disappeared when I ran off.

After jumping up and climbing over a couple of the fences, I realized I couldn't do this for very long while wearing my heavy electrified flying suit and large boots. I dropped down into the next yard and hurried across it. There was a rabbit hutch up against the fence on the far side. Quickly, I looked all around and didn't see anyone. I still had to get rid of my gun, so I whipped it out of my pocket and reached as far back between the fence and the rabbit hutch as I could and hid my .45 pistol.

Unbeknownst to me, people were watching me from inside the houses, looking out of the windows. From the upper window of his home a little boy saw me put my gun between the rabbit hutch and the fence. Later that day he told his father, who that night went out and retrieved it and threw it into the River Noord.

Into the Shed

Once more I shinnied up a tall fence, and then I began to really tire. I looked around again and couldn't see anybody anywhere, so I dropped down into the next long narrow yard. I noticed a shed built up against the back of the house to the left.

The houses were quite odd. The front door opened out onto the sidewalk and the dike road, but the land at the rear was about twenty feet lower. This was reclaimed land from the sea, which the Dutch called a *polder*. The back of the house was a story plus, about fifteen to twenty feet in height. The Dutch normally used the area underneath the house for storage, not for living.

The shed was about ten feet long and eight feet wide. Because it was up against the back of the house, I thought it probably led into the cellar, which in turn probably led into the house. It was made of wood and had a roof that sloped away from the back wall of the house. It also had a wooden door in the side facing the next yard. I made a snap decision and ran over to the shed, opened the door, and hurried inside. On the left wall was a small window, so even with the door closed there was some light.

It was now about 4:45 in the afternoon and dusk was just beginning outside. It turned out there wasn't an entrance or doorway from the shed into the lower part of the house as I had thought there might be. "I'm inside," I figured. "I'm out of sight, and I ain't gonna leave! What's the smart thing to do here?"

There were two tables in the shed. One of the tables stood just inside the wooden door against the left wall. It was about three feet by four feet, and on top of it was a rabbit hutch with two or three rabbits in it. On the right side, immediately inside and against the front wall, was a similar table, also with a rabbit hutch on top. A lot of stuff, including potato sacks, was stored under these tables.

There was a shelf at the back up against the rear of the house. A bunch of things were stored up there as well. There were a lot of garden tools in the shed—shovels, rakes, and so forth. Having played cops and robbers and hide-and-go-seek as a kid, I used my head. I took a handful of rakes and shovels, three or four of them, and pushing the wooden door open a little bit, reached outside and leaned the tools up against the face of the door. Then I brought my hand back in and let the door close. This act probably saved me from being captured.

I looked around and decided that the smart thing to do next was to get into the darkest place, which was under the table on the right side, so I crouched down and hid there.

Outside, the shooting had pretty well stopped, but sirens were still blaring. I could hear cars and trucks roaring back and forth up on the dike road. I did an inventory. I went through everything I had, which wasn't very much. I had the escape packet of money, a survival kit with little odds and ends, and a Boy Scout knife, which I always carried with me. I took the knife and cut off the six-foot cord that was still dragging from my electric flying suit.

A view of the back of the house with the rabbit shed at the right. The steps on the left lead up to the dike road. The photo was taken in 1959. The man on the left is Kees van den Engel, whom you will soon meet.
(Lt. Col. Keeffe collection)

Next, I went through my pockets. We hadn't planned to fly that day so I had gone to bed at midnight. We'd been awakened at 2 a.m. and, because I was groggy from lack of sleep, I hadn't prepared properly for going on a mission (I noticed later that I had mismatched socks on my feet). I had things in my pockets that I shouldn't have had, including some laundry receipts and a tailor receipt for an Eisenhower jacket I'd ordered. These jackets were the big rage. They only came to the waist and didn't have a tail on them like the other officers' jackets. I chewed up all the stuff that might be of importance to German intelligence and buried it in the dirt floor of the shed.

Then I took potato sacks and covered myself with them, and there I sat. I heard a motorcycle roar past. Some minutes later I heard a truck going the other way. Every once in a while I heard people moving around in the house above. Pretty soon I began to hear voices, which came closer and closer. I could tell this was the search party. There were people in the back yards and up on the dike. They were probably soldiers or police. I couldn't see them, so I wasn't exactly sure. But I could hear them coming closer.

All of a sudden there was a lot of shouting. I figured they had just found my parachute hanging up in the tree and my Mae West, which had my name stenciled on it. I heard them in the yard next door. Then suddenly I heard *bang, bang, bang*! on the front door of the house above me. Apparently, the people who lived in the house had opened the door because I could hear hob-nailed boots stomping around up there. At the same time I heard shouting outside the shed. Somebody swept away the tools that were up against the door. The door flew open, and a man stormed into the shed.

I peeked through a slit between the potato sacks I was covered with and was able to see him from the waist down. He had on green riding breeches and black riding boots. He was also wearing a short green tunic and gray gloves with snaps on each wrist, and he had a German Luger in his right hand. The Luger had a cord attached to the bottom, which I suppose went up over his shoulder. Holding the Luger at the ready, he turned around two or three times in the middle of the shed. Somebody started shouting from outside. He yelled an answer and left. I found out later he was from what the Dutch called the Green Police. The Green Police were all Germans, and they were very nasty, bad fellows.

"Why didn't this guy search around the shed more?" I wondered. How surprised and lucky I was! The thing that saved me had to have been those tools up against the door.

"There can't be anybody in here because these tools are here," the man must have thought. The subconscious does funny things, and I'm sure that's what happened. He had stomped in, spun around a couple of times, shouted a response to someone outside, then turned and left—all in the space of a few seconds.

When the German left the shed, the running around upstairs also stopped, probably because the Germans had gone through all the rooms. I could hear the search continue on to the next yard and then move farther and farther away. The sounds of the search finally died out completely, except for the odd motorcycle or vehicle roaring past.

Soon it became quiet. I could hear people moving around in the house above, and I thought I could hear the mumbling of voices. As the light outside faded, it became dark in the shed.

Contact

CLOMP! CLOMP! CLOMP! CLOMP! CLOMP! Somebody was approaching the shed, so I got set all over again. I pulled out my Boy Scout knife, cupping the handle in the palm of my hand and holding the blade between my thumb and index finger. I arranged the slit in the potato sack so I could look out. It was now completely dark. The door opened and an elderly man came in.

He was carrying a small lantern in his right hand. I could see he was wearing Dutch wooden shoes, old ones that were all beat up. He had on tattered wool pants and an old worn-out suit coat. In his left hand, he carried a bowl of fairly large carrots. It was dinnertime, and he had come to feed his rabbits. He put the bowl and the lantern down on the table up against the left wall and more or less had his back to me.

I sized him up. We'd been told never to go up to a well dressed, wealthy person because he or she was probably sympathetic to the Germans. "Go to one person, a simple person, or go to a church and talk to the priest or reverend."

This man was certainly not well-to-do, so I thought I had better do something. I reached out and jerked the back of his jacket. He turned around and just about dropped dead of a heart attack right on the spot. I came out from under the table, where I'd been cramped up for maybe half an hour or longer, and stood up.

He was a little shorter than I.

He cowered back away from me and started to speak, but I put my finger up and whispered "*Shhhhh*," signaling him to be quiet.

We sized each other up for a second or two, and then I turned my attention to the carrots. I was really hungry. By now it was close to 6 p.m., and I hadn't eaten much for breakfast that morning. I pointed to his carrots.

"Jabber, jabber, jabber," he said. I couldn't understand a word.

I reached over and took a carrot and started eating it, and he looked at me with big wide eyes.[4]

"Can you speak English?" I asked him.

"Jabber, jabber, jabber."

"Können Sie Deutsch sprechen?" (Can you speak German?) I asked him, using the little bit of German I knew.

"Jabber, jabber, jabber."

"This isn't getting anywhere," I thought. "What am I going to do now?"

He then pointed to my face. I didn't realize it, but I had caked mud and dried blood on my face and also in my hair. The blood from the shrapnel cut on my face had probably gotten into my hair when my helmet came off. I must have looked pretty wild.

"No, no, no, I'm OK, I'm fine. Don't worry about it," I said.

He took a potato sack, two nails and a stone and went over to the shed window to cover it up. He put a corner of the burlap sack up on one corner of the window, then a nail, and started hitting the nail with the rock, driving it into the wall *BANG! BANG! BANG!*

"Good Lord, the whole neighborhood's going to hear this," I thought in alarm as I rushed over to him.

My First Dutch Word

I grabbed the rock from one of his hands and the second nail from his other hand. My adrenaline was surging again, and I physically pushed the nails into the wood with the rock.

"Quiet! *Shhhhh*," I motioned to him.

I took another nail and, on a vertical post in the middle of the shed, I scratched a *2* and a *0* and pointed to myself, implying I was twenty years old. For the first time, I saw a light go on in this guy's head.

"Ahh," he said and motioned for the nail, which I handed to him.

He then scratched a *58* on the post.

Then he said "*Ik*" and pointed to himself.

I had my first Dutch word—"I." In Nederlands, "I" was "*Ik*."

"*Acht en vijftig*," he then said.

This was close enough to German. He was telling me he was fifty-eight years old. I had my first communication with the Dutchman.

I could tell things were roaring around in his head. By now he realized I was the American they were looking for. "Here he is in my shed!" he had to be thinking, "This is terrible, what am I going to do?"

"Will you help me?" I asked him. I didn't realize how close this was to the Dutch, "*Wilt u mij helpen*?," but he must have understood because he pointed to his watch and indicated he would be gone for half an hour and then come back.

"*Terug, ik kom terug*," he said, which was very close to the German, "*Ich komm zurück*." (I come back.)

"Well," I thought to myself, "either he's a good guy or he's a bad guy. There's nothing I can do anyhow. I have no idea where in Holland I am, so I have to trust him."

Taking the lantern, the man went out and closed the shed door. A short two or three minutes later I heard steps outside again, but they sounded different from those of the Dutchman.

"Well, this is either the police, or he's gone and gotten somebody to help."

But all that had happened was that, while he was gone, he had changed out of his wooden clogs and into shoes. He came back in carrying a plate that had on it a thin slice of bread with a thin layer of jam and two or three little pieces of candy. He grinned and handed it to me.

"He's a good guy," I immediately thought to myself.

He pointed to his watch again and left.

What's a Good German Sympathizer Supposed to Do?

I found out later that Johannes Korteland, the man who owned the house whose shed I was in, was a German sympathizer[5] and he now had a problem; he had an American airman hiding on his property.

His mind was racing! "What the hell do I do with this American? I have to be careful here. The Germans might kill me, or my own people might kill me if I turn him in."

When Korteland left the shed the second time, he went up on the dike road and, in the dark, walked to the village doctor's house, about fifteen minutes away. He wanted some advice about what to do with the American in his shed. He didn't know at the time that the doctor was the head of the local Resistance organization. The doctor's name was Rietveldt.[6]

Korteland arrived at Dr. Rietveldt's house and knocked on the door. The doctor's wife opened it and saw Korteland standing there wringing his hat in his hands. Speaking in a quivering voice he said, "I would like to speak with the doctor, please."

"I'm very sorry, but the doctor is busy right now," replied Dr. Rietveldt's wife.

"But this is very important. I need to talk to the doctor right now!" he said in earnest.

"Well, I'm very sorry, the doctor is busy," she told him again.

Earlier, Dutch Underground people from farther down around the bend in the dike road had seen me go over the fences and into the shed. They had kept an eye on it ever since. They'd seen me put the tools outside the door and thought that was quite clever. They later saw the Green Police man go in. "Well, the jig's up, he's caught the American now," they'd figured.

But as they watched, the policeman came back out empty-handed! They kept watch even after dark, and finally saw Korteland, carrying a lantern, go down along the side of his house and around the back to his shed. They saw him enter, come out twenty minutes later and go back up into his house. Then they saw him come out of his house a second time and go back down into the shed.

After witnessing all of this, they rushed over to Dr. Rietveldt's house. "The American is in Korteland's shed!" one of them said. "This is bad news because Korteland is a German sympathizer." About that time, an additional underground person who'd been watching the shed hurried in and announced that Korteland was on his way to the doctor's house.

A few minutes later came Korteland's knock at the front door. Hearing his wife answer the door and tell Korteland he wasn't available, the doctor came out from a room and walked to the front door.

"What is the problem, Johannes?" he asked Korteland.

Korteland answered in a whimpering voice, "Oh doctor, the American the authorities are searching for is in my shed. What am I going to do? I'm afraid of the villagers, but I'm also afraid of the Germans."

"Well, this is one of the prices you pay for being sympathetic to the cause of the Nazis," said the doctor. "However, to solve this problem, Johannes, you go home. You don't tell your family anything. You close the shutters, go upstairs and go to bed."

"But what about the American?" wailed Korteland.

"Don't worry about the American, don't think about him. You never saw an American. Just go home, go upstairs to bed and forget about the American. He was never there."

Korteland thanked the doctor, turned around and walked back down the dike road to his house.

In the shed, I heard the front door open and close in the house above. Then I heard people moving around and I started to worry. "What had this guy done?" I wondered. He hadn't come back here with police, and he was in the house now.

Pretty soon I couldn't hear any more sounds coming from upstairs. Time went by slowly in the dark shed. It became later and later. I'd had only one carrot, one piece of bread, and some candy to eat.

All of a sudden, I heard shuffling and whispering voices just outside the shed door.

"This is it. Either it's the cops, the German military, or the Gestapo—or it's some good guys," I thought and then braced myself for whoever was going to come through the door.

Going Underground

As I stood in the middle of the shed, the door opened and a little man entered. Standing behind him was a huge man and three or four other men. The little man was Dr. Rietveldt, but I didn't know this at the time. The doctor had a flashlight, which he flashed up and down on me two or three times while I just stood there.

Finally he spoke to me in rather broken English. "We hellup you."

One of the men outside handed in a worn, but clean, man's suit and a pair of shoes. I took off my F2 flying suit and was about to unzip the electric liners from the outer wool jacket and pants. I intended to throw away the electric liners and put the wool suit back on, but the men motioned for me to put on the clothes they had brought instead. I did this and stuffed my uniform and the liners under one of the tables.

Their suit was too big for me! Korteland must have told Dr. Rietveldt that I was a very large man. I had to lap the fly and use some string for a belt. I put on the shoes, which must have been size twelve or thirteen, and stepped right out of them. Taking the laces out of the eyes of the shoes, I tied them around and down across the bottoms of the soles. In essence, I tied the shoes onto my feet. Before I stood back up, I reached under the table and retrieved the money pouch from my discarded uniform and shoved it into the front pocket of my "new" suit.

We then did a lot of hand shaking and hugging and clapping on the back. During our quick conversation Dr. Rietveldt asked if I had a gun. I said I did and told him that in the adjoining yard against the fence was a rabbit hutch, and that I had put my .45 between the back of the hutch and the fence. The doctor turned to the big man and they talked quickly among themselves. The big man nodded, gave me a quick look, and opened the shed door and left, closing the door behind him. Focusing his attention back on me, Dr. Rietveldt said, "OK, you come with us."

Out into the night we went. We walked stealthily along the back of the house and along the left side of it up some steps to the dike road. Directly across the road, on the other side of a fence, was a small boat yard and factory. We climbed over the fence and quickly made our way down to the river.

These men had already prepared a rowboat with a set of oars, and it was rocking quietly in the current. There was handshaking all around again, then one of the men indicated for me to climb into the back of the rowboat. Another fellow pushed the boat away from the shore and climbed into the back with me. The rower, whose name was Johannes Verdoorn, was already in the middle of the boat. The fellow who was escorting me was probably twenty-two to twenty-four years old. His name was Marinus Veth. Johannes started rowing up the dark river called the Noord.

Marinus Veth (l), and Johannes Verdoorn (r) rowed Lt. Keeffe up the Noord River from Noordhoek to Dordrecht.
(Lt. Col. Keeffe collection)

After the big man[7] left Korteland's shed, he went to retrieve the .45 pistol I had hidden, but by then it was gone. The next day he spoke to the owner of the house who told him that his son had seen a man hide the gun and that he had gone and found it and thrown it into the river. The Underground people were not happy. In fact, they were quite angry because they needed all the weapons they could get. That same day they dove in the river for the gun, found it, took it completely apart, cleaned it and put it back together again. The Underground now had another fully loaded, functional gun.

To Dordrecht via the Noord

The Noord is a huge river. The place where we pushed off in the rowboat was on a big bend in the river called Noordhoek. At this time, I had no way of knowing that behind us and across the river, just a couple of miles away to the northwest on the outskirts of the town of Hendrik-Ido-Ambacht, German guards were posted around the hulk of the B-24 heavy bomber I had bailed from just a few hours before.

Johannes rowed us out to the center of the Noord and continued up river for about half an hour. It was pitch black out, yet the night sky was clear, displaying tens of thousands of stars. There were no man-made lights anywhere because the area was under strict blackout orders. The only sounds were the soft swish of the oars and the quiet gurgling and hiss of the river. Johannes kept the oars as quiet as possible and was on constant alert for German patrols because the Germans had orders to shoot on sight and sink any boat found on the river at night.

Neither Marinus nor Johannes could speak a word of English, and my Dutch was almost non-existent. I was very grateful the two of them were risking their lives to get me to safety. Before we got off the river, I gave Marinus my silver Air Force class ring, the class of 43-F.

About a kilometer or two up the Noord, the river branched, forming a "Y." In the middle of the "Y" was a very large town named Dordrecht. Johannes pointed the bow of the rowboat toward the crotch of the "Y." As we came nearer to the town, I could see the silhouettes of buildings against the night sky. Johannes rowed toward a kind of plaza that stood above an eight-foot stone wall rising up out of the river. Stone steps led down from the plaza through an opening in the wall, continuing right into the water so that boats could pull up and discharge people. At this time of night the dark waterfront, the plaza, and all the buildings appeared to be closed up and abandoned. A town under the rules of blackout is a somber and mysterious place. It is also dangerous.

The only sound was the lapping of water against the oars and the stone wall. As he neared the edge, Johannes swung the boat 90 degrees, and we came to a quiet stop at the first step above the water line. Marinus Veth and I got out, shook hands with Johannes and pushed him and the rowboat back out into the current where he was quickly swallowed up by the night.

All the while Johannes was rowing me up the river his wife was at home worried and distraught. Their home was on the dike road just a few houses north of Korteland's house. Her husband had come to her earlier that evening and told her he had to row an American up to Dordrecht. She cried all the time he was gone, fearing the Germans would get him. But he made it back to the boatyard, put the boat away and got home before the curfew.

The Germans had many rules, or *Befehls*, in the occupied countries during the war. One *Befehl* had to do with curfew, which was from ten in the evening until six in the morning. Anyone caught on the streets could be shot, either by the police, a soldier, or any number of security forces. Civilians had to be off the streets, absolutely, during curfew. As in England, everything in Holland had to be blacked out; no light shining from windows or doors, or from vehicles. The Germans would shoot through any window if somebody foolishly or acciden-tally let a light shine out of it. The Dutch were extremely careful to follow the demand of the Germans for blackout.

After we pushed the rowboat back into the river, Marinus and I turned around and walked up the steps, crossed the plaza, and went through an entrance into the town of Dordrecht. The entrance was actually a short tunnel through some kind of a building. As we neared the opening, I looked up. In the dark I could barely make out a steeple on top of the building. Once through the tunnel Marinus guided us out onto a dark street called Wijnstraat. He was humming. It was a strange hum, sort of like "dal, dal, da dal, dal." I started humming it, too. He couldn't speak any English and I couldn't speak any Dutch, but as we walked farther into the dark town we smiled at each other every once in a while and shook hands.

I followed Marinus up Wijnstraat for a few hundred yards, and then we turned right down a cross street named Schrijverstraat. He obviously knew where he was going. At the next corner we turned left onto Kuipershaven, walked a short distance along a dark canal and turned left again onto Aardappelmarkt.[8] The houses along these streets were all three- and four-stories high and were built right up against each other; one house built against the next one, which was built against the next one, on down the block.

Marinus took us down Aardappelmarkt to the fifth home on the left and stopped before a door with #9 on it. The street in front of these homes blended into a broad cobblestone plaza and wharf which bordered the canal. By this time we had stopped humming. Marinus put his finger to his lips while he quickly looked around. Quietly, he opened the door and we went in and climbed a set of stairs up to the living room on the second floor. In the living room was a big Dutch lady. She was close to six feet tall and must have weighed about one hundred and eighty pounds. She and Marinus spoke briefly, and then he nodded and turned to go. His job was done. He had escorted me to a safe house in Dordrecht, and now he had to go catch what he called a *veerpont*, a small pedestrian ferry. He said something in Dutch, which I took to mean goodbye, and left the house. He went back across the Noord and walked home to Papendrecht, a small village near where I had come down.

Marinus Veth was eventually picked up by the Germans and disappeared. Sadly, I was to find out that many of the people I met in Holland died in dreadful ways at the hands of the Germans.

I was left with this large lady who had a very loud, booming voice. She spoke very good English but kept talking and asking questions with such a powerful voice that I became quite concerned. "The whole neighborhood can hear her talking in English," I cringed thinking.

One of the questions she asked me was about when the invasion would happen. Of course I had no idea. Almost to a person, one of the most important things people in Holland wanted to know was, "When is the invasion?"[9]

Aardappelmarkt and wharf. Marinus Veth escorted Lt. Keeffe to his first safe house at #9, the fifth house from the corner on the left. (Lt. Col. Keeffe collection)

It was now about nine or nine thirty in the evening, and after the lady and I talked for a short while, she showed me to a room where I was to sleep. I thanked her, went in and closed the door. Before I lay down to sleep, I stood to the side of the bedroom window and looked out over the dark city. There wasn't much to see, it being so dark out, but I could just make out the shape of a church steeple a short distance away.

The next morning I met the husband. It turned out he was an Englishman—a little shriveled up Englishman, very much a wimp, married to this big-bosomed Dutch lady. It was quite obvious to me that he didn't wear the pants in this house. It was also obvious that he didn't like my being there.[10]

"Please stay away from the windows," he said, "and I hope you're not here very long. This is very dangerous. If you are found here, both my wife and I will be shot."

I felt about an inch high and probably should have left, but I didn't because I had nowhere to go and knew nothing of where I was. It was now the 9th of March, and I had been gone from England for about a day and a half, although it felt much longer.

In the evening, another man, Dr. P.J.G.H. Lemoine, came to the house. He also had a big booming voice. Again I was scared to death that the whole neighborhood would hear him speaking in English! I didn't realize it, but he had arranged for me to be moved. He told me that the next day a couple of *onderduikers* would come for me. Many of the boys and young men in Holland were called *onderduikers*, which means "to dive under." All around Holland the

Dutch were hiding young men and boys because the Germans collected males from age sixteen to twenty-five and hauled them into Germany as forced labor.

Dr. Lemoine and I talked well into the evening. He told me that when he was out making his rounds the previous day, he had watched my airplane circle around and had seen all the parachutes open. Then he told me what had happened to two of my crew, Lt. Moulton and Sgt. Baker.

In a field near the farmhouse where Dr. Lemoine was at the time, Moulton, the bombardier, and Baker, the gunner who had been shot through both legs, had come down on a farmer's property. Baker had been hopped up on the morphine I'd given him and he ended up on the ground oblivious to everything. Moulton had hit the ground stiff-legged and broken both his legs.

A couple of farmers went out and lifted a gate off its pivots and used this gate, called a *hek*, as a stretcher to bring each of the airmen to the farmhouse. Dr. Lemoine first took off Baker's boots and cleaned and dressed the wounds. Then he set both of Moulton's broken legs in crude splints. Afterward, he stayed with both airmen until the German soldiers came. The Germans were angry because they couldn't find any weapons or other items on the airmen, and they became angrier when Dr. Lemoine sent for a car and had Baker and Moulton transported to a hospital where they would get better care.

Baker and Moulton were taken to a German field hospital in Dordrecht where they were reunited with Sgt. Smith and Lt. Stevens. Smith had seriously injured his back, maybe even broken it, when he landed on the ground. Stevens had broken one leg. I asked Dr. Lemoine if he had any news of the other crewmen, but he didn't. He also told me that the place where I had come down was called Noordhoek, which means "Corner of the North River." It was on the outskirts of the village of Papendrecht.

Eventually Dr. Lemoine got up to leave because he had to be home before curfew. We said goodbye, shook hands, and again he said that two young fellows would be by in the morning to pick me up and take me to a new place.

By now I was becoming rather ripe. When you're flying in combat, even though it's cold, you perspire, and I had moved all over our airplane immediately following the German fighter attack and worked up quite a sweat. I sure wanted to take a bath. But I had always been taught by my parents that if you were a guest, you let the other people take the lead. I wasn't offered a bath so I didn't ask for one, but I did wash my hands and my face before I went to bed.

Sure enough, around mid-morning the next day, two young men about my age came to the apartment building with three bicycles. I was taken downstairs and out the back into an enclosed small backyard where I was introduced to them. We all shook hands, and I thanked the Dutch lady and her English husband.

View from Aardappelmarkt looking across the plaza to Nieuwe Haven. (Lt. Col. Keeffe collection)

Then the two escorts and I hopped on the bicycles and crossed Aardappelmarkt to the north side of a small canal that flowed to the southwest. We followed the canal on a cobblestone street named Nieuwe Haven for a couple of blocks and crossed back over the canal before it emptied out into a large river.

We pedaled through the city for about a mile, always paralleling the river, riding past numerous little waterways and small harbors. Small wooden boats and large river barges were everywhere; tied up side-by-side or jockeying for position to pass beneath low-hung bridges. Eventually, we made our way up onto a bridge which took us north over the large river. Halfway across the bridge, one of my escorts gestured grandly at the river calling it the Oude Maas. It joined with the river Noord back near the entrance to Dordrecht where Marinus and I had been dropped off by Johannes Verdoorn just a couple of days before. Once over the bridge, we pedaled northwest away from Dordrecht into the Dutch countryside. It was Saturday, the 10th of March.

North to Rotterdam

We rode our bicycles for about two and a half hours from Dordrecht to the city of Rotterdam. After leaving Dordrecht, we paralleled the main highway on a bicycle path several feet away from the roadbed itself.[11] The sun was out, and the sky was a beautiful blue. I was astounded by many of the things I saw. Holland is a small country, and even during the war the people were very busy. People were everywhere—on the roads, on bicycles, and working in the fields.

The road wound through flat farmland. In every field there were dozens of randomly placed, very tall poles. These poles were about forty feet high and looked like telephone poles. Wires criss-crossed the tops of these poles, and I quickly realized they were there to make it very difficult, if not impossible, to land gliders. At this time, the Germans were very concerned about the potential of an invasion. They were fortifying the coastline all the way from Spain to the northern part of Norway. I don't know how far inland the Germans had put these posts, but they had to have cut down a hell of a lot of trees to wind up with so many of them.

I was surprised how easy it was to ride the Dutch bicycles. They had big wheels, probably thirty-two inches tall. Each bike had a ring bell on the handle bars and a reflector on the back fender, both of which were mandatory. They also had a small generator that could be flipped down onto the front wheel to give power to a light mounted on the handlebars.

We rode past German soldiers who were busy doing many things. There were a lot of German military vehicles on the road. I felt very exposed pedaling along with the two boys, and every time we passed a German soldier I expected the worst. As we approached Rotterdam, I could see several large bridges ahead that crossed over what appeared to be a huge river.[12] Along the way we went through several check points with German soldiers standing guard, but a low level of security must have been in effect at this time because we were not stopped at all. Another German guard was on the approach to one of the bridges, but he just looked bored as he waved us past.

Eventually we crossed over the Maas River and made our way into Rotterdam proper. We cycled out onto a street that ran along the side of the Diergaarde Blijdorp, which one of the boys told me was the Rotterdam Zoo. On one side of the street was a very large park-like grassy area. We rode through it to a street on the other side where there was a long row of apartments. These apartment rows were easily two or three blocks long.

Just like Marinus Veth, the two fellows knew exactly where to go. We went up to a particular apartment where one of the boys knocked on the door. A young lady answered, and I was taken inside and told this was where I was going to stay. The young lady didn't speak English and, of course, I knew no Dutch except for a couple of words and some numbers. My escorts knew a little English, enough that I understood I was to stay at the apartment. We shook hands one last time and then they left. I found out later that these two young men had been issued pistols and had been given orders to "protect and save the American," if necessary with their lives.[13]

It was late morning now, coming up on noon. I still hadn't had a shower and was feeling very slimy and foul. The young lady's husband came home in the early evening, and he spoke English reasonably well.[14] He and I talked about many things while we had dinner. The couple was a little older than I was, probably in their mid-twenties, and had no children.

Samuel Esmeijer, alias "Paul," one of two young men from the Resistance who escorted Lt. Keeffe from Dordrecht to Rotterdam by bicycle. (Courtesy of Mark Lubbers whose grandfather was a member of the Dutch Resistance)

Their flat, or apartment, occupied two floors. They showed me my room, which was upstairs, and where the bathroom and the water closet were.[15] I looked longingly at their bath tub. However, they didn't ask if I'd like a bath so I didn't ask. I went to bed feeling pretty dirty, but I was quite tired and easily fell asleep.

The next morning the young man went to work. His wife and I sat down at the dining room table and began to talk to each other. I wanted to learn Dutch, and she wanted to learn and practice English. We spent much of that day and the next working on this.

The second day things went along a little more smoothly. The wife wasn't as shy, and neither was I. We were making little sentences and beginning to understand each other.

After a while she made some tea. "*Wilt u een douche hebben?*" she then asked me in a very nice way.

By this time I was able to make out "*wilt u*," (will you), "*een*," (a), "*hebben*," (to have), "*douche!*" (Will you have a douche?!) Instinctively, and quite surprised, I jumped up off the chair at the dining room table. "No! I don't want a douche!" I blurted out. I thought, "This woman's crazy!"

After that little shock, I kind of steered clear of her for the rest of the day, and she steered clear of me, too. At the end of the day when the husband came home, he and his wife spoke quickly in Dutch.

Then he came right over to me. "How did things go today?" he asked.

"Oh, fine, just fine. Everything went just fine," I replied pleasantly.

"My wife says you were surprised about something. Possibly you were upset about something?"

"Oh, no. No, no," I said.

"Well, will you come with me?"

He took me into the bathroom and pointed to the tub and said, "*Bad*," (bath), and I nodded my head.

Next he pointed to the shower head, "*Douche*."

Then it dawned on me what the woman had asked me. She had asked me if I would like to take a shower.

"Oh, I'm sorry," I said sheepishly. "I didn't understand that that is what she was asking me. Yes, I would very much like to take a shower." And what a fine, wonderful shower that was.[16]

The next day was my birthday, the 12th of March. Twenty-one years of age and back home I could now legally drink alcohol. I didn't tell this nice couple about my birthday because I didn't want to make them feel like they should do something special for me. It was probably the loneliest birthday I've ever had.

Johannes "Jo" Berlijn was a chemist by occupation, and the district leader of the L.O. in charge of false identity papers and ration cards. (Courtesy of Els van der Meer, Nationaal Monument Kamp Vught)

After staying with this young couple for about three days, a man came and took me to another one of these row house apartments. This home was owned by an older man who was probably pushing fifty years old. His name was Jo Berlijn. The Dutch and the Germans pronounce the "J" like a "Y." His wife's name was Lena, and they had a young daughter named Elsje. I stayed with them for two or three days. Jo Berlijn was in the insurance business. He was also working full time with, and for, the Underground as one of the top level people in the Rotterdam organization. He had connections in City Hall, which was how the Underground was able to make false identity papers for people and get these papers placed into the files in City Hall.

Holland Under German Occupation

The Germans controlled everything in Holland. But they also occupied Czechoslovakia, France, Belgium, Denmark, Norway, and Luxemburg, so they were spread very thin. In addition, they were fighting a war in Russia. Therefore, they had to rely on the Dutch people for many things and set extremely severe penalties for anybody they caught playing games with them.

The Germans tried to have tight control over the utilities in the countries they occupied, especially the "PTT," the Post, Telephone and Telegraph. But in Holland, as in the other countries they controlled, the Germans had limited manpower, so they had to leave many of the local people in their jobs. It might seem that every move made and every word spoken in an occupied country was monitored, but not so.

The telephone was very important to local Resistance groups who helped hundreds of downed Allied airmen like me. It was used with caution, but used nonetheless. Many of the locals also knew someone close by who was in the Underground, the Resistance, and they made contact with them whenever the need arose.

For instance, when I came down, it was necessary to quickly find a safe house for me. The Underground needed to get me out of Noordhoek, and out of Papendrecht, so they took me down the river Noord to Dordrecht. Arrangements were made for me to stay there for one to four days until the Germans stopped looking for me. The safe house people I stayed with had nothing to do with the planning and operations of the Underground. This was all done by somebody else. Dr. Lemoine, who came to see me at the house in Dordrecht, was affiliated with the Underground, so I presume that he'd spoken with Dr. Rietveldt, who was also with the Underground in Papendrecht. One or the other of them had arranged for the two lads to take me to Rotterdam.

I'm sure there'd been a phone call to one of the organizations in Rotterdam. "We're transporting an American pilot by bicycle, and we will put him with so-and-so family for a couple of days until you are able to take him elsewhere."

The Underground organization in Holland was actually comprised of many semi-autonomous underground groups. The military had an underground, the civil servants had an underground, the bureaucracy, all the national provinces, as well as the cities had undergrounds. The Dutch Reformed church had a resistance movement and the Catholic Church had their organization. Everybody, it seemed, had a resistance or underground organization.

The largest organization was called the L.O., the *Landelijke Organisatie*, which translated to something like National Organization. The Dutch authorities had established the Landelijke Organisatie to aid and hide young Dutchmen and

Jews from the Germans. The Germans were short of manpower for their factories. They would surround a huge block of homes, apartments, or row houses and then methodically go through them, normally at night. Any young men they found between whatever ages they were looking for, were hauled out of their homes and thrown into army trucks. Then they were transported into Germany where they were forced to work in numerous slave-labor camps. Frequently these work camps were associated with factories. My understanding is that the L.O. had upwards of 300,000 people hidden throughout Holland during the war. The L.O. was the main, or parent, organization handling the hiding and feeding of all these hidden people, the *onderduikers*.

A much smaller group, separate from the L.O., was the *Knokploeg*, or K.P. for short, and their official designation was L.K.P., or *Landelijke Knokploeg*. The K.P. was the strong arm squad, the "bad" guys, the toughs. Any killing that had to be done, they did it. If the organization needed to rob a bank, the K.P. guys did that. If papers or ration cards were needed, these were the men sent to do the work. They also were involved with sabotage, and led many daring raids to liberate Dutch civilians imprisoned by the Germans. Who controlled all of this, I didn't know; I doubt that even the Dutch knew. It didn't pay to know.

The Nazis picked people up and interrogated them brutally to get information. They wanted to know about these resistance organizations: who belonged to them, who controlled them, who they reported to, and so forth. Usually, when a Dutch citizen decided to become heavily involved in the Underground, he or she left home and "dove," became an *onderduiker*, so as not to put their family in jeopardy. Many of these brave men and women didn't see their families during the entire war, or if they did, it was in secrecy and very brief.

Jo Berlijn was a senior member of the LO. I stayed with him and his wife and daughter for two or three days. The second day I was there, somebody from the Underground brought a young man to the house who spoke very good English and was about my age. His name was Kees (pronounced "Case") van den Engel. We got along very well immediately and become lifelong friends. He'd been a worker in the Fokker aircraft factory on the outskirts of Rotterdam, but the Germans had bombed the factory and put it out of business. I had just turned twenty-one and Kees was twenty-three. His sole job during the war, or, more correctly, until he was captured by the Dutch Nazis, was working for the Underground.

I soon found out that I was to become his protégé. He took me everywhere with him. In the Underground, he worked in a secure room in the cellar of an elementary school in the Spangen district, where he made false papers. Dutch bureaucrats in the town halls were, of course, collaborating with the different underground organizations, and they fed these organizations fake blank forms.

The Dutch could make anybody legal by filling out the forms and roughing up the paper and so forth. This was Kees' job. After he made out the false papers, someone else took them to their loyal friends in the city halls, and those people inserted the false papers into the personnel files of the city.[17] This was very frustrating to the Germans.

Jo Berlijn and Kees worked together. Kees made the papers, and Jo Berlijn was one of the men who interfaced with the various town halls. Jo was also a chemist, and he used his skills to remove the dreaded "J" from the Jewish identity cards that Jews were forced to carry.[18] This helped many Jews become "invisible" and blend in with the normal population. His underground name was Fransen. Everyone working in the Resistance in Holland had fake names. Kees' underground name was Cock. He and Jo formed a fictitious organization they called "Cock & Co," also known as the "Coco Firm," to represent their falsification center.[19]

Because the Germans were looking for him, Kees van den Engel never went to his home in Rotterdam after the start of the war. The Germans would have interrogated his father and mother brutally if they had had the slightest inkling that they might know where their son was located. So Kees stayed away for the entire war to protect his family. By the time I met him, Kees hadn't been home to see his family in four years.

Kees had several "dive" houses where he stayed from time to time, and he moved from one to another every few days. One such place was down in the cellar of the school in the secret room where he made false papers. Another was at the home of a Dutch Marine officer who was away somewhere fighting with the Allies. Kees took me to this home one time, on a street in east Rotterdam named Maria Stuartlaan, and I met the officer's wife and their seven-year-old daughter. I only knew this woman as Mrs. van Rhijn.

Even though Kees never went home to see his parents, he kept in touch with his father in quite an ingenious way. His father was the organist at one of the Dutch Reformed churches in Rotterdam and practiced the organ a few evenings during the week. Kees would walk by the church at a particular time on a particular evening of the week and listen from outside to the music his father was playing. They had agreed that if any Germans or Dutch Nazis were inside or near the church, Kees' father would play a certain hymn as a warning to Kees to stay clear and leave the area. If that hymn was not being played, Kees would enter the church and meet with his father. But, even that was done covertly because they could take no chances of being seen together.

While playing the church organ, Kees' father faced away from the pews, but there was a small mirror attached to the organ woodwork. When it was safe to do so, Kees would enter the church and walk up to within a couple of pews of where his father was playing the organ. His father would be able to see his son in the small mirror, but he didn't dare turn around and face him, or hug him. They would speak to each other for a few minutes, Kees kneeling in a pew with his head bowed pretending to pray, and his father playing the organ, seeming oblivious to anyone kneeling and "praying" behind him. A few times over the next months, Kees took me with him when he went to visit his father at the church.

I'd been staying with the Berlijns for two or three days when Kees came by and moved me to another house, the home of the Broekhuizens, located at Oostzeedijk 130. This man and wife were in their fifties. Albert Broekhuizen was a photographer who did much of the photographic work for the Underground. This included identity photographs. I stayed there for around seven to ten days. Albert's wife, Cornelia, was a wonderful cook. They were Dutch Reformed and very religious people. At every meal in the Broekhuizen family, we'd all hold hands, and Albert would say the Our Father in the Dutch language.

By this time, Kees was finding that there was no problem taking me with him, so everywhere he went he took me along. Somewhere, someone had gotten other clothing for me to replace the ridiculous old suit and huge shoes Dr. Rietveldt had given me.

I wanted to learn Dutch as quickly as I could, so everywhere I went with Kees I badgered him with questions. "*Kees, hoe laat is het, alstublieft?*" (Kees, what time is it, please?) I'd ask him, and he'd smile and tell me the time in Dutch. Maybe I'd catch it, and maybe I wouldn't.

I began riding the street cars with him, and he also started introducing me to his friends. Many times we stopped in coffee shops and met with two or three other underground people. Sometimes they had business to transact. I'd follow along with the conversation as best I could, but mostly I'd just sit and observe. At one of these coffee house meetings, Kees introduced me to his girl friend, Marijke—which of course was her underground name. Her role in the Resistance was that of a courier.

Around the third week of March, I followed Kees to another house and stayed overnight there. This was the home of Theo Elsinga. Theo Elsinga was a union boss in civil life. When I met him he was a very strong, high level leader of the L.O. He had a large family with a lot of kids. I met all the kids and had a good time and a very pleasant evening. Theo's oldest son was a fine young man named Folkert who was deeply involved with the Underground. He was also a member of Cock & Co.[20]

Jose "Theo" Elsinga and his 19 yr. old son, Folkert. (Courtesy of Mark Lubbers)

There were several police organizations and, because the Germans were limited in numbers, they had to keep the Dutch policemen on the force. Although the Germans did put Dutch Nazis in the police force, they still needed the bulk of the Dutch police. The police wore the typical Dutch police uniform. I was told by the Underground that if a policeman was older, say over thirty years old, he was probably OK, but not if the policeman was younger. The Germans were taking young Dutch boys and making Nazis out of them and then training them to replace the Dutch police. They intended to eventually get rid of the entire Dutch police force by replacing them with these boys. Because of all the different police and security organizations and not knowing who to trust, traveling at night after curfew was very risky.

A Condition of Frightfulness

Rotterdam was a huge city with probably over a million people during World War II. By the time I arrived there, a mantle of darkness and fear had settled onto the civilian population. The Germans intentionally pitted neighbor against neighbor, friend against friend. Anyone could call the German authorities and betray somebody. It had gotten to the point in 1944 where people wouldn't talk to strangers. If they did talk to acquaintances, they certainly did not talk about anything political or about the war. People talked only to friends. Everyone had to be very careful because anybody could denounce anybody else, and then the Germans would pick them up and they'd disappear.

The Germans had another *Befehl* called *Nacht und Nebel Erlass*, or Night and Fog Decree, which stated that anyone picked up for "Offences against the Reich or German Forces" in any of the occupied countries including Holland, was to disappear and their families were to be told nothing. Normally, if the Germans picked up someone, they came with blaring sirens and flashing lights in the middle of the night. Soldiers kicked in the door and stomped through the house screaming and shouting. When they found the person they were looking for, the poor soul was dragged out into the night and taken away, never to be heard from again. The captive was usually put in prison or taken to Germany as slave labor, but there was no communication with, or information given to, the family. The family could go to the local Dutch police station and try to get information, but the police would just throw up their hands and say, "We don't know. The Germans don't tell us!" There was no way of corresponding with loved ones and no way of finding out where they were. They just disappeared.

Nacht und Nebel Erlass was one of many brutal decrees spawned by Hitler. The Nazis implemented it with the express purpose of spreading terror in the occupied countries.[21] This decree was part of a larger Nazi policy called *Schrecklichkeit*, which, translated literally, means a condition of frightfulness, awfulness, or dread. The Germans intentionally employed this policy of Schrecklichkeit, which they first implemented in Belgium during World War I, against the civilian populations in the occupied countries in order to create terror and thus disarm or destroy any civilian resistance. It was very effective. Fear is a terrible thing, and these people lived in fear. It's difficult for someone to understand what this was like unless they've lived in a police state.

"Look at Our American!"

On one particular night, Kees and some of his friends took me to a meeting to show me off. Kees and the others were so proud, almost beating their chests.

"Look what I've got. An American pilot!"

They thoroughly enjoyed introducing me to their friends.

A dentist, Dr. Albert Jappe-Alberts, was at the meeting with his wife Jacomijntje. They had had the Underground bring me to the meeting so they could look me over and decide whether or not they would accept me into their home.

I was introduced to the doctor and his wife, and all the others, as the

"American pilot." Everyone was "oohing" and "awing" and fawning all over me, and here I was in borrowed clothes that didn't fit!

As was becoming predictable, the first question I was asked was, "*Wanneer zal de invasie komen?*" (When is the invasion coming?)

I had to tell them that second lieutenants didn't know when the invasion was coming. As a guest, they treated me royally with their minimal amount of food and, in this particular case, a glass of Dutch gin.

Soon after I arrived that evening, someone gave me a large water glass and filled it half full with Dutch gin, "*jenever.*" Boy, what powerful stuff it was! I took a little taste. It burned my tongue and throat, and I started hacking and coughing. I couldn't drink it!

"What in the world am I going to do with this?" I wondered. I looked around and poured it quietly into a plant. I don't know what the proof of that Dutch gin was, but it was pretty high, and for me, it was virtually undrinkable.

Along with meeting Mr. and Mrs. Jappe-Alberts, I also saw Jo Berlijn and Albert Broekhuizen at the party and chatted with them for a while. Well into the evening, there was a knock at the front door, and a man entered the room. What happened next was really interesting. It was as though an electric charge had gone through the room when he walked in. Heads turned his way, conversations hushed briefly, and a feeling of anticipation and awe permeated the air.

This man's name was Bertus, but of course that was his underground name. It turned out he was the leader of the L.K.P., the resistance organization that did all the dirty work: killings, robberies, sabotage, and so forth. He traveled with three or four pistols and probably a billy club. I was very impressed. I knew immediately that he was a strong personality. And he reeked of leadership.

Bertus

His real name was Leendert Marinus Valstar. Before the war, in civilian life, he had been the manager for a big group of farms. The owners were wealthy and needed somebody with a strong personality to manage their farms. That's what Leendert did. After Leendert began working in the Resistance, he never went back to his home. This was for the sake of his family's protection. The Germans knew that someone called Bertus was the head of the L.K.P., but they didn't know his real name. Somewhere along the line they found out that Bertus and Leendert Valstar were indeed the same person, so they picked up his wife and her parents and imprisoned them in Scheveningen prison near The Hague. Then they tacked a sign onto the door of their home:

"Leendert Valstar, alias 'Bertus', we now know who
you are. We've picked up your wife and your parents-
in-law. Beginning one week from today, we will be
executing these people, one every other day, random
choice. We will not do this if you will come and
give yourself up. We will release your family and we
will not bother them, because we have ascertained
that you have not been living at home since the war
started."

Only the efforts from fellow resistance workers, as well as his wife, who
had somehow got a letter out of the prison telling him to continue leading
the Resistance, prevented Leendert from turning himself in to the Germans.[22]
Instead, he went to work in the Resistance with a vengeance.

About two months after our encounter, on the 15th of May 1944, Bertus was
in a park meeting with some of the Underground people. A person from another
organization had shot and killed either a German or a Dutch Nazi, and the police
and the notorious German SD[23] were chasing him. The man ran into the park
where Bertus was having his meeting. The police put a cordon around the park,
and went through the park searching. Bertus' meeting broke up and each person
went their separate way. All but Bertus were stopped and searched as they left
the park, but they had no weapons and were released. When Bertus walked out
of the park, the SD stopped him and discovered that he had two or three pistols
and other fighting equipment with him. They took him to the SD headquarters
in Rotterdam located in a house on the Heemraadssingel.

*Leendert Marinus Valstar, alias "Bertus," leader of the L.K.P, the strong arm of the resistance.
(Courtesy of Mark Lubbers collection)*

The Dutch leadership of the L.O. learned very quickly that Bertus had been
captured. "We've got to get him back," they said. "We need him. We can't let
the Germans cart him off or kill him."

They hurriedly put together a strike force to hit the SD headquarters house and get Bertus back. Unfortunately they were about fifteen minutes too late. When the Germans picked him up, at first they didn't realize who they had, but they knew right away that he was a very big fish. Anyone with the kind of arsenal he was carrying, and who reeked of the amount of leadership he did, had to be important. They decided they needed to get him to a prison, so they took him from the Heemraadssingel to the municipal prison. When the Underground hit the house to free him, he was already gone.

Eventually, he was taken to the concentration camp at Vught, a town southeast of Rotterdam, and on the 4th of September 1944, he, along with sixty other Dutch Resistance prisoners, was murdered by the SD. The 4th of September was also the day Antwerp was liberated, and it happened that the Allies were fighting the Germans that day near the camp where Bertus was killed.[24]

The Home on Eendrachtsweg

The night of the party, the Jappe-Alberts made their decision and invited me to come home with them. They had to be very careful, though, because they were also hiding five Jews in their house.

Dr. Jappe-Alberts was a Dutchman and a dentist. He had been married to a Jewess, and they'd had two children, Gerret and Ans. His wife had died, leaving the doctor with two teenagers.

Mrs. Jappe-Alberts, Jacomijntje, was previously Mrs. Chambers. During World War I she had met a British intelligence officer by the name of Chambers, and they'd fallen in love and were married. After the war, Chambers left the intelligence service of the English Army and took a job down in South Africa. He and Jacomijntje had a son whose name was Malcolm. Then Chambers died. Jacomijntje, who went by the nickname "Jackie," went back to Holland and reconnected with a former school mate, Dr. Jappe-Alberts. Well, she had lost her husband, he had lost his wife, and they were old school chums so they decided to get married. He brought with him to the marriage a boy and a girl, and Jackie brought a boy.

It was agreed that Malcolm would be raised as a Britisher. He was fluent in Dutch and English, and every year he went to England for the school year and then came home for the summer. He was at university in England when the war broke out in Holland on the 10th of May 1940. He was due to return home for the summer two weeks later, but there was no more going from country to country once the war started. Jackie's son spent the entire war in England, where he became a Naval Officer. I think one of the reasons Jackie, along with

Dr. Jappe-Alberts, made the decision to take me into their home was that she saw her son in me. Malcolm was about my age.

Before the curfew, but after it had become dark, we left the party and walked to the Jappe-Alberts' home at 33a Eendrachtsweg, which was kind of on the edge of downtown Rotterdam. The row of houses on their side of the street faced the *singel*. A *singel* is a trench, about one foot deep and three feet wide, that runs down the middle of the green belt of a boulevard and is filled with water. All of Holland is at, or very close to, sea level, and the drainage system is programmed to the half centimeter. *Singels* are an integral part of the fresh water drainage system. Eendrachtsweg was a lovely boulevard with its park-like setting—the green belt with a *singel* filled with water running down the middle and surrounded by trees and grass.

Dr. Albert Jappe-Alberts and Mrs. Jacomijntje Jappe-Alberts. (Lt. Col. Keeffe collection)

The Jappe-Alberts' home was on the east side of the street facing west, and on warm spring afternoons, sunshine streamed into it much of the time. Part of the first level of their apartment building was below street level. Another family lived on the first two levels, and the Jappe-Alberts had the third and fourth levels plus the garret, which was the attic.

Four stone steps led up from the sidewalk to a couple of tall blue doors set into a narrow indent in the building front. The door on the left was for 33a, and the door on the right led to 33b. To get into 33a, a person had to ring the door bell so someone inside could release the catch from up above with a string arrangement that pulled the latch down below. Then the person entered and went up a set of very steep steps to the third level. The Jappe-Alberts' home was to become, more or less, my permanent residence for a while. After I arrived at their home that first evening, Dr. Jappe-Alberts and his wife introduced me to their two children, Ans and Ger, and to the five Jews they were hiding.

Jews in Hiding

Dr. Jappe-Alberts had many friends in the Jewish community in Rotterdam. At the beginning of World War II there were about 140,000 Jews in Holland. After the Germans took total control of the country, one of the first things they did was to round up all the Jews. This took several weeks.

At first the Germans forced Jews to put a six-pointed yellow star on their clothing with *Jood*, the Dutch word for Jew, written on the star. Next, the Germans no longer allowed Jews to go to parks, theaters, and certain restaurants. As time went by, more and more restrictions were put on them. It got to the point where Jews had to stay off the sidewalks and walk in the gutters when a German was present. Finally, the Germans started picking them up and concentrating them in camps near the towns of Amersfoort and Westerbork, in north-central Holland.

When the roundups began, a close relative of Dr. Jappe-Alberts' former wife came to the Jappe-Alberts and pleaded with them. "Please take us in, my husband and myself and our little daughter." And they did. This happened in the spring of 1942. The family's real last name was Cohen, but while in hiding, they were the Bakkers. Their daughter, Helen, was eight years old.

Soon afterwards, a Jewish dentist friend came to Dr. Jappe-Alberts. "I fear for my family. I've got eight children!" he said anxiously. "What am I going to do?" After much deliberation, Dr. Jappe-Alberts said he'd take two of the daughters. So he took two sisters, Aat and Niesje. They were teenagers, just like the Jappe-Alberts' daughter and son. Altogether in this household were Dr. Jappe-Alberts and his wife Jackie, his two children, Gerret and Ans, the two Jewish sisters, Aat and Niesje, and the Jewish family, the Cohens, which I dubbed "The little family."

Then in I came, an American airman. Mr. Cohen didn't like the fact that I was going to be living with them. If the Germans found me, an American airman, in the house, it could result in everyone in the household being lined up and shot. "*An der Wand!*" (Against the wall!) I couldn't blame him in the least.

The Cohen family had been in the Jappe-Alberts' house since the autumn of 1942. I arrived in early spring of 1944. The man and wife and the two sisters hadn't been out of the house in nearly two long years. Mrs. Jappe-Alberts took the little girl shopping or for walks every few days. She didn't have the typical "Jewish" appearance yet that caused many older children to be picked up, so it was fairly safe that no one would look twice at her.

Up in the garret, a sleeping room had been set up for the little family. There was another small room for the two sisters, Aat and Niesje, and a third small room, which was Malcolm's. Since he was in England his room became mine. My little room had a small window, a cot, and a dresser with a bowl and pitcher on it. I didn't have much to put into the dresser, maybe two pairs of socks and two pairs of underwear. Jackie was kind enough to give me a tooth brush. Each evening I took the pitcher downstairs and filled it up with water for washing up. In the morning I carried the bowl downstairs, emptied it and cleaned it out, then took it back up to my room for use that evening.

On the first floor of the Jappe-Alberts' home, which was on the third level of the building, the doctor had one room for his dental chair and clinic and a second room for his son Gerret. Strangely, the kitchen was also on this level. All the food had to be taken up a floor to the dining room on the fourth level and then brought back down for washing and so forth. On the main floor (the fourth level) was a living room overlooking the street. There were two large bookcases by the window in this room. Dr. Jappe-Alberts and his wife had an extensive library of paperback books published by the same company, most of them printed in English. Consequently, I did a lot of reading while at their home. There was also a large table in the combined living room/dining room. The bathroom was on this floor, along with a little cubbyhole like a shop, where the doctor worked on dentures and other things. The next level up was the garret.

The ten of us ate all of our meals together. Occasionally Opa, Jackie's father, came and spent the day. The Jappe-Alberts also had a servant woman come in periodically. Both Opa and the servant woman knew about the Jews and about me. It was a pretty busy place.

I was like a breath of fresh air to everybody except the Jewish man, Mr. "Bakker." I very quickly dubbed him "dude." I was little more than a kid myself, but I came to dislike him, and he didn't particularly like me either. He was a whiner, very bitter and angry. I felt so sorry for his wife, who was a mousy little person. She was scared to death all the time because of his complaining, bitching, pissing and moaning. This got pretty grim after awhile and created tension throughout the household.

These people were living in terrible conditions. By the time I got there in March of 1944, most Jews had been rounded up and cleared out of Holland. They had either been shipped to Poland and exterminated, or they were being held in the concentration camps at Amersfoort and Westerbork, or were in hiding like the family and the two sisters in the Jappe-Alberts' home.

My New Identity

The Germans required the Dutch to carry an identity card called a PB, which is short for *Persoonsbewijs* (Personal Identity Card). The PB was made of heavy paper, about four inches by eight inches in size, with two folds. When folded, the card was much smaller and could be carried in a pocket. It had six spaces for writing—three on one side and three on the other side. On the front was printed Persoonsbewijs. Inside was the required photograph of the holder, plus several pieces of information: height, age, weight, and so forth. The card also listed the holder's *beroep,* which means business or profession.

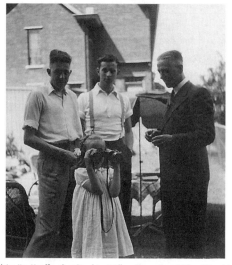

L to R: Kees van den Engel, Lt. Jim Keeffe, alias "Andries Willem Teeuw," and Albert Broekhuizen at one of Kees' dive houses, the home of Mrs. van Rhijn. The little girl is Mrs. van Rhijn's daughter. (Lt. Col. Keeffe collection)

Shortly after moving in with the Jappe-Alberts, I went with Kees over to Albert Broekhuizen's house. Albert led me into his small studio and had me sit on a stool. He took my picture and glued it onto a false identity card he was making for me. My new name was to be Andries Willem Teeuw. The card had an area where other problems could be listed, such as health problems, and Albert typed *doof* and *stom*, deaf and dumb. This was done because I could be found out easily by my obvious American accent if I were stopped by the Germans or the police. My *beroep* was *mandenmaker* (basket maker). Suddenly, I had become a deaf and dumb basket maker! During the months I was hiding out in Rotterdam, the authorities asked to see my identity papers only once.

Frequently Kees came by the Jappe-Alberts and took me places with him. Soon, I got to the point where I was going out by myself. I learned which street cars to take and began to wander farther and farther away. I didn't like being cooped up all day and, when I landed at the Jappe-Alberts, I was given the freedom to come and go as I pleased. Occasionally Jackie and I went shopping. She was responsible for going to the German authorities to get monthly ration cards for food and other things for her legal family, while at the same time trying to make sure that she had enough food and supplies for the six of us who were in hiding. My God, that woman was brave! She was a small lady, tough as nails, and very strong willed. How she fed her crew of ten people three times a day was quite an amazing accomplishment.

The Dutch and Their Tea

Everything was in short supply and rationed under tight controls. There was a ration card for food and another ration card for clothing. Because one of the primary jobs of the Underground was to hide people, they also took on the responsibility of finding ways to feed all those in hiding. The main way this was accomplished was by stealing ration cards. This was absolutely necessary, otherwise people would have starved. The Jappe-Alberts family not only got official ration cards for themselves, but the Underground gave them additional stolen cards. They received one extra ration card for each of the five Jews and two extra ones for me—anybody who kept an Allied flier got double rations.

During mealtime, we each had our own jar of jam at the table. A jar held maybe two cups of jam, and it had to last a hell of a long time. Some had grape, some had white grape, some had strawberry, and some had plum jam. Things were very well organized. The Dutch drank a lot of tea. Everyone thinks the English drink a lot of tea, but I can tell you the Dutch drank a hell of a lot more tea than the English did.

This is how a typical day went concerning tea. The housewife, in this case Jackie, came up first thing in the morning with a cup of hot tea to awaken me. Then I went down to breakfast and shook hands with whoever was there. Whenever someone entered a room in Holland everybody shook hands. It seemed as if the Dutch shook hands all the time and drank tea all the time! (I wore a Dutch wrist watch, and I finally had to take it off my right wrist and put it on my left wrist because all the hand shaking was making my right wrist thicker and stronger.) Tea when I got up, then tea with breakfast. At mid-morning we had tea again, then tea with lunch and tea in the mid-afternoon. Then we had tea with dinner and tea about nine-thirty or ten o'clock at night before going to bed. We had tea seven or eight times a day.

The Dutch hated the tea they had to drink during the war because it was ersatz, not real. All shipping from the Orient ground to a halt after the occupation began. By the time I arrived in the Netherlands, real tea had long since disappeared. The Dutch also drank ersatz coffee. I wasn't a coffee drinker so I never had any, but I sure liked the tea.

Blending In

The Dutch warned me constantly to be very cautious. "Be careful of this, be careful of that. Don't do this, don't do that," they'd say.

I learned to change some of my personal habits and looks. One of the interesting things the Dutchmen did when they tied their shoes was to tuck the laces down into the shoe. They didn't leave them exposed the way we do in America. Another thing I found unusual was their belts. The Dutchman's belt was a foot to a foot and a half longer than necessary. Most of the year the weather in Holland was very stormy and windy and, because most Dutchmen walked or rode bicycles, they wrapped the extra long belt around themselves outside their raincoat to keep it from blowing all over. I presume the weather was also the reason they tucked in their shoe laces.

Sideburns were another thing I had to be aware of. In the States we cut our sideburns horizontally, but in Holland during the war they cut them diagonally. I also had to change my eating habits. The use of the knife, the fork, and the spoon was completely different in Holland from the way I used them, and I quickly adapted to eating food the Dutch way. It was very wise to learn these types of things in order to be unobtrusive and blend into my surroundings. It was anomalies like these that secret policemen, the SD or the Gestapo, or even sadly other Dutch folks, looked for when they scanned a group of people. Many an unsuspecting airman, I'm sure, was picked up because of these seemingly unimportant little things.

A City Built on Sand

The Germans attacked Holland on the 10th of May in 1940, and the Dutch Commander surrendered on the 14th. Yet, on the same day the Dutch surrendered, the Germans firebombed Rotterdam. From the air, they spread magnesium powder over the city and then dropped incendiaries and high explosive bombs. Incendiaries were made with magnesium and once they started burning, the fires couldn't be put out—they kept burning as long as there was oxygen. After the war there was a big controversy over the firebombing of Rotterdam. It had been completely unnecessary because it occurred on the same day the Dutch commander received the German surrender ultimatum. The bombing mission was already underway and the Germans later claimed the airborne commander never received the information that he was to cancel the mission. Regardless of their excuses, they firebombed Rotterdam that last day, burning out and leveling a square mile in the center of the city.

Rotterdam is built virtually on sand. That makes it easy to construct buildings, and when necessary, to rebuild or change things around. But sand, and anything constructed on it, is also easily damaged, particularly road beds, sidewalks, and streetcar tracks. Over the four years after the Germans firebombed the city center, the Dutch people cleared the streets of rubble and got the streetcars running again. However, the streetcar tracks weren't very straight because of the bombing.

The German Luftwaffe nearly destroyed the entire Rotterdam city center on 14 May 1940. This is a view of a small area of that destruction. Shown are the remains of Williams Square, the Victoria Hotel and the Leuvehaven. The steeple of St. Ignatius church on Westzeedijk is in the distance. (Courtesy of Rotterdam Municipal Archives)

When I wasn't staying at the same place as Kees, which was most of the time, either he came to wherever I was and got me or I met him somewhere. He'd telephone to tell me where to meet him, and I'd either walk there or take the street car.

One afternoon Kees and I were standing up riding in the back of a streetcar and I intentionally tried to be macho by not holding on to anything. I spread my legs apart and took the normal movement in stride. This was fine until we got into the bombed out downtown area where the street car suddenly started lurching side-to-side because the tracks weren't straight. I lost my balance and fell right into a woman standing next to me.

Automatically, out of courtesy and habit, I blurted out in English, "Oh, I'm very sorry! Excuse me." At the same moment, I looked at Kees and knew instantly that he realized I had spoken in English. He turned around and quietly moved away from me.

The woman became angry and upset. She read me the riot act, in Dutch of course. "If you young men would hold onto something, you wouldn't be bumping into people and almost knocking them down. *Blah, blah, blah.*"

I stood there silently, looking very humbled. Fortunately that was the end of it, but Kees was afraid somebody else might have heard me.

"You can't ever speak English! Don't do that!" he said firmly when we got off. And of course I said I was sorry. A simple slip like this could very well have been deadly, not only for me, but for those helping me.

Occasionally, German soldiers or German civilians used the streetcars for transportation. Normally they'd just get on, find themselves an empty seat, get off and go about their business. Many German civilian families lived in Holland during the war, and the husbands of these families probably worked in government or occupation jobs. Many of the young boys from these families were members of the *Hitler Jugend*, the Hitler Youth. They wore a black and brown uniform with a neckerchief, short pants and knee socks, and they all carried little hunting knives. They were being brought up as the super race and their arrogance was beyond belief.

I was on a streetcar a couple of times when some of these Hitler Jugend kids got on. First off, they didn't pay. The Germans rode the trams for free in Holland because they were the occupying force. Once on the tram, the kids would look around and pick out a particular person to harass, at which point they'd go up to this person and demand, "We want this seat!"

My immediate inclination was to knock the legs out from under these little monsters and tell them to go fly a kite, but I had to bite my tongue and not make a scene. The person they were harassing would have to get up and move. If the person refused to do so, the tram operator had orders from the German occupation authorities that required him to enforce what these kids wanted. If the person still did not cooperate, the tram operator was required to stop the tram when he saw German soldiers or German officials. They'd get on the tram and take the person away. They were really bad, those little Hitler Youth bastards.

First Contact Home

A few days after I moved in with the Jappe-Alberts family, several of us were sitting around the table having our afternoon tea. "Jim, you can send a letter home to your folks," Jackie said to me. "We'll have to use our name, but I think they will know it's from you."

At this time during the occupation, the only way to communicate with anyone outside Holland was through Switzerland and the Red Cross. The Red Cross had special letter forms, and a person could send a couple of them a month.

Jackie handed me one of these Red Cross letter forms, and I wrote a little note to my family in code. At Jackie's suggestion I signed it with her name. In hindsight, this was probably a very dumb move on my part, but at the time I didn't think of all the possible ramifications. This letter is probably what caused, months down the line, the arrest of the Jappe-Alberts family and the five Jews by the SD. Exactly how this happened I don't know, but I've always thought that the letter played a part.

It took five months for my letter to make its way to my family on Hunter Boulevard in Seattle, Washington. It traveled from Holland to France, from France to Switzerland, and finally from Switzerland to the United States. When the letter arrived at my parents' home, there were several stamps on it from the various stops along the way. The first stamp was dated 29 Maart 1944, another 5 Juin 1944, and another was dated Aug. 12, 1944. By the time the letter reached my parents, I was already a prisoner of the German Luftwaffe.

This letter was the first tangible news my parents received that proved I was still alive. After I was shot down, I'd been classified as "Missing in Action." In fact, this letter was also the first indication the War Department had that I was still alive.

"Lt. Keeffe Was Killed by Our Marines"

After we all bailed out of our B-24 on the 8th of March, everyone but me was picked up by the Germans within a few hours. Many of the crew were wounded. Baker had been shot through both legs. Moulton had broken both his legs when he landed, Smith had injured or broken his back, and Stevens had broken a leg. These four were rounded up and taken to the Luftwaffe hospital in Amsterdam where they stayed until they were able to travel into Germany to various POW camps.

The rest of the crew wound up in the prison in Dordrecht that first night. The next morning when the Germans opened the cells and let the men mix together, Jimmy McArthur counted noses. He counted himself plus four other crewmen: Allen, Hughes, Turlay and Hall. He knew that Miller had been left on the airplane, so that took care of six.

"Where are Moulton, Stevens, Smith and Baker?" he asked, and one of the

German authorities informed him that they had all been sent to the Luftwaffe hospital.

Then McArthur asked, "Where is Lt. Keeffe?"

"Lt. Keeffe took out his side arm and got into a gun fight with our Marines, and they shot and killed him," one of the guards said.

Eventually McArthur ended up at Stalag Luft I, the prisoner-of-war camp up at Barth on the Baltic Sea northwest of Berlin. Once there, he wrote home to his mother. "… Miller was killed in the airplane and ten of us bailed out satisfactorily. Four of them went to a hospital. All of us wound up in Germany, except for Lt. Keeffe. The Germans shot him because he pulled out his .45 and got into a fight with them."

When an airplane went down, the War Department in Washington D.C. created a file for that airplane and assigned that file an MACR (Missing Air Crew Report) number. Everything to do with our crew, airplane, guns, and engines was under the file number MACR 2959.[25]

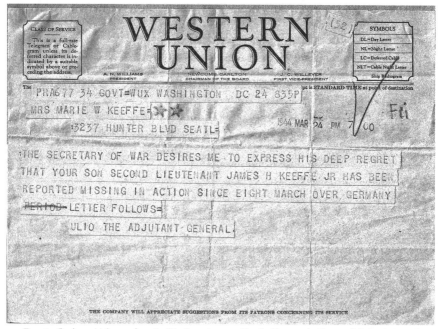

Two star (bad news) telegram from the War Department to Mrs. Keeffe, reporting her son "Missing In Action".
(Lt. Col. Keeffe collection)

One of the jobs of the War Department was to send telegrams to the families of the crew members from a downed plane. The first telegram sent to each family was the "Missing in Action" (MIA) telegram. After that the War Department followed up with several other letters and telegrams to let the families know of any new information that might have come to light, or in my case, assurances that they were still searching and would report anything new once it was verified.[26]

My parents received their first War Department telegram not on the 8th of March when we went down but about the 24th of March, a couple of weeks later. Since I had written home every day while at Hethel, my parents had already become concerned when my letters stopped coming. It took about ten days for mail to come from England. The telegram arrived in an enclosure with a cutout to show the recipient's name and address. Everyone back home in the States knew that a telegram with two stars '☆☆' next to the recipient's name meant bad news. When my mother was handed the telegram, she immediately saw the two stars and knew that something terrible had happened to me.

The War Department also sent each crew member's next of kin a list of the entire crew and the names and addresses of the next of kin of each crew member, so they could correspond. McArthur wrote his mother and told her what had happened to the crew. His mother then wrote to my mother and commiserated with her. "Here's what happened to the other ten crew members," McArthur's mother wrote, "and I'm very sorry about what happened to your son, James."

Of course, my mother wrote back. "What do you mean? We don't know anything. The War Department merely says he's missing in action."

"My son informed me that this is what happened," responded Mrs. McArthur. "He was shot and killed on the ground by the Germans."

"Well, that sounds just like Jim," my sister Jeananne said to Dad after they read that I had gotten into a shootout. "He's gone and we'd better get used to it."

After hearing from Mrs. McArthur, my dad contacted the War Department with the story she had related, and the War Department wrote back. "We have no knowledge of what you are telling us, and as far as we are concerned, we continue to carry your son in the status of MIA. His pay and allowances will continue until we have other information."

This correspondence continued through May and June. "You've got to accept it," my dad kept telling my mother. "Stop all the worrying and praying. We're at war and these things happen."

In the first week of July, my parents received another letter from the War Department's Adjutant General's Office.

Dear Mrs. Keeffe:

As promised you, I am writing again regarding your son, Second Lieutenant James H. Keeffe, Jr.

It has been my fervent hope that favorable in- formation would be forthcoming and that you might be relieved from the great anxiety which you have borne during these months. It is therefore with deep

```
regret that I must state that no further report in
his case has been forwarded to the War Department.

    I want to again emphasize the fact that the
Commanding Generals in all our theaters of opera-
tions are making a continuous effort to establish
the actual status of personnel, who have been re-
ported as missing, or missing in action. In many
instances the War Department must rely upon the
reports by a belligerent government through the
International Red Cross for information.

    You may be certain that when any information is
received, it will be promptly transmitted to you.
In the event no additional information is received
within the next three months, I will again communi-
cate with you.

                    Sincerely yours,
                    J. A. ULIO
                    Major General,
                    The Adjutant General.
```

"Jim, I know Jimmy is not dead," my mother told my dad. "Let's not talk about it anymore. Let's just let it lie. You believe what you want, and I'll believe what I want."

In August, my cousin, Patty Keeffe, happened to be visiting my parents one day when the mail was delivered. She brought it in and put it on the dining room table. My mother sorted through it and pulled out the bills. She pushed the other letters aside, and Patty asked if she should open them up. Mother said yes. One of the letters was from the Red Cross. My mother had received several letters already from the Red Cross, not about me, but asking for money, donations and what not.

Patty opened the envelope and took out a form letter printed in German and Dutch, with the inked writing in English. She called out to my mother. "Aunt Marie, this is really strange. Look at this funny letter."

My mother glanced over and saw the hand writing. "Oh heavens, that's Jim's handwriting!" She took it, and although she couldn't read the German or the Dutch, she could read what I had written.

Mystery letter sent by Lt. Keeffe from Rotterdam, hoping to inform his family that he was alive and well.
(Lt. Col. Keeffe collection)

After I signed the letter "Jackie," I then addressed it. Finally, Mrs. Jappe-Alberts signed and dated it 21-3-44.[27]

"Wait a minute!" my mother said. "He went down on the 8th of March, and this is dated the 21st of March. My God, he's alive! I knew he was alive!"

Then my father made a big mistake. In his joy and exuberance, he took my letter to the Seattle newspapers, along with the news that his son had been found alive and well and was "hiding out with the Underground." A couple of articles appeared the next day. One was titled "Mystery Card Brings Cheer," and the other read:

Flyer, Lost Since March, Works With Underground

Second Lieut. James H. Keeffe, Jr., copilot of a Liberator bomber shot down over Germany March 8, is now playing a new role in the winning of the war – he's working with the underground movement of a Nazi-occupied country.

In a carefully worded form letter, carrying a message in his own handwriting, the airman was able to inform his parents that he had escaped the clutches of the Germans and was safe. The letter, which came through the International Red Cross, arrived yesterday to cheer the hearts of Mr. and Mrs. James H. Keeffe, Sr., 3237 Hunter Blvd.

"Everyone is fine and well," he wrote. "Enjoying holiday. Hope that we may be together soon. Write as of usual. (signed) "Jackie"

A woman had been "found" to whom his mail could be addressed and the form letter which was used revealed he was working with the underground. It was dated March 21, 1944, and the five months that have elapsed while the letter was being delivered failed to dampen the spirits of his parents.

Signature Is a Blind

"We had word from the pilot's mother that all the men had landed safely," the happy father said yesterday, "but the message did not state that they were all prisoners of war.

"The signature on this letter is a blind, because we never called him Jackie, but it's his writing, all right," he said firmly. Then --"It's wonderful to get a direct message in his own writing."

Brother in Seabees

Lieutenant Keeffe landed in England the Monday before last Thanksgiving, and had completed a number of missions. He joined the Air Force in September, 1942, and trained at Santa Ana, Lemoore and Tulare, Calif., and received his wings at Yuma, Ariz. A graduate of Lincoln High School, he was in his junior year at Seattle College, specializing in chemistry, when his studies were interrupted by the war.

A brother, Robert Keeffe, is a machinist's mate, third class, in the South Pacific with the Seabees. The boys' father is chief of the construction unit for the Civil Aeronautics Administration, in the building of the new Seattle-Tacoma Airport at Bow Lake.

It was known that the Germans subscribed to every magazine and newspaper in the United States. They had a huge staff clipping out articles and pieces of information, and they were fanatics about record keeping and cross filing. I'm sure this article came to their attention, was cross-referenced and filed, and eventually may have been instrumental in causing terrible things that happened to some of the people I knew in Holland.

"I Need to Get Back to England"

A couple of weeks after moving in with the Jappe-Alberts, I began to tell Kees and some of the other people that I needed to get going and get back to England.

"Please help me find a way to get back. If you can't help me, just give me a half-loaf of bread, and a hunk of sausage and I'll start walking."

"Where will you go?" Kees asked.

"Well, I'll go to Belgium and then to France, and then I'll go over the Pyrenees."

I knew people were getting back to England by going to Spain. From Spain they'd go to Gibraltar, and from there they'd hop a ship, or be flown back to England.

Shortly after this, Kees came to the Jappe-Alberts' house and informed me that there would be an effort to get me out by boat. Holland was quite small, and Rotterdam wasn't far from the coast. Where the Maas River flowed into the North Sea there was a point of land called the *Hoek van Holland*. One night members of the Underground decided to try a dry run from the Hoek. They would launch a boat to see if they could get out and away safely. Once out of the river mouth and into the open water, they would then turn around and come back. If they were successful, then the next night I would be on my way. Unfortunately, their boat was shot out of the water by a German coastal patrol E-boat, and a man was killed. I was told they weren't going to try that again.

"Just Trim Around the Ears, Please"

During the five months I was in hiding and evading the Germans, I had my hair cut three times.

The first time, Kees took me to a barbershop. It was another beautiful sunny day. As we walked along the busy streets, Kees told me that the man who owned the barber shop was the brother of Jo Berlijn. The name of the barber shop was

"Berlijn's Haar Kapperij," (Berlijn's Barber Shop.) He told me that Mr. Berlijn had already been informed that he, Kees, was bringing a deaf and dumb young man for a haircut.

We entered a building and walked up the stairs to the second floor, crossed the hall, and went into the barbershop. It had a window overlooking the sidewalk and street we had just come in from. The sun was shining in through this window and it lit up the interior of the shop. Several barber chairs faced a mirrored wall, just like in American barbershops, and up against the back wall were some other chairs where a couple of men were sitting while waiting for their haircuts. One fellow was reading a magazine, and the other was sitting quietly with his eyes downcast. I didn't see him look up once while I was there.

I noticed right away that three of the people sitting in the barber chairs were German military officers. Their caps were hanging on the rack, and a couple of the officers weren't covered up with the barber cloths.

"Oh boy, what now?" I thought. "This is going to be interesting."

Kees spoke with Mr. Berlijn, and Mr. Berlijn, having been told I was deaf and dumb, motioned for me to sit down in one of the waiting chairs while he finished up with the fellow he was barbering. When he was done, the man paid him, got his cap and left, all decked out in his beautiful green German officer's uniform.

Mr. Berlijn looked at me and, gesturing with his hand, pointed for me to sit in the middle barber chair. Well, I already knew what was on either side of that chair—two German officers! There were also a couple of Dutchmen in the two remaining chairs. All four of the men, the two German officers and the two Dutchmen, had barbers cutting their hair. And of course the barbers were, as barbers do in a barbershop, talking to each other and to their customers.

I sat down and Mr. Berlijn covered me with a barber cloth and started cutting my hair. Meanwhile, the other chairs emptied out and filled up again. The shop was very busy because of the beautiful day. After Mr. Berlijn finished with me, he removed my barber cloth , dusted me off, and motioned for me to get up out of the chair.

The cash register was to the left of all of the chairs, on a little counter near the window. As I walked over to it, I took out my wallet. Seeing this, Mr. Berlijn started speaking to me and Kees in Dutch.

"No, no, no. It was already taken care of," he said, referring to the payment for my haircut.

But I wasn't really trying to pay him. Actually, I was having some fun. By this time I'd gotten over my worries about the German officers. They hadn't bothered me, and I hadn't bothered them. With my back to all of the chairs, I opened my wallet and pulled out a few English pound notes. I had just gotten paid a few days before our fateful mission, so I had quite a few notes which I riffled with my thumb as I showed them to Mr. Berlijn.

He signaled with his hands again that he didn't want to be paid, but his eyes became very large, and his mouth dropped open a little when he saw the English pounds. He'd seen English pounds before the war when English people visited Rotterdam, but they were virtually non-existent ever since the Germans had taken over. He patted me on the shoulder, and I turned to Kees who was now standing beside me grinning. Kees thanked him, and then we went back down the stairs and out into the warm, sunny afternoon. I suppose what I'd done was pretty silly and foolish, but sometimes that's what it takes to bring a little levity into otherwise tense living conditions.

Two American Airmen and Two Dutch Gold Guilder Pieces

About a week later, Kees came again to the Jappe-Alberts' house and asked me to follow him, saying he had a surprise for me. He was pretty excited as we bicycled through the city, and I kept asking him what was going on and where were we going. All he'd tell me was that he had some people he wanted me to meet and that I would be surprised.

Eventually we arrived at the address of Graff Florisstraat 105, which was a typical Dutch apartment building. We parked the bikes in front of the building and went up the steps. I followed Kees to one of the apartment doors, and he knocked gently. A man opened the door and, upon recognizing Kees, let us in. The man's name was J. J. van Dongen, and he was in the insurance business. Then came the real surprise. I saw two men dressed in very nice suits sitting in the living room. The minute they began to speak, I knew they were Americans!

It turned out they were airmen from the same airplane, a B-17 bomber from the 334th Bomb Squadron, 95th Bomb Group, which had been shot down by an Me-110 on the 22nd of December 1943. J. J. van Dongen was sheltering them, just as the Jappe-Alberts were sheltering me. One of the men was a gunner and the radio operator, Sergeant Richard C. Dabney. The other was the navigator, 2nd Lieutenant Ernest J. Bennett. We all shook hands and were very glad to meet each other. Kees had brought me over specifically to meet these two American airmen. It was a very nice act of kindness.

I visited J. J. van Dongen's apartment several times over the next few weeks. He was very well-to-do by Dutch standards and, because of this, he had good food and good booze. He was quite a nice man and very interested in America. He also spoke excellent English. One time when I was visiting, I told him that

I had a wad of English pound notes. When I showed them to him, he warned me, "It's not very wise for you to be carrying those. Would you like to trade for some gold?"

Of course I said yes.

He led me to an office in one of the rooms in his apartment where he had a fairly large safe. I handed him the roll of English pounds, and he estimated the value of them against the value of some gold coins he had. In exchange, he gave me a very nice 1875 10-guilder coin and a 1912 5-guilder coin. Before I left his apartment, I cut a small vertical slit inside the top band of the pants I was wearing and slid the two gold coins inside the band. Throughout the rest of the war I held onto those two gold coins, through multiple interrogations, strip searches, prison camp clothing exchanges, and on through the years. I have them still.

I found out that Dabney and Bennett never ventured out of van Dongen's apartment. By the time I met them, they'd been cooped up inside for several months. I don't know how they stood this without going crazy.

The two Dutch gold coins given to Lt. Keeffe by J. J. van Dongen. (Lt. Col. Keeffe collection)

One Saturday, I was sitting in the Jappe-Alberts' living room, which also served as a library, reading one of the many books there. I had spent many hours during the past few weeks in this room whiling away the time reading. On this particular day, I got up out of the chair to stretch and glanced out the window. I always looked out of the windows while standing in the corner so I wouldn't be seen by anyone outside. It was another beautiful, warm, sun-shiny afternoon, and the sidewalks below were crowded with people.

Suddenly, in the milling crowd, I spotted two men. They were both cap-less, wearing Army Air Forces A-2 brown leather flying jackets and officer's "pink" pants. I couldn't believe my eyes! In those clothes, I knew they were probably not from a bomber. They had to be downed fighter pilots. I was frustrated because the large window could not be opened. I ran down the stairs, out the door, and down the outer steps to the crowded sidewalk. For several minutes I ran about trying to find them but without success. Finally, admitting failure,

I returned to the house and spent some time explaining my weird behavior. I've often wondered about those two guys; who they were, where they were staying, why they were still in AAF military outfits, how they wound up on Eendrachtsweg.

Meeting the Sanders

Dr. Jappe-Alberts and his wife were non-practicing Protestants and didn't go to church. Kees belonged to the Dutch Reformed church. It wasn't long before Kees and the Jappe-Alberts found out I was a Catholic. They introduced me to a tailor whose name was Anton "Ton" Sanders, and to his wife, "Cocky." The Sanders were in their late twenties and were Catholics. Arrangements were made so that I could go to church with them on Sundays. The Catholic church the Sanders attended was St. Ignatius on Westzeedijk, just down Eendrachtsweg, a couple of blocks south from where the Jappe-Alberts lived.

The Sanders would phone on Sunday mornings to let me know they were leaving their apartment on Breitnerstraat, a street a few blocks away. Walking down Museumpark, they would turn right onto Westersingel, which was directly across the *singel* from Eendrachtsweg. I'd be looking out the third-floor living room window of the Jappe-Alberts' place waiting for them to come into view. When I saw them turn the corner, I'd wave to them, at which point they'd stop and wait for me. Then I'd run down the stairs, go outside the building, walk around the *singel* and join them. Then we'd continue walking down Westersingel a couple of blocks to St. Ignatius. This became a nice routine that I always looked forward to.

After church one Sunday, the Sanders introduced me to the pastor whose name was Pater Hanckx. He and I had many talks together over the next several weeks and, of course, he worked for the Underground. On several occasions, Pater Hanckx and I traveled around the city together. During one trip, riding streetcars through Rotterdam, he took me to meet another man-of-the-cloth, a chaplain, Kapelaan Haanen. This man was in his mid-thirties and even wearing his priestly clothes he looked very athletic and powerful. One of his jobs as a chaplain was to minister to seamen aboard ships that were either at anchor in the Maas River or tied up at various docks lining the numerous waterways.[28]

The Capture of Jo Berlijn

On the 19th of April, about a month after I'd moved from Jo Berlijn's home to the Jappe-Alberts, Kees came over. He was extremely agitated and upset. He told us that Jo Berlijn had been picked up at the Rotterdam police headquarters the day before by the SD and taken away. No one could find out where he'd been taken. This was terrible news indeed. Not only was Jo a wonderful man and a family man, but he was also vital to the Underground. Kees was very upset as he told us what had happened, but he didn't know much other than that Jo had been talking with someone at the police station when the SD stormed the place and hauled him and the other man away in a car.

Kees told us that Lena and Jo's brother had gone to the local police asking for information about Jo's whereabouts, but were told nothing. Jo Berlijn had vanished into the terrible world of *Nacht und Nebel*, "Night and Fog."

It wasn't until the middle of 1945, several weeks after Holland was liberated, that Lena found out what had happened to her husband. Jo Berlijn had been picked up at the police station while trying to convince a fellow resistance worker, a police inspector named Johannes van Tas, to go into hiding. After the SD caught him, along with Tas, he was taken to Scheveningen prison and held there for four months.[29]

In August (1944), he was transferred to the Bunker, the interrogation and torture facility at Vught Concentration Camp just outside of the town of Vught, fifty miles southeast of Rotterdam.[30] There, he had been tortured brutally and then shot and killed on the 30th of August. Johannes van Tas had been murdered by the SD at Vught a couple of weeks earlier on the 11th of August. The SD loved to torture their prisoners. One of the ways they did this was to take a prisoner out to the Bunker courtyard and pretend to shoot him by placing a gun to his head and pulling the trigger. Sometimes the gun had blanks, other times it didn't. The SD had a reputation for pulling this stunt several times on a prisoner and laughing at their terrified reaction.

When Jo ended up at Vught, he was one of those who were taken out and shot in the bunker courtyard, but they hadn't used blanks on him. Before he was killed, he had written a beautiful letter to his wife on a scrap of paper, and hid the letter up on the pipes going through the cells.

One day, after the war was over, a Dutchman who'd been Jo's cellmate in the Bunker at Vught was walking down a street in Rotterdam and saw Lena.

They stopped and spoke. "I'm so sorry about what happened to your husband," he said to Lena.

"What happened to Jo? What do you mean?" Lena asked puzzled. "I don't know anything. He was arrested in April of last year, and none of us have heard one word about him. Please, what do you know?"

"He was sent to Vught where he was interrogated. Then, on August 30th, he was taken out into the courtyard and shot," the former cellmate said. "Did you get his letter?"

Lena was stunned. "What letter? I know nothing about a letter."

The man told her about the letter Jo had written to her, the letter he'd stuffed up on top of the pipes in his cell. "If you like, we can try to find out if your husband's letter is still at Vught," the man offered.

Lena and the fellow went to the Canadian military authorities, who at that time had control of Holland, and spoke to a Major. He put them in a staff car and drove them to Vught, and then to the Bunker. The retreating German soldiers had tried to defend the Bunker for a while, and shelling from the Allies had caused considerable damage to the structures. Now it was being used as a prison for Dutch Nazis.

Jo's former cellmate was able to identify, exactly, the location of the cell he and Johannes Berlijn had occupied. With the help of the Canadian authorities, they broke down a new wall that was blocking the way into the damaged cell. Inside the cell, the man reached up onto the pipes and retrieved the letter Jo had written to his wife and daughter and handed it to Lena. In the letter, Jo told his wife to not hate "our enemies," but to forgive them.

My Dear Wife,

When you receive this letter God has taken me into Heaven. Probably you are then already aware of this fact, but I thought, a letter from me would be of great value to you. The Lord taught me in this prison to love Him and to forgive my enemies. I ask you to do the same.

Elsje too must seek the Lord early. It is so happy to know, that He is our Guard. God will look after you.

Ask Koos, Leen and David to help. The money I still had is mine, so you can use it. Say farewell to Dad, Mam and the boys and also to your Mam and the boys.

Peace comes soon. I hope that this is the last war in your life. Darling don't cry, remember, that God gives relief and made me His child.

Bye-bye darling, an embracement for you and Elsje. Every day I kissed you in my thoughts.

```
So Bye-bye and till we meet again in Heaven.

                      JO.

I did my duty. Three cheers for Holland.

   Bye-bye Lena, bye-bye Elsje, a firm kiss and an
embracement.³¹
```

A week after Jo Berlijn's capture, Folkert Elsinga was also picked up by the Germans. All his father, Theo, could tell us was that his son was seen at a coffee shop with a couple of others from the Underground. A short time later a car pulled up, and two men got out and went into the shop. A minute later they came out with Folkert walking between them, and all three of them got into the car and drove away. Theo had to stay low for a long time after that, constantly worried that the SD or the Gestapo would hit his home, or at the very least, harass and intimidate his family. Inquiries by family and friends to the local authorities about Folkert's whereabouts, or situation, fell on deaf ears. No one knew anything. Folkert, too, had just disappeared.

Mapping German Military Installations

I started spreading my wings more and more in Rotterdam and wandered farther and farther away from the Jappe-Alberts' house. I'd been cooped up before I came to their home, and it was wonderful to be able to travel around.

Before I came to stay with the Jappe-Alberts, I had spoken with the Underground people and let them know that I couldn't stand being cooped up so much. "Look, I can't live this way, stuck inside and constantly told not to look out any windows. Just give me a loaf of bread and some sausage, and I'll go by myself south to Belgium." Luckily the Jappe-Alberts, and later on the Sanders, didn't care if I went outside and circulated.

One of the things I noticed while wandering around Rotterdam was the huge brick walls that the Germans had put up between many of the buildings. The first time I walked with the Sanders to St. Ignatius Church, I saw that one of these brick walls had been built between their church and a building across the street. I looked farther and saw that this wall extended both east and west along Westzeedijk for the few blocks I could see.

The Germans wanted to expand defensive zones from the port area outward into the city. The way they did this was to build tall brick walls between buildings and sometimes connected to the buildings. Any buildings in the way were made part of the wall. These walls were about twelve feet high and five feet thick at the base, tapering to a couple of feet thick at the top. On the top, the Germans put two or three inches of wet concrete and pressed in broken bottles and other shards of glass. I decided to get a map of Rotterdam and identify where German installations and these walls were located.

After getting a map of Rotterdam from somebody, I started riding a bicycle or a streetcar to different parts of the city to take notes. I never took the map with me on these outings in case I was stopped and questioned. I kept it hidden in the room I was staying in, and during the evenings I took my notes and transferred what I had onto the map. I ended up mapping out three concentric rings of brick walls, troop barracks, and a few flak towers the Germans had erected in some of the city parks.

The Dutch hated these walls with a passion. The walls interfered with their mobility because there were soldiers at the pass-through points where the walls crossed major streets. Sometimes the soldiers would check papers, but most of the time they didn't. The Dutch despised these walls so much that one of the first things they did after they were liberated was to tear them all down.

A Couple of Decent German Soldiers

On a sunny spring day near the end of March, I was walking from the Jappe-Alberts' residence to the Sanders' home, which was located at Breitnerstraat 60b. I turned left onto Museumpark, and as I was passing the Boijmans Museum on the left side of the street, I saw several people looking at something going on across the street. I followed their gaze and saw an incredible sight.

Two men with hats on and shotguns were bullying an old grandmother who had just come in from the countryside on her bicycle. They had stopped her so they could examine the contents of a bag that hung over the handlebars of her bicycle. The two men were throwing her butter, some food, and other items into the gutter and out into the street. These were two middle-aged men doing this! They'd also knocked her bicycle over, and one of them was stomping out the spokes. This was terrible because it was probably her only means of transportation, besides the streetcar. She was screaming and struggling with them, trying to prevent them from ruining her bike and her food.

The Dutch people on my side of the street just stood and watched. Not one of them tried to help her. This sort of bullying and brutality had been going on since 1940, and most of the local people were afraid to interfere. The two men doing the bullying were members of the NSB, and their arm bands, which had *Landwacht* (Landwatch) stitched on them, were their badges of authority.

Inwardly I exploded with anger as I watched all that was going on. I stepped off the sidewalk and started across the street; I was going to stop this injustice, and to hell with the consequences! Out of the corner of my eye, up the street on the other side, I saw two German soldiers in uniform walking toward this scene. They were simple soldiers with rifles slung over their shoulders. I watched them stop when they saw what was going on with the old lady and the NSB punks. As I continued crossing the street, I saw the two soldiers unsling their rifles, put them at the ready and run toward all the commotion, yelling as they ran. I didn't want to become involved with German soldiers with rifles, so I stopped. The two soldiers ran up to the three people and started screaming in German at the two NSBers.

A long, high, permanent wall ran along behind the sidewalk where all this was going on, and one German soldier, using his rifle, backed the two bozos up against the wall.

"*Hände hoch*!" (Hands up!) The two men dropped their shotguns onto the sidewalk and put their hands up.

The second soldier went over to the distraught old grandma, who was still yelling and screaming, and tried to help her by lifting up her bicycle. She was so excited and angry that she started screaming at the soldier as well and began hammering on him with her fists. It would have made a great movie scene! The poor soldier was stooped over trying to fend off her fists with his rifle in one hand, while at the same time trying to pick up her bicycle with his other hand. He finally got the bicycle up, but both of the wheels were bent out of shape from the thugs stomping on them.

Grandma cooled down a bit and began scraping some of her food off the pavement where one of the bastards had thrown it. The second soldier helped her a little, then turned around and joined his buddy. They ordered the two Landwacht men to walk down the sidewalk to the right, away from grandma. The punks tried to pick up their shotguns, but one of the soldiers kicked the guns out of the way, all the while jabbing the two with his rifle and screaming at them. He was calling them low-lifes and cursing at them for what they'd done to the poor old grandmother. German is the best language in the world for screaming at somebody, and that German soldier really gave it to the Dutch Nazi punks.

The two soldiers force-marched them all the way down to the corner, about three hundred feet away, screaming at them all the way. Then they slung their rifles back onto their shoulders and walked away from the scene. With the soldiers gone, the two thugs came back and got their shotguns. By this time, however, the poor old lady had scraped up what food she could from the street and put it back in her bag. She was continuing down Museumpark, pushing her broken bicycle. Finally, the people back on my side of the street began to go about their business, and I continued on my way to the Sanders.

Those were two decent German soldiers. They saw something that was wrong and bad; they stopped it and then went on their way.

More Members of the Underground

Occasionally Kees took me to underground meetings held in coffee shops and small cafes where I was introduced to other members of the Resistance. Sometimes Kees' girlfriend, Marijke, joined us for coffee. It was at one of these meetings that I first met a couple of young men named Boy Sissingh and Piet de Beer, who were both members of the KP.

The higher authorities in the Underground used the KP to knock off people who deserved to be killed (like Dutch informants and German collaborators), to raid city halls for food stamp cards and blank forms, to hold up banks, and sometimes to blow up things. Some of these efforts, getting food stamp cards for instance, were done with the complicity of the people in the city hall. These people would act completely surprised and shocked and jump up with their hands in the air when the KP showed up with their guns. Then they would point to the open drawers where the food cards were. There was considerable cooperation between the KP and the workers of the particular place they were hitting; i.e., a bank, City Hall, or another municipal office.

Lt. Keeffe "Andries" visiting Boy Sissingh's home in Hillegersberg. Back L to R: Beppie Sissingh, Boy Sissingh, Piet de Beer. Front: Lt. Keeffe, Jannie Sissingh. Boy and Piet were both members of the L.K.P., the strong arm of the Resistance. (Lt. Col. Keeffe collection)

Another morning while we were drinking tea and coffee together, Boy Sissingh and Piet de Beer, whose underground name was "Witte Piet" (White Pete), began to describe and plan an operation they were going to do that afternoon. The operation was to involve two cars, each with five men. The two cars were to split up and do a couple of "hold ups," one at a bank and one at a city office, to get ration cards. Later on, Kees and I met up with Boy and Piet again and learned that all had gone as planned.

I went to Boy Sissingh's home in the Hillegersberg area of northeast Rotterdam on several occasions. I met his mother, whom he called Mams, his father, and his two sisters Jannie and Beppie. His mother made wonderful apple pie and made sure I ate some each time I came by. I spent some nice quiet times at Boy's home. Piet de Beer was there one time and we all sat in the back yard under some big shade trees and had a relaxing afternoon picnic.

Reprisal Killings

On a much more serious note, when necessary, members of the KP eliminated people. A committee or a big boss would decide whether a particular person was a traitor, and if the person was found guilty, his name went on a list of people to be eliminated. Boy and Piet, and most of the other KP members, each had a list with four or five Dutch names. One of the men I met while in Rotterdam turned out to be a traitor and was eventually eliminated by the KP. Later on in the war the KP stopped killing traitors and Nazis unless it was absolutely necessary because the Germans began to retaliate with a vengeance by rounding up Dutch civilians and shooting them in reprisal killings.

To try and quash the increasing violence against German authorities and Dutch Nazis by the Resistance, the Germans formulated a policy for reprisal killings that was especially evil and terrifying. If a German soldier was wounded, one Dutch civilian was to be shot. If the soldier was seriously wounded, two people were to be shot. If the wounded person was of high rank, the number of civilians to be shot and killed was higher. If a Dutch Nazi sympathizer was killed, ten were shot, and if a German soldier was killed, twenty were shot.

The doomed civilians were taken to the location where the German or Dutch Nazi had been wounded or killed and were shot on that spot. A German soldier stood guard over the bodies for forty-eight hours, running off anyone who tried to get close. At the end of forty-eight hours the soldier left the scene, and, finally, family members and friends could rush in and try to identify the dead and give them a proper burial.

The Germans had a few different ways to select the people to be shot in their reprisal killings. Let's say they needed twelve people. One way to get their twelve was to go to the local prisons, randomly grab their victims out of the prison cells and take them out to be shot.

Another way to get their twelve was to round them up off the busy city streets in broad daylight. This was accomplished by sending a convoy made up of a German staff car, three trucks and a couple of motorcycle guards racing to a busy intersection. The staff car would race through the intersection to the far side and stop. The truck behind the staff car would enter the intersection, turn right and screech to a halt. The truck behind that one would enter the intersection, turn left and stop. Then the last truck approaching the intersection would stop. Thus, the convoy completely blocked off all roads into and out of the intersection. This happened within seconds, and as the drivers jammed on their brakes, all hell broke loose. Armed soldiers would jump out of the backs of the two trucks. Some of them would run to each entry into the intersection to keep people from leaving. A couple of other soldiers would jump out of the third truck and throw the canvas tarpaulin that covered the back end of the truck up and over the top.

Then soldiers, shouting and cursing all the while, would start grabbing people—men, women, children, it made no difference. They would beat them and throw them onto the truck. These poor people would be in an absolute panic; screaming and crying and trying to flee. After a few minutes, an officer would stop this process by blowing a whistle or shooting a round up in the air. Then he'd count the number of people on the truck. Meanwhile, the soldiers at the intersection points continued to block all exits.

Twenty Dutchmen lie where they were shot on May 3, 1945, near Saint Lambert Church, Rotterdam, at the corner of Oostzeedijk Beneden and Hoflaan. The Germans killed them in reprisal for the shooting of a policeman by the Resistance. (Photo taken by Joh. van Bueren, courtesy of Rotterdam Municipal Archives)

If more people were on the truck than the twelve needed for the quota, the officer would reach in and pull extra people out, throw them on the ground and then put guards up to keep the remaining people from trying to jump off the truck. If the count came up short, the officer shouted an order to one of the soldiers and more victims were grabbed, kicking and screaming, and hauled into the truck. Then, at a signal from the officer, all the soldiers would run and climb into the backs of their trucks. The staff car would speed away with all the trucks roaring behind, and they would drive out to the place where the twelve were to be shot. This was another hideous sub-policy of Schrecklichkeit, and before the war was over, it would smash through the lives of the Jappe-Alberts and Elsinga families.

The Home on Breitnerstraat

On the 18th of May, about a month and a half after I moved in with the Jappe-Alberts, Anton Sanders and his wife Cocky asked if they could have me as a guest. I'd been walking with them to the Catholic church on Sundays for a few weeks already and had gotten to know them quite well. So I said sure and went to stay with them. They lived only about a ten minute walk from the Jappe-Alberts on a street called Breitnerstraat, in number 60b. Their flat was more modern than the Jappe-Alberts' place, and Breitnerstraat was a quieter street, lined on both sides with apartments.

To get to the Sanders from the Jappe-Alberts, I walked up Eendrachtsweg a few doorways to the corner and turned left onto a street that soon became Museumpark. I went past the Boijmans Museum and across Rochussenstraat to Mathenesserlaan. One block up was Breitnerstraat, and once there I turned right. The Sanders' apartment building was one of many in a string of four- and five-story buildings that ran solid for two hundred and fifty to three hundred yards, the entire length of the street. In fact, the string of apartment buildings ran virtually non-stop all the way around the three streets forming a large triangle: Mathenesserlaan, Breitnerstraat and Rochussenstraat. Inside this triangle, at the south end, was a group of tennis courts.

Breitnerstraat was a narrow street with a sidewalk that was shaded over its entire length by a thick canopy of tall trees. In front of the Sanders' apartment building was a fence through which a short walkway, with a tiny little garden on each side, led up to the front of the building and a set of broad stairs. This set of stairs rose up into the second level. On the second level landing were four doors: one on the left, two in the center and one on the right. Beginning on the left, they were labeled 60b, 60c, 62a and 62b. The apartments on the left and the right occupied both the second and the fourth floors. The two apartments in the center occupied the third floor only.

The Sanders lived in the apartment on the left, 60b. Once inside, steep stairs bypassed the third floor leading up to the fourth floor where they had their bedroom, a bathroom, a landing and another very small bedroom that was only about 8 feet by 10 feet. This small bedroom had a door opening out onto a balcony that overlooked the tennis courts below. Against the wall on the balcony was an iron ladder leading to the flat roof.

The Sanders didn't have any children, so this little room became my bedroom. The ladder to the roof was my escape route. If the Germans were ever to come, I was supposed to run up the stairs to my room, run out onto the balcony, climb up the iron ladder to the roof, run along the rooftop for about three-quarters of a block to another similar fire escape, then climb down that to a balcony and go into the apartment of Ton's mother.

When I moved in with the Sanders, they immediately warned me about the German officer who lived in 62b. Before the war, a family of Jews had lived in 62b. But soon after the German occupation, the poor family was dragged from their home and carted off to concentration camps, and a German SD agent moved into their apartment.

Anton and Cocky Sanders, and friends, standing on the balcony outside the room they offered to Lt. Keeffe. Hanging over the rail on the balcony to their right are a pair of shorts belonging to the German Sicherheitsdienst (SD) agent who commandeered that apartment. (Lt. Col. Keeffe collection)

Anton Sanders was a tailor. He and his brother owned their own tailoring business at 53a Mauritsweg, a couple of blocks north of the Jappe-Alberts' home. Anton was neither a poor nor an ordinary tailor. He was a Master Cutter, and a well-to-do, upper-middle-class gentleman. The secret to tailoring men's suits was in the cutting of the cloth. The Dutch word for this type of tailor is *kleermaker*, which is different from a tailor working with pins and needles. Anton never did any of that; he did the cutting and supervised others' work.

Before the war, he and his brother operated what had been their father's business, and sold suits for $500 each. Even in 1944, four years after the beginning of the war, Anton was eating very well because of a thriving black market. He had booze and wine. In fact, I gained most of my knowledge about wine while I was at the Sanders.

Anton and I were the same size and build, so he gave me some of his clothes to wear. They were a bit used, but very nice indeed. I became the best dressed deaf and dumb basket weaver in all of Holland.

Escape Attempt by Plane

I persisted in trying to get out of Holland and back to England. One evening, Kees came over to see me at the Sanders' apartment and told me he'd been in contact with a high-level organization that was secretly in touch with the British Intelligence Service. One of this organization's purposes was to help facilitate the pickup and drop off of British agents using small airplanes.

"We have an airplane landing in Belgium tomorrow if the weather is good," Kees said to me that evening. "They are picking up two British agents who need to be returned to England, and the airplane can take ten passengers. That means eight additional people can be sent to England, and we have decided that you will be one of them."

I was given a lot of information and instructions to take back to England. The next day, Marijke was to pick me up at the Sanders' home at ten o'clock in the morning. She would then take me to the train station where we would both board a train to Belgium. A twin-engine English airplane was to arrive from across the North Sea just at dusk.

I figured that this airplane would probably be something like the twin-engine Avro Anson. But this vulnerable little transport airplane wasn't to be alone during its very important mission. The RAF and AAF would be sending thirty to fifty fighters to fly above the little airplane to suppress any ground fire and also to do combat with any airplanes the Germans might send to shoot it down.

It was very important to the Brits to get these two agents back, and since they had empty seats, to bring others out. Frequently it was necessary to save certain people from the Nazis. These people were assigned seats on a pickup like this. In my case, I was an American officer and a pilot in good health. Thus, it was practical for me to go back because I could then hop right back into the war effort and hopefully fly missions again.

The airplane would land at a pre-selected farmer's field and turn around with the engines running. The door to the cabin would be opened and the people would pile in, including me. Then the door would close and the airplane would take off into the night.

Each night at ten o'clock, the BBC aired about fifteen minutes of gobbledy-gook. The announcer read off all sorts of strange little sayings like, "The cat is in the kitchen. The cat is in the kitchen," or, "Tall trees stand straight. Tall trees stand straight." All these repeated nonsensical sayings were coded messages of some sort. I was given a similar message, "The cork is in the jug." If I made it back to England, I was to inform British Intelligence, and they'd put my message out on the BBC to let the Dutch know I had arrived safely.

That evening, I said my good-byes to the Sanders and Kees van den Engel. Early the next morning, the 2nd of May, I walked over to the Jappe-Alberts and said my good-byes to them and to the Cohen family upstairs. Then I walked back to the Sanders where Marijke was supposed to pick me up. Ten o'clock came, and she didn't show up. Five minutes went past, then ten minutes, and she still hadn't arrived. The Sanders began to get antsy. The Dutch were very punctual. If something didn't go according to plan, they became very nervous.

About fifteen minutes after the hour the telephone rang. Anton jumped to answer it and listened for a few seconds. He immediately turned toward me and exclaimed in alarm, "Jimmy, go to your safe house. Go quickly! Marijke has been picked up!"

In a case like this, I was to go to Boy Sissingh's house in Hillegersberg, in the lake area. I grabbed my suitcase and took a tram to Sissingh's house where I stayed until things cooled down. No one had any idea of what had happened to Marijke and everyone was very anxious and tense. That evening at 10 p.m., Boy, Jannie, Mams, Mr. Sissingh, and I gathered around a secret radio and listened to the BBC. We heard the standard fifteen minutes of coded messages. Toward the end was the coded message that confirmed a small airplane from Belgium had arrived safely in England. However, one message was not transmitted, "The cork is in the jug," because I was still in Holland.

I got a call from Kees a couple of days later, and I made my way back to the Sanders' home where I learned the terrible news. Before Marijke was to pick me up that morning at 10 a.m., she'd had a couple of things to drop off for the Underground. She had made one drop off and was supposed to make the second drop at Albert Broekhuizen's home. Somehow the SD had learned of Broekhuizen's involvement in the Underground. They were in a car parked across the street watching his house, waiting for him to come home so they could pick him up. Marijke stopped at the Broekhuizen home, unaware that men from the SD were across the street watching. When she knocked on the door, the SD men saw the door open and watched Marijke go into the house with a briefcase. That was all they needed.

They jumped out of their car, ran across the street and burst into the house. Albert Broekhuizen wasn't there, but the agents took his wife away, along with Marijke. Later that same day, members of the Resistance located Albert Broekhuizen before he went home and told him the horrible news about his wife.

He immediately went into hiding, and it was many years before I saw him again.

It wasn't until after the war that anyone found out what happened to Mrs. Broekhuizen and Marijke. Marijke, whose real name was Hendrika Maria van der Jagt,[32] was sent to a slave labor camp in Gross-Rosen, Poland, where she almost died. She was put to work in horrible conditions making radio tubes. As the war wound down and the Russians closed in from the east, she and the other workers in the factory were transported back to Germany by train in refrigeration cars, although the refrigeration wasn't turned on. These types of cars were well insulated, had no air circulation, and were virtually hermetically sealed. It was a nightmare. She was put it a boxcar full of females. Their body heat increased the temperature in the closed box car to upwards of 95 degrees. To try and cool down a little, the women took off all their clothes. The high humidity caused the ceiling to drip with their condensed perspiration. Their destination was Ravensbrück, the notorious women's concentration camp. Upon arrival there, the guards opened the boxcar door and found about a quarter of the women inside were dead from asphyxiation. When the war ended, Marijke made it back to Rotterdam, but people accused her of having been a whore for the Germans. Catholic nuns took pity on her and brought her into their cloister where she stayed until she regained her health. Cornelia Broekhuizen, sadly, was also taken to Ravensbrück. She died there the 20th of February 1945.[33] Albert Broekhuizen was hidden by the Underground and survived the war. When he made his way back to his home on Oostzeedijk, he found that it had been turned into a whore house.

Noordereiland

One of Ton Sanders' customers, Eduard Hoogeweegen,[34] was the owner of the Hulstkamp gin factory (distillery) located on an island in the Maas River called Noordereiland. The Maas is a huge river that flows through Rotterdam to the sea. It begins in France as the Meuse, flows through Belgium and then through Holland, where it is called the Maas. The long narrow island in the middle of the Maas had no bridge to it from the north side. People had to hop on a small passenger ferry to go to the island.

I met Mr. Hoogeweegen at Sanders' tailoring business one day. He was a middle-aged bachelor, about fifty, and a very wealthy man. Sanders called him "the gin man." He invited me to come to his apartment, which was located in his factory on Noordereiland. There were also several other factories and businesses on the island.

The Sanders had a good bicycle with rubber tires, which was extremely rare. By this time of the war most of the Dutch tires were worn out, particularly the ones people used for work. When the rubber tires were no longer any good, the owner would find a wood worker who'd make wooden tires and screw them onto the rims. These wooden tires made a terrible clatter on the cobblestone and brick roads.

The Hulstkamp Distillery located on Noordereiland (North Island) on the Maas River.
(Courtesy of Mr. Huub Zegers, Hulstkamp Gebouw)

I rode the Sanders' bicycle to the river dike, which was only about half a mile south of the Jappe-Alberts' home. Tied up at the bottom of a ramp was a small passenger-only open ferry boat, which the Dutch call a *veerpont*. I pushed my bike aboard. The ferry ride up river to the island took only a few minutes. I rode to the block where the Hulstkamp distillery was and pedaled around the block three times. Mr. Hoogeweegen was looking out the window and watching for me. He knew when the ferry boat docked and if I wasn't being followed, he was to pull the window blind down. This was the signal for me that it was OK to come in.

He had servants, he had food, he had meat, he even had wine and whiskey! He was definitely tied into the black market somehow, but I never asked. It was here that I became truly familiar with Scotch Whiskey, at the ripe old age of twenty-one years old. In fact, he had Haig & Haig Pinch Bottle, which is the best of the Haig Scotch whiskeys.

I visited Mr. Hoogeweegen two or three times. On each occasion I made sure to leave in time to get back to the Sanders before curfew. Being indoors before curfew was always in the back of my mind, not only because of the risk of getting shot, but also because the city would be in full blackout, which meant it would be difficult to travel around. If necessary, I traveled after curfew, but very carefully. Although it was considered a complete blackout, a few street lights were permitted to burn, one of which was right at the top of the ramp leading down to the ferry.

One time I got a little looped before 9:30 p.m., which was the time for me to leave Hoogeweegen's place. I needed to hurry because the last ferry left at 9:40 p.m. "You stay here tonight. You're a little too tipsy to go back," Eduard said when I told him I had to leave.

"No, I have to go. I promised Cocky I'd be home tonight."

I slipped outside and rode the bike down to the ferry. It was dark, with only a dim street light at the ferry dock. I went aboard with four or five other people—some who were walking, two or three others with bicycles, and the man who piloted the ferry. It took only minutes to cross the dark river. When we reached the other side, the pilot started to tie up the ferry boat at the bottom of the dike ramp.

I looked up the ramp and there, under another dim street light, stood a Dutch policeman in his blue uniform.

"Uh, oh," I thought.

I took the chain off the sprocket of my bicycle and fiddled around with it. I was set to be the first off the ferry but after seeing the policeman I wanted to be last off. The other people got off and went up the ramp. It was quiet, with only the sound of water lapping against the side of the river wall. Up above I could hear the policeman speaking.

"*Persoonsbewijs controle, alstublieft.*" (Identity card inspection, if you please.)

"Crap. If I go up that ramp, he's going to ask me for my PB card," I worried and fiddled around with my bike some more.

"*Opschieten jongeman, u moet er af,*" (Hurry up young sir, you have to get off) said the pilot. He had finished tying up the ferry and was shutting it down for the night.

"*Ik moet terug naar het eiland. Mijn fiets is kapot.*" (I have to go back to the island. My bike is broken.)

"*Nee, hoor,*" he said, "*Nee hoor, u moet er nu af. Ik ben klaar voor vandaag. U kunt morgenochtend terugkomen.*" (No, you have to get off now. I'm finished for the night. You can come back in the morning.)

There was nothing I could do. By now all the other people had been inspected by the policeman and had left, but he was still up there standing under the dim street light. I pushed my bicycle off the ferry with the chain still off the sprocket, and tried to go over into the shadows along the ramp, hoping I could turn left at the top and get past him unseen. Unfortunately he was watching me as I walked up to the street level on the dike.

"*Kom hier. Persoonsbewijs controle.*"

I pushed my bike over to him and noticed that he was middle-aged, between thirty-five and forty years old. In my head, of course, I was sobering up rapidly. I thought to myself the same thing I had thought back in the rabbit hutch. "Either he's a good guy, or he's a bad guy."

"*Persoonsbewijs controle, alstublieft,*" he repeated. (Let me see your identity card, if you please.)

Leaning my bike up against the light pole, I reached inside my jacket pocket, took out my identity card and handed it to him. He looked at me and then looked back at the picture. He looked at me again, and then he looked at my good shoes, my good suit, and my necktie and shirt. He looked at the bicycle with the rubber tires.

I had a good bike and was well dressed. He'd already read, I'm sure, that I was supposed to be a "deaf and dumb basket weaver." He looked me up and down and back to the card, two or three times.

"Oh what the hell," I figured. "*Jawel, het is zo. Ik ben een doofstom manden-maker.*" (Yeah, that's right. I'm a deaf and dumb basket maker.)

He looked at me again. He turned around and looked to the left over his shoulder. Then he turned around and looked to the right over his other shoulder. Everybody was gone, and the pilot down below was still in the process of shutting down the ferry.

After a short time of quiet thought, the policeman folded my *persoonsbewijs* twice and handed it back to me. "*Ga nu weg, ga nu weg,*" (Go away, go away) he said after I took it. Then he turned around, put his hands behind his back and sauntered off into the night, whistling.

I had been warned about the Dutch police, how one could tell their allegiance by their age. I was lucky, very lucky that night, and the warning had been true. I had encountered a good guy.

*A typical passenger-only ferry, or veerpont, in Rotterdam. Photo circa 1935.
(Courtesy of Rotterdam Municipal Archives)*

Being Followed

One day as I was traveling around Rotterdam, I noticed that a particular man kept showing up at various places I was going to. After walking across a street intersection, for instance, I'd turn around and notice that he was starting to walk across the same intersection. A couple of times I looked back up the sidewalk I had just come down and saw the same man standing in a doorway looking off somewhere. He seemed vaguely familiar, and eventually I realized I had met him once, briefly, at J. J. van Dongen's place. His name was de Groot.

To find out for sure if he was following me, I walked around in a rather convoluted route, crossing over several streets and backtracking down others. Sure enough, I saw him pop out around a corner and start walking up the same street as I, but on the opposite sidewalk. This really got my anger up. I decided to end it real fast.

After turning a few more corners, I stepped into the shallow doorway of one of the apartments. About a minute later he walked by. I grabbed him by the collar and pulled his face close to mine.

"If I see you following me one more time, I will break out all of your teeth." I spoke slowly and in a very soft but clear voice. "I don't know what your business is, but I don't like being followed!"

It was indeed de Groot, and he stood there with a shocked look on his face. When I let go of his collar, he nodded his head and walked away up the sidewalk without a word. What I couldn't understand was why this man, who had been in van Dongen's apartment once, was following me. One thing I was absolutely sure of, though. De Groot was not spying on me for the Underground. He could be following me for the Germans, or for other reasons, but be that as it may, I never saw him again.

The Invasion

Not long after, in late May, the weather became warmer and summer arrived. One day in early June, I went out for a couple of hours to scope out another section of the city for any German installations to put on my map. Afterwards I headed back to the Sanders' apartment. I turned off the sidewalk on Breitnerstraat onto the walkway leading to the outside stairs. I was half way up the stair, when the door to apartment 62b opened and out walked the German SD officer. Some days he wore an Army uniform, some days he wore a Navy uniform, and some days he was in civilian clothes. This particular day he came out wearing civilian clothes, and he started down the stairs.

"What the hell am I going to do, turn around and run? He probably has a gun," I thought as I continued up the stairs. (The SD usually carried a 9mm PPK semi-automatic pistol.)

I looked at him, and he looked at me rather sternly as we passed each other.

"*Goedendag, meneer*," (Good day, sir.) I said, nodding my head.

He looked right through me and continued on down the stairs to the outside.

I knocked on the Sanders' door and was let into the apartment.

"Oh! I heard his door open and wondered what was going to happen," Cocky said, obviously frightened. When I told her, she breathed a sigh of relief. "Oh, thank God! I thought for sure you were going to get caught!"

Several days later, after Ton had already left for work, I was in the shower on the upper level. Suddenly I heard Cocky running up the stairs. "Yimmy! Yimmy! Yimmy!" she shouted.

"What the hell's going on? The Gestapo must be here!" raced through my mind as I remembered the run-in with the SD man who lived downstairs. I thought I was busted, and here I was in the shower!

I flew out of the shower, grabbed a towel and ran out of the bathroom onto the landing at the top of the stairs. Naked and soaking wet with soap all over me, I was headed for my little room so I could go to the balcony, up the fire escape and then run across the roof to my safe house. Just as I was turning toward my room, Cocky reached the top of the stairs panting.

"*Nee, hoor, Nee, hoor -- de invasie is begonnen! De invasie is begonnen!*"

Finally, it sank into my head what she was saying, "The invasion has begun! The invasion has begun!"

There I was with a towel, dripping wet and all soaped up, standing in front of the housewife as she told me the invasion that everyone had long been waiting for had begun. The Allies had landed in Normandy, France. It was Tuesday, the 6th of June.

The Smugglers

Prior to the invasion I'd been trying to get the Dutch Underground to help me, somehow or other, get back to England; however, I hadn't worked at it too hard. After the invasion I became rather insistent and told them I had to get back.

During one of my visits with Pater Hanckx at St. Ignatius, the conversation turned to my strong desire to get back to England. Pater Hanckx told me he had an idea, and that very day he took me to the house of a big-time smuggler, way out on the western outskirts of Rotterdam.

Down in the basement of this house, the smuggling operation was in full swing. The basement was full of boxes and barrels of black market goods: booze, brandy, wine, food, and so forth. Interestingly, before the war, smuggling had been illegal. The government and the police had been looking for smugglers, trying to intercept what they were doing. But during the war, the Dutch government and the smugglers worked together.

Pater Hanckx spoke to the man in charge to find out if there was some way they could get me into France. They spoke quickly in Dutch, which I couldn't understand very well, but I got the impression that they weren't able to help me. The man said a final word, whereby we turned around and went back into the city.

A short time later, Kapelaan Haanen mentioned that he knew of an organization in Breda that was moving airmen south, with the objective of getting them out of Holland, through Belgium and into France. My thought was that once across the Belgian/French border, I could hide on a farm or in a town somewhere in northern France until the Allied armies swept through. Then I could surface.

"Give me some time to work out the details, and when I have some news I'll contact you," Kapelaan Haanen said to me.

Left: Pater (Father) Hanckx, Catholic priest and a member of the Underground. Photo taken some years after the war.
Right: Kapelaan (Chaplain) Haanen, curate at a Catholic church in Rotterdam, also a member of the Underground.
He spent much of his time ministering to sailors and merchantmen aboard ships.
(Courtesy of the Catholic Documentation Center in Nijmegen, the Netherlands)

The end of June came, and the weather was quite warm and dry. On two different clear days I saw two condensation trails quite close together at a very high altitude above Rotterdam, around 30,000 to 40,000 feet. They were so high up that I couldn't even see the airplanes making them. These two contrails went to the north and about half an hour later came back heading south. Another half hour or so later they returned heading north again. I was quite sure I knew what was going on. The two condensation trails were made by a plane carrying photo mappers from England. They were mapping Holland during the clear days for the same reason I had made a map of Rotterdam—to find out and mark down where the German installations were.

Finally! On My Way

Several weeks back, Kapelaan Haanen had introduced me to a Catholic family named Ubink. Every so often since then, I took a tram and went to visit the Ubinks for a day at their home in a western suburb of Rotterdam called Schiedam. Sometimes I spent the night and returned to the Sanders the following day. One afternoon I was visiting with them, and during a conversation, I related my experiences of bailing out of the B-24 and hiding out in the rabbit shed. Mr. Ubink became very excited when I mentioned hiding my .45 pistol. He got up and had me follow him into his bedroom where he showed me a pistol he had secreted away. He told me how dangerous it was for anyone, other than the Germans and their cronies, to have any weapons whatsoever, but he had decided to keep a pistol in case he ever needed it.

Mr. Ubink told me that another Allied airman had stayed at his home for a few days. The airman's name was Sgt. Charles E. Zesch, a B-17 waist gunner.

On Wednesday, the 12th of July, I rode the tram to the Ubink's house for another visit. While there, I got word from Kees that Kapelaan Haanen wanted to speak with me. I quickly made my way back to the Sanders' house, checked in with them and then walked to the Catholic church to see the priest. When I arrived at his office, Kapelaan Haanen told me he had everything arranged for me to get out of Holland and into France.

"I can guarantee you the people from here to the Dutch border," he told me. "In Belgium, I can't guarantee this because I don't know the people. But I know the people who deal with them, and I can say it is a legitimate, trustworthy organization."

"Finally!! Thank God!" I exclaimed. "When do I leave?"

"A couple of men will come by to get you at the Sanders' home in three days, which will be the 15th. Have your suitcase packed and be ready to go. Use the next couple of days to say your good-byes, and please be careful."

We talked a little while longer, and then we shook hands and wished each other well. I left the church and went directly to the Sanders and told them the great news. I was finally going to be on my way back to England!

The next three days seemed to crawl by. On the 14th, I was visiting the Jappe-Alberts when Kees came over. He and I walked across Eendrachtsweg, sat on the grass next to the *singel* and soaked up the fine hot July sun. We talked of all that had happened while I was in Rotterdam, and of the people we knew who had been taken away: Jo Berlijn, Cornelia Broekhuizen, Marijke. There was still no word at all concerning any of them. Amazingly though, and to the absolute delight and relief of the Elsinga family, Folkert Elsinga had come home a few days before I got word from Kapelaan Haanen about leaving.

Sure enough, back in April, he'd been picked up at a coffee shop by one of the German security outfits and taken to the Amersfoort concentration camp. While there he was interrogated many times, but they couldn't pin anything on him and eventually he was released.

Kees and I spent about half an hour sitting on the grass. We both knew the war wouldn't last much longer, but until it ended, there was still constant danger as well as the threat of being betrayed. I told him how thankful I was for all the help he and everyone else had extended to me at great risk to themselves. Kees gave me a couple of really fine small silver bookmarks as a parting gift, and then it was time to say goodbye. We shook hands and wished each other well and told each other that when the war was over, we'd look each other up. Then Kees walked away up Eendrachtsweg, and I went back into the Jappe-Alberts' house.

That night I packed a modest suitcase with my clothes and whatever else I had, including the two small silver bookmarks. I slit the lining of the suitcase and hid the map of the German installations in Rotterdam that I had drawn over the past several weeks. Ton had given me a little bottle of Bisquit de Bouche cognac, a very high quality French cognac, and that went into the suitcase also.

Upon awakening the next morning, I put on an old worn suit Ton had given me and walked over to the Jappe-Alberts to say goodbye to them. My emotions were rather bittersweet because I was sad to leave this fine family, but I was also antsy and excited to finally be on the move out of Holland and back to England. I shook hands with Mr. Cohen and said good-bye to him and his family and the two Jewish sisters, Aat and Niesje. I learned later that after I left to go back to the Sanders, Dr. Jappe-Alberts said to his wife, "Jackie, you should have given Jim a big kiss."

Around noon, a couple of young men came to the Sanders' door and asked for me to come with them. They'd been sent by the Underground and would be my escort to Breda, a small town in South Holland near the Dutch/Belgian border. We took the tram down to the railroad station, and one of them bought our tickets. Then we hopped aboard the train and rode south for a couple of hours.

When we disembarked in Breda, the two men and I walked through the town to a large open square called Pastoor Pottersplein, or "Pastor Potter's Square." On one side of the square was a Roman Catholic Church. On the other three sides were apartment buildings and homes.

The three of us walked across the square to #61, directly opposite the church. They took me through the gate and through a tiny little garden to the front door where they handed me over to the Loose family. The husband's name was Jan, and his wife's name was Jeanne. They had two young boys; Johnnie who was four or five years old, and a toddler named Adje. The couple was probably in their early thirties. After introducing me to the Loose family, the two young men left.[35]

The Loose Family in Breda

Mr. Loose welcomed me into their home and led me up the stairs to a small room that overlooked the plein. As he closed the curtains to the window, I could see the church across the square. He warned me to be very careful if I had the curtains open and not stand in front of the window.

"This will be your room while you stay with us," said Mr. Loose. "Please put down your suitcase and follow me downstairs. I would like to offer you some tea and show you around our home."

In the back of their small house was a simple yard with two apple trees. Jan Loose, who could speak English fairly well, told me that in the first year of the war the Germans had gone house to house taking stock of what people had in the way of food production. The Loose family, for instance, had the two apple trees, and the Germans had estimated what the production of these two apples trees would be. "At harvest time you will bring to the following headquarters' address, xx number of kilos of apples," they had told him. Food was very important to the Germans as far as their war machine was concerned because they had to feed their entire military, plus all of their prisoners. Therefore, they were quite detailed in procuring enough food, right down to family gardens and apple and other fruit trees.

I stayed with the Loose family for several days. Most of this time I wasn't feeling well; for four or five days I was down in bed with a high fever. Air raid sirens blared almost every day because the 8th Air Force was flying across Holland, heading into Germany.

By now, the air raids had fallen into a recognizable pattern. First I'd hear the air raid sirens. Then I'd hear automobiles and trucks rushing to the places where they had to be during an air raid. It would then become quiet, and soon I'd hear a hum. I knew where to look, and I would see a little glint, like a sparkler, high up in the blue sky. Then I'd see another glint, and another glint. These glints were caused by the sun's rays reflecting off the glass windshields or other shiny parts of the airplanes. Eventually I'd be able to pick out tiny dots, which were B-17s or B-24s in formation. The sound would grow and swell, and then the formation would fly over us. About this time, the Germans would begin to fire anti-aircraft flak at the bombers.

Jeanne and Jan Loose. (Courtesy of their son, Ad)

One clear blue-sky day, I was lying in bed upstairs watching a bomber stream go over. I saw a B-17 get hit and fall out of formation and then go into a flat spin. In a vertical spin an airplane is pointed almost straight down at an angle greater than sixty degrees, with the airplane turning on an axis. In a flat spin the angle of the airplane is less than thirty degrees and it would pivot on its center of gravity, about where the bomb bay was located.

I watched the B-17 spin in for about four and a half minutes. It was smoking and had flames licking out of it periodically. I saw a few parachutes. The crew would have been nine or ten, but I didn't see that many parachutes. In a situation like this, centrifugal force could plaster an airman up against the fuselage so that only super-human strength could get him to an escape hatch or a window where he could get out.

The spinning B-17 got down to about 3,000 feet and then, all of a sudden, it stopped doing the flat spin and went into a vertical dive straight into the ground. This was heart-wrenching to watch.

To the Border

A couple of days after my fever passed, somebody from the local Underground arranged for me to continue on my journey. Soon afterwards, two young men came to the house with three bicycles. These fellows, whom I presumed to be about my age, escorted me on a very circuitous route down small roadways and paths to the Dutch/Belgian border. They were particularly careful to stay off the main roads. When we got near the border we waited on the Dutch side. I still had on the old suit Ton Sanders had given me, and I had my suitcase.

Years later, I learned that at about the same time we stopped at the border, Kapelaan Haanen arrived at the Loose home. He had pedaled a bicycle all the way from Rotterdam. Through contact with the local Underground near Breda he had heard that I was sick and was still at the house. So he put together a package with some socks and underwear and brought it all the way down to Pastoor Pottersplein, only to find that I had left earlier in the day. That was a very kind act for him to do—and very dangerous.

When we arrived at the border, one of the two young men told me they were waiting for some other people to come and join me going into Belgium. After about half an hour three men showed up. Two of them were uniformed Dutch Border Policemen, members of the *Marechaussee*. They were very fine young men, probably in their late twenties or early thirties. They had an Englishman with them, and we all shook hands. The young escorts and the two policemen spoke quickly in Dutch, and then they spoke in English with us. I found out the Englishman was a Royal Air Force Lancaster bombardier, a sergeant air-crew member. His name was John Jenkins, and he was a Cockney from the south side of the Thames River in London. He'd come down rather recently in eastern Holland during a night raid and had been brought here quickly by the Underground to join up with me.

"Do you have a PB?" one of the policemen asked me.

"Yeah, I've got one," I replied and took out my fake identity card to show him

"Well, we'll take this now because you can't use it in Belgium. They'll take care of you there and issue you a new one. What else do you have?"

I told them I had some money.

"That's OK, you can keep it. What else?"

I opened up my suitcase and showed them the two silver bookmarks and told them they were a going-away present, and they said those were OK. Then I pulled out the little half liter bottle of Bisquit de Bouche.

"Where in the world did you get this?" one of the *Marechaussee* asked.

"I got it from my friend in the tailoring business up in Rotterdam."

"Nobody in your situation would have a bottle like this. I am sorry, but you cannot take it with you."

"Fine," I said. "Let's drink it." They thought this was a good idea, so the six of us finished that little bottle of cognac. Once again they asked if I had anything else. By this time I had come to trust them. "Well, in the lining of my suitcase here, I have a map of Rotterdam with all of the German installations I was able to locate."

Both of the *Marechaussee* became very concerned, and one of them warned me, "Young sir, do you realize that you are no longer a military officer? You are now a spy? If the Germans capture you with this map, they will not treat you as a military officer. They will treat you as a spy and horribly. You should not take that with you."

I asked them what they recommended and if either of them wanted the map.

"No, we don't want the map. Let's burn it, get rid of it and leave no evidence." One of the men pulled out some matches and we started a little fire and burned the map. This simple action probably saved my life.

"I'm sure the intelligence people will debrief me when I get back to England, and I will tell them about my map and the installations. If they show me the aerial photographs taken by the air mappers I watched awhile back, I can work off those and point out the German installations."

The policemen dealt primarily with me because I was an officer, a great big 2nd Lieutenant. The Englishman was a sergeant who knew no Dutch because he'd only recently come down. The two young men who'd brought me had already left by the time I produced the map. They'd taken the third bicycle and gone back to wherever they'd come from. I never knew their names, and I never saw them again.[36]

Nearby was a little bridge over a tiny canal called a *sloot*, that was just two or three feet wide. "What you do is walk across that bridge," one of the *Marechaussee* said. "On the other side is Belgium. Just keep going on the path until you come to a road. Turn right onto that road, which is west, and walk for two hundred meters. It's a small road, following a grain field. On your left, keep looking for an opening into the field. When you see this opening, go in and follow the path to a beaten down area in the tall grass. Wait there, and by one in the afternoon (it was late morning when we arrived at the border) a young lady will come into the field. She will have a bicycle and will give you instructions as to what to do."

Into Belgium

Sgt. Jenkins and I shook hands with the Dutch policemen. I saluted, and they saluted back and wished us good luck.[37] As they stood watching us, we followed their instructions. We walked across the little foot bridge, continued along the path, then turned right onto the single-lane dirt road and walked down it for a couple of hundred meters. On the left side I saw the opening into the grain field. It was near the end of July and the grain was very high, almost ready to be harvested.

Jenkins and I turned off the little dirt road into the grain field and followed a path that sure enough, after a few turns, led us into a beaten down kind of a circle about twelve feet in diameter. We lay down in the grass and soaked up the nice warm sunshine. And we waited. Eventually, a young woman walked into the area where we were secreted. She introduced herself as Anna, which was probably a false name.[38]

We didn't waste any time. Anna led us back out of the grain field and picked up her bicycle, which she'd left on the narrow road, and we all walked south for about 1.5 km into the little town of Meerle. There she bought tickets for us on what I would call a country tram of about three or four cars. It wasn't a train, but it wasn't a streetcar either. She handed each of us a ticket.

"We will all get on now," she told us. "I will sit by myself and you will sit by yourselves, and we will all hope that we are not controlled. If we are controlled, you are on your own; I do not know you."

To Antwerp

We hopped on one of the small cars and sat on separate benches, and soon we were on our way. Anna sat behind Jenkins and me and never looked overtly at either of us during the trip. We rode the country tram from Meerle on into downtown Antwerp, about thirty miles away. Antwerp is a huge port city, although not as large as Rotterdam. We stopped at a small station in the middle of the city. Anna got up and walked past us, tapping me on the shoulder as a signal to us to get off.

Anna walked us west a few blocks to a street named Lange Gasthuisstraat where we entered a building. This building contained shops on the bottom floor and living quarters on the second and third floors. I only entered this building once, and two or three days later I left it, so I don't remember much about it. The woman who was there spoke English reasonably well. After the war I found out that her name was Mrs. Gyphis Rommens. She and her husband, Valere Rommens, were both members of one of the Undergrounds in Antwerp. Her husband ran a little restaurant called Petit Paon, but I never met him.[39]

Anna took us up to the top floor where there were a couple of bedrooms, and she left us in one of them. This was the 23rd or 24th of July, and it was very hot! We had to have the windows open, and I have never seen mosquitoes in my life like we had in that room. They ate Jenkins and me up.

We stayed in this upstairs bedroom for two days. Mrs. Rommens brought food up to us because we couldn't go downstairs. She came up the second day, very nervous, and told us she'd just had a close call. She said that a German *Hauptmann* (the German military rank equivalent to Captain) had knocked on the front door and told her he understood that she and her husband had two bedrooms, and he wanted to have one for himself. He needed to have a place to stay while he was in Antwerp. She made some excuses, but he wanted to go up and look in the room, the one where Jenkins and I were located. She told him her daughter had come home and was now in the room asleep. The captain was decent enough not to force it, and he left.

The Big Boss

During the evening of the third day, Anna came to pick us up. She and Mrs. Rommens spoke together and a few minutes later we left with her. "I'm taking you to the Big Boss' flat," Anna told us. "We'll have dinner there and then they'll see about your going on."

It was about six o'clock in the afternoon when Jenkins and I walked out of the place and went with the young lady to the Big Boss' apartment, about a mile away on a street named Van Eycklei.[40] This street was lined on one side with tall apartment buildings and on the other side with a large tree-covered park. About halfway down the long row of apartment buildings we went inside a main entrance and climbed the stairway to the fourth floor.

Van Eycklei street, circa 1939. (Courtesy of Stadsarchief Antwerpen)

Anna led us to a door and knocked on it. A woman in her late twenties answered the door and invited us in with a big smile. It was a very nice apartment, and once inside we were introduced to a second woman. The first woman,

Pam, offered Jenkins and me a glass of wine and invited us to sit down. Not long afterward, a short man came in and was introduced as the Big Boss of the Underground. I immediately didn't like him. He was shifty-eyed and while talking with us, he wouldn't look us straight in the eyes or hold eye contact.

In this apartment were some escape maps and some dog tags. The Big Boss showed Jenkins and me some aircrew insignia—pilot wings, gunner's wings, bombardier wings and other items, and he was very proud of them. "These have been given to us by airmen we have sent on down to France," he bragged.

"Gee, this is great," I thought. "These guys really know what they're doing."

Anna stayed with us for a while, and then she left. The other two ladies prepared some food, and we had a very nice dinner. The Big Boss broke out plenty of alcohol, and we all sat back and enjoyed a relaxing evening. Eventually it became dark outside. After a while, there was a knock on the door and two men entered.

It was obvious the two men who entered knew the Big Boss and vice versa. They told us they were smugglers and that they were going to put us into a sealed motorcar and drive us to France. I knew all about sealed motorcars from my time in Holland. This was how the German wheeler-dealers and officers shipped stuff back into Germany. After a car was loaded with whatever was being transported, seals were put on the car handles. With the papers the drivers had, the Germans at the check points could not search these vehicles. The smugglers transported not only legitimate goods but also girlfriends and stolen contraband this way. Presumably, if people had enough money to pay their way out of captivity, they were transported this way as well.

Belgium, like Holland, was under curfew. People had to be off the streets by 10 p.m. Around 11 p.m., one of the men said it was time to leave and that we had to be very careful once we got outside. We stood up and shook hands all around. I thanked the ladies profusely for the fine dinner. Then I shook hands with the Big Boss, but I still didn't like him. My intuition was correct because, as it turned out, he was a traitor to the cause of the legitimate Belgians.[41]

We walked down the stairs from the apartment and out onto the dark street. With me and Jenkins were the two smugglers, whom I thought of as Big Guy and Little Guy. Little Guy spoke English very poorly, and he kind of paired off with John Jenkins. Big Guy had lived in the United States for almost fifteen years. His American English was just like mine. In fact I closed my eyes and couldn't catch any fault in his speaking, so I knew he had lived in America. But he was very clever. I realized later that he was trying to prove how knowledgeable he was about America.

"Did you go to the Chicago Fair?" he asked me.

"No, I didn't," I answered, and he told me all about the Chicago World's Fair.

"Did you go to the New York World's Fair?"

"No, I didn't." I said again.

Then he told me all about the New York World's Fair.

Left: The "Big Boss," Rene van Muylem. Right: Pauline "Pam" Vlaming. This photo is from her NSB identity card. (Courtesy of Michael LeBlanc collection)

When we left the apartment, each of them took out a PPK pistol and chambered a round. "Boy, these guys really know what they're doing. They're cautious and they're careful," I said to myself.

There was no light at all outside due to the blackout, but there was enough ambient night light that I could make out building silhouettes on our side of the street and the park on the other side. We walked a short distance, only five to seven minutes down to another apartment row, where we went up the front steps, into the foyer and over to an apartment door. Little Guy unlocked the door, turned on the lights, and we all went inside. The apartment was furnished but completely empty of people. Little Guy took Jenkins into one room, and Big Guy took me into what was the dining room and closed the door.

"Young American officer, have a chair," he said. I sat down and was wondering what in the world was going on.

He sat down in another chair at the dining room table and started talking to me. "We now need to find out that you are what you say you are, you and your friend the Englishman, before we deal any further with you," he said and proceeded to try to interrogate me. Fortunately I had been down long enough to know about interrogation and how to resist it.

"I'd like to know the names of the people you were staying with up in the Netherlands. I understand you've come from Breda. I need to know when you came down."

"Well, I'm happy to tell you when I came down. I came down on the 8th of March. I'm a B-24 copilot with an eleven-man crew. I'm sorry though, I intentionally did not learn any names of people because, as you probably well know, they all have false names. I intentionally did not learn where I was staying. I stayed away from windows and I did not go outside. Beyond that, there is nothing I can tell you."

Big Guy tried different approaches to get me to answer his questions, but I kept going back to my first response; I didn't know anything. This went on for half an hour, maybe forty minutes. Big Guy finally accepted that I wasn't going to tell him anything else. He said that was enough, and we went out of the room and found the other two.

"Now we're going to take you and put you in the sealed motor car," Big Guy said to Jenkins and me. "We're going to walk along the edge of a park. We'll be in the middle of downtown, and we'll walk to a building. The door to this building off the sidewalk will be open. When we go up the step into the building, through the door, a German soldier with a rifle will be standing by the elevator and the stairs. We will not speak to him, and you don't speak to him either. We'll go right past him and up the stairs."

"Boy, these are cool guys," I kept thinking. "They've even bought off a German soldier."

"We'll take you out the back of the building and into the garage area," Big Guy continued. I knew what he was describing. In European cities there are triangular blocks or square blocks of buildings, and one can drive through an archway in one of the buildings into what they call a *hof* (courtyard), an open area inside the block.

The four of us went back out onto the dark street, crossed to the other side and walked along the edge of the park. We travelled through a couple of large intersections and turned left onto a fairly good-sized boulevard. We were the only people outside that I could see. The streets were completely empty of traffic except for a couple of German staff cars that motored silently through an intersection up ahead of us. They looked like ghost cars, black shapes moving through a slightly less black night.

We continued to walk furtively up the left side of the boulevard to a building with double-entrance doors, and one of them was open. The two men led us through the entryway inside to a dimly lit foyer. To the right side of the foyer, an open door led into a dark room. Directly across from the entrance was an elevator with a stairway to the right of it. Sure enough, a German soldier was standing by the stairs with his rifle. Nobody spoke to anybody, and the four of us just walked right past the soldier and climbed the stairs.

The stairs turned two times before we got to the second floor. We went to the left down the hall. Little Guy opened the door to a small office and turned on the lights. "Come on in," he invited pleasantly and we went in.

Once inside, Big Guy closed the door. "Have a chair," he said.

This was a very small office with two or three chairs, a desk, and a couple of filing cabinets. Little Guy and Big Guy immediately stopped speaking in English and started speaking to each other in German. I knew the difference between German and Dutch, and I was a little puzzled. I noticed a calendar on the desk, and the calendar was not in French. Nor was it in Flemish or Dutch. It was in German. The words were different for the days of the week and the months. I just observed these things and thought about it a little bit, but not much.

About that time, Big Guy turned around, "You and the people you've been with think you're so smart. For your information, you are now our prisoners. We happen to be the Secret German Police."

He walked over to a filing cabinet and took out a file. "Here are the people who have preceded you, coming down through Holland," he said and he read off a bunch of names.

I didn't recognize any of them until he came to two names. One was Ernest Bennett, and the other was Richard Dabney. They were the navigator and radio operator I had met in J. J. van Dongen's home in Rotterdam.

When Big Guy finished reading off the names, he slapped the file down on the desk. He leaned on his knuckles and looked directly at us. "Sorry," he said. "You're not going to France tonight. You're going to prison."[42]

End Notes
Evasion

1. C. P. Vanderplank mistakenly wrote "…March.", implying that the bomber had gone down in March of 1945, when in actuality it had gone down in March of 1944.

2. One of the farmers found and took my heated flying gloves and a few .50 caliber machine gun rounds. When I met him years after the war, he gave me one of the gloves and one of the rounds. He also gave me a pendant he'd made from a piece of the airplane's Plexiglas. He had fashioned it into a pendant for a necklace for his wife. Embedded in the plastic are two Dutch dimes called *dubbeltjes*.

3. The man wearing the fedora was Adriaan van Wijngaarden.

4. The Dutch didn't usually eat carrots as large as these, they fed them to the animals. They only ate carrots that were no more than three inches long. Their word for carrot was *wortel*, and the little carrots they ate, which were tender, were called *peentjes*.

5. In Holland there were Dutchmen who were very loyal to the crown—the House of Orange and Queen Wilhelmina. Then there were loyal Dutchmen who wanted to get rid of the monarchy but were still loyal Dutchmen, just the way, today, a lot of the English want to get rid of their monarchy but are still loyal English citizens. Then there were the workers who were upset with the government. There were also Socialists and Communists. The workers and the farm people were frequently somewhat sympathetic with the Nazis. In fact, there were a lot of Dutch Nazis. I didn't realize how many during the war because I never dealt with them.

    To understand how someone in an occupied country could sympathize with the Nazis, one would have to realize that Hitler did a lot of good things. He put all of the German people back to work. He began to tear apart the horrible Versailles Treaty, which the French, the English and the Americans had rammed down the Germans' throats at the end of WW I. The Nazis were doing remarkable things in Germany, and many people in countries bordering Germany liked what they said. But, of course, it was all headed toward making Germany "number one," and heading them down the road of conquest, expanding the German empire as it were, taking over countries.

6. In Holland, as in much of Europe, doctors operated out of their homes. They had fair-sized houses. One room was an interview room, another room was a little office, and a third room was for simple operations like fixing and setting bones. They did quite a bit of work in their homes.

7. The big man was Willem Verdoorn, Johannes' older brother. At that time they both lived a few houses north of Korteland's house on the dike road, at Nordhoek 10.

8. *Aardappel*, or "earth apple," is the South Holland name for potato, and *markt* is market, because very close to this house in a row of houses was a wharf area along the river. Apparently in the old times they had food markets there. So this house was located on Aardappelmarkt, the site of an old potato market.

9. She was referring to the Allied invasion that everyone knew was being planned, but where and when was unknown. This was the Normandy Invasion, D-Day, which eventually happened on the 6th of June 1944.

10. The man's name was E.A. Gomm, and he was an advocate, or lawyer.

11. It's really very nice because in Holland, in many of the cities and towns, there is the street, and then next to the street is something like a curb. On the other side of the street curb is a very wide bike

path, maybe ten feet wide. Then, on the other side of the bike path is about a two meter wide sidewalk; so, pedestrians, then bicycles, and then vehicles.

12.   This is a huge river that has its origin in the French Alps. In France the river is called the Meuse. During WWI there were ferocious battles in the Meuse Argonne forests. The Meuse travels north out of France, through Belgium and then into Holland where it is called the Maas. It then empties out into the North Sea.

13.   One of the young men was named Samuel Esmeijer. He was a brave and daring man who eventually became leader of the Rotterdam L.K.P. Unfortunately, he was caught by the Germans and killed the 28th of November 1944.

14.   In Holland, the school kids go on to high school. Of course they learn the Dutch language first. The second language they learn is German, and the third language is English. Then if they are going on to university, they also learn French. This does not necessarily make them proficient in all of these languages, but normally anybody who graduates from high school there can speak Dutch, English, German, and possibly French.

15.   In most of these apartments, the toilet is in a separate small room. In that same room is a small wash bowl to wash your hands after you've finished using the toilet. There is another room with a medicine chest, mirror and bath tub.

16.   The Dutch have an instant water heater up over the bathtub, a small thing that is gas fired. It is called a geiser, and is very efficient. As you take your shower or draw your bath water, this thing is firing and quickly gives you a flow of very hot water. As soon as you turn the water off, the heater stops heating the water, which is a smart use of energy.

17.   Many European countries are completely different from the United States. For instance, Holland is democratic in some ways, but in other ways it's not. In Holland anytime you move, you have to inform the police. Your papers from your former town are then transported to your new town and become part of that town's records. Your personnel papers follow you your whole life.

18.   Information source: Nationaal Monument Kamp Vught (www.nmkanpvught.nl).

19.   Thanks to Mark Lubbers for this info. Mark also clarified the difference between the L.O. and L.K.P.

20.   Info supplied by Mark Lubbers.

21.   See Appentix A for official wordage of the Night and Fog Decree.

22.   From two Dutch sources who researched this for the author. (a) Rene van Heijningen, who works in the Information Department of the NIOD - Netherlands Institute for War Documentation, found it in "Het grote gebod: gedenkboek van het verzet in LO en LKP" 1979 edition, pg. 356, and (b) Hans Budde.

23.   The SD, Sicherheitsdienst, was the German Security Service. It was primarily the intelligence gathering service of the SS (Schutzstaffel) and the Nazi Party, initially charged with rooting out enemies of the Nazi leadership and eliminating them. Both the SD and its sister organization, the Gestapo, were under the control of Reichsführer-SS Heinrich Himmler.

24.   On the 31st of August 1944, Leendert Valstar's father was murdered by the Germans – possibly in order to force Leendert, who was in prison in Vught, to give up information about the underground. Even though Leendert was beaten and tortured, he never gave up any information. Leendert's wife died in the 1980s.

25.   See Appendix D for MACR documents.

26. See Appendix E for War Department letters sent to Mrs. Keeffe, Lt. Keeffe's mother.

27. Most European countries reverse the first two elements of a hyphenated date. This could be confusing for Americans if the first two elements were 12 or lower. For instance, in Holland 12-3-44 is the 12th of March 1944. However, in the United States it is the 3rd of December, 1944.

28. Kapelaan Haanen's Catholic ministry was with the Apostolaat der Zee, the Apostleship of the Sea. The AOS was founded in Glasgow, Scotland, in the early 1900's and provides for the pastoral care to all those who live from seafaring and fishing, their dependents and communities. The agency is also known as Stella Maris, Star of the Sea. www.stellamaris.net

29. Information from *"Het grote gebod: gedenkboek van het verzet in LO en LKP"* 1979 edition, pg. 284 (provided by Rene van Heijningen, NOID).

30. Camp Vught – The Germans began construction at this site in 1942 primarily to house Jews prior to transporting them into Germany. This facility became known as Concentration Camp Vught and was the largest SS torture camp in northwestern Europe. (www.nmkampvught.nl)

31. I was told this story by Kees van den Engel when I visited with him after the war. He had a copy of Jo Berlijn's letter to Lena, and he made this translation for me.

32. Marijke's real name, Hendrika Maria van der Jagt, was revealed to us in 2009 in an e-mail from her and Kees' son, Frank van den Engel.

33. Information about Mrs. Broekhuizen's death found in *De Rotterdamse gevallenen van het verzet 1940-1945* (published in 1997), page 90. (Provided by Rene van Heijningen, NOID).

34. The Hoogeweegen family has been the owner of the Hulstkamp distillery for over two hundred years. During the war years, Eduard Hoogeweegen and his older brother were the owners. They, along with the older brother's son, Berni, worked daily at the distillery and were active members of the Resistance. Information provided by Mrs. Iris Lamers, daughter of Berni Hoogeweegen.

35. One of the young men, Nico, was eventually captured by the Germans and died in a German concentration camp.

36. These young Dutch fellows were from the Resistance group named Group Andre, located in the town of Sprang-Capelle, and they came to escort me to the Dutch/Belgium border.

37. The two Marechaussee young men were Gradus Antonius Gerritsen and Adrianus Theodorus Joannes van Gestel. They were staying at the home of Maria Cornelissen-Verhoeven, a mother of five boys and three girls, when they were betrayed by Pauline Vlaming, the 'girlfriend' of the Big Boss (Rene van Muylem). All three were executed by the Germans on the 10th of September 1944.

38. "Anna" was a Dutch girl who was working for the Germans. Her real name was Maria Verhulst-Oomes.

39. During the winter of 1945, the Rommen's home, along with several other buildings on Lange Gasthuisstraat, was destroyed by a German V2 rocket.

40. This was located at Pauline Vlaming's apartment at Van Eycklei 17. Pauline's alias was "Pam."

41. The 'Big Boss' was Rene van Muylem. His 'girlfriend' was Pauline Vlaming. Big Guy was Karl Helmer, alias "Stahl." Little Guy was Luftwaffe Oberleutnant Dr. Werner.

42. See Appendix B for description of the fake escape line.

Interrogation

This Can't Be Happening!

I was stunned! "They must be testing us or playing games with us to see if we'll get upset," were my immediate thoughts. Then came an even greater shock.

"I think you will be interested in this other list," Big Guy said to me as he pulled out another sheet of paper from the file. He began reading the names of people he said I had met in Rotterdam. Many of the names were unfamiliar to me, yet some of them were very familiar. The names I recognized were Anton Sanders, Jan Loose and Kees van den Engel. A feeling of dread washed over me.

"So you see, lieutenant," bragged Big Guy, "we know all about you and where you've been since you came down. We know the people you've stayed with and we know what they do. But we're not going to do anything at this time because we want them to keep sending us evading fliers like you." He was watching me intently to see how I reacted, but I kept my face and body language neutral.

"Now, empty your pockets," he ordered.

When I put the money I had on the table, he took it and stuffed it in his pocket.

"You won't need this," he said.

Then he noticed the two silver bookmarks Kees had given me.

"I'd like to keep those," I told him.

"Where you're going you won't need them. I can use them," and he put the bookmarks in his pocket, too.

"Open up your suitcase."

I opened up the suitcase, and fortunately the map wasn't in there. Thank

God the Dutch Marechaussee had talked me into burning it! Big Guy rummaged around but only found some socks, some underwear, a shaving kit and a tooth brush.

"This can't be!" I kept thinking. "If there was a break, where had it occurred? Could it have been the girl? It couldn't have been her, she was too nice. Could it have been the lady with the place on Lange Gasthuisstraat where we had stayed the last couple of days? No, she was genuine. It could have been the Big Boss, he was shifty-eyed."

Both men were speaking in German but, even though I caught a word here and there, I couldn't follow their conversation. Little Guy took Jenkins and left the room.

Big Guy finally closed the file. "OK," he said, "It's time for you to have your ride in the car."

He took me out of the room, back down the hall and down the stairs. Off to the left, just inside the building's entrance, was a large entryway into an office. The lights, which a short time ago had been very dim, were now burning brightly. It was obvious that we were in a police station.[1] Back behind a counter near the far wall were several people doing what workers do when running a police station 24 hours a day.

By now it was about one o'clock in the morning on the 27th of July. When we came down the stairs, Big Guy poked the German soldier in the stomach, and they both started laughing. The people in the police station office were all laughing, too. I was steaming mad and quite confused. We stepped outside and watched a sedan with a driver pull up to the curb.

Big Guy opened the door for me. "Young lieutenant, climb in."

I still couldn't believe it—for five months everything had been working so perfectly! The driver started up the sedan, and we drove down the darkened, blacked-out street. Even the headlights had covers. (These light covers had slits about the width of a finger that allowed some light to escape so the driver could see where he was going.) We drove down a couple of streets and then turned off the road and stopped in front of a gate. A German soldier came out and spoke to the driver and Big Guy in German. He opened the gate, our driver drove through, and then the gate closed behind us. We stopped in front of a building just inside the gate.

"OK, get out," Big Guy ordered.

We walked into the building through the entryway. Just inside, across the foyer from the entry door, was a table. Suspended from the ceiling above the table was a light cord with a wide conical lamp shade and a single bulb. This was the only light source. Big Guy spoke to the German soldier sitting at the desk, and then he signed in. Next he opened a satchel he was carrying and took out a piece of paper and handed it to the soldier. They spoke to each other some more in German. The soldier read the document, looked at me and then signed at the bottom. It was a transfer document from the Green Secret Military Police requesting the Army War Prison on Begijnenstraat to take custody of me.

When they were finished, Big Guy turned to me and said, "OK, walk down that hall there." I looked to the right down a long hallway that was very dark at the end. Then I looked to the left down another long hallway with several doors, and it too faded into darkness. I started down the hall Big Guy was pointing to, but after a few steps, I turned around and looked back at him. He motioned for me to keep moving.

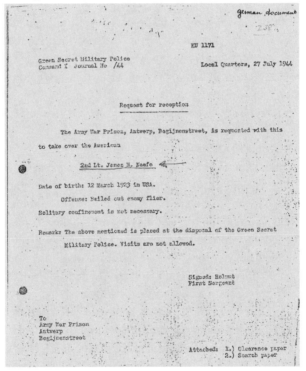

Green Secret Military Police transfer paper. Translated by U.S. Intelligence staff after the war. (Lt. Col. Keeffe collection)

"Where am I supposed to go?" I wondered.

The hall was lined with doors on both sides, but they were all closed. Big Guy stayed a few paces behind me and, as I turned to look at him again, I noticed he had his pistol out. This didn't look good at all. The feeling of dread thickened and I felt a knot form in my stomach. The sound of our footsteps seemed far away.

By now my eyes had adjusted to the darkness. We finally came to the end of the hall and another door. Again I turned toward him.

"Open the door," he said with his Walther PPK at the ready.

I turned and opened it. The door led to the outside. It was so dark that I could hardly see anything. A faint bit of light from the low-wattage bulb way back up the hall where we'd just been shone feebly through the open door, across fifteen to twenty feet of beaten earth, and up a few feet of a brick wall. Otherwise it was pitch black.

I looked at my captor.

"Go on out there," he said, motioning with his gun.

I looked back outside, my mind racing.

"This bastard's going to kill me. Am I going to plead for my life? Am I going to beg him not to do it? No! If I'm going to die, I'm going to die."

A couple of steps down and I stood on the packed earth outside. I picked up one foot, reached out and put it down. Then the next foot, reached out and put it down. I could see Big Guy's shadow along side of me in that little patch of light, and I could tell he still had his gun pointed at me. My mind was going a million miles an hour.

"What does it feel like when a bullet hits your head?" was all I could think of.

He didn't come out into the blackness but remained standing in the open doorway while I walked slowly across the packed earth, one foot at a time. It was a clear night out and I could see the stars. I could also see high walls. I was in some kind of an outside enclosed area. Because of the dim light coming from the open doorway, I was able to see that I was heading toward a brick wall.

Big Guy was still standing in the doorway behind me.

"No, no, no. Move to the left and open the door there," he said.

I was able to make out the frame of a door in the brick wall. Running, I grabbed that door and yanked it open, and out poured bright light. It was like being thrown a life ring from a boat while drowning.

Only then did Big Guy finally come out into the dark open area. He crossed over and followed me inside to a large round room. It dawned on me that he had been afraid I would attack him out there in the dark! That's why he had remained in the open doorway, trying to appear coolheaded, holding his gun at the ready in case I jumped him.

Coming into that brightly-lit room was like being saved from a death sentence, and it took a few seconds for my heart to stop racing.

In the middle of the round room was a kiosk. It was enclosed in glass and had counters on the inside. A German soldier, another guard, was inside the kiosk and he came out when he saw Big Guy and me enter the room. I began to wonder where I was.

It turned out that this area was like a hub from which the four wings of the prison emanated. Big Guy and the guard spoke for a minute or two in German.

Then he put his pistol away in his pocket and turned to me.

"Well young Lt. Keeffe, maybe after the war you and I can sit down and drink a beer together."

He put his hand out to shake hands with me. I must say that my response to him was not very officer-like. I just looked at him and hissed, "I won't shake hands with you, you son of a bitch."

BOOM!! He hauled off and hit me hard on the side of the jaw, knocking me flat. Then he turned on his heel and went right back out across the yard.

That was the hardest I'd ever been hit, and I lay there on the floor a little dazed. As I started to get up, the German sergeant came over and helped me to my feet.

"You are a very brave and a very foolish young man," he said in English.

"*Kommen Sie mit mir*," he said. (Come with me.)

Located around half of this room were entrances into the wings of the prison. The German sergeant took his keys, opened the door to one wing and we went in. It was dark except for a couple of dim light bulbs. We went up the stairs to the left to the second level and out onto a balcony that had a tier of cells along its length. We walked along the balcony and stopped at the fourth cell. The sergeant unlocked the door and opened it.

"This is your new home," he said, and motioned for me to go in.

After I went inside, the guard closed the door and went back down to his post.

To my surprise, the Englishman John Jenkins was already in the cell. There was also another man who introduced himself as Bill Coedy. It turned out his full name was Herbert John Wellington Coedy. He was a Canadian bombardier/navigator. I was 21, and I think Jenkins was two years younger at 19, and Coedy was about 29. He'd been a math teacher in Canada before the war.

Inside the Begijnenstraat Gefangnis

The prison was a monstrous building with high, thick brick walls and several wings radiating out from a central hub. Right next door to the prison complex was a Catholic Carmelite nunnery. My understanding is that when the Germans occupied Belgium during May of 1940, they opened the doors of this provincial prison and ran everybody out into the streets. Then they took it over and turned it into what they called the Army War Prison.

Our cell was on the left side of a wing up on the second level. The cells in this area were used only for captured Allied airmen. In the cells closer to the stairs were other Americans.

The cell was supposed to hold only one person. It was about seven feet wide and fifteen feet deep. The only things in the cell were four very old palliasses, which were mattresses made of long potato sacks filled with straw. These had been used for nearly four years and were now compressed down to about half-an-inch thick. We stacked them in the corner during the day and did not sit or lie on them because that would further compress the straw. When the four of them were spread out they took up most of the floor space. We agreed not to use them except to sleep on at night.

There was also a bucket that we used for bodily wastes, both liquid and solid. We had no toilet paper—in fact we had nothing. Near the back of the cell, about a foot off the floor and about a foot in from the exterior wall, was a four-inch pipe that ran the width of the cell. I presume this pipe was filled with steam during the wintertime to bring heat into the cell.

The ceiling was close to ten feet high with one window on the back wall up near the top. To look out, one of us had to hold another fellow up. This was August and it was hot while we were there. Some of the window glass was broken out, which made it more bearable, but I thought this must be pretty grim in the winter.

When I arrived it was about two or three o'clock in the morning. Little Guy had brought Jenkins to the prison about ten or fifteen minutes earlier. After we introduced ourselves to each other, we chatted for a bit, then went to sleep. I was very happy to see my young English friend again.

Early the next morning around seven o'clock the cell door opened. The guards took us downstairs for medical examinations and check-in; first the Canadian, then John Jenkins and me. Jenkins and I were taken first to an administration room where a German fellow opened up two large folders and had us examine the contents. Inside one of the folders were most of the items Big Guy had taken from me: a wrist watch, a fountain pen, and that was about it. Big Guy had kept my two silver bookmarks and the little bit of money I'd had, but he never found my two Dutch gold coins.

Most Germans were very methodical and actually quite honest. This one displayed the contents of my packet and asked if I agreed they were mine. Then I signed a piece of paper and he put my things in an envelope. Those things, I understand, followed me everywhere I went during my captivity. The German also filled out a card with my information: name, rank and serial number, and my address in Seattle, Washington.

After we were finished with that little chore, we were taken to the first floor of our wing. At the bottom of the stairs was a two-room dispensary for sick or wounded prisoners, operated by a German sergeant. The dispensary held a mix of prisoners: Americans, Brits, officers, non-coms and civilians. There were even Germans in the room who were inmates of the prison. In fact, when our cell door was opened every morning for about half an hour, I noticed that there were German officers in the prison cells across the wing from us. Their buttons and medals had been taken, as well as all marks of rank. Everything had been stripped from their uniforms. I don't think they had belts either.

When my turn came in the dispensary, the fellow acting as the doctor spoke to me.

"You are an American?"

"Yes, I am," I told him.

"Why are you not in uniform?"

"Well, I've been walking around the area for a while."

He laughed.

"How are you feeling? Are you all right? Do you have any problems, any medical problems? Are you on any medications?"

"No, no, no—I'm fine."

"Would you like to stay and talk with me?"

"What's this guy after? Is he going to interrogate me somehow or other?" was my immediate thought.

"Sure, I'd like to."

"Well, sit over there until I'm finished with my sick calls," he told me.

When he was finished, everyone had left except me. "Would you like a cup of tea?" he asked.

"Sure. Why not."

He brought out a couple of mugs of tea and handed one to me, along with a cookie or two, and we talked for a while. I was very wary because I was afraid he was going to try and get information out of me, but he didn't.

After we'd spoken for a few minutes he said, "I have enjoyed talking with you. Would you like to speak with me again?"

"Sure. OK, why not."

"Alright, good. Every morning you come on sick call. Even if the guard indicates to you that you don't look sick, just say to him, '*Ich bin krank.*'" (I am sick.)

So every morning I went down on sick call. I sat off to one side until the orderly was finished, and then he and I would talk. I think he was the equivalent in rank of staff sergeant. He began to unload his troubles and I listened, but I stayed wary. He told me that Hitler was no good for Germany. He was very angry, he told me. He had wanted to become a doctor, but while he was in medical school he had been inducted into the Army and was made into something less than a doctor. He had been trained very quickly in how to take care of battle wounds, and they wouldn't let him finish medical school. He was quite bitter and very unhappy with the Nazis.

One day when I went down to see him he said, "Lieutenant," (he called me by my rank, even though I was still in the same civilian clothes I'd worn down from Holland), "there is an American sergeant in a prison cell in one of the other wings who refuses to eat. He thinks we are trying to poison him, which we are not. He is psycho, and I am concerned about him. Would you be willing to speak with him?"

"Sure," I said.

The next day the sergeant was brought down to the dispensary, and he really was psycho. He wouldn't believe me when I told him I was an American officer.

"You're not an American officer," he growled. "You're not even in uniform."

"Well, I was walking around for a while and had to wear civilian clothes," I explained to him, but he wasn't convinced.

"You've got to eat," I told him. "I'm eating the same crap as you're getting, and you've got to eat it or you'll deteriorate and become extremely sick."

He refused to believe anything I told him, all the while claiming he was being poisoned with the food and that he wasn't going to eat anything under any circumstances. There was nothing I could do for him, so he was taken back to his cell.

A day or two after I arrived, at around noon, a big guard brought a fourth person to our cell. He was a little Jewish fellow from the Bronx, New York, named Maxie Weinstein. I had never before seen a person who looked green, but Maxie Weinstein looked green and scared. The guard opened up the cell and ordered Weinstein inside. "*Hier ist ein Jude*," he said. (Here is a Jew.)

There were now four of us crammed into a cell designed for one. Our only piece of furniture was an eighteen inch deep by two foot long old slab of wood that was somehow affixed to the wall with two braces running down to the floor. The only thing we used it for was dividing up our food.

Our morning routine began when a guard came by, opened the cell door and shouted for us to set our buckets on the walkway just outside. Then other prisoners, probably civilian, came along and emptied the contents of the buckets into a larger container.

We ate only twice a day. I don't remember what we drank out of, but there must have been tin cups or something of the like. At each meal all food for the four of us was brought into our cell on one large tin plate. Dividing the food up became a bit of a problem.

In the morning we were each given a bitter hot liquid to drink and one thin piece of bread with a little jam spread on it. That was breakfast. Late afternoon of the first day, we each received a dried herring well-caked in salt. I had trouble even looking at it, so I didn't eat it.

When the civilian prisoner who distributed the food came to pick up the plate and saw that I hadn't eaten it, he was quite surprised.

"You haven't eaten your fish."

"No thank you," I said to him, "I don't care for it."

"There's a guy, a bad boy, in another wing who's on bread and water, and he needs some food. Could I take this for him?"

"Please, go ahead. I can't eat it."

He took it and presumably gave it to that fellow prisoner.

Cell Psychology

An interesting psychological phenomenon emerged amongst the four of us in our prison cell. There was Coedy, the Canadian, a very nice man and rather studious, a former school teacher; there was myself, the American officer; there was Jenkins, the English bomb aimer; and then there was Maxie Weinstein.

After realizing he wasn't going to be killed or sent to the gas chambers, Maxie Weinstein became what I would call a typical street kid from the Bronx, bragging about everything and stretching the truth. The day he arrived, Maxie blurted out all sorts of things about his flying career. He was a B-17 bombardier and he told us about all the missions he'd been on. After a while he started re-telling parts of his story, but facts would change; like how many missions he'd been on, or how much flying time he had. Eventually he paired up with John Jenkins, while I paired with Coedy.

"How many missions have you flown?" Weinstein asked Jenkins.

"Eighteen."

"Well, I did twenty-three."

"Maxie, when you came in you told us you were on your first mission. How do you have twenty-three?" I interjected.

"Well," he told me, "I was on secret missions."

"How much flying time do you have?" I asked.

Jenkins had said he had x number of hours, say 300 hours.

"Well," Weinstein said, "I've got 700."

"Weinstein, please tell us how you have 700 hours," I asked.

"Well, I went to pilot training and was washed out. Then I went to navigator training and was washed out. Each of those was 300 or 400 hours."

"Nonsense," I replied, "I flew as a pilot cadet, and I had 219 hours when I graduated. You didn't have 300 or 400 hours."

Everything was a lie, or a gross exaggeration. When Weinstein told us about his last mission, he said that the pilot and copilot had bailed out first, then he and the rest of the crew had bailed out. I couldn't believe that a pilot and copilot would ever be the first to bail out of a stricken airplane, so I chalked that up to another lie.

After a lot of questioning, this was the final story we got out of Maxie about his last mission:

When his group of B-17s first encountered flak and fighters on their bomb run into Emden, a city in northwest Germany, their plane suffered considerable damage and the navigator who was up in the nose with Maxie was severely wounded. The intercom was knocked out and a couple of engines were on fire. Maxie shot down a German fighter, then went up to talk to the two pilots. He discovered that the nose access door was gone, and so were the two pilots and the flight engineer/top turret gunner! And they hadn't activated the bailout horn!

As the plane was doing gyrations, Maxie climbed into a pilot's seat, straightened out the flight of the plane and put it on automatic pilot. He then went to the rear of the plane to see what he could do for the five crewmen there, some of whom were wounded and a few of whom were dead. On his way to the back, because the plane was under fighter attack, he utilized various gun positions to shoot down a few more fighters. After seeing to it that the wounded bailed out OK, he made his way back to the nose to get his parachute chest pack. He exited via the door-less nose hatch and wound up on the ground in Holland after surviving attacks by Luftwaffe fighters during his descent. He kept these at bay by shooting at them with his trusty .45 caliber pistol, which he'd been issued for the main purpose of protecting the aircraft's TOP SECRET Norden bombsight.

It was inconceivable to me that two officers, two pilots, would abandon their aircraft without warning those in the back to bail out. An aircraft commander should be the LAST one out of the airplane after first making sure that all live crew members were out. Their actions, if true, were completely unacceptable and cowardly and were court-martial offenses.

I caught Maxie up on a few points of his story, but on others I couldn't because I hadn't been there. Most of his bravado was directed at John Jenkins, who had about twenty night combat missions to his credit. He, Maxie, was an OFFICER, and a Bombardier utilizing the TOP SECRET Norden bombsight, which he had to protect with his life! And so it went, on and on.[2]

The big trouble started when it came time to divide the food. The first time we were handed a plate of food after Maxie arrived, it had two or three pieces of bread with some jam.

As we took the food, Maxie complained. "That helping is too big. This one is bigger and that one is smaller."

He complained like this the next day when we were given food in the morning and in the afternoon, and I became very irritated. "Alright Maxie, you divide it up," I told him after the third time he bellyached about the portions.

He divided up the food. Then he grabbed a pile he had intentionally made a little larger than the others. Maxie pulled this stunt a couple of times.

Finally I grabbed his hand and told him to put down the food.

"Stop breaking everything up. You're turning the bread into crumbs."

He'd crumble the bread up to even the piles out, always keeping an eye on making one larger.

Then I had an idea.

"I'm dividing the food," I said the next time the food came in.

"I don't trust you," Weinstein complained.

"Well that's tough," I told him as I divided the food on the narrow board that was nailed to the wall.

"All right, Weinstein. Come and take your pick."

"What are you trying to pull, Keeffe?"

"I'm not trying to pull anything. You're first, and I'm last. Come and take your pick," I told him.

He started picking up the portions to weigh them in his hands, and I had to snap at him. "Stop handling all the bloody food!"

"I want to hold them!"

"Nope! Just look at them on this board."

So he eyeballed the portions and got down to the level of the board to check the horizontal mass, or something. It was crazy.

"You're trying to pull something," he said finally.

"Just take one. Choose one."

This was getting ridiculous! Finally he chose a portion and scooped it up.

"OK, John, take one," I said to Jenkins.

"Coedy, take one," and Coedy took a portion.

There was one pile left, and I took it.

"OK, Maxie. Tomorrow you divide up the food, and from now on that's the way we're going to do it. The guy who divides up the food gets his last."

"You're trying to pull something, Keeffe," he said. He just couldn't let it go, but that's the way we divided up the food for the remainder of our stay at the Begijnenstraat Gefängnis.

Maxie complained about everything. Each one of us had identified one of the palliasses as our own, and we kept them stacked in the corner out of the way during the day.

When he came into the cell, Maxie got the fourth palliasse.

"That's not fair. You gave me the worst one."

"It is fair because you were the last one in, and that's the end of it," I said to him.

Weinstein immediately wanted to sit on them during the day.

"No, we don't do that," I said. "Besides wearing them out, they take up too much room in this little cell."

One of the reasons that Coedy and I had paired up was that we both liked to play chess. I had gotten a piece of newspaper and a pencil stub from the medical sergeant, and we had made a chess game.

When Bill and I first started playing chess, Weinstein made comments.

"No! No! No, no. Don't make that move."

"Weinstein, shut up!" someone would tell him.

We eventually divided our cell down the middle the long way, all fifteen feet of it. I had had enough.

"Weinstein, you stay over on that side, and Bill and I will stay on this side."

The psychology of group incarceration was very interesting.

Every couple of days when the air raid sirens went off, the entire German staff headed down into the air raid shelters in the lower part of the prison. But they left us prisoners in our cells.

"We hope you get bombed by your own bombers," the guards sometimes said to us.

I began to tap on the four-inch pipe in the cell sending Morse code. I used a pebble I'd found, and I dragged it for a dash and rapped it for a dot. I began communicating with some of the Americans in the other cells this way.

The door to our cell was about three inches thick, and there was a small round peep hole at eye level with a flip-up metal flap on the outside of the door. Occasionally we'd see an eye through the glass peep hole. One day during an air raid while I was sending Morse code to an American, the cell door suddenly banged open, and there stood a huge German guard shrieking at me. "If you do that one more time, I will shackle your hands and feet to that pipe!" he yelled as he stormed in,

I don't know why he didn't hit me, he was furious enough. But I didn't send any more Morse code after that.

Every morning, after a little breakfast and after sick call, we were taken outside to one of the triangular patches of beaten earth, the same type of place where I had thought Big Guy was going to shoot me. This was an open area between two wings of the prison with a twenty-foot-high brick wall at the end. We'd do calisthenics, or some of us would walk in a circle around the perimeter.

We had some fun with this at times by letting Weinstein lead us. The German guards thought it was hilarious that the little Jewish kid from the Bronx was leading all the rest of the prisoners. They never laid a hand on him, though. To my knowledge he was never touched because he was a Jew.

One bad thing happened after I'd been at the prison about nine or ten days. Somewhere along the line we were told that if we wanted a haircut, we could get one. At the far end of our wing of cells was a cross-over U-shaped walkway that connected both sides of the gallery along the back wall. On this walkway, along the back wall, was a chair where a prisoner cut hair.

I went down and had my hair cut, and there I made a very big mistake. The barber was Flemish and also a prisoner. When I learned that he could speak Dutch, I asked him if he could get a message out of the prison to a resistance group. Ever since Big Guy read the names of some of those I'd met in Holland—Sanders, Kees and Loose—I tried desperately to find a way to get word to them that they were in grave danger.

The barber said he could get a message out. I asked him to have an Anton Sanders in Rotterdam warned that I had been betrayed to the Germans, and the barber said he would do that. Being just twenty-one I was not very worldly-wise, and my desire to warn the Sanders of my capture may have set in motion consequences for him and his wife. I don't know if this resulted in the raid on the Sanders' home and the pickup of the Jappe-Alberts that December. I don't think so because I didn't tell the barber about the Jappe-Alberts or anyone else. Yet, the SD hit the Sanders and the Jappe-Alberts on the same day and at the same time, the 5th of December 1944. I think their information had to have come from someone other than me, perhaps from a traitor there in Rotterdam. At least, I hope and pray that was the case.[3]

Another Truck Ride

The day we left the prison, the 4th of August, guards brought a large group of about fifty of us down into one of the outside triangular areas between the prison wings. There was a huge gate in the wall at the end, and a truck had been brought inside. It was like a medium-sized furniture van with a cab for two people and a box with a door in the back end of it. Inside the box were five benches and a single small window that looked into the front cab. A German soldier holding a rifle sat next to the driver.

A couple of German guards herded us into the rear of the truck. Single file, we walked up two steps onto the floor of the box where another German guard was inside with a burp gun hanging around his neck. They filed us in and had us sit on the benches facing forward. We were told to put our hands behind our heads and keep them there.

I was one of the last ones in, and another guard with a rifle climbed inside behind us. He closed the door to the box. Then he said something to the other guard who signaled the driver through the window, and we immediately started moving. As the driver ground through a couple of low gears, the truck slowly picked up speed and moved through the gates of the outer prison wall. We turned onto the street and I heard the gate clang shut after us. After we drove for five or ten minutes, turning several corners, the truck stopped.

Outside the truck I could hear a lot of traffic noise and hubbub from normal street business. The door opened, letting in bright sunlight, and we were all warned again to keep our hands locked behind our heads. Because I was on the rear bench, I was able to bend down and look under my left arm to see what was going on outside the truck door. I could see the street, the curb and the sidewalk, and lo and behold, I could see the entrance to the police station where Jenkins and I had been informed that we were prisoners. Both of the entrance doors were open at this time of day.

About five minutes later, Big Guy and Little Guy walked out of the building with two Americans. Both Americans were smoking small cigars, and it was quite obvious that they thought this was a joyful occasion. The Americans were happy, and Big Guy and Little Guy were happy. The Americans were smiling and patting the two German agents on the shoulder as Big Guy pointed to the truck.

When they reached the back of our truck all four shook hands.

"We'll get together after the war," one of the Americans said. "We really appreciate all you're doing for us."

"No problem at all, we're happy to help our American friends. But right now you're going to join your companions and go down into France and be free again," Big Guy told them as everyone laughed.

The first American stepped up and came into the box. He still had the small cigar in his mouth. "Hi fellows!" he said.

WHACK! The guard inside hit him on the back of the head with a rifle butt. Of course, we were all sitting silently on the benches, looking toward the front of the truck with our hands behind our heads. Not a peep out of us, because we'd been told to be quiet.

The fellow got the idea very quickly. He sat down next to me, still with that cigar in his mouth, and put his hands up behind his head. The second American, who'd been saying his good-byes outside, climbed up into the truck.

"Hi, Guys!"

WHACK! He got hit on the back of the head with the rifle butt too. I don't know if he was still smoking a cigar or not, but he sat down quickly and became real quiet. They both had stunned looks on their faces, and I could just imagine what must be going on inside their heads as they realized they weren't going to freedom, but were instead prisoners.

Transferred to the German Luftwaffe

We drove for about forty-five minutes south from Antwerp to Brussels. Finally we stopped and when the back door was opened again, we were told to get out. I noticed we were in a courtyard surrounded by brick buildings. We had driven through an archway in one of the brick buildings into a *Hof* (inner courtyard).

It turned out that this was the German Luftwaffe Headquarters-West. We were ordered out of the truck and officially handed over to the receiving authorities. Up to this point we had been in the hands of the Abwehr, the German Security Service, and the Green Secret Military Police, both intelligence agencies. Now we were in the control of the German Air Force, the Luftwaffe.

Our entire group was taken up to the third floor and into a very large open room. This room was divided into cubicles with only sheets, or cloths, hanging and forming the cubicles. Somehow or other there were frames holding up these sheets. We each wound up in a separate cubicle with a bed.

"Absolute silence. No talking. No whispering," a guard told us. However, some of the men wouldn't keep quiet. They continued to talk and whisper amongst themselves. Suddenly, all hell broke loose. The guards came stomping and screaming and shouting into those cubicles, and after that there was no more talking. In fact it became absolutely quiet. The stomping and screaming was very effective.

We were there maybe two days. They took me through the routine again: my envelope was opened; I inventoried my watch and my fountain pen; I signed the piece of paper, and then they put everything back into the envelope.

The second day, I was taken out for interrogation. The interrogator sat at a little table in the doorway of a small office. He had a long form titled, "International Red Cross Form." We'd been warned about these forms during briefings back at Hethel.

"We need this information so we can notify your family that you are safe, blah, blah, blah," was a typical line we'd been told might be used on us. And that's exactly how the interrogator started the questioning with me. "I need your name, your rank, your service number, your place of birth, your mother's name, your wife's name, your organization, and when you went down."

I got partway down the form and refused to go any further.

"I'm sorry, but I'm not giving you any more answers. You know and I know that the only thing that's required by the Geneva Convention is name, rank and serial number, and you already have more than that."

The interrogator then said, "OK."

It was almost a joke, certainly a formality with no coercion whatsoever. I stood up and, before I left, I glanced into the office and noticed a calendar on the far wall. It was Sunday, the 6th of August 1944. I realized I had been a prisoner of the Germans for eleven days now.

Into Germany

Later that afternoon about fifteen of us were brought out into a hallway where several Luftwaffe guards were waiting for us. When the guards told us to pick up their backpacks, some of us refused. We were officers, and the guards shouldn't have asked us to do this. The situation almost turned very nasty.

After arguing back and forth with the guards, a few of the men said "to hell with it!" and picked up the guards' packs. I wouldn't and didn't. I think if we'd hung together the guards would have backed off. The guards then marched us out of the building into the *Hof* and into a couple of closed trucks in which we were driven to the train station.

We were put into third-class train cars and transported eastward across Belgium, our destination being Frankfurt, Germany. I remember that while we were still in Belgium, our train had to cross over a river on a very rickety bridge that the Germans had pieced together because the Americans had bombed out the main bridge that had been parallel to the one we were on. I was scared to death our train was going to fall off the bloody thing.

I struck up a conversation with one of the Germans, a medical orderly, and he and I talked all the way into Germany. His English was pretty good, and boy was he unhappy with Hitler. I was amazed that some of these Germans spoke to the extent they did against the war, against Hitler, and about what was going on. I came to realize that not all Germans were Nazis.

I remember one incident at a station where we were changing trains. German soldiers traveled with their bags and their rifles. I saw one such soldier carrying a lot of luggage, and the poor guy dropped one of his bags. I heard glass break, and then I saw something leaking out of the bag. I felt sorry for him. He probably had a bottle or two of cognac or wine in his bag, and now it was broken and leaking all over the place. He just stood there, seemingly at a loss as to what to do.

We crossed into Germany at Aachen, and from there we continued eastward to Frankfurt, arriving at the train station late at night. There were fifteen of us and four guards. When we got off the train, we were taken down into the bowels of the station to a workmen's area where we slept on the bare floor. There were a few wooden benches, but the guards slept on them. I actually think we had it better on the floor because those poor guards had a difficult time of it trying to stay on the narrow benches.

I noticed an interesting thing about the German guards once we got to Frankfurt. All of them had burp guns, the German *Schmeisser* or "machine pistol," attached to straps hanging around their necks, which allowed the guns to lie flat against their chests. In Belgium the guards had all stood and faced us. Or maybe every other one faced us. But in Germany all the guards stood with their backs to us, facing the people on the platforms. We soon found out the reason for this behavior.

"Terrorfliegers!!"

Very early the next morning we were brought back up onto the platform. I could see that the station had been badly damaged by some very accurate bombing. We were in sorry shape ourselves. We had had only a little bit to eat back at the Luftwaffe Headquarters in Brussels the day before. We had not been given any lunch or dinner, and then we had slept on the hard floor down in the hole below the station. Without any breakfast to eat and no toilet equipment—I don't think any of us even had a comb—we were brought up onto the platform to wait for the commuter train to come in from the north, which it finally did around seven o'clock.

The train chugged to a hissing, screeching stop in the huge covered station and disgorged an entire fleet of factory girls going off to work somewhere. They all carried lunch buckets and wore the same type of clothing, a gray one-piece overall.

Among the lot of us, I was probably the only one in civilian clothes; the other men were wearing a mish mash of flying clothing. Some of them had bandages on their faces and elsewhere because they had sustained burns and other injuries. Two or three were pretty badly banged up.

The girls spotted us with the guards and knew immediately that we were enemy fliers. They flocked over to us and started getting all worked up. I had never seen hatred and mob action get out of hand as quickly as it did here. These girls were spitting on us and shouting at us. Some of them were swinging their lunch pails, trying to hit us with them. They were screaming at the guards in German, calling us *Terrorfliegers* (terror fliers). To them, we were murderers of women and children.

"*Schweine! Terrorfliegers!*"

"*Geben Sie uns vier oder fünf von ihnen!*" they begged the guards. (Give us four or five of them!)

Each of the guards took hold of both ends of his schmeisser and used it broadside to push the girls away from us.

The girls finally wound up shrieking as loud as they could, some shaking their fists, and others frantically trying to reach through the guards at us, "*Geben Sie uns ein! Nur eins! Nur eins!*" (Just give us one! Just one! Just one!)

Again the guards pushed them away and muscled us over to a door in the train. The cars were now empty, and the guards forced us quickly into a compartment and slammed the door closed. When we were all inside, the factory girls quieted down and went off to their factory. These women would have taken us apart. They were clawing at us with their finger nails, trying to tear our skin apart. It was just like a cat and dog fight, only it was all cats against some poor dogs.[4]

Finally, the train pulled out of the Frankfurt station and headed northwest up to the town of Oberursel, which was located at the foot of the Taunus Mountains. The countryside we passed through was quite beautiful. In fact it was difficult to imagine there was a war going on when we were traveling in areas away from the cities and installations like train stations. But one look at the guards with their guns brought everything back into focus.

The trip from Frankfurt to Oberursel took only a short 30 minutes. After disembarking in Oberursel, we were lined up and marched through the town. We were lucky because we found out later that the prisoners in most of the other groups had been ordered to take off their shoes, tie the laces together, and hang them around their necks before they were marched through the town. Some of the prisoners had even been required to keep their hands behind their heads all the way through the town, just to humiliate them.

The German people all knew what we were. They stopped and stared and spoke quietly among themselves and then went on about their business. As we walked through this small town, I was struck again by how pleasant everything looked, there being no war damage whatsoever.

On the far side of the town, to the northwest, was a small grassy park shaped like a teardrop, surrounded by a residential area. In this park was a kiosk where newspapers, magazines, candy, cookies and other small items were sold. A few shade trees dotted the park, and part of its perimeter was used as a turn-around for the streetcar that went up into the Taunus Mountains. We were to wait for the street car to come and take us up the road a piece to an interrogation camp.

"At Least They're Fighting for Their Country!"

By now it was around nine o'clock in the morning. I still had on the modest suit I had worn all the way from Holland. I hadn't had my socks off, or any of my clothing, for almost two weeks. But it was warm out, so I had my jacket draped over my arm and my sleeves rolled up above my elbows. Two or three of the wounded and burned guys, and most of the other fellows, were sitting or lying on the grass. The guards had come together, burp guns hanging around their necks, and were chatting amongst themselves while smoking cigarettes.

There were ten or fifteen civilians here and there, walking on the sidewalks and waiting in the little park for the tram. After soaking in the sun for a while, I noticed a well-dressed middle-aged man with a cane walking towards us from across the street. He began to walk around our group, looking at us all the while. He had a limp, which was probably why he had a cane. As he walked, he became more and more agitated, just the way the factory girls at the train station had done.

Pretty soon he was shouting and screaming in German, yammering about "terror fliers" and "murderers of women and children." I remained standing with my arms folded as I watched him get all worked up. He became angrier and angrier, and he finally stopped directly in front of me, about a foot from my body. He stood there screaming at me, and I just stared right back at him.

All of a sudden he tilted his head back and then flung it forward, spitting me in the face! This was the first time in my life I had ever been spat at or spat upon. I immediately dropped my jacket and went into a boxing stance; I was going to cold-cock this guy! He raised his cane then, getting ready to beat me with it. All of this happened very quickly.

Out of the corner of my eye, to the right, I could see the guards. One of them spat his cigarette out of his mouth, grabbed his burp gun, and ran over to us.

I wanted to hit the angry man and knock him flat, but a voice inside warned me. "You let it fly, Jim, and you're dead. The guard will shoot you. He has a loaded gun, and he's running over here."

Surprisingly, as I stood there quivering with my fists up, the guard ran right past me. By then he had his machine gun at the ready. He jabbed it right into the middle of the chest of the German civilian and started shrieking at him in German. He kept jabbing the man with his gun, forcing him to back up. He backed him across the little park, out onto the road and across it, to a high curb on the far side. The middle-aged man fell backward over the curb, flat onto the ground.

"You damned civilian, get away from these people and leave them alone," screamed the guard. "At least they're fighting for their country! That's more than I can say for you, you worthless old man!"

There were a lot of Germans on the sidewalk, and a few in the park, watching this. When the guard finished screaming, he just turned around and let the burp gun hang back onto his chest. He came back into the little park and walked past me with a wink. Then he went over and picked up his cigarette and started chatting with his buddies again.

I stood there by myself for a bit, amazed at what had just happened. Slowly, I calmed down. The middle-aged man rolled onto his stomach and got to his knees, then to his feet. He picked up his cane and walked off, brushing the dirt from his suit.

Soon after, a two-car tram showed up. I was busy talking with a couple of the other men and didn't notice if the tram had been spun around 180 degrees when it stopped, but it was pointing back toward the mountains when we boarded. The guards hustled us onto the tram, and we rode on it for only five or ten minutes as it made its way up into the Taunus Mountains. On the left side we passed by a small factory that we later found out made propellers for German airplanes.

Newly arrived Allied airmen POWs at Auswertestelle West 'Evaluation Center West' near the German town of Oberursel. Many of them are still wearing their flying outfits. (Courtesy of Raymond Toliver, author of The Interrogator, *the story of Master Interrogator Hanns Joachim Scharff)*

Auswertestelle West

Shortly after passing the small factory, the tram stopped and the guards ordered our small group to get off. We walked across the road and went up a smaller road to the right. The area was all relatively flat farmland except for that little factory. The land began to rise to form mountains another half a mile up the road. Actually they were only hills, but the locals called them mountains.

As we marched up the road, we could see the camp up ahead of us. The German name for this camp was *Auswertestelle West*, Evaluation Center West. This was the Luftwaffe interrogation center for captured Allied air crewmen.

We were taken through the barbed wire entrance gates and into a building on the left side of a road inside the camp. The main floor of this long building was rather high off the ground, and we had to go up a dozen steps to get to it. We were then led into a large open room, and another German guard came in.

This shows the outside stairway leading into the cooler at Auswertestelle West, where all arriving POWs were stripped and searched. (Courtesy of Raymond Toliver, author of The Interrogator)

"Well, here we have another bunch of terror fliers. OK, men, strip naked please. We have to search you," he said in perfect English. It turned out this guy had lived in New Jersey for many years.

Standing right in the middle of this large room we all stripped naked. The guards checked our clothing. I don't recall any of the men carrying anything, but we were examined and searched. Somehow I was able to move my clothing around, while standing there naked, in such a fashion that the guards never found the two gold coins J. J. van Dongen had given me back in Rotterdam.

After the search, we were taken singly down a hall and put into tiny individual cells. As he shut the door to my cell, the guard ordered me to be silent. The small cell was about 12 feet long by 6 feet wide. It had a door at one end and a window at the other end, which had been painted over to make it opaque.

The only things in the room were a radiator underneath the window, a cot and a chair. There was also a little gadget that went through the wall by the door. Whenever I had to go to the john I pulled the little handle on this gadget that dropped an arm outside the door, where the guard in the hall could see it. He would open the door and ask what I wanted.

That first day, after going to relieve myself, I was able to go into a wash room and wash my face for the first time in about a week. There were no towels or soap, just water, but it sure felt good to rub water over my face.

This was an interrogation camp, yet I wasn't interrogated by the normal interrogation staff, probably for two reasons. One, they may have had too many American officers to deal with who'd recently come down, and two, my form that followed me from the interrogation at the Brussels Luftwaffe West Headquarters most likely stated that I had come down the 8th of March because I had told them that. Here it was the middle of August, and the interrogation staff already had the information that I had refused to go through the whole Red Cross form in Brussels, so they may have figured it was a waste of time with me.

They fed us very little here, only bread with a little smear of jam on it. The heater in my cell, which I think was steam operated, was always on and couldn't be turned off. The window was closed and couldn't be opened, so it became stifling hot, almost unbearably so. I ended up kicking the heater and breaking something on it, but at least it no longer produced heat.

Across the internal camp street from the building of cells was a large compound used as a holding area for men who had already been interrogated. Once this group of men reached a certain number, the Germans moved them out of the camp and on to the next stage of their journey. I must have arrived there just as a group was ready to be moved because I never had to stay in the holding compound.

After two nights in Auswertestelle West, I was brought outside with about fifty other prisoners. The guards lined us all up and marched us back down to the town of Oberursel where we were put on a train and taken up to the town of Wetzlar, about an hour away.

Dulag Luft

Wetzlar was famous because the Carl Zeiss factory was located there. This company made very fine lenses and cameras. We didn't go into the main part of Wetzlar; instead, our train took a siding track to a small village. Here we all got off and were marched through the village and up the side of a hill to another German camp. This camp was called *Durchgangslager der Luftwaffe*. *Durchgang* means "pass through," or "transit," so this was the Transit Camp of the Air Force; *Dulag Luft* for short.

The main entrance to Dulag Luft, Wetzlar. (Courtesy of Claudio Michael Becker)

The area we were taken to was a tent city that had been hastily constructed, probably within the last six months or so, to hold temporarily the flood of American airmen coming out of the skies from fighters and bombers that had been shot down.[5] There were a few permanent buildings in this part of the camp with more in various stages of construction, one of which was used principally for a mess hall. It was here that we were finally given a decent square meal. Although German guards were present, Allied fliers operated this mess hall. An American Lt. Colonel, a West Pointer, was in charge.

At Dulag Luft we were all examined medically to make sure we didn't have any major problems. The wounded and burned men were taken care of. Afterward, we were each issued a two-piece cardboard box, about 14 inches high and 10 inches wide, sent by the Red Cross. These boxes reminded me of the famous suitcase-like boxes used in America during the 1930s. They were made of very thin, brown pressed board, less than an eighth of an inch thick. They had two straps to hold them together, and a handle. Rural American boys and girls who'd gone to work in the towns during the Great Depression had used boxes like these to send their laundry home by bus. Their mothers did the laundry and then sent it back.

Inside our boxes was a treasure trove! When you don't have a handkerchief, when you don't have a comb or a toothbrush, when you don't have a damn thing except two gold coins, when you haven't eaten for a few days, when you've been wearing the same clothes for about three weeks with no change or washing, anything is nice.

Each box contained a large olive-drab knitted wool sweater, four or five pairs of socks, a couple of sets of underwear, a shirt, a comb, and a razor with a little package of razor blades. There was a bar of soap, for God's sake, and a towel! It was like Christmas!

We were all in one room together going through our gift boxes. One guy held up his sweater and it was huge! "Wow," he exclaimed, "Look at this tent!"

I had already taken the sweater out of my box and unfolded and looked at it. I'd noticed that it was considerably smaller. In a way I was lucky that I'd been down since the 8th of March because during this time I had learned how to get by on one square of toilet paper, how to conserve soap, how to conserve paper, how to conserve everything, and I already knew that wool was warm. The more wool you had, the warmer you were going to be, and winter wasn't far away.

"Here, this looks about your size. I'll trade you," I said to the man.

I gave him my smaller sweater, and he passed me his huge one. I started to put the sweater on, and as I pushed my arm down one of the sleeves, I snagged something. I took my arm out, turned the sleeve inside out, and found a small piece of paper, a note pinned inside the sleeve. Written on the note was, "Knitted by Miss Mae Arduini, Rural Valley, Pennsylvania." After reading it, I filed the information away in my head, crumpled up the note and threw it away. However, I kept the safety pin because as a prisoner I was learning to keep everything I could get my hands on.

While at Dulag Luft, I was finally able to shower and shave, wash my clothes and eat reasonably well three times a day. After three days, a large group of us, one hundred and fifty to two hundred men, formed a purge (a group of men being sent somewhere was called a purge), and we were marched out of Dulag Luft, back down the hillside, through the little village and back to the train siding. This was Tuesday, the 15th of August, another bright warm summer day.

A purge of Allied POWs marching out of Dulag Luft to the local train station en route to various permanent camp destinations. Many POWs are carrying cardboard suitcases issued while at the transit camp. (Courtesy of Claudio Michael Becker)

One Furious Strutting German Officer

A very funny thing happened on the way to the train siding. We were marching towards the little village in a column four men abreast and forty to fifty men deep, and the guards were walking alongside us. The village had one main street made of packed dirt with a very high crown. Apparently, horses and cows were herded through the town frequently because there was horse and cow manure on this street.

Just before we entered the little village, the German officer in charge of the detail called out to the guards. He was a brand-spanking new *Zweite Leutnant*, a 2nd Lieutenant. He looked as though he had just stepped out of a band box. His green uniform was really spiffy, and his brand-new black boots were beautifully shined.

He stopped our entire column, and while we waited, he took out a cigarette holder about a foot long. He produced a cigarette, put it in the holder and motioned for one of the guards to light his cigarette. Instead of holding the thing the way one would normally hold it, he held it strangely, the way a person would hold a fencing sword with the closed hand palm up and the elbow tucked into the side.

After taking a couple of long slow pulls on the stupid-looking cigarette holder, he ordered the guards, "Ready, march!"

And into the village we went.

People were out on the sidewalks and hanging out of the buildings and houses along the road, watching our parade of prisoners. They had done the same thing on our way through the first time. This little rooster of a brand-spanking new *Zweite Leutnant* was up on the sidewalk walking parallel with us. He was certainly not going to march through all the manure like we had to!

He was walking along, bowing to the left and bowing to the right to the young maidens, occasionally taking a puff on his long cigarette holder. When we came to an intersection, he stepped down off the curb, bowing to the left and to the right, still walking parallel with us. He went up over the crown of the cross street and back down again approaching the curb on the other side.

The curbs were over a foot high, and as he neared the far curb, he misjudged his footing and fell forward onto the walkway with that cigarette holder, unfortunately, between his face and the sidewalk. When his body hit the ground, his head snapped down, and his cigarette holder got all smashed and broken up. He rolled over, and I suppose he was a bit injured, but he was still hanging onto the smashed up cigarette holder.

Guess what all the fliers did, all of us prisoner *Terrorfliegers*. We all started to laugh. We just roared! The lieutenant got to his feet, and he was furious! His beautiful uniform was now dirty. His sparkling, highly-polished black boots were scuffed and smeared, and his high-class cigarette holder was all mangled.

Turning red in the face, he started to scream in German. He retrieved and put on his soiled cap. He ordered all of us, the guards included, to run, and we had to run the rest of the way, about two or three blocks, down to the railroad siding. "*Laufen! Laufen!*" he screamed every few seconds.

We weren't going fast enough for him, so he bellowed even louder, "*Schnell! Laufen!*" And we continued to laugh!

He screamed and shouted the entire time we were being put on the train. Funny things do happen even in the worst of times.

All the trains we boarded, this one included, were passenger trains with second-class and third-class cars. On one side of the car was a passageway, and off that long passageway were compartments. Bench-style seats faced each other inside each compartment, and there was a window to the outside. It was mid-morning when we boarded the train, and we traveled on it for most of the rest of the day as it carried us farther and farther eastward.

Arrival at Permanent Camp Stalag Luft III

Water tower and buildings at the Sagan train station, view looking west. Most arriving POWs were detrained east of these buildings onto a concrete platform and from there marched through the woods to the main camp. (Author's collection)

After several hours of traveling across Germany and into Upper Silesia, we finally arrived at our destination outside the beautiful little castle town of Sagan. This region was comprised of principalities, and Sagan was the seat of what they called a *Furst*, a Prince. Our train pulled into the south side of Sagan's large railroad station. Just south of the tracks, a narrow road disappeared into a forest.

View looking east at Sagan train station. The concrete offloading platform can be seen just past a brick machine gun defensive block down along the right side of the tracks. (Author's collection)

It was late afternoon when we arrived, and after we disembarked from the train, the guards formed us up and marched us down the road through the forest. It was only about half a mile to the permanent camp, and as we neared the end of the woods, the camp opened up to view, extending to the left and to the right. It was huge! It was obviously a very permanent camp because there were barbed wire fences, and twenty-five-foot-high guard towers had been placed at intervals all around the camp's perimeter.

We followed the narrow road out of the woods, crossed over a wide cobble-stone road and entered the camp through a main gate. We had arrived at our final destination, the German prisoner-of-war camp called *Stalag Luft III. Stalag* is a contraction of two German words, "*stamm*" and "*lager*." *Lager* translates as "camp." *Stamm* is more difficult to translate; it literally means in English, "stem of a tree." In this case *Stamm* is interpreted as "main" or "central" camp. *Luft* is short for Luftwaffe, the German Air Force. So *Stammlager der Luftwaffe Nummer III* was shortened to *Stalag Luft III* and referred to the Permanent Camp of the German Air Force number III.

We could only see a small portion of the camp because it was so large. It turned out there were five sub-camps, or compounds, plus the German personnel camp. Each area was separated by its own single barbed wire fence. The outside perimeter fence of the entire complex was actually two parallel barbed wire fences. A five-foot area filled with a jumble of barbed wire separated the two parallel fences.

The main gate through which we entered opened into an area called the *Truppenlager*, which means "soldiers camp" or "troop camp." I learned later that the Truppenlager housed the German camp personnel: the guards, the officers and the ferrets. The administration offices of the camp commandant were also located in the Truppenlager. Once inside the main gate, we immediately turned left and were marched into the next area called the *Vorlager*, which means "before the camp." To get to the main compound from the Vorlager, we had to go through another set of barbed wire gates. The prisoners in the main compound were able to watch our purge come into the Vorlager through the barbed wire fence.

It seemed that I alone was in civilian clothes while all the other incoming prisoners were wearing a mixture of various military uniforms, and we were all carrying the little brown cardboard suitcases we'd been given back at Dulag Luft. The POWs inside the compound knew that we were a new purge, and the word went out. Soon, they all lined up along the warning wire inside the main compound and began shouting instructions to us.

"Fill your palliasses up with as much fill as you can!"

"Smile for the camera!"

Top half of Lt. Keeffe's POW ID card. The bottom half (not shown) describes his physical characteristics. Figure: slender, Height: 1.81, Age: 12.3.23, Face form: small, Jaw form: small, Eyes: brown, Nose: straight, Hair: brown, wavy, Beard:, Teeth: grade A, Other Marks: see above (which states 'tip of right thumb missing'), German Language Knowledge: hollandisch (Dutch). (Lt. Keeffe collection)

One of the first things the Germans did was to form us into a line to have our pictures taken for our permanent POW ID cards. Outside one of the Vorlager buildings was a stool, in front of which, about eight feet away, was a reflex camera with a cable release mounted on a tripod. The guards took one man at a time from the line and had him sit on the stool. The photographer turned the crank on the camera to bring up another negative and took a picture.

Then he shouted, "Next!"

While I was standing in line waiting to be photographed, a B-24 flew overhead at about 2,000 feet. The bomber was flying low, and I could see a couple of German fighters playing with him. One fighter would get up a little ahead of the bomber and turn in, shooting at it. Then the next fighter would do the same. I was really steaming because I could just picture the airmen wounded and all smashed up inside that airplane. I knew they were going to be shot down.

By the time my turn came, I was really angry. I had watched the Luftwaffe soldier who was running the camera, and I didn't think he was very bright. When they sat me down on the bench, he turned the crank and brought in a new negative. I watched him take hold of the cable release and then watched as his thumb started pressing it—and "*Ah-chew*!!"

Right as my head went down with the fake sneeze, he snapped the picture, and of course he got the top of my head. So he turned the crank to try it again.

A guard with a rifle was standing next to me and shouted, "Look ahead and don't do that anymore."

Then the soldier, with a new negative in the camera ready to go, started pressing the cable release again. Just as he was about to squeeze it, I turned around to the soldier with the rifle next to me.

"Was hast Du gesagt?" (What did you say?)

Snap! This time the cameraman took a picture of the side of my face.

The German soldier really let loose this time, screaming and shouting at me. He straightened my head around and threatened me, spitting all the time while he shouted.

I did this again, and another negative was wasted. The fourth time, the guard standing next to me took his rifle by the barrel and belted me over the back of my head with the butt end. The not-so-bright soldier with the camera cranked it up again and took hold of the plunger, and I watched his thumb. Well, I didn't want to get shot, so as his thumb started down, I moved my eyes clear off to the right while keeping my head straight forward. This is the picture they put on my ID. I still have it to this day, and there I am, looking way off to the upper right and scowling at the guard standing next to me.

After all of our pictures were taken, we were registered and issued German POW metal dog tags. On mine was stamped "Kgf.Lg.Nr.3.d.Lw 7412," which stood for *Kriegsgefangenen Lager Nummer 3 der Luftwaffe 7412*. In other words, I was the 7,412th Allied prisoner to have the "honor" of being a registered occupant of Lager Number 3 of the German Air Force.

Lt. Keeffe's German POW dog tags along with his trusty P-38 can opener. Both were connected together with a long GI boot lace, the end of which was always secured to one of his front belt loops. (Lt. Col. Keeffe collection)

Our next stop was at another building, the clothing store, where we were given prisoner clothing. I wound up with a French beret, GI pants, a Polish battle jacket and a horrible Royal Air Force overcoat. Most of these clothes were tight and too short, which would be no good when the weather turned cold.

This was the end of the civilian clothes I'd worn for so long. I played the shell game once again because I had to get the two gold pieces out of the hem of my old pants and into my new pants without being seen. I don't recollect exactly how I did a lot of these things, but somehow I must have cut the waist band of my new pants and stuck them in there, or I put them in my pocket and hid them in the pants later on. I don't remember. But I kept my gold pieces. I was also issued black boots, or rather high shoes that were workmen's boots. The soles looked like they were made from the tread of automobile tires.[6] As it turned out, these were the best boots I've ever had. We were also each given a potato sack, about seven feet long to be filled with wood shavings and used as a mattress.

After we were issued our clothing, the guards opened another set of gates and told us to go into the main compound, which was called Center Compound. As I walked through the gates, I realized that this was going to be my home for quite some time.

End Notes
Interrogation

1. This was the *Geheime Feldpolizei* "GFP" (Secret Field Police) Headquarters on Belgielei.

2. Many years later I found out that, even though most of what Maxie bragged about in the cell was either gross exaggeration or completely made up, his story about his pilots abandoning the airplane first—and without alerting the other crew—was true. So, too, was he truthful when he said he helped the wounded navigator exit the airplane. I'll refer more to this later.

3. After the war, Mrs. Jappe-Alberts wrote that suspicions ran high toward a man named de Groot as being the traitor who betrayed her family and the Sanders. (See letters in Appendix F)

4. I was very lucky that the German guards warded off the angry civilians as they did. Later on in 1945, as the war ground on, high ranking German officials made a policy, which they enforced, ordering German authorities, military personnel, local town officials, etc., not to interfere with civilian ire directed against captured enemy fliers. Arthur Durand described the German response to civilian attacks against downed enemy pilots in his book, *Stalag Luft III, The Secret Story,* pages 50 - 52.

5. The original location of Dulag Luft was at Oberursel, but it was bombed in March of 1944. Its damage was so extensive the Germans moved the camp to Wetzlar, to the site of an established Flak training camp. Information provided by Claudio Becker.

6. It turned out these were CCC boots. During the early 1930s, the depression years in the United States, there were many young men whose families couldn't feed them any longer. There were no jobs for them, so the government set up a program called the CCC, the Civilian Conservation Corps, to put them to work. The Army ran the CCC camps in a semi-military fashion.

    The CCC built roads, lavatories and amenities in many of the national parks around the country. Timberline Lodge at Mt. Hood was built by the CCC, as was the original Paradise Inn on Mt. Rainier. If you go to Mt. Rainier National Park, or any of the other national parks around the country, you will see stone bridges that they also built. They worked hard and their work was very good. These young men lived in a semi-military environment. They had three square meals a day, slept in tents or in barracks and were given clothing. The CCC was a wonderful program for these people who had no employment during the Great Depression.

On Sept. 17, 1944 a reconnaissance airplane took this photo of Stalag Luft III prison camp. Lt. Keeffe was in Center Compound. The Sagan train station is just beyond the wooded area to the NE. Compound designations added by author. (Courtesy of U.S. Air Force Academy archives)

POW

Stalag Luft III and Center Compound

The construction of Stalag Luft III began in April of 1942 with the Truppenlager and two prison compounds. One of the compounds, designated East Compound, was for prisoners who were officers. The other one, located between East Compound and the Truppenlager, eventually came to be called Center Compound. It was for sergeants or NCOs (non-commissioned officers). The distinction the Germans made between the prisoners who were officers and those who were sergeants showed up in the design of the blocks, or barracks, in each of the compounds; the blocks in East Compound had rooms for officers, and the blocks in Center Compound had open bays.

The trees had all been left in the Truppenlager with the exception of those that had to be cut down to make room for the buildings. It was a lovely place right next to Center Compound on the west. We could see in there because there was no wall, only the double barbed wire fence.

The first prisoners housed in Center Compound were French, Polish, Yugoslavian, and English aircrew sergeants. As more and more Americans flooded out of the skies, the Germans had to increase population densities in the existing compounds and build new compounds.

Late in 1942, the Germans began building a much larger compound to the west of the Truppenlager, which they eventually divided, calling one part North Compound and the other South Compound. East Compound became so full of officers, that many of them, both American and British, were transferred to North Compound in early 1943. When South Compound opened in the fall of 1943 most of the American officers from North Compound were moved into South.

By this time, most of the NCOs had been transferred out of Center Compound and sent to Stalag Luft VI in the Baltics, so Center Compound became strictly for American officers.

West Compound was the last compound the Germans built. It started receiving American POWs in the spring of 1944. By then, Stalag Luft III had grown to nearly seventy acres. A satellite camp to the northeast of the town of Sagan, called Belaria, was also constructed. When it opened, several hundred prisoners were transferred there from Stalag Luft III.

By the time I arrived, the 15th of August 1944, Center Compound held nearly 1,950 officers and a few sergeants. The other American officer compounds were West and South, with North and East strictly for British officers. Altogether, more than ten thousand men were being held as prisoners of war in the German Luftwaffe camp known as Stalag Luft III, with more arriving almost weekly.

I did not see John Jenkins the English bombardier, or Bill Coedy the Canadian, after we left the cell back in Antwerp. I did know that they both had been shunted off to other camps. Coedy probably wound up in East Compound or North Compound here at Stalag Luft III. Jenkins, being a sergeant, was sent to one of the many NCO prisoner-of-war camps spread throughout Germany.[1] Earlier, when we were walking through the forest from the train station to Stalag Luft III, I had seen Maxie Weinstein for the first time in many days. He was jabbering to anybody who'd listen to him. I wanted nothing to do with him, so I steered clear of him.

A prisoner who was a member of the American camp administration staff was waiting for our group as we walked through the gates from the Vorlager into Center Compound. He led us in, advising us to follow him.

We didn't march in, but kind of straggled in. Maxie Weinstein was up in front, and I made sure I stayed behind him. He was grinning from ear to ear. I think he was very happy to be alive.

Between the buildings, I could see guys lined up looking to see if they recognized any of us newcomers or could maybe find someone from their own bomb group or fighter group.

"Hi Tom! Aw, you got it. You got shot down, too. Well, welcome to Stalag Luft III!" one man shouted. "You're a Kriegie now!"

Kriegie comes from the German word *kriegsgefangener*. *Krieg* means "war" and *gefangener* means "captive." So, translated literally, the German term means "war captive." To shorten *kriegsgefangenen,* the plural of *kriegsgefangener,* we just called ourselves Kriegies.

Another POW ran up to a fellow walking close to me.

"You're a sight for sore eyes, Bob! I haven't seen anyone else from our crew.

You're the first!" he shouted. "Anyone else with you?"

Most of the men in our purge were recognized, but nobody recognized me.

A 'purge' of new Allied POWs arriving at Stalag Luft III being scrutinized by other POWs looking for old friends and aircrew members. (Courtesy of U.S. Air Force Academy archives)

As I walked past one of the wooden buildings, I noticed a couple of second lieutenants standing off to the left side watching our purge come in.

"There's that little bastard Weinstein," one said.

Hearing this, I walked over to them. "Do you know Maxie Weinstein?"

"Do we know Maxie Weinstein!" one replied, "Yes, he was our bombardier."

"I need to talk with you," I said. "Where are you staying?"

"We're in Block 51, Combine 4. Look us up. My name's Ed Pollock. I was command pilot, and this is Milo Raim my copilot."

I filed this away in my head because I was determined to talk with them about the story Weinstein had told us.

We continued in and were led to a building that turned out to be the compound theater. As we filed on inside, we were told to find a seat and sit down. Then one of the American officers shouted, "Attention!"

All the chatting and shuffling of chairs and feet died down, and the group became silent. In walked a full colonel, Colonel Delmar T. Spivey. He had been shot down and made a prisoner like the rest of us and, because of his rank, he had become the Senior American Officer (SAO) and the commander of Center Compound. We all jumped to attention. We were back in the military now.

Colonel Spivey marched up onto the stage and turned toward us. "At ease. Please be seated, gentlemen." He gave us a nice welcoming speech. He told us about the camp and about what would happen to us.

"Each of you will be assigned to a block and to a combine in that block. A block is the same as a barracks, and a combine is the same as a room. We operate in a military fashion here, but on a relaxed basis. In your combine you will have a Combine Führer, the Combine Leader. Your block will have a Block Führer. We have a chain of command here in Center Compound, and it will see to all of your needs. If you have any problems, use your chain of command.

"We have people waiting outside this room. As you go out, they will escort you individually to your new quarters. We will have more meetings, but the main thing now is to get you settled. Before you go, we will issue you a few things to take with you to your new quarters."

Colonel Spivey continued on, explaining about the Goon boxes—the guard towers. (We called the German guards Goons.) He also explained about the different types of German guards. He told us about the warning wire, which was thirty feet inside the double concertina barbed wire fence. The warning wire was just that—a warning. The thirty feet between it and the barbed wire fence was a literal death zone. The German guards could, and would, shoot anyone found in that area. After Colonel Spivey was finished, he left the stage and we all snapped to attention.

One of his assistant officers stood up and addressed us. "As the Colonel mentioned, you will receive some things as you leave. Take your newly acquired treasures and somebody will be waiting outside to escort you to your new quarters."

We were each issued a ceramic bowl, about two quarts in volume, a knife, a fork, and a spoon, all of which were German military issue. The ceramic bowl was cheap stuff, rather light and colored brown. We were also given a heavy white enamel mug, like a coffee mug, but without a finger hole. This was the type of mug you could drop, throw or kick, and it wouldn't break. The bowls didn't last long—being ceramic, they didn't take much abuse before they broke. And lo and behold, I was given one roll of toilet paper! You haven't lived until you've been without toilet paper for two or three weeks.

With my arms loaded with goodies, I stepped outside. An officer came over to me.

"Hello, and welcome to Stalag Luft III. My name is Billy Lawrence."

I introduced myself and we shook hands.

"Come with me. You're going to be in our combine."

Block 43, Combine 7

It was a nice, bright and warm summer afternoon. I followed Lawrence to Block 43 and into Combine 7, which happened to be at the south end of the building on its west side. Combine 7 was a room about 15 feet square. In it were four triple-deck bunks and one double bunk, which made it capable of housing fourteen of us.

Inside the combine, a couple of men were sitting at a wooden table. Lt. Billy Lawrence introduced them to me—Lt. Dale Tipton and Lt. Elmer M. Brockmeier. Brockmeier, from Denver, Colorado, was a B-24 bombardier. Dale Tipton was a B-24 pilot, a big fellow from Los Angeles. Lawrence was a B-17 pilot from Texas and was the oldest Kriegie in our combine. That made him the *de facto* Combine Führer.

I unloaded all the stuff I was carrying—my bowl, mug, knife, fork, spoon and toilet paper—onto a wooden table in the middle of the room and shook hands with the two men. Lawrence then took me to an empty bunk where I stowed my suitcase. Then the four of us chatted for a while. Soon other fellows began to arrive because it was getting close to dinnertime. As they came into the room, Billy Lawrence introduced me to each one and pointed out their bunks.

Immediately to the left upon entering the combine was a triple bunk. Lawrence had the bottom bunk. The middle belonged to Lt. Vernon L. Burda, a B-24 navigator from Dickinson, North Dakota. Brockmeier had the upper bunk.

Continuing clockwise around the combine, against the outside wall was a double bunk. Tipton had the bottom bunk. Lt. Jim D. Magargee, "Mac," a B-17 bombardier from Pennsylvania, had the top one. Next was the window. Around on the right side wall was a triple bunk that only had two guys in it when I arrived. The bottom bunk belonged to Lt. Chad W. Stephens, and above him was Lt. Buryl C. Heffron. They were both very quiet types and stayed close to each other all the time.

Next was another triple bunk. I had the middle bed, Lt. H. C. Schauer, a B-24 pilot, had the bottom one, and another copilot, Lt. Dwaine E. Gould, had the one above me. Schauer and Brockmeier had crewed together and flown with the 451st Bombardment Group, 726th Bomb Squadron, which was part of the 15th Air Force based out of Italy. The fifth bunk, another triple, stretched along a row of lockers that formed the wall separating our combine from the hallway. Lt. Emerson Jones Jr., navigator, had the top bunk, and Lt. Roy D. Bartley, a P-47 pilot from Muncie, Indiana, claimed the middle one.

During the next couple of months, two more officers showed up and took the remaining two bunks. Lt. Francis J. Hasek, bombardier, climbed in above Heffron, and Lt. Millard E. Mulry filled the bottom bunk of Bartley's tier.[2]

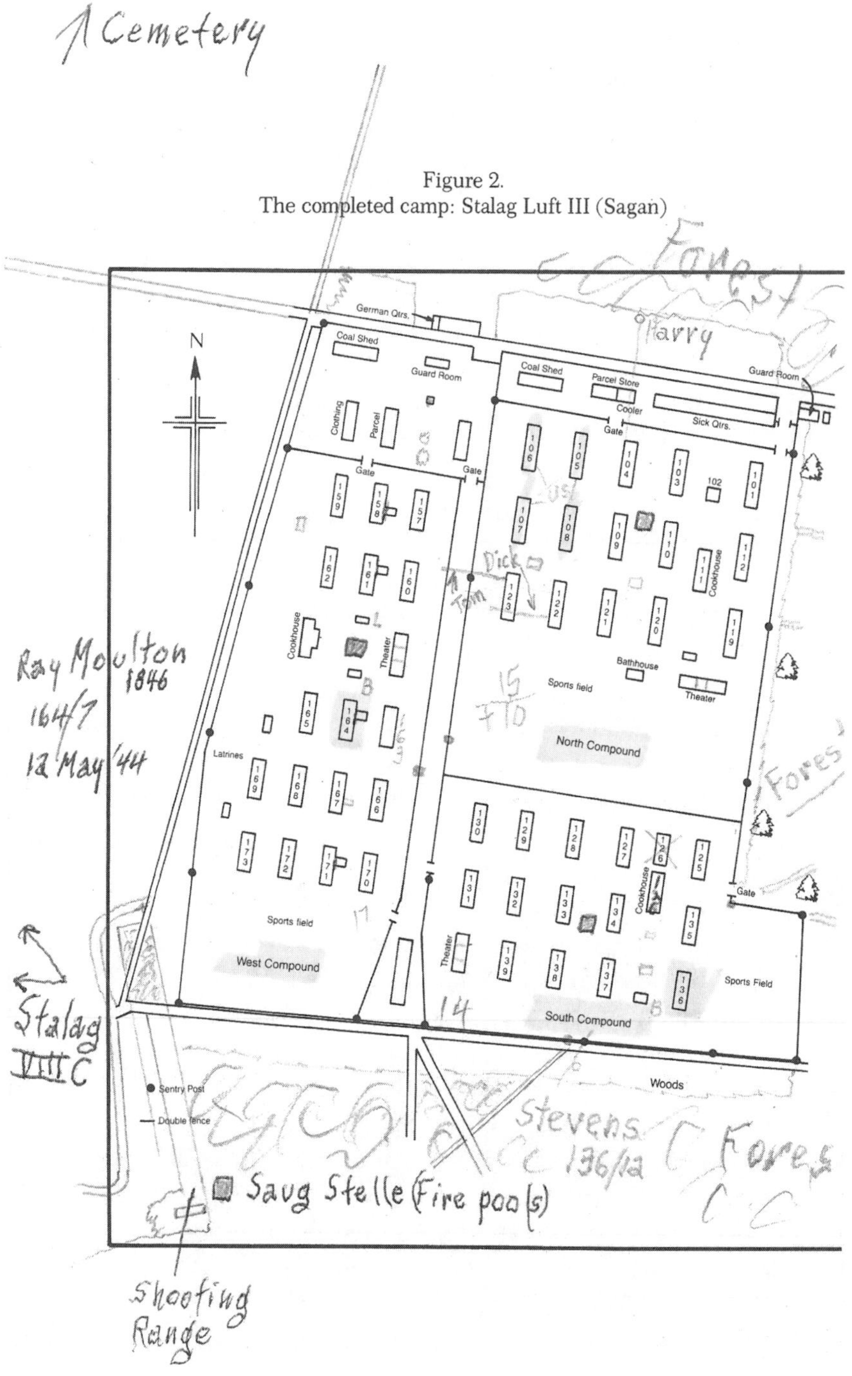

↑ Cemetery

Figure 2.
The completed camp: Stalag Luft III (Sagan)

Ray Moulton
1846
164/7
12 May '44

Stalag VIII C

Saug Stelle (Fire pools)

Shooting Range

stevens
CC 136/12

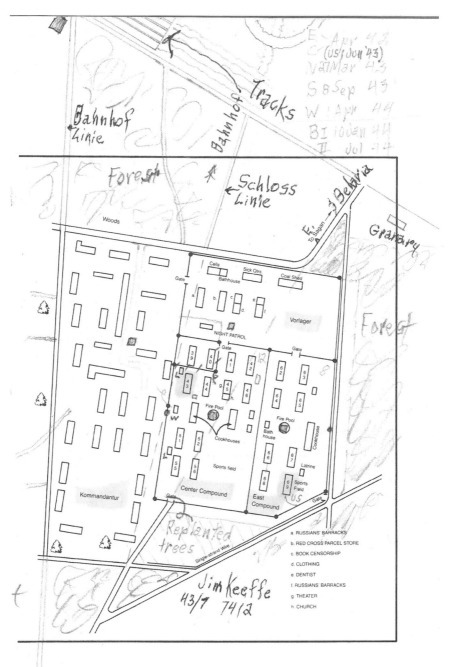

Diagrams of Stalag Luft III showing the various compounds and the Kommanduntur (Truppenlager). Enhancements and notes added by Lt. Col. Keeffe (Ret).
(Courtesy of Arthur Durand, author of Stalag Luft III – The Secret Story, *pgs 112 & 113)*

Lawrence finished all the introductions, and soon dinner was prepared. The men had long since established a routine that I quickly learned and took my place in.

"We'll take your bowl and your knife and fork. You can keep the spoon. Here's a tin plate you can use for all your meals," one of the guys said.

The tin plates were all the same and had been made out of tin cans. They were about eight inches long, five inches wide, and had sloping sides about one and one-half inches high made out of either two or three tin cans.

Everything we did in this camp was done on an expert basis. Among the thousands of men at Stalag Luft III were representatives from almost every type of profession and skill. Almost anything could be done by somebody in camp who had the know-how, and could teach others. This included the ability to make things out of tin cans—not only make them, but also to seal them so they were waterproof. The tin plates were all the same size, so they nested evenly because of the sloping sides. The workmanship in these plates alone was amazing.

During my first dinner in the combine, Dale Tipton told me that he and Burda were from the same crew. They had flown with the 781st Bomb Squadron in the 465th Bombardment Group, also part of the 15th Air Force. They had been stationed at Panatella Air Base in Italy. After they had already been shot down once and their entire crew had returned safely back to their base, they chose to keep flying missions. On the 16th of July 1944, they had formed up once more for a mission to a suburb of Vienna, Austria. Their airplane, the "Crescent of the Half Moon," sustained such heavy damage from attacking German fighters that they had to bail out once again. This time they were all captured.[3]

Over the next several days, I learned the layout of Center Compound and became familiar with the daily routine. Believe me, it was daily, and it was routine.

Our block, number 43, was structured the same as most of the other blocks in Center Compound. The building was about 120 feet long and 45 feet wide. In the middle, half way from either end, was a wall with a door, which I presumed to be a fire break. Each end of the block had an entrance door. The entire building was raised about two and a half feet off the ground by concrete piers that had wooden beams pier to pier. One of the reasons for this was so the security goons, whom we called ferrets, could crawl underneath to look for tunnels.

Just after entering the building from our end, on the right side, was a ten by fifteen foot room that was called the kitchen. In it was an iron stove with four burner holes and a very small oven. The stove was vented up through the ceiling and through the roof to the outside. On the far right wall of this room a bench was built into the wall.

Across the hall from the kitchen were two other rooms, one behind the other, separated by a wall. Together they were the same size as the kitchen. The first room, the smaller of the two, contained a small table with a hand-crank bread slicer on top that was used by the entire Center Compound.

Having the only bread slicer for the entire compound in our block had some plusses and some minuses. One of the plusses was that we sometimes had extra bread. The German black bread, called *Kriegsbrot* (war bread), was pretty horrible stuff. After the bakers made the loaves, they rolled them in sawdust and then put them into a large baking pan that held maybe twelve to fifteen loaves. The sawdust kept the loaves from sticking together. It was tough to eat, but we ate it anyway.

There was a cardboard box by the side of the table with the bread slicer. When food was relatively plentiful, the men ran the loaves through the bread slicer and then cut off the pieces with the sawdust, which dropped down into the box. We'd go in and pick up these pieces and make what we called scrounge pudding for dessert.

To make scrounge pudding, we soaked the bread ends in water and added some sugar, powdered milk and prunes. To make a frosting, we took some margarine, put it in one of the ceramic bowls and whipped it with a fork. After about ten minutes of whipping, the margarine would suddenly begin to inflate with air. Next, we sprinkled sugar in it and kept beating. This took 20 to 25 minutes, but lo and behold, we had frosting.

The second room took the balance of the space and was used for what we called "the night pisser." Along the inside wall was a long urinal with a pipe that ran down through the flooring to the outside and over to the abort, the pit latrine. There was also a pail or a can in the pisser for use by anyone who needed to defecate at night.

After passing the kitchen on the right and the bread slicer/night latrine rooms on the left, there was a second door that opened up into the central hallway where the combines were.

Originally, when they were occupied by the sergeants, the blocks in Center Compound didn't have combines—only open bays filled with lots of beds and, therefore, lots of people. After taking over this compound, the officers turned the open bays into combines. They accomplished this by first creating a central hallway that ran from the door that opened into the hallway at one end to the center fire break wall in the middle of the building. The hallway was made by lining up wooden lockers along each side, thus creating walls. Each locker was about three feet wide by seven feet high and sixteen inches deep. It had two doors, one beside the other. Two Kriegies shared one locker. So, for the fourteen spaces in our combine, there were seven lockers. They were lined up so we could access the locker doors from the hallway. Breaks in the rows of lockers became the entrances into the combines.

There were three combines on each side of the central hallway. These six combines made up our end of the barracks. Combine 7, which I was assigned to, was the first combine on the left after entering the central hallway from the area where the kitchen and the bread slicer/night latrine rooms were. The other two combines on the left were 8 and 9. Across from 7 was Combine 6, then 5 and 4.

Our combine had the only heater in our end of the block. It was a large rectangular Tyrolean heater with a smoke stack that went up through the ceiling. The outside of this heater was covered with tiles, and we burned briquettes in it. We also ironed our clothes on it. We'd wad up a towel, put it inside a wet shirt or a pair of pants and then rub this up and down against the hot tiles. Men from the other combines in our block came in and used the stove, too. Some could rub a darn good crease in their pants. One of the reasons we ironed our clothes was for the Saturday inspection that our SAO, Colonel Spivey, instituted as one of many good ideas to maintain discipline and military protocol.

Initially there had only been single bunks in the combines, but eventually they were converted into double bunks. When I arrived, the Germans were in the process of changing the double bunks into triple bunks.

The walls that separated the combines were made from cardboard Red Cross boxes. These boxes were opened carefully and flattened out meticulously so they could be put between the bunks to act as a wall. In other words, a triple-decked bunk in one combine was placed next to a triple-decked bunk in the next combine, and these two bunks were separated by one of these quarter-inch cardboard walls. The two bunks served to hold these walls in place.

A typical combine room with triple bunks.
(Courtesy U.S. Air Force Academy, USAFA, Special Collections Branch, General Clark collection)

The cardboard walls didn't go all the way up to the ceiling. They were fashioned to end a couple of feet above the third bunk, roughly eighteen inches below the ceiling. This open space helped with air flow and also permitted sound to travel between the combines. However, the men in one combine were not able to see the men in the next combine unless they went out into the hallway. This provided a measure of privacy and helped to alleviate the feeling of never being able to be alone. Some of the other compounds had blocks of actual rooms with doors and with walls made of wood. Two of the blocks in Center Compound also had rooms instead of combines. The combines like ours didn't have doors, just open entrances formed by making spaces between the rows of lockers. Frankly, I liked it better that way.

A cord hung from the middle of the ceiling of each combine, with a 40-watt light bulb at the end. This single light bulb was covered by a broad, round green shade and was the only source of light after dark for all the men in a combine. Each combine also had a window that could be opened. The window had two vertical panes of glass, each in its own frame, which could be pushed open and pulled closed. There were wooden shutters on hinges on the outside of each window that could be closed. Under the window was a wooden counter where we prepared the food and did the dishes.

On the floor underneath the light bulb in the middle of our combine was a wooden table with fourteen stools. The table was about three feet wide by five feet long. The stools came in two different styles, having been made by two different manufacturers. We ate our meals at this rather small table. Two men sat at each end and five men sat on each side, for a total of fourteen men.

We used the stools in other ways besides sitting on them. The top of each stool was made of four pieces of wood with cracks between. We'd hammer a nail diagonally across a crack, and then use a table knife as a cutter. This was how we cut our metal tin cans. First, we'd take the lid off and empty out the contents for cooking or whatever. Then we'd cut off the bottom lid. These lids were put into a box and saved until we needed them to make something else.

One of the required jobs in the combine was "tin bashing." For three days running, each person had to bash tin. This meant cutting the beads off the tin cans and cutting the soldered strip away, then flattening the tin with a wooden mallet and putting it into a box kept hidden under somebody's bed. The tin would be used later to make a myriad of things. The mallet was made out of a broken baseball bat with a hole bored in the broken-off section for a handle. Sometimes bats were broken intentionally when we needed more mallets. The metalsmiths taught us many tricks, including how to make seams and how to roll the tin.

Every combine had rules, or SOPs, "standard operating procedures." In our combine we had two important rules. We could have guests, but they could not smoke Elegante cigarettes. Somehow, in the past, some French cigarettes had made their way into our combine. I don't know where the hell they came from, but they were called Elegantes, and they stank to high heaven. We also had a rule that nobody could fart intentionally while in our combine. Good German black bread is very tasty, but the Kriegsbrot we were given was horrible stuff. I don't know what was in it, but it created tremendous gas in our stomachs. When someone passed gas it was terrible. Anyone who broke either of these two rules didn't get dessert that night.

Generally everybody got along. But human nature being what it is, tensions sometimes built up and occasionally a fist fight broke out. We got along pretty well with each other in our combine except for me and Schauer, who bunked below me. Right from the first, he and I didn't like each other. To get into my middle bunk I had to step on his bunk, and when this happened he'd make some snide remark. I didn't appreciate this sort of behavior. Between him and me, life was a matter of a truce, "You don't bother me and I won't bother you." He had virtually nothing to do with me, and I had virtually nothing to do with him.

There were definitely fourteen different personalities. We had a few bookish types in the room, we had some real talkers, and we had a couple of men who were stand-offish. It was actually a wonderful mix of people.

At the opposite end of our building was another kitchen room like ours. The room across the hall from this kitchen was used for a different purpose than at our end. Instead of being divided by a wall with one side for the bread cutter and the other side for the night latrine, this entire room was the living quarters for the senior officer of the block. He and two of his buddies had this nice, rather large room—large compared to what the rest of us were in.

We could pass freely through the door between the two halves of the block, but we had a rule that the men had to close the door once through in order to keep the noise of one side out of the other.

The dynamics and the politics of socializing in a block were very interesting. There was a huge difference between our end of the barracks, which was neat, tidy and clean, and where the men got along well, and the other end of the barracks. I was very happy that I lived where I did. There were a lot of difficult-to-live-with people who kept the other end of the barracks in turmoil. Fortunately, we didn't experience what was going on there. The only time any of them came into our end was when they needed to use the bread slicer or when they needed the night latrine.

Someone Finally Recognizes Me

Every new prisoner in our compound had to be personally identified within a few days of arrival by at least one other prisoner who wasn't new. This was done to make sure that each new prisoner was just that, a legitimate prisoner, rather than a spy planted by the Germans.

The morning after my first night in Combine 7, a couple of POWs showed up asking for me. They said they would take me around and show me Center Compound.

"Gee, what a remarkable organization this is," I thought. "Here are these guys taking their time to show me around."

Three days in a row the same two men came and took me around. On the third day we were walking the perimeter track just inside the warning wire. This area was where we all got a lot of our exercise. There were nearly 2,000 of us POWs in Center Compound, so there were guys walking around the track in a counter clockwise direction all day long. For some reason or other, we always walked in the same direction.

As we walked past the south end of Block 42, I noticed a man sitting on the stoop that led up to the floor level of the barracks. I recognized him as a fellow I'd been in training with.

"Hey, John, is that you?" I asked him.

"Jim Keeffe! You finally got here along with the rest of us."

"Do you know Lt. Keeffe?" one of my escorts asked him.

"Oh yeah! He and I went through Primary together."

The two escorts immediately excused themselves and walked away. They were finished with me, and I never saw them again. I never knew who they were. Later, I learned that they'd been assigned to escort me around and keep me away from anything sensitive. I also found out that different people from different barracks had been asked to walk past us as we made our way around the camp so the escorts could see if anyone recognized me.

Right after John recognized me, the escorts went back to a committee and told them I had been positively identified. Soon after this, somebody else came and took me to meet the colonels in "the Eagle Squadron."[4]

"Come with us, Lt. Keeffe. It's time you met X."

"What the hell is X?" I asked.

"You'll find out."

I was taken out to the fire pool—a large concrete square pool full of water—where three colonels were waiting.

"Lt. Keeffe, we were becoming very concerned about you," one of the colonels said after introductions were made. "Your story is rather weird. You were down in Holland for five months you say?"

"Yes, sir."

"Well, you've been identified now. But if it had gone on another two or three days, we would have asked the German Command to take you out of here. We wouldn't want anything to happen to you, like disappearing at night. Would you care to tell us your experiences?"

I then told my entire story and they believed me.

It was very important that everyone in the camp was proven to be legitimate. Later on, I heard that the Germans had inserted people into some of the incoming purges of new prisoners. These people were to act as German spies and report back everything they could. But other prisoners had discovered them and reported them to the German staff with the recommendation to, "Take these people out of here because we can't be responsible for what might happen to them."

The X Committee, sometimes referred to only as X, was responsible for the following within the compound: intelligence gathering—both German and POW, camp security, and covert operations that included all aspects of escape activities. Each compound had its own X Committee. These committees were well organized at the time I entered the camp. I had dealings with X only one other time while at Center Compound. Other than that, I never saw or heard anything about them.

Black Arm Bands

Upon my arrival in Center Compound, I noticed right away that some of the prisoners were wearing black arm bands made of four-inch strips of black cloth around the upper left arm of their jackets or coats. I asked about the arm bands and was told they were being worn in memory of, and in protest of, the murder of fifty prisoners who escaped the camp and then were recaptured by the Germans. I asked further questions about this and was told of the massive escape that occurred from North Compound just six months earlier, on the night of the 24th of March, 1944. Seventy-six men had escaped through a three hundred and thirty-six-foot tunnel that turned out to be eleven feet short of the safety of the woods. This was the largest escape attempt by Allied prisoners of war, and later became known as The Great Escape. The Germans diverted huge numbers of soldiers and other personnel into the effort to round up as many of these escaped men as possible.

When Hitler was informed of the huge escape he became furious, screaming that he wanted them all captured and killed immediately.

"How many were there?" Hitler shouted in the presence of Feldmarschall Wilhelm Keitel, chief of the German High Command (OKW), Reichsmarschall Hermann Goering, the head of the Luftwaffe, and Foreign Minister Joachim von Ribbentrop.

"We think there were about eighty," he was told.

"Fine, kill them all!"

"You can't do that," Goering cautioned. "The world will never accept it. And don't forget, they have our prisoners. They have our airmen, our pilots, in England, Canada and the United States."

"*Fünfzig!*" Hitler shouted. "Then kill fifty of them!"

In Berlin, a German Gestapo general by the name of Artur Nebe was given the files of the seventy-six escaped prisoners and the task of selecting fifty of these men to be shot. Of the seventy-six who escaped, three actually did get away, fifty were shot, and twenty-three were returned to Stalag Luft III.

The commandant of Stalag Luft III, Oberst (Colonel) Friedrich von Lindeiner-Wildau, a decent professional and honorable soldier highly respected by the senior prisoners of Stalag Luft III, surrendered to his superiors after the massive escape and was arrested. He was replaced by Oberst Franz Braune, who was the commandant when I arrived.

The murders had shocked and angered the decent German guards and officers, including Major Gustav Simoleit, the deputy commandant. They had made it clear that the Luftwaffe had had nothing to do with the killings. Even six months later, when I arrived in camp, a quiet somber mood filtered through everything.

Left: Colonel Friedrich Wilhelm von Lindeiner-Wildau, Commandant of Stalag Luft III until he was court-martialed after the massive POW escape from North Compound in March, 1944. (Courtesy of USAFA Special Collections Branch, General Clark collection)

Right: Major Gustav Simoleit, Deputy Commandant of Stalag Luft III, was a professor of history and geography before the war and fluent in four languages. He was a decent man, highly respected by the Allied senior officers of all compounds. (Courtesy U.S. Air Force Academy archives)

More about Center Compound

Center Compound had twelve blocks, eleven of which held about one hundred and seventy Kriegies each. Just inside the gate from the Vorlager was the first row of blocks. These were numbered, starting on the west side, 39, 40, and 41, 42. Directly behind this row was a second row with blocks 43, 44 and 45, 46.

Block 45 was a special building. It was the same shape and size as the other blocks that housed us prisoners, but it was not divided into combines. The compound theater took up the largest section, the entire north half. The prisoners themselves had built much of the interior of the theater. There were dressing rooms, equipment rooms, the main stage area and the seating area. They had obtained some materials from the Germans, and they had also used Red Cross shipping boxes. The Red Cross boxes were roughly three-foot-square plywood boxes with wood stiffeners all the way around, and they were used for many things. Most of the chairs in the theater were constructed using the wood from Red Cross boxes. The south end of Block 45 contained various rooms, one of which was the chapel where Sunday services were held. Other rooms housed our compound commander, Colonel Spivey, as well as General Vanaman and some other high rankers, along with a few sergeants who acted as their orderlies. Finally, a couple of small rooms had been set aside for use as classrooms.

A large pathway that we called the Avenue led from the Vorlager gate south between Blocks 40 and 41, and Blocks 44 and 45, to the area of the compound where the square concrete fire pool was located. The fire pool was filled with water, and we called it the "swimming pool." The Germans called it the *Saugstelle*, literally the "suction place" because they could pump water from this pool to fight fires. The pool was probably twenty feet square and four feet deep. Occasionally we swam in it, but the medical people told us we shouldn't because most likely the pool contained bugs and bacteria. The Germans never used the fire pool while I was there, that I recall.

Behind the second row of blocks were two large, long buildings called cook houses, one on either side of the fire pool. These were the two largest buildings in the compound. The building on the west side of the fire pool was the kitchen, and the one on the east side was a combination of several things. It held the mail room, another classroom, and Foodacco. Foodacco, short for Food Account, was a room for trading food, soap, cigarettes, and other things. It had several shelves full of items for trade, and a Kriegie was in charge of its operations.

The "Situation Room," also in the east cook house building, had maps and news reports posted on all four walls. This room was kind of like a war room, and it was where we kept track of what was going on in the various theaters of operation. The Germans took exception to us calling it a war room, hence the name Situation Room.

This was all done out in the open. In fact, German guards and officers often came into our Situation Room because we had more accurate maps than they did. There was a large wall map of Europe and another of the Pacific. Thumb tacks and yarn showed the various battle fronts—the East Front, the West Front, the Italian Front and the Balkans Front. We moved the front line across the maps according to the news.

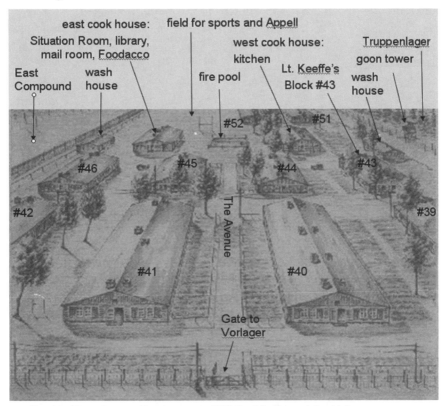

Drawing of Center Compound by an anonymous POW. View is looking south from Vorlager entrance gate. Notes and block numbers added by author. (Courtesy of USAFA archives)

I guess at one time the Kriegies had used the cook houses for cooking food, but there had been complaints because, human nature being what it is, one person's idea of how to cook differed from another person's idea. Anyhow, they'd long ago elected to have cooking done in each block.

In the east cook house was where we boiled water. Each combine had a pitcher made of lead. This thing stood about two feet high and had a ten-inch diameter base, a five-inch diameter neck, and a handle and a pouring spout. Riveted onto the side of the pitcher was a little metal band printed with the words "*Kein Trinkwasser* (not [for] drinking water). We used these pitchers to carry our drinking and cooking water from the east cook house to our combine. We weren't supposed to use them for drinking water, but they were all we had. I imagine that if we had remained prisoners for longer than we did we would have picked up lead poisoning.

Both of the large buildings had long, Texas-style porches that faced the fire pool. On the west cook house porch, the Germans had wired one (for sure or maybe two) speakers up to a radio. The only channel the Germans played on this radio was the official channel of the OKW, *Oberkommando der Wehrmacht*, the German High Command of the Armed Forces. The Germans would play music over this radio at times. They also broadcast news, propaganda, and Hitler's speeches.

Hitler was a masterful speaker and was usually screaming by the end of a speech. Even for those who didn't understand German, he was still quite mes- merizing. A loud fanfare of large trumpets preceded each of Hitler's speeches and lasted about five minutes before he came on and spoke. The man was a master, however, very few of us paid any attention to him.

The OKW radio also broadcast news of the war effort, always from the viewpoint of the Germans and never with anything negative. The Germans never admitted to losing ground, but instead spun the news in a positive light. For instance, we heard statements like:

"Along the Dniester River, the German Sixth Army executed a strategic withdrawal to better consolidate their forces for a massive offensive against the heavily weakened Third Ukrainian Front."

They always had a myriad of Nazi excuses for retreating, yet they never called it that. But it was perfectly evident by the way the war was going that things were not in their favor on either the Eastern or Western Fronts.

Most of the time, the OKW played music over the speakers. They played light classical and regular classical, but never any music by Jewish composers. As the Nazis lost countries they had once occupied, music from those countries would cease to be played. When the Germans lost Hungary, they stopped play- ing Hungarian music. When they lost Poland, they quit playing Polish music. Pretty soon we were hearing only German music, and we eventually got sick and tired of Wagner.

When the Germans in the camp had announcements to make, they turned off the radio and used the speakers as a PA system. They also used the PA system to announce the approach of an air raid within a certain radius of the camp. It would sound something like this:

"*Achtung! Achtung! Die Luftlage Meldung. Es gibt Nordamerikanische bomber Flugzeuge über Magdeburg.*" (Attention! Attention! The air situation report. There are North American bomber aircraft over Magdeburg.)

The Situation Room in South Compound. Kriegies, and at times German staff, keep up with the various battlefronts that are displayed on numerous wall maps. (Courtesy USAFA Special Collections Branch, General Clark collection)

Soon after hearing the air raid announcement blare over the loud speaker, we'd hear local sirens. When this happened, we had standing orders from the Germans to go inside our blocks and close the doors and shutters because they didn't want us standing outside cheering. The Germans didn't like it when we cheered, and occasionally a guard up in a Goon box would become angry and shoot down into the compound. I heard that the previous April a Kriegie in South Compound had been shot and killed by a German guard from one of the Goon boxes. The prisoner had been standing in an open doorway during an air raid and was killed instantly.[5]

One way the Germans attempted to spread propaganda among us Kriegies was by bringing in copies of newspaper articles and magazines with photos that described how the wonderful military machine of the Third Reich was dealing a mighty blow to American bombers. These articles were printed in English and aimed directly at us American and British airmen. One article from the German Luftwaffe magazine, *Der Adler* (The Eagle), contained a set of photos of shot up B-24s with the following description:

> "A north-american Liberator bomber during its flight over English territory. Trusting in their supposed superiority the terrorist bombers frequently flew into the German area, until our fighter groups and anti-aircraft units struck them heavy blows."

```
    "In addition to the enemy losses quoted in of-
ficial German reports there are the so-called "cold
down", i.e., those terrorist bombers that have been
damaged by the German defence, must go down over the
sea, crash over English territory, or are smashed up
during the landing. Their number is extremely high. A
picture taken by an enemy correspondent shows a heav-
ily damaged Liberator bomber whose undercarriage was
so shot up that it had to make a "pancake-landing" on
its airfield."
```

We Kriegies thought the German attempts to dismay us through this type of propaganda, or any of their propaganda for that matter, were pretty funny. Most of us had seen the smashed-up industrial and rail centers as we were transported across Germany to Stalag Luft III, and some of this damage was the direct result of the missions we'd been shot down on. We also knew through the news from the BBC, and from other downed officers arriving weekly into camp, that the Germans were losing. It was just a matter of time.

In the southwest corner of Center Compound were the last four Blocks: 51, 52, 55 and 56. Between Blocks 52 and 56 and the east wire was a large open area where we had appell (roll call) formations twice a day. We also used this area for sports. Finally, a few latrines and wash huts were located along the west and east perimeter warning wires.

East Compound and "Gen"

A wooden board fence about nine feet high separated Center Compound from East Compound, where British officers were located. From our side we were able to see the very tops of the buildings and chimneys in East Compound. I don't think there were any trees over there, but we did have a few remaining in our compound.

On our side of the fence was the thirty foot "death zone" with a little warning wire running along its edge, and on the other side of the fence, in East Compound, was the same thing. A prisoner could be shot if he crossed the warning wire and entered this thirty foot forbidden area. Thus, the total distance from the warning wire in Center Compound to the warning wire in East Compound was sixty feet.

Long before I arrived, the prisoners in Center Compound had come up with a way to communicate with the English next door. This was accomplished by putting a stone in a tin can with a message and throwing it over the fence. Arrangements were made for the transfer of the news, all done by notes thrown over in a can. For example, a note might have written on it: "At 7 p.m., somebody will be whistling a tune near such-and-such section of the fence. When the whistling stops, be ready to receive the can."

Then, precisely at 7 p.m., a tin can would be thrown over the fence containing a stone and a note. Whoever threw the can had to have a pretty good arm to clear the sixty-foot gap with the solid wooden fence in the middle.

For a long time this was how we got the news from the English. They had a secret radio receiver over in East Compound, and their people took down the news in short hand that they picked up from the BBC, which was broadcast from England. Someone else then wrote it out in long hand. Then someone took a copy of that, folded it up, put it in a tin can with a stone and heaved it over the fence. We called the news from the BBC "gen."

A view of East Compound taken from the goon box at the south end of the fence separating East from Center Compound. This part of the fence wasn't solid like the section further north where the blocks were. POWs are walking the perimeter near the warning wire. A granary dominates the skyline to the NE near the Sagan rail yards. (Courtesy of USAFA archives)

Each block was required to designate one of its men to bring the news from the tin can to the other men in his block. At a certain time, say ten o'clock in the morning, all of these designated men met ostensibly for a class, but what they were actually doing was meeting with the man who'd received the news in the tin can from the English the night before. He'd read it to them, and they would all write it down. Later in the evening, each of the designated men would go back to his own barracks. Security guards were posted at the doors, and then these men went from room to room and from combine to combine to read the news. This routine was done every day.

So we had two things to compare all the time: the OKW news that came over the loud speaker, and the news from the BBC. The differences between the two were frequently quite significant. We certainly trusted the BBC much more than we trusted the OKW.

The Vorlager Shower Parade

At the north end of Center and East compounds was the Vorlager, which both compounds shared. One gate, the gate our purge had passed through, led from the Vorlager into Center Compound, and another gate from the Vorlager led into East Compound. The Red Cross food parcels were stored in one of the buildings in the Vorlager. In another building, the mail and book parcels were opened and censored before delivery into and out of the compound. This building also contained the clothing store.

Russian prisoners of war were made to do the dirty work in our compound, and they were housed in the Vorlager in two barracks surrounded by a small, wired enclosure. The Russians did any hard work that had to be done, including cleaning out the pit latrines. We had virtually no communication with them. However, they were just on the other side of the fence from Blocks 39 and 40, and occasionally we heaved chocolate D-bars and other things, like cigarettes, over to them because they were not given any Red Cross parcels.

One of the only reasons we prisoners ever went into the Vorlager was to take showers. Inside one of the buildings was a large boiler and a shower room. The shower room was about 15 feet square with a concrete-lined, depressed floor with drains in it. A string of pipes up on the ceiling fed ten shower heads placed every four feet or so. We weren't able to bathe in the main compound because there was no place to do it. The only hot water available was for cooking. Every day there was a shower parade where a group of Kriegies was brought into the Vorlager to take their showers.

Once every four or five weeks, Block 43 came up on the rotation schedule for our turn in the showers. The guards took twenty of us at a time on what we called a shower parade. We gathered up our soap, towels, and washcloths, if we had one, and went to the gate to form up. Then a guard came into our compound, counted us, and marched us through the gate and into the shower building. Then we all stripped. Normally we wore overcoats and just shorts, instead of a full uniform or whatever we had in the way of clothing. After shedding our clothes, we stepped down into the depressed concrete area and stood in pairs under each of the ten shower heads and waited for the guard to turn on the hot water. Once the water came on, we went to work.

We had to move quickly because they didn't leave the water on very long. Each of us got wet and then, for instance, I'd soap up my front while my partner soaped up my back. Then we'd turn around and I'd do his back while he did his front. If the guard was pissed off about anything that particular day, he'd shut the water off early while some of us were still covered with soap. The good guards didn't do this, but we had a few bad eggs. Because we had to be fast, there was no enjoying the shower. Some of the men also took cold water bucket showers in the wash rooms in the main camp.

The shower parades were one of those things that broke the routine; we were glad for any opportunity to do something different.

The Daily Routine

One chap in each combine of fourteen was designated as the brew guy for the day. In the morning, around 7 a.m., our brew guy got up out of the sack, dressed, and took the *kein trinkwasser* over to the east cook house and lined up with all the other brew guys to fill his pitcher with boiling water.

'Brew guys' line up at the cook house with their lead 'kein trinkwasser' pitchers for morning hot water. Each combine had one pitcher for roughly fourteen men. (Courtesy of General Clark CD collection at Maxwell AFB. Thanks to Marilyn Walton, author of Rhapsody in Junk*)*

Each block had about twelve combines. That made close to one hundred thirty combines total in our compound, so a lot of men were lined up for water.

In fact, everywhere in the compound men lined up for something or other throughout the day.

After filling his lead pitcher with boiling water, the brew guy returned to our combine and placed the pitcher on the table. Then he woke somebody up to help him with KP. The night before, the shutdown crew in our combine had gone to the bread slicer room and sliced the bread for the next morning. While the brew guy filled everybody's mug with hot water for either tea or coffee, the other man put a tiny bit of margarine on each slice of bread and then spread a thin film of jam across each one—one slice for each person. This was our breakfast.

The rest of us got up and went out to the latrine and then to the wash house to clean up a bit. Every day I washed myself from the neck up plus my hands, and every two days I washed my feet. Then we came back to the combine and drank our brew and had our piece of bread.

South Compound Kriegies forming up for evening appell.

Around 8 a.m., all two thousand of us Kriegies emptied out of the blocks and went to the parade ground in the southeast corner of the compound for appell. We lined up by blocks, with the eleven blocks forming a large U-shape, and stood at attention. There were approximately one hundred seventy men in each block. Each block was a separate formation five men deep and about thirty-four men long.

The Germans then came out to our formations. All of these proceedings were done in a military format. We were called to attention and then our SAO, Colonel Spivey, saluted the German Lager Officer. Then two guards went over to the first block's formation. One went to the rear of the formation and walked along counting, while the other walked along the front counting. When they reached the end of the formation, they came together and compared their counts.

"*Ich habe 170, wie viele haben Sie?*" (I have 170, how many do you have?)

"*Ich habe 170.*" (I have 170.)

"*Prüfen!*" (Check.)

Then the two guards went to the next block formation. If everything checked out OK, appell took about a half hour. Sometimes, if it was a nice day and the Germans had caused us some trouble, we caused them some trouble by increasing or decreasing our count. There were several ways to do this.

In the past, the prisoners had made an arrangement with the German Luftwaffe staff whereby prisoners who were sick did not have to go out and stand to be counted. Therefore, if we needed to hide the fact that someone from a block had escaped or was not going to be at appell for some other reason, another man from the same block would claim to be sick and lie in one of the beds in that block. He'd make sure he was in a bed up against a cardboard wall that separated two combines. Ahead of time, someone would have made a separation in the cardboard. The "sick" man could hear when the guard came into the building and walked along the wooden floor, *stomp, stomp, stomp*. The guard went into each combine to see if anybody was there, and when he reached

The last block can be seen marching into place on the sports field. (Courtesy of USAFA Special Collections Branch, General Clark collection)

the combine with the "sick" man, the "sick" man would say, "Here I am," and the guard would add him to the count. Then the guard would leave the combine and head down the hall to the next combine. At that same moment, the "sick" man would roll quickly through the separated cardboard into the bunk on the other side, a quarter of an inch away, and be counted again. This was one way we could increase the count.

Another way was for a tall skinny man to put a broom with a folding cross stick attached to it inside a large overcoat. This fellow would place himself in the middle of his block's formation at appell, unfold the cross stick, place the broom inside another large coat he was concealing, and hold the contraption up next to him. With the extra overcoat and a fake head made out of something, he'd have a dummy POW. The guards wouldn't notice this fact, and they'd count the dummy.

Sometimes we played around with the appell count just to bother the Germans. They couldn't stand it when the count didn't add up to the correct number. If the count was off during appell, they started screaming and shouting at each other and then did the count again. That time the number would be OK. Then they'd count a third time, and it would be off more than it had been the first time. The Japanese would never have tolerated this. To us it was like fun and games but, occasionally, the Germans became so angry they kept us out there for two or three hours.

If fellows escaped, or if the Germans thought someone had escaped, they made us go through what we called a "picture parade." Everybody would have to come out of the barracks, including those who were sick. Then one by one, combine by combine, the men in each barracks would file past a table set up outside with several guards around it. Each had to be identified by the locator card with his photograph on it.

After morning appell the Germans dismissed us, and we returned to our combine for another slice of kriegsbrot with a thin covering of jam, kind of a second breakfast. Then we each went about our day, taking care of whatever responsibilities we had. We also had an afternoon appell around four o'clock. Rain or shine, sleet or snow, we were counted twice every day.

In the mornings we usually didn't sit together to have our brew. After the brew guy made the brew and filled all the cups on the table, we each took our own cup and drank the brew while getting ready for the day. Eating after morning appell was also very casual. Some of the men picked up their piece of bread and went to lie down on their bunks to eat it. Others would sit outside if the weather permitted.

For lunch we usually sat down together to eat. However, if the weather was good, I took my food outside and sat in the sun with my back up against the block wall.

Around four-thirty in the afternoon, following the afternoon appell, things settled into the routine of preparing for and cooking dinner. After dinner was prepared, we all sat down at the single combine table to eat. It's rather interesting when you have fourteen people sitting on stools around one fairly small table. Then, of course, there was cleanup. Normally we finished with cleanup about seven in the evening.

Cooking and washing dishes, as with all other duties, were rotated through the combine. We had made a sink over by the window and used it to wash our dishes. After the last people were finished cooking on the stove, we used it to heat water using the *kein trinkwasser* or other tin can pots we had made. We used the heated water for dish washing. The one good thing about cooking was that the cook didn't have to do any cleanup. The least desirable job, but the easiest one, was washing up afterwards. We washed our own mugs and our own spoons, but the plates and anything used for cooking were washed by the washing detail.

In the evenings we did many things. We played cards or chess, worked on log books and diaries, or read books. After the kitchen crew was finished, some of us went into the kitchen to sing quartettes, barbershop stuff. We also went into the kitchen room because it was warm from the stove that still had dying coals in it. Sometimes we brought in a dictionary or an encyclopedia so we could learn words, pronunciations, and spelling.

Don't Say It, a book by John Updike, a professor at one of the eastern universities, was very good. He used a technique he called SPUM—an acronym for *Spelling, Pronunciation, Use, and Meaning*. The words he discussed in his book were words that university students back east had trouble with. For instance, I remember very clearly the word "carbine." Many people pronounced it "carbeen," but this was incorrect; the proper pronunciation was "carbine" with a long "I." I found learning words with other men quite interesting and enjoyable.

Some of us Kriegies held bridge tournaments and chess tournaments. At times these tournaments became very tense. One such time was when our half of the block held a bridge tournament in Combine 4. The final two teams were playing their last game. Kibitzers (people who watch the game and chat, and at times become bothersome) were permitted into the combine, but absolutely no emotion was to be shown—no body language, no talking, no whispering, no jostling, and no looking around from one guy's hand to another's. The kibitzers had to be perfectly still. This game was for the championship, and nothing would be tolerated that might jeopardize the game's integrity.

I was a kibitzer standing behind one of the four players. At one point he got up and went out to the toilet, which was located between Block 39 and Block 43. While he was gone the cards were dealt. When he returned he picked up his hand, and I just about fell through the floor. He'd been dealt all thirteen hearts— the entire suit of hearts! The odds of this happening are absolutely astronomical. His own heart probably stopped, but he kept a complete poker face.

Somebody started the bidding, and by the way the bidding was going, it seemed the other three players also had good hands. This made sense because they had no hearts. The man with all the hearts passed every time the bidding came around to him. I forget what the other three were bidding, but this man's partner had a very good hand and was becoming visibly angry with him because he kept passing.

The final bid wound up something like seven diamonds. His partner passed, and the partner of the final bidder passed, and then it was up to the man with all the hearts.

For the first time, he spoke. "I bid seven hearts."

His partner became quite angry and slammed his cards on the table.

Then the man holding the hearts, figuring it was a joke, turned his cards over and said, "OK, who's the wise guy?"

The other three truly hadn't known what he had. During the entire hand, we kibitzers had had to just stand there with our hearts pounding. If we'd shown any emotion, they would have tossed us out of the room. We knew the game hadn't been rigged. However, no one could convince him of this.

"This is impossible!" he exclaimed when the other players assured him no one had messed with his hand. He won because he bid seven hearts. The other side doubled him, and then he re-doubled. I'd never seen anything like this.

Settling in for the Evening

One of the look-forward-to items of the evening was when the gen reader came around. We had to post guards out in the hall while he read the BBC news from the night before. This was the highlight of the day. One of the problems in the camp was the spreading of rumors. Rumors got started, and then they got amplified. Getting the news everyday through gen, even though it was almost twenty-four hours old, kept us kind of on the straight and narrow and kept our morale up. Eventually, we got the news through our own crystal sets.[6]

A lot of classes were held during the evenings, and many of the orchestra and band guys practiced their music. Every once in a while a production was put on at the theater. Sometimes in the evening I wandered over to other barracks to visit friends I had met. As summer turned into fall, and fall into winter, it became dark earlier and earlier in the evenings. The few lights outside in the compound were bright enough that I could see to walk around. Up in the Goon boxes the German guards had spotlights, which they used periodically. There were also lights around the outside of the barbed wire enclosures.

Typical goon box (guard tower) situated around the perimeter of all compounds. Each was equipped with two search lights, a machine gun, hand weapons, and a telephone.
(Courtesy of USAFA Special Collections Branch, General Clark collection)

Around nine o'clock in the evening, we started getting ready for bed. We did a final washing up out at the wash hut, brushed our teeth and so forth, and headed back to the combine. Eventually the lights went out.

One of the nice things we had in our end of Block 43 was a wind-up record player from the YMCA. I don't know where the YMCA got the records, but we had popular music from the 1930s and early 1940s that the Germans permitted in the camp. When the lights went out, one guy would stay up and play the records for a while. Because our cardboard walls didn't go all the way to the ceiling, the music drifted throughout the combines in our half of the block. We all kept quiet after going to bed. We listened to the music and became lost in our own thoughts.

Our own commanders required that the windows be opened at night to preclude sickness. Body heat from so many men was quite a bit of heat and did a pretty good job of heating the inside of the barracks, but this also permitted sickness to spread. Opening the windows at night allowed for air circulation, which lowered the risk of sickness.

We kept our windows open until ten o'clock in the evening, when the Germans came around and banged on the outside walls of the building shouting, "Close up! Close up!"

We closed up the shutters so the light wouldn't spill outside, but after the lights inside went out, usually by eleven o'clock, we opened the shutters again for the fresh air. Later on in the fall and during the winter the brew guy closed the windows before he went to fetch hot water in the morning, but the shutters stayed open all day.

When lockup was completed, the *Hundführer* (a German guard who used dogs) came into the compound with his dogs, usually two or three German Shepherds, and turned them loose. None of us wanted to be outside when those dogs were around.

German Guards and Officers

Center Compound was assigned a German officer called the Lager (Camp) Officer. He was the liaison between the German colonel and his staff and our senior people. If there were any problems, if we had any squawks, our senior people went to the Lager Officer.

Two types of guards came into the compound off and on throughout the day. One type we called ferrets. They always wore one-piece, very dark gray coveralls. Their job was to crawl around under the barracks, up in the attics and other such places to look for contraband, tunnels, or any other forms of illegal work that we prisoners might be involved in. The ferrets never bothered us unless they found something going on. Very few of the ferrets spoke English. It wasn't necessary because they were camp security and had no reason to speak with us. The man in charge of all camp security, including the ferrets, the one responsible for uncovering dozens of escape tunnels, was Oberfeldwebel (Master Sergeant) Hermann Glemnitz. He had been a pilot during the First World War and was very tough. He was also highly respected by most of the prisoners because he was a fair and honorable man.

The other group of German guards worked for the Lager Officer. They were German NCOs, most of whom spoke English. They were a kind of interface between our people in the compound and the German staff. These guards had a special purpose, which was to make reports of what was going on in the camp. Also, one of their main duties was to oversee appell.

This a photo of several German guards called 'ferrets.' Their job was to snoop everywhere in the POW compounds for any sign of illicit activity. (Courtesy U.S. Air Force Academy archives)

Left: Sergeant-Major Hermann Glemnitz, senior NCO of Stalag Luft III and head of camp security. Photo taken with hidden camera by POW in South Compound. (Courtesy of USAFA Special Collections Branch, General Clark collection)
Right: Sergeant Wilhelm Stranghöner "Popeye" senior NCO of Center Compound. (Courtesy of USAFA Special Collections Branch, Arthur Durand collection)

The highest-ranking German NCO of Center Compound was Feldwebel (Sergeant) Wilhelm Stranghöner. He had also served in the German Army during WWI and had been a farmer during the intervening years. Somewhere along the line he'd lost an eye and had a glass eye put in, so we called him Popeye. He, too, was an honest, honorable soldier who did not hate Americans, but who had a job to do and did it reasonably well.

Duties and Responsibilities

There were many responsibilities and duties in Center Compound: block responsibilities, combine responsibilities, and individual responsibilities.

Individual responsibilities included making up your own bunk, taking care of your own clothes, washing your own clothes, and washing yourself. Combine activities were written up on a roster. We rotated the cooking, washing up of our eating utensils and the like, and sweeping out the combine, which meant sweeping out into the hall.

Fifty or sixty of the two thousand Kriegies in Center Compound were sergeants. They were there ostensibly as orderlies for the senior officers, but they were given only light duties to perform; for example, sweeping out the hallways in the blocks. These sergeants were in the compound by choice. In mid-1943, when all the sergeants were moved out of Center Compound, some were asked to stay on as orderlies to the officers. Most of those who were asked agreed to do so. I suppose they figured they'd fare better if they stayed with the officers, and actually they did fare better.

Occasionally we had some trouble with these sergeants.

"We're not in a military organization," they figured. "You, sir, are not my commander. You have no direct authority over me, and I'll do what I damned well please, so buzz off and leave me alone." Some of the junior officer prisoners had the same attitude.

These people had to be dealt with. They were taken aside and spoken to, initially, in a friendly fashion. If they remained intransigent, Colonel Spivey used some very tough people. On rare occasions it was necessary to take trouble makers out and "instruct" them, whatever that required. This happened two or three times to those sergeants who had decided they were being imposed upon and that they shouldn't have to work if officers didn't have to work. This didn't happen very often, but it did happen.

Colonel Spivey was a West Pointer and, even though he called us "his boys," he saw to it that everything we did was according to military custom. He knew the importance of maintaining discipline and, for the most part, the other Kriegies agreed with him. For instance, he instituted standby room inspections on Saturday mornings. One reason for this was that some of the prisoners, like two or three of them at the other end of our barracks, were turning into animals.

Inspections brought military discipline back into our living quarters. We put in a lot of effort to get our clothes, shoes, bunks, and combines in order.

On a block level we also had requirements. Each block had to furnish what was called a duty pilot. A German did not enter or leave Center Compound without having his every move monitored and recorded. The duty pilot was responsible for this. The only gate for the compound that led in from the Vorlager was near Block 41. One room of 41, the corner room, was set aside for the duty pilot. The duty pilot stayed in this room for his tour of duty, which lasted maybe four hours. I never pulled duty pilot, so I don't know what time they started or how long the shift lasted, but I'm sure there was someone on duty from the time the German guards came into camp until they closed up at night.

The duty pilot was able to see everyone who entered the camp from the Vorlager. He knew every one of the Germans by name and rank, and he kept a record of all the Germans on a clipboard he carried. He logged them in and he logged them out.

A few Kriegies who were gofers, or runners, lounged in the same room with the duty pilot. If a particular ferret or German officer came into the compound, and if there was secret stuff going on, like an escape effort in progress, or papers being made, or tunnels being dug, these runners alerted the people involved, who then carried out their shut-down procedures. Everything we did in camp was done with a very high level of organization and security.

Combine-level duties also pertained to the kitchen located at each end of each block. Each kitchen had a small iron stove and there was a duty roster for the six combines using that stove. With eighty-four people all needing the little wood stove, a schedule was absolutely essential. Not only was use of the top of the stove scheduled, but use of the little oven was scheduled as well. Each combine had a person designated as the toast maker. That person used the stove to make toast for all the men in his combine.

We learned how to toast the awful kriegsbrot by taking a slice of bread and sticking it onto the side of the iron stove. When that side was toasted the slice fell onto the floor, unless it was caught in time. Then we turned it around and stuck it back on again.

Not only were the sides of the stove scheduled and used for toasting, the pipe running up into the ceiling was also scheduled and used for toasting. It was quite a sight to see the stove and the pipe covered with slices of kriegsbrot.

Whiling Away the Time

We did all sorts of things to amuse ourselves and pass the time. Many Kriegies attended classes held in the east cook house. The students could even earn university credits by taking some of these classes, which included recreational programs, bird watching, and "how-to" classes on a myriad of subjects.

Anyone who could teach anything was asked to conduct classes. We even conducted vacation tour talks. For instance, I gave talks on skiing. I put together a lecture called, "Ski Talk Pacific Northwest—Mt. Rainier and the Evergreen Playground," which I held in the theater at 7 p.m. on a Monday evening. The art Kriegies made up an advertisement for my ski lecture and posted it on the cook house bulletin board.

Flier for Lt. Keeffe's class titled 'Ski Talk' posted on cook house bulletin board. (Lt. Col. Keeffe collection)

Bulletin boards were attached to the outside of the east cook house wall, running the entire length of the covered porch. These bulletin boards advertised classes like mine and offered other kinds of information. Most classes were held in this building, but other small rooms scattered among the various blocks were also used as classrooms.

One special bulletin board was where some Kriegies posted their "Dear John" letters, some of which were really tragic. I remember one from a girlfriend writing to her fiancée: "I did what you suggested. I contacted your father, and I am sorry to break it off with you, but your father and I have decided to get married."

We also had a hand-drawn map of the United States on the outside of the east cook house wall. It was about two feet wide by three and a half feet long, including Alaska and Hawaii. Tacked on the wall alongside the map was a sheaf of papers listing the names of prisoners and the location of their homes in the United States. When a new POW came into camp, a pin was placed on the map showing where the new POW was from (unless that spot already had a pin). The pin signified that at least one prisoner in the compound was from that city. The new POW's name was also written on the list that contained the names of the POWs from his home state and town. For example, when I came into camp, someone stuck a pin on the map where Seattle, Washington, was located. My name was then written on the sheet of paper that listed those from Seattle. Periodically, we would look through this sheaf of papers to see if someone from our own state or town had been brought into camp. I added a pin for Sioux City, which is where I was born, and another for Salt Lake City, where I had gone to high school.

We played a lot of sports, and we had sports organizations. For instance, each end of each block had a team—either baseball or basketball. A lot of the men, myself included, played sports on the dirt field at the southeast end of the compound. Football, basketball and baseball were the most popular.

Another room in the east cook house was the library. POWs who had been in camp for a long time received book parcels. They read their books, then their buddies read the books, then their friends read the books, and finally the books went to the library. The library not only contained books, but it also had a few tables where prisoners could sit down and study or do research. I did an awful lot of reading, and I kept a word book. Anytime I encountered a word I didn't know I wrote it down, and later I looked it up.

Many of the guys were involved in the arts. We put on stage productions, had two dance bands or pop music bands, and one mostly complete symphony orchestra that was quite good. Two or three of the men in the orchestra had been musicians with Glen Miller or Tommy Dorsey. Some men also formed a choir. Different groups were creating stage productions all the time—for instance, *Pirates of Penzance* and *Arsenic and Old Lace* were produced. These men were very good. Of course, they had to play the female parts and dress up. My God, they were funny!

The Germans helped us get equipment and costumes in quite an open fashion. Although we were supposed to be paid by the Germans, as outlined in the Geneva Convention, our leadership elected to receive credits rather than having the problem of dealing with money, and therefore, gambling in the camp. We'd send the Germans a detailed list of what we wanted, and they'd fill our list. These items were paid for by using the credits we accumulated with the Germans. Some of the things we asked for and got were magazines, newspapers, and costumes such as dresses, pith helmets, and uniforms.

During my stay at the camp we ate meat only once, right around Christmas time. A request was put in for the meat, and it too was purchased with credits. Each man's portion was the size of a hamburger. But it wasn't hamburger, it was horse meat. Also, for New Year's we purchased party favors, caps, and whistles using credits.

The main thing we had to fight was boredom. Some of the prisoners spent most of their day in their bunks, if they didn't have a duty to perform or weren't involved in sports. In one half of a barracks of roughly eighty-five men there might be three or four oddballs who did nothing but hang out in their beds.

Then there was the ever-present track around the warning wire. Walking around and around and around the compound along the wire was a favorite way to chat with friends and keep our muscles toned. I made it a point to walk the perimeter every day, regardless of the weather.

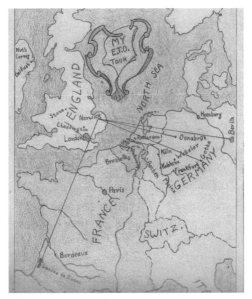

One of Lt. Keeffe's drawings done while at Center Compound. (Lt. Col. Keeffe collection)

Elmer Brockmeier and Jim Magargee came up with a unique way to stave off boredom—they went into the laundry business. Somehow they came up with a tub, and with that, together with hot water and the awful German soap, they set up shop. They couldn't charge money for their services because there wasn't any in the camp, so they resorted to the most useful form of currency a POW had—cigarettes and D-bars. They even had a marketing department by the name of H. Schauer, the guy who bunked below me. He went around to the other blocks and advertised for them. These guys ended up with quite a business.

I often drifted over to the Situation Room to see what was going on in the war. Over time, the positions of the various strings on the wall maps changed, and the probable outcome of the war became obvious as the fronts kept shrinking inexorably inward.

On Sundays I went to Catholic Mass, which was held in the theater building, and I served as an altar boy a few times. There was a Catholic priest, as well as a couple of ministers, in Center Compound.

A few times I sat in my bunk and drew diagrams and maps using colored pencils from the library. One drawing I titled "My ETA Tour," which showed my four bombing missions. Amazingly, I was able to bring a couple of my drawings home with me.

Pollock and Raim

A week or two after settling into life in the compound, I decided it was time to look up Weinstein's pilot and copilot, Lieutenants Pollock and Raim. After lunch one day, I walked over to Block 51 and went inside to the entrance of Combine 4. There I found both Pollock and Raim sitting at their table talking to each other. I introduced myself and asked permission to come in.

"Sure, come on in and sit down," Pollock answered, pointing to a stool.

"No thanks, I'd rather stand. First off, I need to be clear that Maxie Weinstein was a member of your crew."

"That's right, he was our bombardier," said Pollock.

"I'm here on serious business because of some things Weinstein told me. He was brought to the same jail cell as me in Antwerp and, if his story is true, I will bring charges against you two when this is all over."

This got their attention. I then related to them everything Weinstein had told me about his mission to Emden and how his two pilots had bailed out first without pushing the bail-out horn to alert any of the other crewmen.

When I finished, Pollock, the pilot, spoke.

"Now let me tell you what really happened. As our group was approaching the target, we ran straight into the thickest flak I'd ever seen. After one exploded close to the front of our airplane, I called the nose on the intercom and asked if they'd suffered any damage. The navigator replied that as soon as flak began exploding close to our airplane, Weinstein had put on his chest pack, scrambled away from his bombsight position, jettisoned the nose hatch and bailed out, all without saying a word."

Pollock then told me the rest of his story: how he sounded the bail-out horn, checked on the crew and found a couple of them dead, then proceeded to get out of the airplane, and how, once on the ground, he and Raim hid out with the Dutch until their eventual capture.

After hearing this, I dropped all thought of bringing charges against either of them. Pollock looked me straight in the eye when telling me about Weinstein being the one who bailed out first without letting anyone know. I didn't really know what to make of Raim during all this because he wouldn't hold eye contact with me at all. In fact, Pollock was the one who did most of the talking, with Raim just nodding every once in a while. After that, I thanked them for clearing things up, we shook hands and I went back outside.

It wasn't until years after the war that I found out the truth about what had happened on Pollock's B-17. Truth always matters, and in this case, learning the truth caused me to completely change my opinion of Maxie Weinstein.[7]

» *Timeline* «

25 August 1944: Rotterdam — Kees van den Engel is captured by the SD, brutally interrogated and sent to Concentration Camp Vught.

(Author's note: The German occupation of the Netherlands was still in full force and the noose of betrayal, arrests and reprisals began to tighten. I make note of such incidents as they relate to the people Lt. Keeffe met during his months with the Dutch Underground, as well as other historical moments toward the end of the war.)

Camp Newspapers

A group of Kriegies started up a newspaper called the *Gefangenen Gazette*. Eventually they were putting it out every day. This newspaper consisted of only one page, but it looked like the front page of a real newspaper. The headlines and the masthead and so forth were all done by hand. The Germans permitted us to use typewriters under parole; we had to promise we wouldn't use them for making escape papers. The newsmen typed up their articles, then cut them out and pasted them onto one big sheet. Then they posted this sheet, or newspaper, on the outside of the west cook house. The newspaper contained international news, national information and camp stories.

Later on, another group started their own paper, the *Kriegie Times*, because they didn't care for the political opinions of the *Gefangenen Gazette*. The

Kriegie Times reporters were always looking for scoops, and eventually they started publishing a full page of cartoons that came out once a week. This too was put up on the wall of the cook house porch.

The cartoons were absolutely outstanding. One of the funniest was of a square cut diagonally by a line. On one side of the square was a person brushing his teeth and holding a small square package with "Dr. Vierling's Zahnpulver," (Dr. Vierling's Tooth Powder) printed on it. Of course the character was brushing away, smiling and happy and holding up this lovely package of Dr. Vierling's Zahnpulver. In the lower triangle was a fellow brushing his teeth and holding a tube of Ipana toothpaste in his hand. (Ipana toothpaste was popular during the 1930s and during the war.) The tube was all wrinkled up and dripping toothpaste. The fellow looked quite unhappy; in fact, he was glowering and maybe drooling. Down below was the punch line, "Why take a paste in the mouth, when you can take a powder? Use Dr. Vierling's Zahnpulver."

We all looked at this cartoon and just roared with laughter! The German guards and officers came over to read the cartoons. When they saw this one, they couldn't figure out what in the world we were laughing at. "Why take a paste in the mouth, when you can take a powder?" That made no sense to them at all. They just shook their heads and walked away.

The Germans, as part of the camp issue, gave us this Dr. Vierling's Zahnpulver. I don't know what the devil the toothpowder was—some kind of pumice—but it had no taste, no flavor, nothing. It was like brushing your teeth with ground-up sand, and nobody used it. The Germans complained bitterly, "We give you things and you don't even use them!"

Another cartoon I remember showed a night scene. In the picture was a bent lamppost with its lamp lit up. Hanging onto the lamppost was a drunk. He was holding a cigarette, had crosses for eyes and a big red nose, and he was completely snockered. The punch line was, "Light up and get lit up. Smoke Elegantes."

The Story of David Wolter

One day I was at the east cook house checking out the map of the United States and found out there was a fellow by the name of David Wolter in camp who was from Seattle. It turned out David Wolter was in my own block. In fact he was in Combine 5 right across the hall and down one from mine.

After breakfast the next morning, I walked down the hall and looked into his combine. One fellow was working at the table, and another was sitting on a bunk.

"Is this the combine of Lt. David Wolter?" I asked the officer sitting at the table as I stood in the entryway.

"Why do you want to know?" he replied, looking up at me.

"Well, I noticed on the map out on the cook house wall that he's from Seattle, and I'm from Seattle too. I thought I'd come and chat with him. Maybe we went to school together."

The fellow stood up. "Come with me," he said and, puzzled, I followed him outside the block.

"Did you see that man sitting on the bunk?" he asked once we were outside.

"Yes, but he didn't speak," I answered.

"Well, he can't speak, or he speaks very little."

Then he told me Wolter's story.

"Lt. Wolter was a P-47 pilot. He crash landed somewhere, I think maybe in France, and got all scrambled up in the wreckage. That's why his face is all banged up. In the process he lost almost all of his memory. All he remembers is his name, his girl friend's name, his mother's name, and the fact that he's from Seattle, Washington. That's why I brought you out here. I didn't want to say these things in front of him. He's almost a vegetable.

"We wake him up in the morning and get him started dressing, and then he can finish on his own. Then we take him by the arm and walk him out to appell. After we're dismissed, we take him by the arm again and bring him back here to the combine, sit him down on a stool and get him started eating. Once we get him started with something simple, he can finish. But there is very little he can do for himself. One thing we don't want to do is upset him."

"Well, it's very decent—what you guys are doing for him. Maybe I can help a little bit by taking him out and talking about Seattle," I said after hearing the unfortunate story.

So I began to do that. When I had spare time, I went over to Wolter's combine and took him by the arm and got him started walking. Then he'd walk along with me around the perimeter track. Sometimes when it was nice and warm we sat in the sun with our backs up against the cook house wall. I started calling him Davy and tried to have small talk with him.

"Davy, I went to Lincoln High School and Franklin High School, and I graduated in '39. Where did you go to school?"

He wouldn't answer me. For two or three of these get-togethers, I got nothing out of him.

"Have you ever gone to Lake Wilderness, to the dance pavilion?" I asked him one afternoon.

For the first time he nodded his head and said, "I've been to Lake Wilderness."

Encouraged, I continued. "I went to Lincoln. Where did you go to school

Davy?"

"I went to Garfield," was his reply.

Slowly, little pieces began to come out. One day I was talking with him about something while we were sitting in our usual spot against the cook house wall. It was nice and warm and quiet. Suddenly, he became very tense. He tightened his fists and began trembling. Then tears began to stream silently down his cheeks.

"Davy, are you all right? Davy, what's the matter? Tell me, what is it?" I asked gently.

The tears kept rolling down his cheeks, and his trembling jaw was clenched tight.

"Those bastards! Those dirty bastards," he finally hissed.

"What are you talking about, Davy?"

"Those dirty bastards," he growled. "Look what they did to me."

"What do you mean, Davy, 'what they did to me'?"

"Look what they did to my face. Look at my face, those dirty bastards."

Davy was really shaking now.

"Davy, what are you talking about?"

"The Gestapo! The Gestapo did this to me!"

"Davy, no," I told him. "You were a P-47 pilot, and you crash landed and got all banged up."

"That's a damn lie! I'm a B-17 copilot!"

Then the dam broke, and it all came out.

Davy was a B-17 copilot flying with the 95th Bomb Group. He'd been shot down on the 4th of March, four days ahead of me. Somehow he wound up in France and stayed for a few months with a Countess in a castle. Eventually, arrangements were made to take him by car to the south of France and over the Pyrenees into Spain, and from there to Gibraltar where he would board a ship back to England.

Three French resistance people picked him up in an automobile to drive him to southern France. A couple of hours later, German guards stopped them at a road block. The three Frenchmen, who all had guns, were shot and killed right on the spot.

Davy didn't have a weapon, so he was taken to the nearest military police headquarters and turned over to the Gestapo. The Gestapo took him to Fresne Prison, a huge prison they had taken over just outside of Paris. There they tried to interrogate him.

He'd been told by the French Resistance:

"If you ever get caught, don't say a word for twenty-four hours because if you open your mouth and say one word in French or German or anything, they'll know you're not from that nationality. We'll need those twenty-four hours to cover our tracks because we won't know whether or not they will have forced you to give information about our operation."

So Davy did this. The Gestapo offered him food if he talked, but he refused. Finally, after twenty-four hours, he answered his interrogators and told them he was an American officer. He gave them his name, rank, and service number, and told them this was all he needed to tell them.

"We know who you are," the Gestapo said. "We know you came down on the 4th of March and that you've been somewhere these last several months. You might as well tell us where because one way or another, we're going to get it out of you. You can make it easy on yourself, or hard on yourself. We want to know where you've been and who you've been with."

Davy refused to respond, so they tortured him. The torture involved being beaten up, either by fists or by kicking. They would drag him out of his cell and ask where he'd been in France and who he knew. He'd refuse to answer, so they'd beat him up and throw him back in the cell. That's how his face got all smashed up.

About a month after the Normandy invasion began, the Allies broke north out of the beachhead area and started pouring into France. The Germans evacuated their prisons, including Fresne Prison. Davy was taken to Gestapo Headquarters in Wiesbaden, Germany. The cells in this prison were like closed caskets, about seven feet long, two feet wide, and about eighteen inches high. The prisoners were put in head first at one end, in a horizontal position. Davy told me he could turn over, but he couldn't sit up. The Germans put a pan in his cell that he was supposed to relieve himself in, but it was nearly impossible to do that.

He said the cells were made of wood, with the result that he could talk with the fellow on his left and with the fellow on his right. The person next to him on one side was a Catholic priest from Belgium, and the fellow on the other side of him was an American sergeant who was off his rocker. Virtually twenty-four hours a day, the Gestapo tortured people in that building. Davy told me that the screaming went on all the time.

He now remembered with horror what had caused him to internalize, to shut down. "I came to hate them so much that I wouldn't tell them anything, even to the point of being killed. But the thing I couldn't take was the screams of the women being tortured. I could stand the screaming of the men, but not the screaming of the women."

Every day they took him out of this cell box he was in, beat the hell out of him and stuck him back inside. After he shut down, the torturers knew something was wrong with him mentally, so they had several doctors look at him.

"This man has lost his memory, and he'll never regain it," the doctors concluded after testing him.

I'm sure that was the only reason Lt. Wolter wasn't killed. For some weird reason, the Germans were so methodical about everything. The Gestapo turned him over to the Luftwaffe with the story that he was a P-47 pilot who had crashed landed in France. The Luftwaffe took control of Davy and put him in a hospital. When he recovered a little bit, they shipped him to Sagan where he was put into Center Compound.

After Davy told me his entire story, I began to worry. "My God, if that's what happened to him, what would happen to me if the Gestapo found out how long I was evading? I came down four days after Davy did and was loose in Holland for five months!"

I went to the X Committee and told them David Wolter's story. "I'm concerned that the Gestapo will come and get me. I don't think I can take what he took."

They made arrangements in case any Germans ever inquired about me. If that ever happened, I was to become a ghost.

After Davy opened up and told his story, he began to get better, and eventually his memory came back completely. We were able to talk about many things, although he remained very quiet and reserved and introverted.[8]

Ghosts

The X Committee reassured me they had places to hide people in the camp, such as up in the rafters in a few of the buildings, or in false walls where contraband was hidden. "We'll be on the look-out, and if the Gestapo come looking for you, we'll put you in hiding."

Here and there, over a period of time, a prisoner became unmanageable. Some of these people just got to where they couldn't stand to be around other people—they had to be alone. When a prisoner got like this, he was put in one of these hidey holes and became a "ghost". Normally, after three or four days, the prisoner simmered down and could come back and function.

After Davy's story came out, I began to have nightmares because I realized what could happen to me if the Germans ever found me out. I'd dream that the Gestapo was dragging me away, and I'd wake up pulling on my arm. Occasionally I'd wake the guys in the combine because I'd be shouting, "No! No! No!"[9]

From Garbage to Diary

Paper was a scarce commodity in Stalag Luft III. In our Red Cross parcels, we received, among other things, cigarettes. I never smoked, so I used my cigarettes for bartering. Some of the guys who did smoke threw their empty cigarette packages away into brick garbage bins. These bins were placed at various spots around the compound, and that's where we threw stuff we wanted to get rid of. No food was thrown out, rest assured, but we did throw away unused cardboard, transparent wrapping, and other junk. The Russian prisoners cleaned these bins out once a week.

Many times I pawed through the garbage and pulled out empty cigarette packages. I pulled the cellophane off each package and laboriously opened up the package paper. I either steamed it open or used a knife. Once I got the paper opened up, I flattened it out and used it for writing paper. In fact, I made a notebook by stitching some of the cigarette papers together. I kept my diary in this little notebook, which I brought home with me after the war.[10]

"We're From the 389th, Too!"

One morning after appell, I wandered over to the Situation Room to check out the map and see what was going on that day. Quite a few other Kriegies were milling around on the porch outside, reading letters and talking amongst themselves. I could hear a few of the conversations, but I wasn't paying attention to any of them until I heard someone say "the 389th."

I turned around and noticed a couple of guys in conversation with another guy, and I became curious. Walking over to them, I could tell the two Kriegies were relating their shot-down story to the other one.

When there was a lull in the conversation I asked one of them, "Did I hear you mention the 389th?"

"Yes, you did," he answered, "that's our outfit."

"No kidding," I said. "I flew with the 389th also. What squadron were you in?"

"The 564th," replied one of the fellows.

"Well, let me introduce myself," I said. "I'm Jim Keeffe, and I was copilot with the Jimmy McArthur crew in the 566th."

"Well I'll be!" said one of the guys. "I'm Al Seamans, and this is Bob Owen. Our pilot's name is John Kendrick who, unfortunately, was really mangled up when we came down over Holland. What mission were you shot down on?"

Come to find out these two had flown on the same mission to Berlin as I had, back on the 8th of March. The story of how their B-24 became crippled virtually paralleled my own. They, too, lost an engine to flak. As they were flying away from the target, a second engine was hit, forcing them to drop out of formation. Somewhere over Holland they ran out of fuel, just as we had, only instead of the crew bailing, John Kendrick decided to take the plane down in an emergency landing.

Unfortunately, things didn't turn out very well for Kendrick and his copilot, Stephan Judd. Upon landing, their B-24 struck a windmill and came to a stop. The nose of the airplane smashed inward, severely mangling Kendrick's legs and badly injuring Judd. Later, as local Dutch people cared for the rest of the crew, Seamans and Owen learned that the Germans had taken Kendrick to a hospital and that Judd had died of his injuries. I remembered back to our own stricken airplane when Mac and I were looking down at all the little canals and country roads, trying to decide whether to bail out or ride the airplane down. Hearing of the terrible fate of Kendrick and Judd, I decided we had made the right decision to abandon the airplane by bailing out.

We talked throughout the afternoon relating our stories to each other. Al Seamans, navigator, and Bob Owen, bombardier, were the only other crewmen from the 389th Bombardment Group that I met as a POW.[11]

Red Cross Parcels

We received food distribution based on the number of men in a combine. When I arrived at Stalag Luft III, our food came from two sources. One source was the Germans, and believe me that wasn't much; a watery something they called soup, little half-rotten potatoes and kohlrabi. These weren't small kohlrabi; they were about as big as a very large cantaloupe, and they were just like eating wood. The Germans also gave us some sugar, some margarine, and the stomach-turning kriegsbrot.

The other source of food was from Red Cross parcels. Actually, this food was paid for by the United States and transported by, and through, the Red Cross. Life would have been grim without these Red Cross parcels. Each parcel was about one foot square by four inches deep and designed to augment the German food for one man per week. We were never given fresh food during the entire time I was a POW.

Parcels came in once a week. Each combine had a designated parcel man, and each block had a Block Parcel King. Once again, everything was well organized. Red Cross parcels were stored in one of the buildings in the Vorlager and distributed from there to the Block Parcel Kings.

Red Cross parcels contained canned food, and the Germans were concerned about our saving this food for escaping. By the time I arrived, an order had come down from the German High Command that we could no longer receive canned food, probably due to the fallout from the massive escape several months before. So each time food was to be distributed, a group of Kriegies had to go to the parcel building in the Vorlager and, under German supervision, open the lids of every tin can in the parcels to be distributed that day. This was done so the food would begin to spoil within a day or two, thus making it fruitless to horde.

After many discussions between the SAOs and the camp commandant, the Germans relented a little and allowed the Kriegies to make just a two or three inch cut in the lid of each can. But every can had to be cut and then put back in the parcel cardboard box. The parcels were then taken to the blocks and distributed to the combines.

AN AMERICAN RED CROSS STANDARD FOOD PARCEL

FEBRUARY - 1944

1 6-oz. carton of Type K-2 biscuit	1 16-oz. tin of Vitamin A fortified oleomargarine
1 8-oz. carton of processed American cheese	1 6-oz. tin of Jam
4 2-oz. bars of chocolate	1 12-oz. tin of pork luncheon meat
1 2-oz. tin of soluble coffee	1 7-3/4-oz. tin of salmon
1 12-oz. tin of corned beef	1 8-oz. carton of white lump sugar
1 16-oz. carton of dried prunes	5 pkgs. containing 100 cigarettes
1 6-oz. tin of liver' paste	2 2-oz. bars of odorless soap
1 16-oz. tin of whole powdered milk	1 pkg. ascorbic acid tablets (Vitamin C)

Contents of an American Red Cross parcel. (Courtesy of USAFA Special Collections Branch, General Clark collection)

We always had two men in our combine ready and waiting for the parcel man when he arrived with our parcels. Their job was to use margarine to seal the cuts in the cans immediately so the contents wouldn't spoil. Someone had already figured out the shelf life of the different foods in these opened cans. For instance, we didn't save a can of salmon even overnight; we ate it the same day we got it. We found out the hard way with salmon. We kept it too long once, and some of the guys got sick. The other stuff, like spam, could be kept almost a week if we did a good job of sealing up the can; liver pate, the same thing.

Two other men in our combine divided up the cigarettes, the soap, and the "D-bars" (military hard chocolate ration bars), which went to each individual. Other items, like margarine, raisins, coffee, sugar, Klim (powdered milk), meat products, and biscuits went into the combine larder, which was the responsibility of one of the men. The cook drew on these supplies for our meals. Again, everything was very well organized.

As the war ground on, transportation into Germany became difficult. After D-Day, a lot of railroad stations were bombed, and the Allies were also strafing trains. This cut down on the number of Red Cross parcels that arrived at our camp. By August the ration had gone from one parcel per man per week to one parcel per two men per week. All the time I was at Stalag Luft III, we were on half-parcels a week.

» *Timeline* «

30 August 1944: Rotterdam - Johannes Berlijn is murdered by an SD firing squad at Concentration Camp Vught.

The Cooler

The punishment for Allied officers who got out of line with the Germans was solitary confinement. There was one building in the Vorlager with cells that we all called "the cooler." It was just a cell, period, and one got very little to eat while in there.

If a prisoner did something that upset the Germans, the maximum sentence they were allowed to give him was thirty days in the cooler, per the Geneva Convention. If a prisoner destroyed property, the Germans could treat him as a criminal, but if a prisoner was just giving them a hard time or refusing to do something, the punishment was solitary confinement for so many days. For example, say a prisoner was sentenced to seven days in the cooler. If he got smart with the man handing down the sentence, it could become fifteen days, or up to thirty days. We had a few men who gave the Germans a really hard time, and they spent a lot of time in the cooler. I never gave the Germans any trouble so I never wound up in there.

Making Some Friends

For some reason, I never became close friends with the men in my combine. Tipton, Burda, Brockmeier, Lawrence, and most of the others were quite friendly, decent men, but we just didn't go much beyond that. Perhaps this was because my story was much different from theirs, since I was on the ground in Holland for several months before being captured and sent to Stalag Luft III.

But I did strike up conversations with many other guys while walking around the camp, and I became friends with a number of them, many of whom were from Block 39. One such fellow was Leonard (Lenny) W. Bughman from Ligonier, Pennsylvania. He lived at a place called Tagshinny Farm. Lenny had been at Center Compound since he was shot down the 16th of August, 1943, a year before I showed up. He was a B-17 copilot and flew with the 546th Bomb Squadron in the 384th Bombardment Group, 8th Air Force.

I also became close with a couple of other fellows from Lenny's combine—Andy Anderson and Bob W. Keller. Andy was a B-24 copilot with the 345th Bomb Squadron, 98th Bombardment Group, 9th Air Force, who was shot down during one of the Ploesti oil field raids.[12] He and the aircraft commander spent almost two weeks adrift in a life raft in the Mediterranean Sea before bring picked up by Italian soldiers. Eventually, after recovering from their ordeal at sea, German soldiers came and transferred both of them to Stalag Luft III

Then Andy spent a bit of time in a Romanian jail and was eventually transferred to Stalag Luft III. Andy was from New York and wanted to be an actor before the war. He played parts in several of the POW stage productions held at the compound theater.

Bob Keller, from New Jersey, also did some acting in the theater, where he and Anderson did a few productions together. Bob was a B-24 copilot with the 330th Bomb Squadron in the 93rd Bombardment Group, also of the 8th Air Force. For a period of time, the 93rd was transferred to North Africa where Bob flew three bombing missions. His group participated in the 1943 Ploesti raid, but he and his crew were delivering a damaged B-24 to Egypt for repairs on the day of the raid, so he didn't go on that mission. He, along with the entire 93rd, was sent back to England after Ploesti. On his first mission from England he was shot down over France. He'd been in Center Compound since October of '43.[13] All these fellows were in the same combine in Block 39, but I palled around mostly with Lenny Bughman. Quite often he'd come by my combine, and we'd go hang out somewhere. He and I became pretty good friends.

Another fellow I met was Jimmy Blackstock who was in Block 40, right next to my block. He was only a year or two older than I and was a Douglas A-20 pilot. He flew with the 47th Bombardment Group (Light) out of Vesuvius

Airfield in Italy.[14] His luck ran out on the 15th of March 1944, a few days after my last mission, and he went down while flying a mission near Arce, Italy. Many years later, Jimmy was best man at my wedding. Jimmy Blackstock was quite the artist I found out, and one day I asked him if he would draw a picture of me free-falling to earth after bailing out of my B-24. A few days later he presented me with a very fine drawing.[15] (See p. 88).

» Timeline «

3 September 1944: Belgium — The liberation of Brussels by the Allies.

4 September 1944: Belgium — The liberation of Antwerp by the Allies.

4 September 1944: Rotterdam — Leendert Valstar "Bertus" is murdered by an SD firing squad at Concentration Camp Vught, along with sixty other Dutch Resistance prisoners.

5 September 1944: Netherlands — Dolle Dinsdag "Crazy Tuesday," German troops begin fleeing toward Germany as Allies advance northeastward through Belgium.

5 September 1944: Rotterdam — Kees van den Engel is transported from Vught to Oranienburg-Sachsenhausen concentration camp in Germany.

10 September 1944: Belgium — Two Dutch Marachaussee, Gradus Antonius Gerritsen and Adrianus Joannes van Gestel, and a mother of eight, Maria Josepha Cornelissen-Verhoeven, are murdered by the SD on the outskirts of Breda, after being betrayed by the traitors "Pauline" and "Anna."

The Germans

When we had evening stage productions, plays or variety shows, or when the orchestra was going to play, we invited the German commandant and his senior officers, and they always came.

The German personnel in the Truppenlager didn't have entertainment like we did. They didn't have enough people to put on different programs, whereas, with two thousand prisoners in our compound, we had the talent and manpower to accomplish things like entertainment for ourselves. Also, we prisoners had a huge credit account with the Germans; therefore, we could purchase or rent whatever we needed, as long as it was available.

Our plays, variety shows, and music productions caused the German soldiers to become very nostalgic. Most of them were far away from home and families, and they missed the normal pleasures of life. They became especially nostalgic around Christmastime when we sang "Silent Night" and other Christmas carols.

Even in some of the small things we had it better than the Germans did. For example, we had decent soap, Swan Soap, which came in our Red Cross parcels. The German soap during the war was terrible. I have no idea what it was made of, but when it became wet, the soap turned very soft and no longer held its shape. Also, the Germans didn't have any chocolate, and their cigarettes were terrible.

As mentioned before, we prisoners conducted ourselves in a military fashion that included hierarchy of rank and position and obeying orders. The German soldiers could sense the difference between how their military organization operated and how we operated. Theirs was very strict, playing out at times with the upper rankers throwing their weight around with their subordinates. Ours was much more relaxed. This was quite an education for the smarter guards. Many of the German guards were just simple farm boys—peasants, while we had some highly educated officers and NCOs.

We were under orders to be correct and proper with the Germans at all times. We had to salute their officers, and they in turn saluted our officers.

One of the rules we had in the camp was that nobody was to deal with the Germans except those people identified and selected by our own X Committee. These were usually Kriegies who came from German communities in the United States and could speak German fluently. I did, however, have a few friendly conversations with one of the guards whose name was Walter. He was a simple family man who only wanted the war to end so he could go back home.

Occasionally, when one of the guards did something wrong, his superior dressed him down. He'd stand toe-to-toe with the poor guy and scream at him. And, of course, we laughed, which made it even worse for him.

When you're being chewed out by a German, you're really being screamed at. The German language is harsh sounding, and it's the best language in the world for yelling and screaming at someone. English doesn't do it. French doesn't even do it. But believe me, being chewed out by a German is quite the experience. When these German superiors got worked up into a lather, spittle sometimes came out of their mouths. Normally they didn't do this sort of thing in our presence because they considered it losing face. But occasionally, it did happen.

» Timeline «

25 September 1944: Netherlands - The Allied offensive to

secure a bridge over the Rhine River at Arnhem, "Operation Market Garden," fails with the tragic result that the German military returns to occupy all of Holland north of the Maas River—including Rotterdam.

White Sheets in the Snow

After the massive escape from North Compound the previous March, and after Oberst von Lindeiner, Stalag Luft III's former commandant, was removed and court-martialed, the new commandant, Oberst Braune, gathered together all the senior Allied officers from each of the compounds.

"I must inform you that in the future, any time an escape of five or more prisoners is discovered, I have orders to call in the Gestapo. You are not going to like this, and believe me, we won't like it either. So please be advised."

After this announcement, our X people instituted tighter controls over escape attempts. They were to approve everything about an escape—whether or not a prisoner was allowed to escape, who else was allowed to go with the escapee, when the escape attempt was to happen. If they decided someone could go, they'd help by supplying him with information about train schedules, money, identity papers and clothing. There were no more mass escapes from any of the compounds after the one in March, but there were other attempts.

I witnessed an escape one night in the middle of December. I went out to the wash hut, right outside our barracks, to brush my teeth before going to bed. There was about four inches of snow on the ground, and as I walked into the wash hut, I saw some guys inside playing musical instruments.

"What the hell are these guys doing out here in the dark and the cold playing their instruments?" I wondered.

There was no light in the wash house, and very little filtered in from the little bit of light outside. One musician motioned with his head for me to look out the window, and when I did, I saw two guys in the process of escaping.

They were lying in the snow alongside the building and covered with white sheets. They timed the searchlight sweeps, then darted toward the warning wire, hopped over it and crossed the thirty foot death zone to the barbed wire fence. Using homemade wire cutters, they cut the wires and got out and away.

The next morning all hell broke loose. As we were getting up, the Germans ran through the compound shouting,

"*Alle raus! Raus!*" (Everyone out! Out!)

They ran us all outside and conducted an appell. Even the sick men had to go. After the count, they found out that two prisoners were missing. To find out who these two prisoners were, they set up a picture parade. We had to stand out there in the snow for about two hours while, one by one, we filed past the desk and were compared to the pictures on our individual locator cards. After the Germans determined who the two prisoners were, we were permitted to go back to our barracks. The two men were eventually caught, returned to camp, and sentenced to time in the cooler.

There was another escape attempt that I knew of. Electrical power was brought into the compound by two wires strung from a power pole outside the main double barbed wire fence to another power pole inside the compound. Wires strung from this pole to other power poles within the compound took electricity to each of the barracks.

One of the prisoners had come up with an escape plan whereby he would go hand-over-hand along one of the electrical wires and over the large, double-barbed wire fence. He got started along the electrical wire, got away from the block itself, but just as he crossed over the warning wire, the electrical wire he was holding onto broke. His escape attempt failed, and much of the compound was darkened when the wire broke.

Even if a man couldn't escape physically, he often wanted to escape to somewhere within the compound to be alone, but it was nearly impossible to find such a place.

There were several times when I just wanted to be alone. "Oh, it would be so nice to just be by myself, with nobody around," I'd think. "Where's a place I can be alone? Maybe I can crawl under the cook house."

I thought of a few places, but each time I went to one of them, several other guys were already there. Fourteen men crammed into a fifteen by fifteen foot square living space among two thousand men imprisoned in a place the size of Center Compound—that didn't leave many spots for me to be alone. Some of the men who were imprisoned much longer than I cracked under the strain, and I'm sure much of their mental anguish came from never being able to be alone.

A New Set of Wings – Kriegie Style

Long before I arrived in camp, several enterprising Kriegies had worked up a pretty clever and ingenious way to reproduce Army Air Forces wings. They gouged out a rectangular depression in a piece of wood, one by three by five inches long. This formed the base of a mold. The mold composition itself was made by taking a brick and rubbing it on rough concrete to get red brick powder. This powder was then mixed with a small amount of Klim and poured into the depression in the wood base. Before this mixture hardened, a real set of wings was pressed into it. After the mix hardened, the set of wings was carefully removed, and what was left was a mold ready to have molten lead poured into it.

Kriegie USAAF pilot wings made for Lt. Keeffe while in Center Compound. (Lt. Col. Keeffe collection)

The lead was collected from the South American Corned Beef and Klim cans that came in the Red Cross parcels. (Klim, milk spelled backwards, was powdered milk and came in a four-by-three-inch round can.) Each of these cans had a hole near the bottom on the side that was sealed with a lead ring. The lead was removed and melted down and poured into the mold. Many times the heat of the lead cracked the mold, and the process had to be started all over again. Once the lead wings cooled and were removed successfully from the mold, a safety pin was soldered to the flat bottom. It was all very labor intensive and time consuming. But if there was one thing we didn't lack, it was time.

I met the fellows who made the wings and asked them how I could get a set made. They told me that if I collected enough lead and ground enough brick powder for two sets of wings, they'd make a set for me and sell the other one. Over a period of a couple of weeks, I went around to the brick garbage bins and searched for tin cans. Eventually I gathered enough cans, about thirty-five or forty of them. I removed the lead and took it to the guys. I also ground down a couple of handfuls of brick powder for them. A short time later, they presented me with a nice set of Kriegie-made wings that I wore from then on.

Unfortunately, there was a bit of a dust up with one or two of the senior officers concerning these wings. They wanted to have sets of wings made for themselves, but they weren't willing to do the dirty work needed to collect the lead and grind the bricks. The chaps making the wings refused to just give the wings away because of the arduous, time-consuming work involved. I sure couldn't blame them.

Mail

According to the Geneva Convention, warring nations had to allow prisoners of war to send mail to and receive mail from their homelands. Methods were set up through a neutral country and through organizations like the International Red Cross to accomplish this. In a situation like a POW camp, mail assumed tremendous importance.

Telegram to Mrs. Keeffe describing her son as "a prisoner of war of the German Government." The telegram arrived two months after Keeffe arrived at Stalag Luft III. (Lt. Col. Keeffe collection)

I went down the 8th of March and was captured on the 27th of July. About the middle of August, I sent my first postcard home. It didn't get there for quite some time.

The first knowledge my parents had that I was even alive and not in a "Missing In Action" status was when they received the Red Cross form letter I had mailed from Rotterdam, from the Jappe-Alberts' house. They received that letter much later, around the time I arrived at Stalag Luft III, five months after I mailed it.

After my purge arrived at Center Compound, the German camp administration at Stalag Luft III sent a list of us new prisoners through their channels to the International Red Cross in Switzerland, and from there the U.S War Department was informed. Eventually, on the 16th of October, the U.S. War Department sent my mother a telegram notifying her that I was a prisoner of war.

The Germans provided us with two-fold letter forms and postcards to use for writing home. The German military produced the postcards, which were not picture postcards. Each prisoner was allowed to send up to three letter forms and four postcards per month. I used my entire allotment. Incredibly, some of the prisoners didn't use up their monthly allotments because they couldn't find enough to say. I had no trouble at all. I mailed my first postcard the day I became Kriegie #7412. It arrived at my parents' home in Seattle not long after they received the telegram stating that I was a prisoner of war.

First post card sent home from Stalag Luft III showing various censor stamps. Two months later, the letter arrived at the Seattle address. (Lt. Col. Keeffe collection)

On November 23, I mailed home another letter. Another post card followed in December.

```
Kriegsgefangenenlager      Datum: Dec. 29, 1944
                           Friday
```

    Dearest Ones -- The New Year is almost here, so
I'm getting off my last Dec. card. Let's hope the
year of '45 will see us all united once more. As yet
I've received only your Xmas card, Mom, the others
should be along soon.

    Peg gave me most of the news, tho. I was so glad
Bob has been OK. Well chums, Love till next time,
                           Jim.

It's interesting to note how many stops a letter made along its route from camp to home and vice versa. Some of the letters had four or five different stamps on them from various German, Swiss, French, and American centers. The "secret" letter I mailed home from the Jappe-Alberts' address on the 21st of March was stamped first by the Dutch Red Cross, then by the French Red Cross on the 5th of June, and finally by the American Red Cross on the 12th of August. Almost five months en route! That particular letter didn't go through any censors, but all the mail from the prison camp did, not only German censors, but U.S. censors also.

We were briefed upon arrival as to what we could and should write about, and what we could not and should not write about. After we wrote our letter forms or postcards, our own people censored them. Somebody in the X Committee was responsible for this. The letters and postcards were taken to the Vorlager, where the Germans who could speak and read English censored our mail. The Germans used a broad-brush and India ink, which worked quite well, to cross out whatever they didn't want to be read. Two or three of the cards I sent home were censored. After the war, I was able to figure out what the Germans had blacked out on one of these cards: "You may write as often as you want." They weren't particularly interested in being swamped with incoming mail, I suppose, so they blacked that statement out.

After the German censors did their censoring, the letters and postcards were packaged up and sent to Switzerland, where the Red Cross then sent them on to the United States, to the War Department. People in the War Department scrutinized each letter and postcard for information, and perhaps censored some of it. When the War Department finished with the mail, it was finally distributed to the addressees. All of my cards and letter forms had *Gepruft*, meaning "checked," stamped on them by the Germans. They also carried the stamp of the American censors.

30 Nov 44
Thanksgiving
Thursday

Nov 30 ?

Dearest Keeffe Family ~   Nov. 23, 1944.

As we are only allowed to send 3 letter forms and 4 cards each month, I've saved most of mine till now in hopes that I could immediately answer your first letter. It hasn't arrived, tho, so I'll write anyhow. Things are routine here, and we're all well.

You might include 4-5 pairs of white wool sweat sox in your next parcel, and 6 handkerchiefs. Send whatever candy you can obtain (I love it) — no cookies or perishables 'cause it takes a long time for parcels to arrive. Don't forget photos of the family and Pat. The weather is chill and rainy. Last week we had our first snow tho it lasted only 3 days. We're indoors considerably due to inclement weather, and as a result play bridge, monopoly, chess, etc. — You should see some of the confections we cook up — and we eat them, too. Cooking may be a woman's art,

but I'll lay money you couldn't do as well considering our utensils and raw material. A year ago today I sent you a telegram, remember? Lots of water has passed under ye olde bridge since then. Say hello to all my friends, and please don't worry. Write often, and don't forget — make those parcels total 11 lbs. (Mercenary cuss, aren't I?) Have a swell time, folks.

A typical three-fold letter sent home from Stalag Luft III. (Lt. Col. Keeffe collection)

I came into the camp in the middle of August, and well into December I still hadn't received any mail. But lo and behold, on the 23rd of December I got my first mail from home! What a wonderful day that was. There were five letters and several pictures of my family!

One of the letters I particularly remember was from my Uncle George. In it he pontificated on how I should bear up under life in a prison camp. He suggested that I do mental arithmetic. I guess he must have thought our situation was more like a concentration camp than a prisoner of war camp.

Families were permitted to send a book parcel of four or five books every few months, and they could send clothing parcels on a limited frequency basis. They were also allowed to send food parcels.

In our letters home, we told our parents, or our next of kin, what we'd like sent to us. There was one very big problem—the lead time. For example, if one of us wrote in the wintertime and said it was cold and it would sure be nice to have some wool socks and flannel pajamas, well, normally the things would show up in July or August. It was very important to think in terms of lead or lag time—from the time a letter was mailed to the time it might take to receive what had been requested.

I didn't receive several of the parcels sent from home until after the war. They had been sent to Switzerland, but by the time they'd gotten there, the war was over, so they'd been returned. I must say, my mom had really done a wonderful job of finding food items to send me. She'd even gone to a store somewhere in Seattle and purchased a vanilla bean for vanilla flavoring. The bean was almost a foot long! That would have made quite a sensation if I had received it while still at Center Compound.

Mail had another level of importance. There were intelligence organizations affiliated with, and operating out of, the Pentagon, and these organizations had secret methods of getting materials in to us, such as information, silk maps, money, parts for radios, and so forth. They sent such items in personal parcels and even in games. But they never involved the Red Cross parcels. If the Germans had found contraband in the Red Cross parcels, they probably would have shut them down.

The Story of Charlie Zubarik

In camp, we heard a lot of stories about other fliers' exploits. A fellow Kriegie by the name of Lt. Charles "Shorty" Zubarik had a very interesting story. He was a simple kid from the coal fields in Pennsylvania. He became an aviation cadet, went through pilot training, and because he was rather small, became a fighter pilot in P-38's. He wound up in the 96th Fighter Squadron, 82nd Fighter Group, one of the first P-38 outfits to go to Africa. They operated out of North Africa, carrying out attacks over Sicily and Italy.

During 1943, there were a lot of labor problems in the United States. The AFL and the CIO were very powerful. The United Mine Workers of America, whose president was John L. Lewis, controlled all of the miners along the east coast. Even though the United States was involved in a war, the union leaders still had their people go out on strike if they felt it was warranted. Of course this angered the citizens, the US government, and the POWs being held in camps. This also angered the men fighting the war because the strikes were delaying the delivery of critical spare parts.

Zubarik and two or three of his friends decided to do something about this, so they went AWOL (Absent WithOut Leave) and flew their P-38's back to the States from North Africa. When they arrived, they put on their uniforms, went to John Lewis' headquarters and somehow got into his inner office. They carried with them a small shoebox-sized parcel wrapped up like a present. They approached Lewis' secretary and said, "We have a gift for Mr. Lewis from the combat people over in North Africa."

The secretary took them into his office. Lewis was there, along with a few of his henchmen. My understanding is that one of the pilots started to present the box to John L. Lewis, but instead of handing him the box, slapped him in the face.

"That's from the people fighting the war in Europe and what we think of you and your people going on strike while we're being shot at and killed. You're interrupting the production of war materials...," and so forth.

Lewis's henchmen immediately jumped on the pilots. Lewis was smart enough to say to his guards, "Don't beat them up. Just escort them out of the building." The pilots were escorted out of the building and then they went back to where their P-38's were parked. They hopped into their planes and flew back to North Africa.

Back at their base, the pilots were court-martialed and kept under house arrest in their tents. Their commander wasn't quite sure what to do with them because he needed them to fly combat in a push into Italy that was already in progress. The commander went over to their tent to speak with them.

"We'd like very much for you to fly combat, and I'll be happy to parole you from your house arrest," he said to them.

I don't know about the others, but Zubarik said, "Sure I'll fly combat. That's why I came over here." So, he went on a mission, ran into some trouble and had to bail out. He wound up a POW at Stalag Luft III and became one of the compound-leadership people.

After the war was over and we'd all returned to the States, the charges against Lt. Charles Zubarik were dropped. It was incredible that some Americans would strike during a war, when other Americans were getting shot at and wounded or killed.

"Good Luck, Yank"

I heard another story that also warrants telling from a chap I met after the war. It was after the D-Day invasion, and Allied troops were already up in Belgium. This chap was also a P-38 fighter pilot and flew on missions out of England. The P-38 had Allison engines, which didn't do well in England's cold, damp weather. He had been on a mission over Germany, and on his way back to England, an engine went out over Holland. He decided to take the plane down rather than bail out.

Leaving his landing gear up, he crash-landed his airplane in a field outside a little town in southern Holland. The local villagers were involved in a soccer game about a quarter to a half mile away from where he landed.

The soccer game came to a halt when the villagers saw his plane come whispering in with both engines feathered and then skid to a stop in the nearby field. Most of the villagers ran to see this strange-looking American airplane with the twin booms and big white stars on it. Some of the other people at the soccer game were smart enough to know that the German police or military would be there in short order, so they headed away from the soccer game, back toward their village.

The P-38 had made a soft belly landing, and the pilot wasn't hurt at all. He unstrapped himself from his harness, climbed out of the cockpit, and started walking away from the plane. Some of the villagers were running toward him, but they were more interested in taking a look at his airplane than at him, so they ran around him and continued on toward the plane. He just wanted to get the hell out of there, so he walked over to the soccer field where several of the villagers had left their bicycles and clothing. He picked out a raincoat and put it on over his flying suit, then got on one of the bicycles and started following the people who were headed toward the little village.

Just as he was pedaling the bicycle onto the road, German soldiers came roaring past him in trucks, going in the opposite direction. Somehow or other, by using triangulation, the Germans had figured out where his plane had come down and were on their way to capture the pilot and secure the airplane.

A young lady who'd been watching the soccer game was also on her bicycle heading back to the town. The pilot pulled up beside her, and they rode all the way into the village together. Occasionally she turned and looked at him, and he smiled back at her. As they approached an intersection, she turned to him and said, "Good luck to you, Yank." She turned left, smiled once more at him and pedaled off. He waved to her and kept on going, right through the little village. He headed south, and within two or three days he was spirited across a major river in South Holland and made contact with the Allied forces in Belgium. He was one of the lucky ones who made it back to England to fly and fight another day.

The Days Turning Cold and Gray

Snow was already in the air by the end of November. The days were mostly gray, wet, and chilly, and I could tell that it was going to get a lot colder as we moved into winter. Earlier I had picked up a U.S. Army GI greatcoat from the clothing store in the Vorlager. I wore it most days now. The GI greatcoat was made from about eight pounds of thick wool. It came to just below the knees, and believe me, it was warm.

The 30th of November was just one more gray, cold, and windy day. But it was Thanksgiving, and some of the guys really went out of their way to make it a memorable time. The day before Thanksgiving, a couple of the fellows in our combine made up fourteen personalized invitation cards, one for each member of the combine. Each card was a four by six inch piece of paper folded left to right. On the front was a drawing of a can of spam placed lengthwise on a plate. The can had a cooked turkey neck, wings and drum sticks attached to it.

The menus for all three meals of the day were on the inside of the card: Breakfast—Orange Juice, Cream of Wheat, Toast, Coffee; Lunch—Toasted Cheese Sandwich, Noodle Soup, Cookies, Tea; Dinner—Spam, Whipped Potatoes, Creamed Peas & Carrots, Toast, Chocolate Pie & Whipped Cream, Coffee. Brew, Raisin Cake, Tea. All fourteen of us signed our names on the back of each invitation. The next day was Thanksgiving, and even with the dreariness outside, it turned out to be a very nice day inside.

On the16th of December, the Germans fired off their last main offensive in the West, an offensive that became known as the Battle of the Bulge. This was Hitler's last desperate effort to split the Allied armies and push on to Antwerp. He launched his surprise attack through the Ardennes, a heavily-forested mountain region in southeastern Belgium. As news of the battle came into our camp, we followed it closely on our war map in the Situation Room. At times like that, rumors flew around the camp like wildfire.

"Be careful about what you say," the senior officers always warned. "Don't start rumors because they can make morale go way up, or way down."

Thanksgiving Day personalized invite card for the Kriegies of Combine 7, Block 43. All the menu items were made from the contents of Red Cross food parcels. (Lt. Col. Keeffe collection)

As soon as the Battle of the Bulge began, morale went way, way down. During the next two weeks it went down even further.

On the other hand, the Germans' morale spiked up a notch or two. They began to laugh and joke more and strut around with the confidence they used to have. To them, the battle was a sign that maybe, just maybe, Der Führer (Hitler) was going to pull out his "secret weapons," which he was always proudly proclaiming his experts were working on.

There were some very intelligent people in Center Compound, including a general, four or five full colonels, some light colonels and majors, and, therefore, a lot of capability. These people held lectures for us and explained that if the German offensive thrust was successful, if the Germans got all the way to Antwerp, we wouldn't be going home soon.

We had several jingles in camp that we used to boost our morale by telling ourselves when we might be liberated:

"Home alive, in 45."

"Fort Dix, in 46."

(I forget 47)

"Golden Gate, in 48."

All we could think about was liberation and going home.

» *Timeline* «

5 December 1944: Rotterdam (2 p.m.) — The SD hit the house

*of Dr. Jappe-Alberts and the entire family is imprisoned
at Scheveningen Prison in The Hague. The Jewish Cohen
family is sent to Westerbork concentration camp, northeast of
Rotterdam.*

*5 December 1944: Rotterdam (3 p.m.) — The SD hit the house
of Anton Sanders. Anton and wife Cocky "dive" into hiding.*

*19 December 1944: Rotterdam — Folkert Elsinga is captured
by the SD while operating a secret radio transmitter. He is
sent to Scheveningen prison in The Hague.*

Christmas and New Year's, 1944

The battle in the Ardennes was still raging on Christmas Day. Although the Germans had stalled far short of Antwerp, our spirits were still very low. BBC news broadcast that the Americans were surrounded in the strategic Belgian city of Bastogne.

Christmas place card for Kriegies in Combine 7. (Lt. Col. Keeffe collection)

The German camp staff, though, made an effort to raise some Christmas spirit by bringing in the only meat I ever saw while a POW. It wasn't much per Kriegie, and it was horse meat, but it was meat nonetheless, and we appreciated their effort. Sometimes, I felt that we actually ate better than the average

German guard because we at least had the contents of the Red Cross parcels to supplement the monotonous German food.

Our combine had another invitation printed up outlining the Christmas meals, beginning at 1930 hours December 24, with a final meal of Brew, Raisin Cake and Coffee at 2100 hours the next day, Christmas Day.

Instead of eating the evening meal on Christmas Eve, I went to the theater to watch a stage production. When I returned to the combine no one was there. I noticed that a little present had been placed on each person's bunk. They were wrapped in paper and tied with a string. I picked up the small package on my bunk and untied the string. Inside I found a pack of cigarettes, a few pieces of D-bar, and a note from Brockmeier, Burda and Schauer with the simple words, "Merry Christmas." Tears welled up in my eyes and I felt very humbled. These three men had saved up packs of cigarettes and D-bars from their laundry operation—who knows how long that took—all for the purpose of giving each of their combine fellow officers a small gift for Christmas. I felt rather small right then as I held my gift because I had kind of made fun of their operation a few times in the past. When the three of them showed up later that evening, I told them how much I appreciated their very thoughtful gift. The next day, Christmas Day, many of us Catholics went to mass.

New Year's arrived, and with it came more cold and snow. Some enterprising fellows packed down the snow in a large flat area out in the exercise field and somehow made an ice skating rink on it. They'd gotten clamp-on ice skates from the International Y.M.C.A. in Switzerland. (A Swedish man named Henry Soderberg was the representative for the International Y.M.C.A. in Geneva, Switzerland, and it was through his efforts that band instruments, athletic supplies, and many of the books for the libraries in the compounds were brought in.)

The Kriegies in Block 55, located at the far southwest corner of Center Compound, threw a New Year's Eve party for the entire compound. The men in one half of the block put forth a tremendous effort and moved all of their combine structures up against the inside of the main wall separating the two barrack halves, thus creating a large open area. The compound band set up at one end and played music all evening long, while Kriegies came and went from all the other barracks. It was a great time and brought some good cheer to us, as most all of us were feeling pretty low and very homesick.

The Russians Rolling Westward

By December, it was clear to us that the Russians were on the move in the East. They stalled for a few weeks at the end of the year but began advancing westward again in January. I spent a lot of time in the Situation Room next to the library, and it was obvious from listening to the daily news that the Russians were pushing back the Germans relentlessly. Over the OKW radio, the German news spoke of "strategic relocations," but from the BBC we got the more believable news that the Germans were in a fighting retreat. It wasn't unusual to see a German officer or two in our Situation Room looking at the map and reading the news posted from the BBC; they knew they couldn't rely on the news coming from their own OKW.

Rumors began to circulate in early January, and our senior officers began to warn us to prepare ourselves.

"You'd all better get your clothing in first-class order, and you'd better start exercising."

Kriegies walking the perimeter next to the warning wire. Looking west from South Compound into West Compound. It didn't matter what the weather conditions were. Most important was staying in shape, mentally and physically. (Courtesy of USAFA Special Collections Branch, General Clark collection)

We all began to walk extra rounds around the perimeter track.

During the previous couple of weeks the German guards and camp administrators had become increasingly nervous and antsy. They weren't dummies. Stalag Luft III was directly in the path of the advancing Russian Army, and the Germans knew it was only a matter of time before they arrived. There was collaboration between the American and British senior officers and the camp commandant, Oberst Braune.

The Allied senior officers let Braune know in no uncertain terms, "The British government and the American government will hold you and the

Luftwaffe responsible if any attempt is made to eliminate the prisoners. We would hope that this will never happen because there has been a reasonable respect between the Allied Air Forces and the Luftwaffe."

Oberst Braune alerted our senior officers, "Please get your people in good physical condition and prepared equipment-wise because we don't know what will happen."

By late January, the level of activity and nervous energy increased noticeably and we prepared for whatever lay ahead. Clothing was a big concern. Winter had already hit with a vengeance, and it was cold and snowy. By now most of us had acquired a heavy wool GI greatcoat, wool army glove liners, and a couple of pairs of wool socks. I was very fortunate because I had been issued first-class boots when I arrived in Center Compound, back in the middle of August.

I wanted to make some sort of a carrying bag, so I took a summer long-sleeved khaki shirt, buttoned it up and sewed the bottom closed. Then I over-lapped the two sleeve cuffs and sewed them together to form a closed loop. This made a nice makeshift bag into which I stuffed my spare clothing, papers, and other odds and ends. I packed a couple of letters I'd received from home but left the rest on my bunk to save weight. I've always regretted not bringing all the letters with me. When my makeshift bag was full I could put my head and one arm through the loop made by the sewn-together sleeves, and the bag would hang down my side. I also planned to roll the two thin blankets I had length-wise, then tie them together and hang them on my other side. We had been issued GI wool scarves, and some of the Kriegies made hoods out of them.

A few of the more enterprising men made suitcases out of tin cans. Others swiped wood and made sleds. The sleds, however, weren't very good because we had no metal for the runners, but as long as the snow lasted, using them would be better than carrying things.

During those last hectic days, we led kind of a dual life—a normal prison camp life on the one hand, while at the same time we were preparing ourselves physically and mentally and getting our clothing and equipment ready in case we were to be handed over to the Russians, or worse. We had a contingency plan if the Germans were to try to kill us. Each compound had come up with a plan for using table legs and other items to fight the Germans, even though we knew we'd be massacred, because we had no guns.

Day by day we didn't know what was going to happen, but we certainly knew that whatever it was wouldn't be long in coming. One of the big questions on everyone's mind was whether or not the camp guards would shoot us if the order was given.

After the war, I found out a bit more about the workings of the German SS and the Luftwaffe, regarding the running of the Luftwaffe officer camps, including Stalag Luft III. Following the massive escape from North Compound on the 24th of March 1944, Hitler had become furious.

"You and the Luftwaffe are incapable of keeping these people penned up! I want the Waffen-SS to take over!" he'd shouted at Goering.[16]

So Reichsfuhrer-SS Heinrich Himmler, head of the Schutzstaffel (SS) and its security arm, the Sicherheitsdienst (SD), appointed SS General Gottlob Berger, his trusted hatchet man, to take charge of all the Luftwaffe POW camps. Soon afterwards, General Berger came to Stalag Luft III on an inspection.

"If I bring my SS guards in here, there is going to be a war with the prisoners, and only one side is going to win, us! There is no way my SS guards are going to take what your Luftwaffe guards have been taking from these prisoners," Berger informed Oberst Braune. Berger was referring to the prisoners' snide comments and occasional laughter toward the guards that he had witnessed during his inspection.

Berger was definitely one of the bad guys. He was especially brutal to thousands of Russian prisoners under his charge. But he wasn't a stupid man. He could see where the war was headed, so he set about working both sides to his advantage. One thing he knew for certain—he couldn't allow his Waffen SS troops to guard Allied officer POWs, no matter what Hitler ordered. There would be an absolute massacre of prisoners, and that would go badly for him after the war ended. So he set up a front office in Berlin as a shield between Himmler's SS and the actual security operations of the Luftwaffe camps. Arrangements were made with the Luftwaffe senior people in Berlin.

"You keep running the camps. Information from you will pass through me to Himmler, and from Himmler, through me to you, and I won't bring SS troops in to control your camps," he told them.

This was acceptable to the Luftwaffe, and Himmler never found out that the SS didn't take direct control of the Luftwaffe camps.

Had Hitler put out the order to exterminate us at that time, Berger would have had to bring in his SS troops, and they'd have had to wrest control away from the Luftwaffe guards. The Luftwaffe guards were mostly old men who had been wounded in combat or who weren't front- line soldiering material any longer. They wouldn't have put up much of an argument. A percentage of the guards were physically capable, but mostly they were second- or third-class soldiers. Once the SS was in charge, all hell would have broken loose. This scenario was a distinct possibility, and our camp leadership had planned for several options. One option was to fight the Germans however we could.

On Saturday, the 27th of January 1945, Hitler was informed that the Russians were on the move again and were only fifteen or so miles from Stalag Luft III.

"Well, move them! Today! And take away their trousers and their boots!" it is said that he shouted.

Hitler had decided to keep the POWs as hostages to bargain with when dealing with the Allied command, and he certainly didn't want the Russians liberating them. He ordered the camp evacuated and all POWs moved into southern Germany, about four hundred miles away. Goering passed the information on to Luftwaffe Headquarters but told them to forget about taking away our shoes and pants.

That same Saturday, we had about six inches of snow on the ground in Center Compound. In the evening, I went to a stage production at the theater. The play ended around 8:30 p.m., and I made my way back to my combine. When I entered the barracks, everything was in an uproar. I was immediately informed that the word had come down that we were to prepare to move out in half an hour. Half an hour!

Hitler's orders had traveled quickly to Stalag Luft III's commandant, probably arriving in the early evening. The German Lager Officer for each compound was sent to inform the senior officer of each compound that they had to be ready to move within half an hour. It didn't actually happen that soon, thank God.

We had our gear ready for this situation. Each of us gathered up whatever we'd put together. I quickly stuffed all my spare clothing inside my makeshift bag and slipped it over my head, followed by my two rolled up blankets. Somehow, I managed to store some paper work and drawings safely in the shirt bag, but I don't remember how exactly. All I know is they made it out of the camp with me and eventually home.

Then we waited.

The evening wore on with lots of nervous small talk. Shortly after midnight, we were called to form up outside. Snow had been falling all evening long, and the wind had picked up considerably. Outside in the dark and cold, we all stamped our feet and shuffled around as well as we could, trying to stay warm.

About thirty minutes later, the guards ordered us back into the barracks. By this time the Kriegies in some of the other compounds had already been marched out and away into the dark, cold, miserable unknown.

End Notes
POW

1.   Sgt. John Jenkins was taken to Stalag Luft VII located near Bankau, Silesia (Poland). Later, during the January 1945 evacuation of the eastern German POW camps, he was marched to Stalag III A near Luckenwalde in NW Germany.

2.   Some of the hometowns were verified by Elmer Brockmeier on his web site at http://www.littlestar.com/brock /story10.htm

3.   The airplane name and mission details are from *Tipton's Crew* by P. La Ferriere and Vernon Burda. Copyright 1994 by Beautiful America Publishing Co. Permission granted by Vernon Burda's daughter, Lezlie Burda Beach.

4.   'The Eagle Squadron', in this context, was what the Kriegies in Center Compound called their senior officers. There were also official Eagle Squadrons that were made up of American officers who were fighter pilots and who'd flown with the British RAF (Royal Air Force) during the early months of the buildup and organization of the U.S. 8th Army Air Force in England.

5.   Actual facts from *33 Months as a POW in Stalag Luft III* by Gen. Albert P. Clark (pg 121)

6.   A crystal set is a very simple radio receiver. It requires no external power, only that which is supplied by radio waves collected by a wire antenna.

7.   In April of 2008, I finally learned the truth about what had happened during Maxie Weinstein's mission. Through corresponding with a Dutch man named Alexander Tuinhout, who had researched the downing of Maxie's B-17, I became convinced that Pollock had looked me straight in the eye back in Center Compound and had lied to me point blank.

   All these years, I'd held less than pleasant thoughts about Maxie because of what Pollock had told me in his combine. I knew that Maxie was a BS'er, and I'd caught him in quite a few lies of his own, but regarding who bailed out of the stricken airplane first, Maxie was the one telling the truth. I feel badly about harboring such ill-feelings toward him all these years, and it sickens me to think that Pollock lied straight to my face. Aircraft commanders have a duty to their crew to insure that they are all out before they themselves leave a stricken airplane. Pollock's actions were shameful and cowardly, and he should have been brought up on charges. My understanding is that someone did bring charges against him, but they were quietly dropped. By whom and for what reason, I do not know.

   Not only did Maxie NOT bail out of the B-17 first as Pollock said, but he had stayed in the stricken bomber long enough to help the navigator, whose right arm was disabled from flak shrapnel, attach his parachute chest pack. Then, before he jumped, Maxie made sure the wounded navigator had exited the airplane. This was AFTER Pollock and Raim had already jumped. Maxie Weinstein showed great courage by his actions in helping the navigator before himself.

   There is a mystery concerning Pollock and Raim. I know that I met them in Center Compound and that we talked about Maxie Weinstein. The two men I met confirmed undeniably that they were the pilot and copilot of the B-17 Weinstein crewed in when they were shot down on a raid to Emden.

   However, in the ledgers compiled by Ewell McCright, their names are recorded as being in South Compound, Block 130. McCright, a B-17 bombardier, was given the task by then Lt. Colonel 'Bub' Clark, South Compound's "Big X," of interviewing and recording the particulars of every POW in South Compound. When the camp was evacuated at the end of January 1945, McCright secreted out the journal volumes that contained information on all 2,194 South Compound prisoners. He was posthumously awarded the prestigious "Legion of Merit" medal for his actions concerning the journal.

How Pollock and Raim could be in Center Compound AND South Compound makes no sense. I never heard of any officer airmen being transferred between compounds. This is one of those mysteries that may never be solved.

Author's note: Other sources mention that POWs, on occasion and for various reasons, did indeed move from one compound to another. Val Burgess, niece of Vernon Burda, has recorded many oral histories of ex-POWs, and agrees that POWs did in fact transfer between compounds. Arnold Wright, who published Ewell McCright's ledgers under the title Behind the Wire, *in 1993, also agrees that POWs were moved between compounds.*

8. After the war, David Wolter left the military, went through medical school and became a doctor, an obstetrician, delivering babies. He eventually went back into the Air Force as a medical doctor and ended up stationed in Wiesbaden, Germany. My recollection is that he was able to visit the Gestapo compound where he had been brutally tortured. This compound had been completely rearranged after WW II. Later on, he left the Air Force and became an obstetrician again on Mercer Island, Washington. David Wolter's MACR number was 2795.

9. I was still having these nightmares when I went back into the Air Force, and they lasted until about 1955. I scared the hell out of those sleeping near me when I had them. When my B-29 group from Fairchild Air Force Base over at Spokane went to Okinawa, we officers were put in open bay Quonset huts with steel cots. One night I woke up screaming. My left arm had gone to sleep, and I was yanking on it with my right arm and shouting, "No! No! No!"

If I had been picked up by the Gestapo, or the Gruenepolizei (the Secret [Green] Field Police), or the Feldgendarmerie (the Military Police), or the Kriminalpolizei (the Criminal Police), I probably would have been killed outright or brutalized like David Wolter.

Instead, I was betrayed to Abwehr, German Counterintelligence. Abwehr is kind of a silly word. After WWI, the Germans were not permitted to have any kind of a military organization, except for a very small self-protection unit. No airplanes, no artillery, no navy, so on and so forth. They surreptitiously created a complete military organization, but used funny names. German Counterintelligence took this term 'Abwehr', which means defense.

10. When I got home, my mother had me take all the items she had saved, my letters and the contacts from the government, and put them all together in a scrapbook. I took my diary made from cigarette papers and typed it out on normal paper and then threw the cigarette papers away. I wish I had kept the original diary.

11. John Kendrick eventually had both his legs amputated and, although he survived combat and the crash landing of his B-24, he was killed when the hospital plane taking him home from Europe crashed. Reprinted with permission from Dr. Ray L. Sisson who wrote "Al Seamans' Story."

12. The oil fields around Ploesti, Romania, supplied Hitler's military machine with 30 percent of its petroleum requirements. The first major low-level bombing attack on the refinery complex, in August 1943, temporarily reduced the output of oil, but it was a strategic disaster for the 15th Air Force, resulting in the loss of fifty-four bombers and over six hundred airmen. A second wave of bombing missions against Ploesti, between April and August 1944, was highly successful, this time permanently destroying 85 percent of its capabilities.

13. Thanks to Stowe Keller, the son of Bob Keller, for much of the information about his dad. Stowe also supplied some good information about Andy Anderson.

14. "Light" refers to twin-engine bombers like the B-25, B-26 and A-20. Four-engine bombers like the B-17 and B-24 were referred to as "Heavies." Their squadron and group numbers were designated with (H); i.e. 566th Bomb Squadron (H), 389th Bomb Group (H).

15. Jimmy Blackstock drew a lot of pictures while at Stalag Luft III, and later at Stalag VII A. He was able to bring them all home with him after the war, but sadly, the briefcase he had them in was stolen.

16. The Waffen-SS was the fighting arm of the Schutzstaffel, which was better known as the SS. In many battles it fought along side of, but was never absorbed into, the regular German army.

The March

Evacuation

The first group out was South Compound. They were probably moved out first because they had caused the Germans the most trouble. After being ordered to form up, they were marched out about 11:30 p.m. This was no small group of people. Each of the six compounds held around 2,000 POWs, plus quite a few guards and camp staff. West Compound followed South Compound, another 2,200 men. The next to go was North Compound.

The poor old guards were all dressed up in their heavy woolen winter uniforms and boots, and they were carrying packs and rifles. With their rifles weighing close to ten pounds including ammunition, the guards were overloaded.

About four o'clock in the morning, we in Center Compound were brought outside again into the snow, formed up, counted, and then marched out into the biting cold teeth of a blizzard. I pulled my long woolen coat tighter around me and tucked my head down to minimize the effects of the blowing snow. We all had some sort of bag or case to carry what precious little we had, and some of the men pulled these on their makeshift sleds. I had slung the loop of my shirt bag over my head and onto my right shoulder, letting the rest of the bag hang down my left side. My blanket roll was over my left shoulder and hung down my right side.

We went through the gate into the Vorlager where things were pretty chaotic. Even though it was the dead of night and the snow was blowing, the camp was fairly lit up because everyone had turned on the lights in their combines and many of the blocks had outside lights turned on. As we went past the parcel building, there were two or three men inside heaving Red Cross food parcels out to each one of us. The SAOs had convinced the Germans that we would need the food if the call to evacuate was given, and the Germans had agreed.

I caught the cardboard box pitched to me and got right back into formation. No one stopped as these parcels were thrown; we just kind of broke ranks, caught a parcel and then formed up again, all the while on the move. Each block marched in its own column, three men abreast and about fifty-five men deep. We moved through the Vorlager and then through the west gate into the Truppenlager. Most of the Germans in the Truppenlager had already been moved out. The wooden buildings stood empty and looked hurriedly abandoned, just like the ones in our compound. We continued through the Truppenlager to the main gate. Once through that we immediately turned left and headed west along the dark northern perimeter road. Popeye had mustered about a hundred and fifty Germans guards and they were waiting outside the Truppenlager. Many of them spread out along the outside edges of our column as we came by. I suppose the other guards fell in at the tail end of the long column.

As we marched, we tore the Red Cross boxes open and threw away everything except what we wanted to keep. For instance, I threw away the cigarettes and the soap. I didn't want to carry the Klim powdered milk, so I pitched that also. I kept the Spam, the prunes, the corned beef, and the D-bar and crammed those into my coat pockets. I also threw away the coffee mixture and a few other items.

The road was completely covered with litter and junk. By the time Center Compound was on the move, six to seven thousand men had already passed down the main road out of camp. Like us, most of these men had also been given food parcels and they'd thrown away the stuff they didn't want. It was like marching across a garbage dump in the snow, except it wasn't garbage, just tons of unwanted items from freshly opened Red Cross boxes.

Center Compound was followed by East Compound, probably at about five o'clock in the morning. Belaria, located across the railroad tracks on the other side of Sagan, left about six o'clock in the morning.

Not everyone left Stalag Luft III, however. In the Vorlager of North Compound was a long building used as a hospital. There were quite a few sick prisoners there who couldn't make the march. They were left behind with a few guards for a couple of weeks. Because they were the only people left at the camp, they had at their disposal all the food they could eat, plus plenty of coal to stay quite warm. They were also able to wander around inside the different compounds because the gates had all been left open and the Germans guards did nothing to stop them. Eventually trucks arrived at the camp and picked up the sick prisoners. They were taken to a railroad station at Sorau (the modern Polish name is Zary) where they were put on railroad cars and eventually rejoined us.

I found out much later that the Russians didn't show up at Sagan for another two weeks. What they would have done if we'd still been in the camp is a good question and is open to much speculation. They would have had a problem because we were all officers in Stalag Luft III. There were several very high-ranking American and British officers and sons of high officials in the camp. The Americans and the British were supporting the Russian war effort by providing them with war materials and funding. The Germans would have gotten word to the Allies that they had abandoned the camp and that the Russians had taken it over. The Russians might very well have tried to move us all into Russia and use us as a bargaining chip. It would have been very interesting.[1]

As we headed west along the northern perimeter road, we passed the rest of the Truppenlager. Next we passed the Vorlager of North Compound. One of the barracks in North Compound was burning. I imagine that one of the British fellows had intentionally left a candle burning around a heap of paper so the building would burn down.

Barracks 104 in North Compound where tunnel Harry of the Great Escape began. It was set on fire by Kriegies as they were marched out of camp, as a final protest for the murder of fifty captured escapees.
(Courtesy of Maxwell Air Force archives and Marilyn Walton)

We continued on to the west and marched passed West Compound. This was the first time I had seen any of the compounds west of us, and for the first time I realized just how big Stalag Luft III was. It was huge! Then we passed portions of another large German prisoner of war camp named Stalag VIII C that we didn't even know existed. Soon after this, we intercepted a narrow little highway connecting Sagan to a town farther south named Halbau. We turned left (south) and began what turned out to be a very long walk down the road.

It was snowing hard and bitterly cold. By the time we headed south, there was about a foot of snow on the ground. The people marching before us had compressed the snow, so it wasn't too difficult to walk. By now we were far away from any camp lights, and it was black as Hades except for a faint ghostly glow, probably from the snow reflecting what little light there was. We traveled along the road, passing through two or three small villages.

We in Center Compound were very lucky because Center Compound, besides having all the surplus full colonels, had General Arthur Vanaman, the highest-ranking Allied officer in camp. The other American and British compounds only had senior officers in the rank of colonel or group captain. General Vanaman had been the American Army Air Attaché to the Germans in Berlin prior to WWII. He knew the senior Luftwaffe officers and was familiar with the Luftwaffe manuals. One of these manuals contained the rules for conducting a march, including a reference to how much rest time men were to be given while on a march—"ten minutes of rest for every fifty minutes of marching." He made the Germans adhere to their own manual's instructions during our march.

The previous evening, when we were told we'd be evacuating the camp, Oberst Braune had offered General Vanaman a motor vehicle to drive him along the marching route.

"Do you have vehicles for all of my 12,000 men?" Vanaman asked.

Of course, he'd been told that that was impossible.

"Well, if they march, I march," the General stated.

Hitler had ordered the Luftwaffe to take our boots and our trousers and to shoot anybody who couldn't keep up or tried to escape. The Luftwaffe refused to take our boots and our trousers, which was extremely fortunate for all of us because we wouldn't have survived even the first night. I didn't hear of any case where the Germans shot a straggler or someone attempting to escape.

Before we left Stalag Luft III, General Vanaman told Oberst Braune that he wanted stragglers picked up, and the German colonel agreed to do so. Then, General Vanaman passed the word to his senior officers that if anyone fell out and couldn't keep up or if there was any shooting, he was to be informed immediately. He took his place at the head of the column and set the pace of the march. Every fifty minutes by his watch, he stopped the column. The German officer in charge wasn't very happy about this, but since Vanaman was a general he grudgingly gave in.

After a couple of hours, the men quieted down and settled into the march. There was some chatting among us, but mostly we kept our thoughts to ourselves. We were all very happy to be outside our cage, outside the camp. But it wasn't a pleasant experience. We didn't know where we were going, and we didn't know how long we'd be marching like this; we'd been given no information. We were just brought out into the snow, counted, and marched off. All night long the snow fell in heavy thick clouds of cold, stinging flakes. The temperature must have been near zero. I have never been so cold and miserable in all my life

After a few hours, the dark night slowly began to lighten, signaling the approach of a gray dawn. It was still snowing heavily. As it became lighter, I began to make out the other men I was marching close to. They were carrying every type of pack imaginable, stuffed with whatever each man had chosen to bring. They were pulling all sorts of makeshift sleds. A few guys were even dragging wooden benches they'd flipped over for sleds. Some of the sleds pulled more easily than others, but they all seemed to be better than nothing. The Goons walked beside our column with their own rucksacks, and some of them picked up the food and clothing items many Kriegies had discarded.

We progressed through a few little villages. At one point during the morning, we came to what seemed to be a big hill. Actually, it was merely a vehicle overpass that crossed over the major divided autobahn from Berlin to Breslau. To me, in the weak light that filtered through the thick gray clouds, it looked like a snow-covered hill as I chugged up the incline along with the rest of the men.

As we came down the other side, I saw several buses parked along the side of the road. Standing in the snow and sitting in the buses were German soldiers on their way to the front. They were wearing white snow uniforms over their regular army uniforms. Some of us spoke to them and gave them cigarettes. We told them we were Allied prisoners being marched west. There was no animosity between us, and there was no trouble. In fact, our hearts went out to these soldiers because they were being bused to the front lines to try to stop the Russians. I figured that ninety percent of them wouldn't live very long.

After a brief rest we continued on. The snow was still falling heavily, but the temperature was warming up a bit. Fifty minutes marching, ten minutes rest, and then up again for another fifty minutes of marching. Somewhere along the line, I managed to eat some graham crackers and prunes from two of the Red Cross boxes.

When we were first marched out of camp, we were a fairly tight column of three men across and maybe a couple of hundred yards long. By now, I wouldn't have been surprised if our column stretched out a half mile or more. We were all extremely tired and God-awful cold, but I think the German guards were worse off than most of us Kriegies. We were all fairly young, in our twenties and early thirties. Most of the regular guards were, I'm sure, in their late forties and fifties. We had been warned and encouraged for several weeks to get in shape and be ready to go, but the guards had not. Most of them were WWI soldiers, or soldiers of the current war who'd been wounded, or they were farmers and not in very good condition. They were having a real tough time carrying their heavy rifles and rucksacks.

A couple of guards asked the Kriegies marching next to them to carry their rifles for a while. One old guard up a little way from me had been muttering a single word all morning and into the afternoon. I thought he was saying *Mutter* (mother), but he was saying *müde* (tired).

He was walking hunched over, and every few steps he said *müde*, took a few more steps and said *müde*, and then again and again, almost like a mantra. This poor man was nearly exhausted, yet he had to plod on with the rest of us.

Taken with a secret camera, this photo shows POWs, some pulling make-shift sleds, marching south from Stalag Luft III. (Courtesy of USAFA Special Collections Branch, General Clark collection)

The Lutheran Church in Halbau

All day long, as we marched down the snowy road, I noticed snow-covered lumps on the ground in front of some of the tightly-shuttered, closed-up houses we passed. We found out later that these lumps were the bodies of civilian refugees who had been fleeing west and had tried to get into the houses looking for help and sustenance. They had died right there, exhausted and frozen, because the people inside wouldn't open their doors to give them help.

We finally reached the town of Halbau[2] well after dark. South Compound had been force-marched very quickly past Halbau long before we arrived, and West and North Compounds had also already gone through.

Just before entering the town, we were stopped and told to wait while Popeye scoured the town for a place large enough to hold all of Center Compound's

2,000 POWs for the night. He finally located such a place, and we were marched into town a short way. Then we turned left up a side street to a Lutheran church. The church was in a walled enclosure with graves and mausoleums in the back. All during our march, Popeye never left the column until every single POW had been put to bed, one way or another. Frequently, bed was outside in the snow.[3]

We were fortunate in our combine of fourteen guys because we were among the first ones into the church. We wound up in a pew on the left side about a quarter of the way back from the altar area. Behind us more and more Kriegies moved in through the double entrance doors, and the small church filled up quickly. About five hundred to six hundred of us were crammed in, making the church look like a beehive. There wasn't nearly enough room for all the prisoners, but Popeye didn't stop until he found places for all of them. Some of them camped in the snow up against the lee side of the church, quite a few got into the mausoleums in the back graveyard, and others were taken to a school a block away. Somehow, Popeye came up with a few bundles of straw for those outside to sit and lie on. It was miserable for those outside. Inside it wasn't much better, but at least we were out of the weather. It was so crowded in the church that we had to sit up in the pews all night long.

The Lutheran church in Halbau, and a mausoleum behind it, where the 2,000 POWs from Center Compound spent their first night during the march. (Author's collection)

Some of the men had diarrhea. On either side of the church about midway to the altar were small doors to the outside. Those darn doors opened and closed all night long as fellows moved outside to relieve themselves, so it didn't stay very warm inside. General Vanaman, Colonel Spivey, and the other full colonels of the Eagle Squadron took over the sanctuary area of the church. The general slept right in front of the altar.

I'd been sitting in the pew with my feet under the kneelers for about twenty minutes when I felt them becoming hot. My first thought was that I had frostbite. I reached down to massage my feet but quickly withdrew my hand because I had touched a very hot pipe. The Lutheran minister, a German, had fired up the boiler and it was sending steam through a pipe under the kneeler. That was a very kind, thoughtful thing for that chap to do.

After getting as settled into the pew as I could get, I started writing a little diary in the notebook I'd made out of cigarette papers while in Center Compound. I had acquired a couple of pencils back at camp which I stashed away, and these came in handy now. The word went around that the Goons were going to get us some hot food, but nothing came of it. C'est la Guerre.

It was so miserable and cold in the church, even with the steam pipe at my feet, that I didn't sleep a wink all night. The next morning we were rousted out of the church around eight o'clock and we stood around outside stamping our feet and flapping our arms, trying to get warm. It took almost an hour to form up all 2,000 of us again into a column. Then we were marched back to the main road we'd been on the day before, heading southwest, and struck off again.

We marched all day and occasionally passed columns of refugees the Nazis had ordered out of their homes in larger cities like Breslau and Sagan. The refugees we saw were in very bad shape. They had farm carts heaped with their belongings, old people and children. They were slowly trudging to the west as well, fleeing from the advancing Russians. Somewhere along the way, Vern Burda came up with a sled and several of us from Combine 7 piled our belongings on it and took turns pulling it down the road.

Diary Entry

4 km West of FREIWALDAU, Monday evening - 29 Jan

> *...we marched until 4:30 pm—a total of 14 kilometers today. The blizzard increased in intensity, and the wind velocity increased to about 30 mph. Tonight 600 of us are housed in a barn 50' x 150'. God—what hell on earth this is. It almost seems as tho we'd be better off dead. I ate a can of cold corned beef, a few prunes, and a couple of crackers during the entire day. Again we were supposed to have been fed by the Goons, but their supply trucks didn't arrive. I understand that all the Sagan Kriegies—12,000—are all on the road marching. God alone knows where we're going. The fellows are throwing away much of their food and clothing*

*because their packs are too heavy—the Goons pick it all up
to trade for food, etc., for themselves in the villages through
which we pass. The road along which we're marching looks
as tho garbage trucks had driven along it and thrown tin
cans, rags, papers, books, scraps, etc., out in front of us. I
don't think it will be too difficult for the Russians to follow us.*

Diary Entry

Still in the barn, Tuesday evening - 30 January.

*We remained here in the barn today because the road
ahead is crowded with those Kriegies who left Sagan before
us. I slept intermittently from 6 p.m. last night until 10 a.m.
this morning—awakening only when cramped limbs cried
out louder than usual. It was necessary for us to sleep in 14s,
with our feet between the knees of the fellow facing us. That's
how much sleeping room we have here. My shoes were frozen
this morning—But I have a pretty good pair, luckily. My feet
were completely wet last night and I suffered with chilblains
all night long. Somewhere along the line I've lost all the sox
I had, except for the 2 pair I'm wearing. Some of the fellows
are wearing rags around their feet because their shoes have
broken apart. More crackers and prunes today, and still no
Goon food. Today three of us bargained for a sled from a
civilian, and we are going to use it together.*

There were a couple of farmhouses next to the two barns we were in,
and some of the big time operators among the Kriegies made contact with
the Germans who lived or worked there. We had some guys who could speak
German, and they made exchanges—food for cigarettes or whatever we had.
We were also able to get cups of hot water that the farmers boiled up. We stayed
there an extra day, partly because the other columns of POWs were jamming up
ahead of us and partly because General Vanaman raised hell with the Germans,
trying to make life easier for us. Somehow he convinced them to let us stay
another night.

Diary Entry

Muskau, Wednesday afternoon – 31 January.

Last night we slept comparatively well – because of

overexhaustion. We were able to stretch out by overlapping our blankets with three other lads so that our feet came up past their knees—and vice versa. Today we marched 34 kilometers. The cold weather broke and the temperature rose to about 35-F, consequently the sled didn't work too well. The three of us took turns pulling it—2 kilometers on and 4 off. The sled weighs approximately 120 lbs. Tonight I'm so bleary eyed I can't think too rationally. We're housed (the 2,000 of us) in a pottery factory. It's quite warm, and we have the lights on, so it's not too bad—except for the clay dust which is all over everything. My shoes and sox are completely wet through from today's march, but as yet, thank God, I haven't gotten any blisters. We were told that four men from the West Camp died of exposure the first night they were away from Sagan—they slept in the snow because there were no facilities in the area for housing them. The Goon guards have been quite decent, and as liberal as possible. The civilians have given us water and hot coffee when they could. One old man about 80 years old stood in the street while we were marching through Priebus—he was passing out hot water from a bucket—tears were streaming down his face, and he kept repeating over and over, "The good God take care of you boys."

A long column of POWs entering a town. The line of Kriegies stretches around to the left and back past the man who quickly stepped into the field to secretly take this photo.
(Courtesy of USAFA Special Collections Branch, General Clark collection)

I recall that earlier that day, during one of our ten-minute breaks, the men from East Compound came into sight on the road behind us. It was around two o'clock in the afternoon. We'd just come through the small town of Priebus and were resting on the side of the road. They caught up to us, walked right through our ranks and kept on going. East Compound wasn't as large as some of the other compounds at Stalag Luft III. I don't know exactly how many men were in there, but I think it was around 1,200. After they passed through us, we moved back onto the road and continued on our way. Eventually we went down a hill with a river at the bottom. A bridge crossed the river, and the town of Bad Muskau was on the other side.

Popeye had gone ahead of us into this town and arranged for a place for all of us to stay. He met our column as soon as we crossed the bridge and had us turn right and go along the river for a few hundred yards to a series of large buildings that turned out to be a ceramic factory complex. This factory produced ceramic bowls, sauerkraut containers and the like. We were put inside the main factory building and found that it was nice and warm in there. In fact, it was not only warm, it was hot. The men from my combine found a kind of platform half way up a wall, and that's where we located.

Diary Entry

Muskau, Thursday, Feb. 1, 1945.

> *Today we remained in the pottery factory. If they had marched us this morning I'm afraid we'd have lost several of the lads. Many of them have fevers and others have such large blisters and chilblains on their feet that they can't even put on their shoes. This morning when I awoke I was more tired and stiffer than I've ever been before in my life. Last night the Goons finally came through with rations for us—1/5 of a loaf of bread per man. This is the first Goon food we've received in 5 days. Later—We went around to all the electric motors here in the factory and took the grease from the bearing boxes for our shoes. Now they won't be quite so damp (I hope) inside. This evening we received ¼ loaf of bread, ½ lb of margarine, and 2 tablespoons of soup per man. Muskau, Friday evening. 2 Feb. We're still in the pottery factory and as a result the morale is much higher than here-to-for. The sick have been cared for, and we've all taken advantage of the much needed rest. The Goons gave us ½ lb of margarine and ½ a cup of burned barley soup per man. We now have*

more margarine than bread!! Rumor says that we're to march
18 kilometers tomorrow—the Eagle Squadron seems to think
this rumor authentic. We are certainly fortunate to have the
General with us. Our Center Compound has suffered less and
has been treated better than any of the other Compounds. The
war news has been excellent the past few days—this, more
than any other one thing has kept our morale up.

It was very foolish of the Germans to give us so much margarine. If people aren't eating properly, and they eat margarine, it coats the intestines and they wind up with diarrhea. By the time we left the factory, quite a few Kriegies were in pretty tough shape with the runs. Fortunately, I wasn't one of them.

We ended up staying a third night, Friday night, in the ceramic factory, all because of General Vanaman and his officers. The next day we finally marched out of Muskau. We went up the hill in a northwesterly direction away from the river and onto a plateau area. The temperature was well above freezing, probably around 40 or 45 degrees, and the sky was filled with broken clouds. It wasn't bad marching as long as your feet were in good shape. Some of the men weren't so fortunate, though, such as those whose boots had come apart and some who were pretty sick. Luckily for them, the Germans had a couple of horse-drawn wagons at the end of our column and they were able to ride instead of walk.

We were back to 50 minutes of marching and 10 minutes of rest all throughout the morning. We passed through the small villages of Jamlitz, Tzschernitz, Wolfshain, and Schönheide. All along the road we continued to see German civilians all bundled up, pushing and pulling every kind of cart imaginable loaded with their possessions. Many times these poor people just waited by the side of the road, or in a field next to the road, for our column to pass. Late in the morning, we stopped near the town of Graustein and the guards marched us onto a side road that had farmhouses on either side. They broke us up into small groups and put us into barns and stalls. During the day a lot of horse-trading went on between us and the German farmers. That evening, I settled down in the straw and wrote in my diary again before going to sleep.

Diary Entry

Graustein (7 km east of Spremberg) Saturday evening. 3 Feb.

This morning we marched about 20 kilometers to the
barns where we're staying in this small village. During the
past two days most of the snow melted, and consequently the

roads were very wet and slushy. Once again we had to pack
all our things on our backs because the sled wouldn't work in
the slush. 150 of us are staying in a small barn for the night.

It was out onto the road again the next morning. The day was filled with bright sunshine and the temperature was very pleasant, up around 50 degrees or so. We were marched to the town of Spremberg and through a major portion to the northern part of it. The German civilians had already seen South Compound come through town, then West Compound, then North Compound followed by East Compound, and now finally Center Compound. They stood silently and stared at us as we marched past them. I'm sure they knew the Russians were coming.

When we reached the northern edge of the town, we turned right and went up a hill, heading back in an easterly direction. At the top of the hill the road passed underneath a small railroad trestle. We marched another hundred yards to a German military compound that turned out to be a Wehrmacht panzer training establishment and maintenance facility for tanks.

South Compound Kriegies arriving at the Spremberg marshalling yards three days before Center compound arrived.
Boxcars and railroad buildings visible to their left. Photo taken with secret camera.
(Courtesy of USAFA Special Collections Branch, General Clark collection)

The guards brought our long straggling column to a halt on the road just outside the gate to the compound and ordered us to compress into a tighter unit. They wanted us to form into a tight column again. A German soldier who had come through the gate stood watching us. After we formed up, the soldier, speaking in English, instructed one of the POWs in the front of the column to follow him, and he had the rest of us follow along behind in single file. Off he went, leading us through the entrance gate and into the Wehrmacht panzer compound.

It was shortly before noon. As we marched in, more German soldiers came out to gawk at us. They'd already seen thousands of other POWs move through during the past few days, so as far as they were concerned, we were just another group passing through.

We were led between two long buildings and on into the center of the facility where there was a large, hard-packed dirt field about 70 yards long by 35 yards wide. When the soldier leading us reached the edge of the field, he stepped to one side and directed the line of POWs to keep moving clockwise along the perimeter of the field and to spiral inward in an ever-tightening circle. This was done to insure that all two thousand of us would fit on the field and also to get a count of how many of us there were. It was actually a pretty good idea.

As the last POW in line came through the compound gates, a pair of German soldiers swung the gates closed and stood guard on the outside. Eventually, all of us were wound onto the field and brought to a halt.

Around the outside of the field were several large buildings with garage-like doors standing open. Shortly after that last POW walked onto the field and the Germans had their count, we were told to go into one of these buildings and wait while some food was prepared for us. The building was a tank storage garage, but was empty at the time. It wasn't as roomy as the ceramic factory back in Muskau, but it was better than the cramped barns in Freiwaldau. At least we were out of the weather. I imagine the garages were empty because the tanks, and all the other fighting equipment the Germans had had in the area, were being thrown against the Russian advance east of us.

About an hour later we were told the food was ready. Once again we formed a line and walked to another building that must have been the kitchen. The front door was open, and a German was standing behind a table just inside the door. On the table were a couple of ten-gallon cooking pots. Single file, we walked up the steps to the open front door, and he ladled a portion of barley soup into whatever we had to put it in. I carried with me an empty food can whose top lid I had bent back to form a crude handle. The ladleful of soup almost filled my can. As we each got our portion, we turned around and went back to the tank garage to sit on the floor and eat. This was only the third time we'd gotten any food from the Germans since leaving Sagan.

Late that afternoon we were rousted up and moved out. This time we were formed into a column of four men abreast. We marched out through the compound entrance and turned right onto the main street. It was almost dark and a misty wet fog had settled in. I distinctly remember walking back under the train trestle soon after we'd started down the road. It loomed up out of the darkening fog and passed overhead, and then it was behind me. This is one of those images that are forever impressed upon my memory: the sounds of many men moving through the dark, no voices, just the rustling of clothing and the scrape of boots on the ground, wrapped in near darkness but with a slight glow reflecting through wet fog, and the darker vague shape of the trestle moving backward overhead.

After coming out from under the trestle, the column turned left onto another road that paralleled the train tracks of the marshalling yard. All this happened within a couple of moments and maybe a hundred feet of walking, yet I felt like I was frozen in time, as if I'd been walking forever through the dark mist on that portion of road.

As soon as we turned the corner onto the road paralleling the railroad tracks, the surrealism of the moment passed. I hitched my greatcoat tighter around me, pulled the sleeves of my shirt bag higher onto one shoulder, straightened my blanket roll more firmly over my other shoulder and continued on with the rest of the column down through the dark fog to the train yard.

Forty boxcars such as these—known as 40 and 8s—were required to transport the two thousand POWs from just Center Compound alone. Over two hundred forty cars were necessary to haul all twelve thousand Stalag Luft III POWs and their German guards. (Courtesy U.S. Air Force Academy archives)

Not Quite the Glamorous Orient Express

Diary Entry

On the train, Sunday, Monday, Tuesday, and Wednesday.
(4,5,6,7 Feb)

> *On Sunday we marched the 7 km into Spremberg, ate*
> *some barley soup at a Wehrmacht training garage and were*
> *then marched through the town to the railroad station where*
> *we were herded into French 40 Hommes & 8 Chevaux cars.*
> *This war, however, they're putting 50 of us Kriegies into one*
> *boxcar with two guards. The ensuing three days were as*
> *close to Hell as I have yet been. It rained for two days—the*
> *roof leaked—most of the fellows were sick with dysentery,*
> *chilblains, or bad colds. During the three day trip we*
> *received only 7/10 of a loaf of bread per man, and water was*
> *officially passed out only twice. At each stop we traded our*
> *cigarettes and soap for bread and water. No one slept, except*
> *for those who passed out from sheer exhaustion because there*
> *wasn't room for more than half of us, had we all tried to lie*
> *down. We have lost all semblance to civilized beings. We're*
> *filthy dirty, unshaved, and many of us have picked up lice and*
> *fleas. All the clean clothes we had are now filthy dirty…*

Printed on the side of each small four-wheel boxcar was Hommes 40, Chevaux 8, which translates to "men 40, horses 8." In other words, this type of boxcar could hold up to 40 men, or 8 horses. After cramming fifty of us Kriegies inside, the two guards who hopped up into our boxcar had two apple boxes to sit on. We had the floor, which was filthy. The guards slid the door shut with a dull thunk, and we waited. It took a long time to load all 2,000 Kriegies into the string of boxcars.

After a while, probably around six o'clock, the train began to move. We were to be in those stinking, cruddy boxcars for three long nights and three long days. It was really tough because many of the men were sick.

When we first got into the boxcar, the guards sat on their two boxes by the closed sliding door facing us. They swung their rifles in an arc in front of them, ordering us to stay back. We prisoners quickly arranged to have one third of the men standing and one third of the men sitting down with their legs spread out with the next guy sitting between the open legs with his back against the chest of the fellow behind him. That way, the last third, the sick fellows, were able to lie down. We rotated standing and sitting every-so-often so we wouldn't cramp up too much.

All during the night and into the next day men were vomiting and having diarrhea. There wasn't one bucket to be had. We asked the guards to slide the doors open to let some fresh air in and to at least let the sick guys vomit while hanging out the door. In response, they took their rifles and swung them at us in an arc.

"Nein, nein nein! Streng verboten!" (No, no no! Strictly forbidden!)

We quickly sorted out who were the senior officers among us, and these men came to a decision. That's one good thing about having military training. One of the Kriegies spoke good German and he addressed the guards in a very stern voice.

"You're going to open the doors, and you're going to throw those damn boxes out. You're going to put those damn guns down, and you're going to have the same amount of space as we do, which isn't much. Or, you're going to have to shoot us as we rush you. Now, you have bolt-action rifles and, at the most, you might each get off two shots before we get to you. That's a total of four shots. Because we're at close range, you might even be able to kill two of us with each shot. Four times two is eight, so with any luck you might be able to kill eight of us. By then, the rest of us will be upon you, and we'll take you apart ear by ear, joint by joint, eyeball by eyeball. Now you've got one minute to decide what to do."

The two guards, both upper middle-aged men, were pretty shaken up by the force of those words. They put their heads together and spoke quickly to each other. Then they began to cry and plead with us.

"Please don't hurt us, we're just following orders."

"We won't hurt you, just open the damn door!"

With that, the two soldiers quickly unlatched the door. They pushed it all the way open, and we threw their apple boxes out. They were then told to put their rifles down, which they did. We got along just fine after that.

Over the next couple of days, the train stopped two or three times. Each time it stopped, all 2,000 of us got out, dropped our pants and crapped on Germany. It was quite a sight.

At one rail yard our train came to rest alongside a similar train filled with German soldiers. We were allowed off our train, as usual, to relieve ourselves. Some of us exchanged stuff with the German soldiers. We gave them some of our canned food, and they gave us some of theirs. They were SS troops, probably headed toward the front somewhere.

One night we stopped short of a big city that may have been Nürnberg.

During the night, the English bombed the hell out of it. We could clearly hear the bomber stream come and go and the explosions of the tons of bombs that fell.

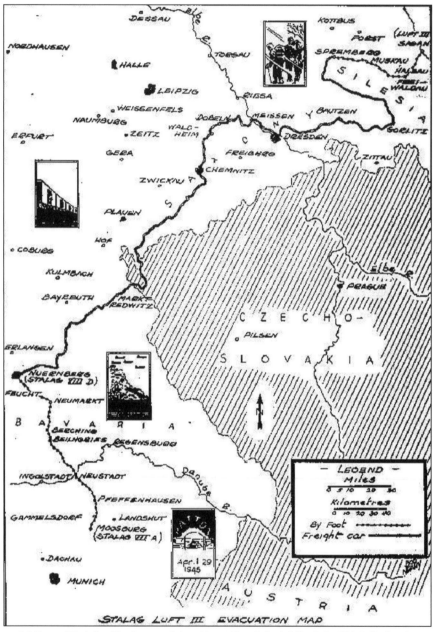

Bob Neary, a Kriegie from West Compound, drew this route from Stalag Luft III to Stalag VII A. Unlike the other compounds of Stalag Luft III, West Compound trained from Spremberg to Stalag XIII D, south of Nürnberg. Several weeks later, they set out on foot and arrived at Stalag VII A the first week of April.
(Courtesy of Bob Books, webmaster of www.b24.net)

We spent three nights in the boxcars on that train as it traveled through the country, and still we had absolutely no idea of where we were going. Each one of us was wrapped in our own individual, miserable, cold, hungry, lonely world. I was absolutely the filthiest I'd ever been in my life. The miles and hours of constant noise as the boxcars clattered down the rails, the rain leaking down through the cracks in the roof, other just-as-miserable men getting sick on themselves and on others—this all fed into our misery and turned those days into a numb haze. Three days and nights is an eternity under such conditions.

The train eventually reached the city of Munich and then headed back to the northeast a few miles to a town called Moosburg.

The Snake Pit

Diary Entry

...This evening (Wednesday) we arrived at the Non-com camp of Stalag VIIA at Moosburg in Bavaria, which is 30 kilometers north of Munich. We're staying in two large stable-like buildings—it's almost as bad as the train.

Stalag VIIA, Moosburg, Thursday & Friday (8, 9 Feb)

Boy what a hole this place is. By common agreement we're all calling this cozy little nook the 'Snake Pit.' The Goons gave us soup (fri.) that I wouldn't feed my dog. 75% of us have diarrhea, stomach cramps, and fits of vomiting. Tonight about 20 of us weren't able to make it to the latrine in time (myself included) when the "urge" caught us unawares. Some of the lads couldn't get outside in time, and vomited all over the fellows sleeping on the ground. Doc Hall says that the excessive amounts of margarine we've been eating has coated the walls of our intestines, rendering them practically useless. General Vanaman and his "staff" left us in Spremberg at the order of the OKW. Wednesday night when we arrived here all the officers from Captain and up were taken away. Now there are only the 1st and 2nd Lieutenants left with a handful of enlisted men. There is no semblance of order left—chaos alone reigns supreme. Here at Moosburg I have seen, for the first time, American and British Non-coms doing labor— Germany's slave workers.[4]

It was early afternoon when the train stopped at the Moosburg station, but we had to stay in the boxcars for a few more hours of filthy misery. Finally, toward dusk, we were unloaded for the last time and marched a short distance through the mud to Stalag VII A. It was a huge camp! We were marched through what must have been the main entrance, past a large, two-story wooden watchtower, and then left up to the far north end of the camp and into a barbed wire, fenced enclosure like a stable area. At some time in the past the Germans had kept their horses here, and it sure smelled like it. Two of the long buildings inside the enclosure had stalls with straw in them, and we were put into these buildings; a thousand of us in each building. We quickly dubbed this place "The Snake Pit."

For outdoor latrines, someone had dug trenches four or five feet deep and two feet wide. A pole, supported by crossbeams a couple of feet off the ground, had been laid lengthwise over the trenches. To do our business we dropped our drawers, turned around and sat on the long pole. But we had no toilet paper; in fact we didn't have much of anything.

Once again our combine was relatively lucky. Because we were among the first into the building, we had to go clear to the far end as it filled up. This was advantageous because we didn't have people walking across us, which happened to those who ended up near the door.

I hadn't been sick the entire trip until the first night in the Snake Pit. I was wearing two-piece long underwear, a pair of wool pants, a wool shirt, an overcoat, and a French beret I'd gotten somewhere. After we all moved into the stable and scoped the place out a bit, we bedded down for the night. There were only one or two low-wattage light bulbs hanging from the ceiling so there was a little light, but it was very dim.

After a time, most of us fell asleep. A few hours later I woke up feeling the urge. I got up quickly and pulled my boots on, and then my bowels began to move. I peered through the gloom toward the door clear across on the other side of the stable. The entire floor between it and me was covered with sleeping men. I started tiptoeing out, trying to miss people, trying to not step on anyone. Finally, as the stuff started pumping out of me, I ran. I ran across many bodies, and they were screaming and shouting at me. With every step I took, more effluent pumped out of my body.

I wound up outside in the dark in what was probably the lowest moment of my life.

"What am I going to do?" was all I could think of as I stood there in long johns that were completely soiled. For once, my mind had gone completely blank. I'd never felt lonelier, dirtier, or more shut-off from the sane world than

I did just then.

It was cold, damp, and very dark outside. Frankly, I was wishing I had a gun. If I'd had a gun, I might have pulled the trigger. But this feeling of desolation didn't last long.

Through the darkness, over near the fence a few yards away, I could just barely make out two or three men standing around what looked like a fifty-gallon drum full of water. They had the same problem I did. They had their trousers off and were trying to clean themselves up. I walked on over to them and quickly came back from my dark mental situation.

My mind snapped back to the present and I realized that I had to get my good pants off immediately, or my soiled long johns would dirty them. I took off my boots, then my pants, and then my totally fouled long-john underwear. I tried to throw them over the barbed wire fence, but the fence was too high. The long johns got stuck up on the barbed wire near the top. I joined the other men and put my hands into the cold water in the drum so I could clean myself up as best I could. When I finished, I put my boots and pants back on, returned to the stable and tiptoed back to where the guys from my combine were sleeping. Seeing those other men outside around the water drum was a God-send. It's amazing how just being around another person in the same condition helps ease one's own misery.

We stayed in the Snake Pit for the next three days. To counteract the boredom, I took several walks each day around the wire fence enclosure. Rumor had it that in order to make room for us, the Germans were moving French POWs out of an area in the main camp that contained four barracks.

I ran into Lenny Bughman from Block 39, and he and I spent time together walking around the wire, catching up on all that had happened since leaving Sagan.

"Jim, why don't you come and join us?" he said during one of our conversations. "When they take us into the main camp, come with me and join my combine."

I said, "Sure, that would be great."

Later on that day, I searched out Dale Tipton and Billy Lawrence and informed them of my decision, not because I needed anyone's permission, but out of respect.

For meals the Germans brought in garbage cans full of soup that we called "green death," and we distributed it accordingly. During one meal, after the soup had been distributed, I leaned over one of the empty garbage cans to spoon up whatever little bit of soup might be left in there. I had my head and arm down in the can and was scraping up maybe half a spoonful of soup when two German officers and two Neutral Power people came around the corner, inspecting the camp. I think the two people with the Germans were Swiss.

When they saw what we prisoners had to use for taking a crap (the pole over the slit trench in the ground) and when they saw me with my spoon in the bottom of the garbage can, the two Swiss men exploded and chewed out the German officers, lambasting them for treating fellow officers so despicably. I smiled and just kept right on spooning away.

After the war, I learned what had happened to General Vanaman and Colonel Spivey. When we boarded the boxcars at Spremberg, the Germans took the General and Colonel to Berlin, where they put them into a huge camp. Eventually they met with SS General Gottlob Berger, the man in charge of all prisoners of war.

SS-Obergruppenfuhrer and General of the Waffen-SS Gottlob Berger.
(Courtesy Bundesarchiv Bild 183-S73321 Wikimedia Commons)

Berger, who was playing both sides of the street, negotiated with Vanaman and Spivey. Berger knew the war would be over soon, so he was looking out for old Gottlob. He exclaimed to the two men how Hitler was insane and that for Germany to survive, Hitler must be eliminated, and that he had a plan. Berger asked if Vanaman and Spivey would be willing to take coded messages to the American forces in Switzerland. His plan was to establish secret negotiations with the Allies to insure a peaceful outcome between them and Germany. In return for their cooperation, he promised Vanaman and Spivey that he would make sure Red Cross food shipments made their way to the POW camps like Stalag VII A.

The Allies had huge storage buildings in Switzerland filled to the rafters with Red Cross food parcels, but they couldn't get them transported into Germany because of the mess the rail system was in from our own bombing. Because of the negotiations with General Vanaman and Colonel Spivey, Berger helped arrange for columns of trucks to bring in medical supplies as well as the food. In fact, some of the Kriegies from Stalag VII A were "recruited" to drive the trucks. I'm sure the two Swiss men were at VII A as a direct result of the negotiations with Berger.

Back in the Snake Pit, the two Swiss men raised hell with the result that the Germans hurried and cleaned out the compound in the main camp that they had been clearing out for us.

A couple of days later it was raining outside with the temperature around 40 degrees. In the late afternoon, as darkness approached, the guards came into the Snake Pit and marched us out in a column and back down through the main complex of Stalag VII A.

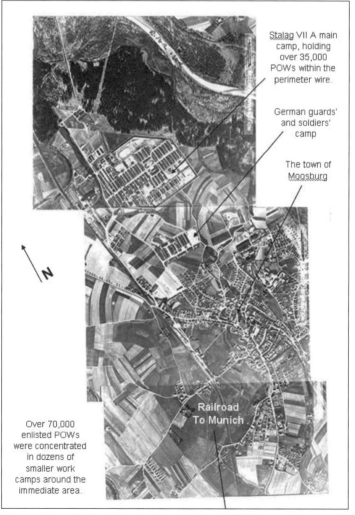

Stalag VII A main camp, holding over 35,000 POWs within the perimeter wire.

German guards' and soldiers' camp

The town of Moosburg

N

Railroad To Munich

Over 70,000 enlisted POWs were concentrated in dozens of smaller work camps around the immediate area.

Three aerial recon photos spliced together to show the entire Stalag VII A POW camp and the town of Moosburg. Notes added by author. (Courtesy of USAFA Special Collections Branch, General Clark collection)

Stalag VII A

Shortly after Germany invaded Poland in September 1939, a prisoner-of-war camp called *Kriegsgefangenen-Mannschafts Stammlager VII A* was established just to the north of the town of Moosburg in southern Bavaria. *Moos* translates into English as moss, deep green moss.

*Front entrance sign to Stalag VII A. War Prisoner - Enlisted men Main camp VII A.
(Courtesy of Jim Reeves whose father, Robert Reeves, was a POW)*

The main watch tower and front gate of Stalag VII A. (Courtesy of Werner Schwarz, co-creator of www.Moosburg.org)

The camp eventually covered nearly 85 acres and was originally designed for around 10,000 prisoners. Outside the main camp of Stalag VII A, there were satellite camps, or work details, in different towns and villages. The camp was intended for enlisted men, but later in the war when the Russians began rolling westward toward Berlin, it became necessary for the Germans to empty all of the prison camps in northern and northeastern Germany and in Silesia (Poland). They brought these prisoners to Stalag VII A. By the time we arrived at VII A, more than 100,000 POWs of all nationalities were spread throughout the complex: British, French, Belgian, Dutch, Greek, Yugoslavian, Russian, and American.

Diary Entry

Stalag VIIA, Moosburg, Sunday (11 Feb.)

> *Today we moved from the "Snake Pit" to our permanent barracks in the camp proper. Prior to being taken to our barracks we spent an hour in the Goon de-louser. All our clothes, blankets, etc., were de-loused for one hour in a cyanide gas chamber. In the interim we Kriegies had our first showers in 5 weeks. Boy, what an experience. It rained all the time while we were waiting our turn in the de-louser, and consequently we got out of wet clothes, showered, and then got back into the same wet, filthy clothes. Our barracks (ha ha) are absolutely the filthiest hovels I've ever entered in my life. There are 15 tiers of beds—with 12 men sleeping in one tier. We have no cooking facilities at all—and no hot water. The abort is positively the bottom, and is indescribably filthy. The protective power men came through while we were still in the "Snake Pit," and said that never in their experiences had they seen men—officers at that—subjected to such humiliating, filthy, sordid conditions. It was at their insistence that we were moved today instead of next week. Little did they realize that we were being moved from Purgatory to Hell.*

We stood in line in the rain for about an hour before entering, one small group at a time, a building containing showers and a hermetically sealed delousing chamber. When our turn came we went into the shower room, took off our wet clothes and hung them on horizontal poles attached to dollies. These dollies were then rolled into the delousing chamber that the Germans filled with cyanide gas after closing the doors. Then we moved to another room and showered.

Newly arrived POWs at Stalag VII A being taken to the delousing buildings.
(Courtesy of USAFA Special Collections Branch, General Clark collection)

There were no towels, so after we showered we just brushed ourselves off as best we could. We stood around naked and dripping wet until the workers opened up the gas chambers and brought our clothes back out, reeking of gas. I climbed into my stinking wet clothes and nearly choked from the fumes. Then we went out the other side of the building and milled around for another hour in the rain while another group went through the process.

Lenny Bughman's combine went through the showers after I did. When he came outside, I left my combine and went and stood with him. Andy Anderson and Bob Keller were there also, and we shook hands all around. Finally, when all two thousand of us had been deloused, we were marched in the rain farther through the main camp to the compound that had been cleared out for us.

Stalag VII A was similar to Stalag Luft III in that the main camp was surrounded by two parallel, imposing barbed wire fences with the six-foot space in the middle filled with a jumbled mess of other barbed wire. As at Luft III, this main camp was divided into several smaller compounds, each surrounded by a single wire fence. A main street ran west to east from the wooden watchtower at the main entrance to the eastern perimeter.

The delousing building was halfway between the "Snake Pit," at the north end of the camp, and the main street. In a steady downpour, we were marched south from the delousing building to the main street. There we turned left and continued on for about four hundred yards. A guard unlocked the gate into a wired enclosure on the right side of the street, and in we marched.

This was the area that had been hurriedly cleared out for us. Awaiting us were four huge stucco barracks that filled the north half of the compound. The south half was open ground with a single large latrine building in the middle. South Compound had moved into a similar enclosure just to the east of us several days earlier.

It was bad enough that these barracks were filthy, cold, and downright disgusting, but they were also infested with all kinds of bugs. Talk about irony. After delousing, they then took us into a place filled with lice, bedbugs and fleas! The worst of the three, as far as health was concerned, were the lice. They were very small, but they bit. Their bite would fester very badly for many days, however. The bite would eventually heal, but it would leave a permanent depression about the size of a half dollar. I was lucky because the lice never bit me. Fleas could drive a person crazy with their constant crawling around, but their bites didn't last long and the marks weren't permanent.

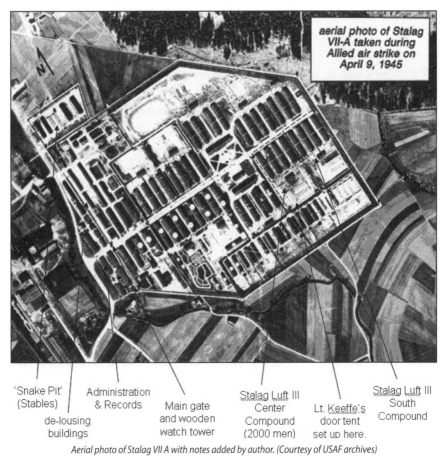

aerial photo of Stalag VII-A taken during Allied air strike on April 9, 1945

'Snake Pit' (Stables) de-lousing buildings — Administration & Records — Main gate and wooden watch tower — Stalag Luft III Center Compound (2000 men) — Lt. Keeffe's door tent set up here. — Stalag Luft III South Compound

Aerial photo of Stalag VII A with notes added by author. (Courtesy of USAF archives)

The barracks didn't contain rooms; instead they were large open bays. At Sagan, we had had triple-decked bunks; here we had tiers of bunks. Each bunk tier had three levels, and each level contained four bunks. If you draw a rectangle and then draw a line through the middle of this rectangle lengthwise, and then draw a line through its width, the rectangle will then be divided into four smaller rectangles. Each of these smaller rectangles represents one bunk. So, on the first level of a tier were four bunks. The level above this had four more bunks, as did the third, or top, level. Therefore, there were twelve men in each one of these tiers.

The tiers were placed in rows separated by a cramped aisle two feet wide. There were roughly twenty of these twelve-man tiers in each half of each long building, and each half had one small table and two benches for all of the people. There was no place to put anything. Living in such tight quarters with so many people was rather grim.

At Sagan, each two prisoners had shared a vertical double locker. Each individual locker had had a shelf and a bar for hanging things. They weren't very big, but at least there was a private place to put the few things we had. Here at VII A we had no place to put our things. What little we had we had to keep on our bunk, either beside us while we slept, or on the bunk when we were elsewhere.

Some of the men had brought their decks of cards with them, and very quickly a bridge game sprang up. Men were playing cards all the time. One of these men was from a very wealthy and famous Pennsylvania family. He was a high-class kind of snob and not very sanitary. In fact, one of the senior people finally ordered him to wash at least his hands, his face and neck, but he refused. He was eventually taken out by the muscle boys and scrubbed with a German GI brush. After that, his personal hygiene improved a bit.

From Bad to Worse

» *Timeline* «

> » *14 February 1945: Rotterdam—An order is sent from the German authorities to the Scheveningen Prison in The Hague, to pull out ten prisoners to be shot in reprisal for the killing of a Dutch Nazi farmer by the Resistance. Dr. Jappe-Alberts is one of the ten men taken to the outskirts of the small town of Heinenoord and murdered in cold blood.*

» *20 February 1945: Germany – Cornelia Broekhuizen, wife of Albert Broekhuizen, dies at Ravensbruck Concentration Camp.*

The Germans gave us no fuel at all, or anything else to cook with. Eventually, things got so bad in the barracks that men were tearing up the floor and the walls to get little pieces of wood to burn in our burner cans. One of the amazing contraptions we made out of tin cans was the Kriegie stove.

A Kriegie stove had a blower and could burn just about anything. It consisted of a firebox made out of tin cans attached to a board. A square tube, also made from tin cans, connected the firebox to the blower, which was an impeller wheel with a hand crank made from a wire. It was like a forge. You could increase the heat by feeding more oxygen; the faster you turned the hand crank, the hotter the fire.

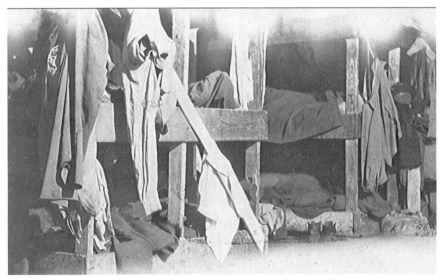

Typical triple-deck twelve-man bunks; four men per level with about two feet of space between tiers.
(Courtesy of USAFA Special Collections Branch, General Clark collection)

The stoves were neat. The firebox had something like a screen half way down in it for ashes to drop through. We'd build a little fire in the top half and put a tin can pan on top to cook in. Andy Anderson traded a lot of D-bars for one of these stoves, and we used that for cooking from then on.

Andy Anderson and Bob Keller staked out a couple upper bunks in our twelve-man tier. Lenny Bughman and I grabbed two of them on the lower level. We didn't have enough blankets, and the ones we had weren't made of wool; they were made from some kind of wood fiber.

Lenny eventually became sick with pneumonia, which was pretty rough on him. When he had the chills, I slept up against him to keep him warm. At Stalag Luft III, he would have been able to go to the hospital building, but not at VII A. A prisoner had to be really sick to go to the hospital here. So Lenny had to tough it out on his own, but eventually he did get better.

After a couple of weeks, Lenny started to become clingy. He wanted to know where I was all the time. Because of this, I began to drift away from him. It was really too bad because I liked Lenny.

Other personality conflicts developed as well. There was a big fellow from Lenny's combine who I didn't get along with at all. I finally exploded one day because he was messing around with the dividing of the food, and I challenged him to a fight. I pointed my finger at him and snapped, "Come on, we're going outside and settle this!"

He was bigger and stronger than I, but I was more determined. He backed down, and afterwards tried to be buddy-buddy with me, but he was not my sort of person.

The Mexican Standoff

Free-standing ceramic toilets in Latrine 9. (Courtesy of USAF archives)

At the south end of our barracks was another building that was the abort. It was a stucco building, set up pretty high off the ground that contained our latrine. On the outside were the characters *Latr. 9.* Inside were two or three rows of stools and then a urinal against the back wall. The stools had no lids and no seats. They were just ceramic base toilets, but without the curlicue traps and they dropped straight down into a large holding chamber below.

Periodically, the Germans brought Russian prisoners in with a honey wagon and had them pump out the abort effluent. Then they took it out and gave it to the farmers for use in their fields and on vegetable gardens.

As time went on, more and more things broke down in the camp. When the Germans didn't send the Russians in to clean out the abort a couple of times, the sewage filled up the lower chamber to the floor level. Then the gas expanded it, which forced it up and out of the stools onto the floor so that it began to run down the steps and pool up on the ground outside. The stage was set for a classical, and potentially deadly, Mexican standoff.

Diary Entry

Stalag VIIA, Moosburg, Sunday (11 Feb.)

> *Today we all (2,000) went on strike. Conditions here have gone from bad to worse. Last night the stools in the abort overflowed onto the floor—the urinals overflowed, too, and the mess is about two inches deep on the inside of the building; and consequently has run out the doors and covered a considerable area of the grounds. Most of us are still sick with diarrhea, and now there's nothing to do but act like animals. The Goons ordered us to fall in for appell this morning, and we refused. As a result they brought in troops armed with machine guns—as well as several of their police dogs. They again ordered us to fall in and again we refused to do so. The Goon Hauptman was in a rage. He wanted to order his men to fire on us, but didn't dare to—we were officers, and more than that, the war wasn't too far from its conclusion. After about three hours of parleying, they finally agreed to clean up our barracks and the Abort. With these promises we formed and submitted to an appell. We have no coal or wood, either for heating the barracks or for cooking our food. We receive one cup of hot water a day per man—all other water is cold—and as a result of these conditions, most of us still have diarrhea, and many cases of the flu have been noted. I only hope and pray that we don't catch typhus. The Goons will furnish us no medical supplies. Most of us are lousy with fleas, lice, and bed bugs. The camp at Sagan was a paradise compared to this place.*

As the Mexican standoff over the appell continued, guys from South Compound below us were watching through the wire. Had this happened a month or two earlier, the Germans wouldn't have hesitated to use their guns and a lot of us would have died, of that I'm sure.

A Russian prisoner pumping out the abort with what the Kriegies dubbed 'the honey wagon.'
(Courtesy of Stowe Keller, son of Bob Keller, POW)

It became even worse in the barracks, but the Germans weren't paying too much attention to us. Previously, when prisoners broke or destroyed camp property, the Germans got really tough with them because it was "Third Reich property!" and anybody damaging it "would be dealt with severely!" But now, the Kriegies began tearing everything up to get wood to heat food or water. Not only were the barracks filthy, full of lice, bed bugs, and fleas, but they became choked up with the smoke from all the wood and paper being burnt inside and from all those who smoked cigarettes. There was also a constant flow of men tramping in and out; consequently, it was never quiet.

Some of the guys started sleeping outside. There were slit trenches in the earth for people to hide in if it ever became necessary to defend the area, or for protection from air raids. These prisoners put covers over the trenches and then lived in them so they could get away from the mobs and the disgusting conditions in the barracks.

At Sagan, we couldn't go out of our barracks at night. Here, as order began to break down, the Germans didn't really care. At Sagan, we had a building for washing clothes. But here we didn't. All we had for our compound of 2,000 men was one water spigot sticking up out of the ground between the two middle barracks, at the south end. It was just a pipe with a turn-on, turn-off handle. There were always a lot of men at the water pipe getting water for drinking and cooking, or for washing themselves. We didn't have shower parades like we did at Sagan; here all washing was done around the water pipe. Men stripped down to their shorts and washed their bodies and their feet while stomping on their clothes to clean them. I usually filled a tin can with water and went off to the side somewhere to wash my hands and face, and occasionally my feet. Thank

God that pipe never ran dry.

» *Timeline* «

» *8 March 1945: Amersfoort Concentration Camp, the
Netherlands – Folkert Elsinga is murdered – he is one of
nearly three hundred Dutch civilians shot and killed by
the Germans in reprisal for the attack two days before on
Polizeiführer Hans Albin Rauter, the Chief of the German
Police Forces in The Netherlands, by members of the Dutch
Underground.* [5]

Diary Entry

Stalag VIIA, March 8, 1945 Thurs.

*One year ago today I got the chop. Here in Moosburg we
Kriegies are having a very bad time of it. The camp has run
completely out of Red Cross parcels, and consequently we're
living on Goon rations alone, which for today (an average
day), consisted of:*

1 cup of hot water in the morning

1 cup of soup at noon (a la Skid Road)

*4 medium sized potatoes which had been frozen & then
boiled*

*1/7 of a loaf of bread per man (Small loaves of black
bread)*

2 tablespoons of Limburger cheese

3/4 of a teaspoon of sugar per man

*These are the daily rations we've been receiving from
the Goons. No more and no less. The fellows are tearing
all the stripping, etc., from the barracks, and are using
their bed boards to burn in their tin can stoves. The Goons
refuse to give us any fuel—either for cooking or for heating
the barracks, so-o-o, this is our only recourse. Most of us
have no bowls, cups, etc., (they would have been too heavy
to carry with us on the march) so consequently 9/10 of our
'china' consists of tin cans—just like in Hobo town. I know
now why dogs scratch themselves so persistently when they
have fleas. It's almost humorous to see how very many of us
stay up as late as possible so as not to go to bed any earlier
than necessary. I dread going to bed each night—the fleas*

and lice keep me in a fever of torment for hours. If they would
only bite me and then leave I would never begrudge them
the blood, but their incessant crawling is almost maddening.
There's absolutely no way of ridding ourselves of them. We
air our clothes and blankets, wash our bodies as well as
possible in cold water—and still they keep up their incessant
crawling. Believe me, I'll always sympathize with any dog I
ever see in the future which is furiously scratching itself.

Four days later, I turned twenty-two years old. Just like a year earlier, while I was at the young couple's safe house in Rotterdam, I didn't mention to anyone in camp that it was my birthday.

"Come Fight With Us Against the Barbaric Asiatic East!"

The Germans became desperate as the Russian offensive pushed farther and farther into the German countryside. Their losses were mounting, and they were running short of fighting men. For a few days a very up-beat and friendly German made the rounds through the various compounds of VII A, passing out full-page fliers to any of us Kriegies who would take them. He had a stack of these fliers, and he'd grin and smile and act as if he was actually on the winning team. Whenever he handed a flier to a curious Kriegie, he'd pat him on the back and shake his hand, never losing his ebullient smile.

Curiosity got the better of me, so when he was making the rounds through our compound, I walked up to him to get one of the fliers. I got slapped on the back and had my hand shook, and walked away to read the thing. The heading was addressed to "Soldiers of the British Commonwealth! Soldiers of the United States of America!" and it went on to explain how we were all—Germans, English and the entire Western world—in a decisive battle against the Red tide from Moscow and we must "choose between submission under a most brutal Asiatic rule—or a national existence in the future under European ideas, many of which, of course are your own ideals."

I had to laugh. The Germans were trying to recruit us to fight with them against the Russians! The German fellow became even more enthusiastic when some of us went up to him to get more of these fliers. No one that I know of actually took this German offer seriously. But when properly crumpled up and smoothed out, the paper the flier was printed on made better toilet paper then we had had for a long time.

The first week of April the weather started to improve a bit. It was the beginning of spring but it was still cold, miserable, and damp, and it still snowed at times. Whenever the sun did come out and the temperature went above 50 degrees or so, most of us stripped down to get some sun and vitamin D.

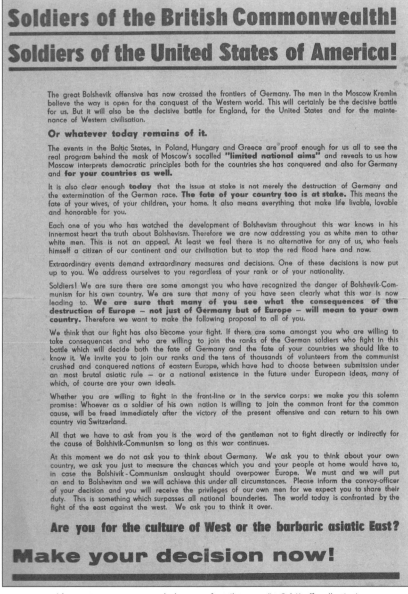

Soldiers of the British Commonwealth!
Soldiers of the United States of America!

The great Bolshevik offensive has now crossed the frontiers of Germany. The men in the Moscow Kremlin believe the way is open for the conquest of the Western world. This will certainly be the decisive battle for us. But it will also be the decisive battle for England, for the United States and for the maintenance of Western civilisation.

Or whatever today remains of it.

The events in the Baltic States, in Poland, Hungary and Greece are proof enough for us all to see the real program behind the mask of Moscow's socalled **"limited national aims"** and reveals to us how Moscow interprets democratic principles both for the countries she has conquered and also for Germany and **for your countries as well.**

It is also clear enough **today** that the issue at stake is not merely the destruction of Germany and the extermination of the German race. **The fate of your country too is at stake.** This means the fate of your wives, of your children, your home. It also means everything that make life livable, lovable and honorable for you.

Each one of you who has watched the development of Bolshevism throughout this war knows in his innermost heart the truth about Bolshevism. Therefore we are now addressing you as white men to other white men. This is not an appeal. At least we feel there is no alternative for any of us, who feels himself a citizen of our continent and our civilisation but to stop the red flood here and now.

Extraordinary events demand extraordinary measures and decisions. One of these decisions is now put up to you. We address ourselves to you regardless of your rank or of your nationality.

Soldiers! We are sure there are some amongst you who have recognized the danger of Bolshevik-Communism for his own country. We are sure that many of you have seen clearly what this war is now leading to. **We are sure that many of you see what the consequences of the destruction of Europe — not just of Germany but of Europe — will mean to your own country.** Therefore we want to make the following proposal to all of you.

We think that our fight has also become your fight. If there are some amongst you who are willing to take consequences and who are willing to join the ranks of the German soldiers who fight in this battle which will decide both the fate of Germany and the fate of your countries we should like to know it. We invite you to join our ranks and the tens of thousands of volunteers from the communist crushed and conquered nations of eastern Europe, which have had to choose between submission under an most brutal asiatic rule — or a national existence in the future under European ideas, many of which, of course are your own ideals.

Whether you are willing to fight in the front-line or in the service corps: we make you this solemn promise: Whoever as a soldier of his own nation is willing to join the common front for the common cause, will be freed immediately after the victory of the present offensive and can return to his own country via Switzerland.

All that we have to ask from you is the word of the gentleman not to fight directly or indirectly for the cause of Bolshivik-Communism so long as this war continues.

At this moment we do not ask you to think about Germany. We ask you to think about your own country, we ask you just to measure the chances which you and your people at home would have to, in case the Bolshivik-Communism onslaught should overpower Europe. We must and we will put an end to Bolshevism and we will achieve this under all circumstances. Please inform the convoy-officer of your decision and you will receive the privileges of our own men for we expect you to share their duty. This is something which surpasses all national bounderies. The world today is confronted by the fight of the east against the west. We ask you to think it over.

Are you for the culture of West or the barbaric asiatic East?

Make your decision now!

A lousy attempt at propaganda, but great for toilet paper (Lt. Col. Keeffe collection)

One warm day we took the table from the end of the barracks and set it up outside. We were all hanging out in little groups with some of us cooking food, when along came a wonderful air raid.

During the air raids at Stalag Luft III, and in the beginning at Stalag VII A, we had to run into the barracks. The German guards would close the shutters and lock the doors with a bar. They didn't like us outside because we'd cheer the bombing raids as they flew across. However, by the time of this particular air raid, the Germans had stopped forcing us into the barracks when an air raid was announced.

So here we were, outside preparing what little we had for our evening meal, when the full might of the U.S. 8th Air Force flew across overhead on their way to bomb Munich. We could hear the dim rumble of the bombs as they hit their targets, which I presume were the rail yards of that big city. This was certainly a maximum effort of close to one thousand bombers.

Diary Entry

Stalag VII A, April 10, 1945. (Tues.)

> *Boy, what a flap our camp is in today! The big Allied push is on, and consequently the Goons have been evacuating all their Oflags[6] into our camp here at Moosburg. All the enlisted men who were camped here have been put on the road to make room for the influx of Officers. Evidently the Goons are concentrating all the Officer POWs in one area for some diabolical reason. Today the Goons erected 7 tents inside the perimeter of our camp, and this evening they moved 3,000 officers of all nationalities into them.*
>
> *LATER: This shall sound unbelievable—but here goes. This evening we cooked and ate our supper outside because the sun was so warm, and too, because the barracks are in such a flap due to the arrival of all these new men. During the preparation of our meal the entire 8th Air Force passed directly overhead at about 20,000 feet, using Moosburg as its I. P. for a bomb run on Munich—20 miles South of here. It took approximately 1 hour for the 1,400 odd bombers and their fighter escort to pass over in Group formations. The sky was perfectly clear and consequently we saw the entire show—preparing and eating our dinner all the while. We watched a few Goon jet jobs attack the formations— watched each Group's bombs fall from the ships right into Munich—saw the flak barrage over Munich account for 5 or 6 of our bombers, which fell to earth like huge birds killed*

while in flight—some in flames, and some just smoking. It takes approximately 3 minutes for a bomber to spin in from 20,000 feet, so you can well imagine that every one of us in the camp spun in spiritually as each of those ships fell from its formation. We watched as the contrails from the fighter escort and the smoke from each of the Mickey ships'[7] bombs accumulated in a wild maze over Munich as Group after Group dropped its bombs and then turned back toward England. The barracks shook and rattled as each stick of bombs plummeted into the now badly burning city—and all this while we ate our meal, just as though we had been out in a park on a picnic watching an air show!

As we watched this air battle unfold, it WAS like being out in a park on a Sunday afternoon at a picnic. The entire event was an awesome sight to behold. The first thing that alerted us was the sound of the air raid sirens blaring from several loud speakers mounted on the sides of two or three of the barracks. Next we heard radio announcements in German, announcing where the bombers were coming from. Then there was a lot of activity. All the Germans and some of the Kriegies either ran to an air raid shelter or to their posts, or to slit trenches in the ground, or to the barracks. But in our case, we kept right on enjoying our evening meal outside. When the noise over the loud speakers subsided things became quiet, and we all waited.

It was a clear day out. As we looked to the northwest, we first saw a little glint, then another little glint, and then another little glint off in the distance. The glints of light were the sun's rays reflecting off the glass windshields and unpainted metal of the airplanes. Then we heard an intermittent high-pitched hum, but the volume was very low. Soon the hum became a continuous, ever-increasing noise. Little dots began to appear in and around the small sparkles of light. These grew slowly into the shapes of either B-17s or B-24s. Soon the lead airplanes reached Moosburg and changed their heading to due south. It turned out we were the IP of their bomb run to Munich. The din built in volume and became a roar as section after section made their turn directly over us.

The buildings and tents and any loose items began to shake. Then everything shook. The roar became so loud we had to shout in order to be heard. The sound was overwhelming, and it seemed as if even the ground was shaking. This lasted until the entire bomber stream passed over us.

As squadron after squadron flew by overhead, the bombers at the front of the stream reached Munich and began dropping their loads on the target. The dull thrump and thunder of hundreds of explosions rumbled back to us for many minutes, and still the bomber stream roared past. Then the reverse took place. The last of the bomber stream flew over and the roar lessened; then it became a hum; then it became an intermittent hum, and suddenly it was quiet. A few minutes later, an "all clear" siren sounded. The entire bombing raid, from when we first caught sight of the massive formation to the fading thrum of the last receding element, lasted for nearly sixty minutes.

I don't think the Allies understood the psychological impact of this magnitude of sound. The Germans, however, understood quite well the terror this kind of sound could instill in people. They purposefully built this audio capability into their dive-bombers, like the Stuka.

Around the second week of April, some of the Kriegies started taking down the barbed wire fencing that separated our enclosure from South Compound's enclosure. The Germans didn't seem to care at all and certainly didn't try to stop us from mingling. Old buddies met up with each other, and a lot of bartering and haggling started up. Again, the Germans didn't seem to care, so we had complete freedom to trade and barter as we liked.

I found it incomprehensible, but all kinds of rackets got started—rackets concerning food, rackets concerning the chocolate Army D-bars and rackets for cigarettes. The number one item of exchange in the prison camp was the Army ration D-bar, which was a high-energy chocolate bar. The second most important item was cigarettes. Everything was valued in D-bars or cigarettes. The number three item was food.

Andy Anderson had traded a of couple dozen D-bars for our Kriegie stove, but this was before the rackets started up. Everything changed once these got going. The Kriegies who set up these rackets formed their own Goon squads. One had to go through the Goon squads in order to get in and dicker with these fellows. It was like watching a corrupt city government in operation.

Shortly after the inner wire came down, I wandered through South Compound's area and spotted Lt. Donald Stevens through the crowd. I don't know if he saw me, but I immediately turned and walked away because I didn't want anything to do with him.

During the month of April, as the war drew near to its end, housing had to be found for the influx of additional officer POWs. The men from West Compound finally arrived from their long trek out of Stalag Luft III. They had been taken to Stalag XIII D, just southeast of Nürnberg, had stayed there for over three months and then were ordered to march south to another camp, which turned out to be VII A. To make room for them the Germans set up huge white canvas tents next to our barracks, moved us out of the barracks into these tents and moved West Compound into our barracks.

Major Simoleit, Deputy Commandant of Stalag Luft III, travelled with West Compound from Nürnberg. When he arrived at VII A, he was made the de facto camp commandant because he outranked the current German commandant. This happened on the 20th of April.

One of the big white tents erected to accommodate the arrival of West Compound. (Lt. Col. Keeffe collection)

The Door Tent

Andy and I, Lenny Bughman, Bob Keller, and another Kriegie didn't like the tents at all. They were horrible! The ground inside was damp and soggy. I don't remember who the instigator was, but the five of us decided we weren't going to stay in the tents.

The entrance to the wooden barracks from either end was through an outside door into a little entryway, then through another door into the main barracks. Why they had those entryways, I don't know; probably to keep heat in during the winter. But they didn't need two doors, so we decided to grab a few to make a structure outside to sleep in and to get out of the stench and smoke. These doors were made of rough wood, not at all like house doors at home.

The five of us went to different barracks and pulled the hinge pins out of six doors. We used the doors to make a tent right up next to the south fence of our compound and placed a blanket at each end. A captain became very angry because we'd taken the doors off his barracks. He stormed out to our new tent and made us give back one of the doors, so we had to put a blanket over the hole that created.

Somewhere, we scrounged up a few nails and used them to tack the blankets to the doors. I grabbed a couple of board planks from the barracks and placed them on the ground outside our door tent so we could put the few items we had on them: a couple of Red Cross boxes, one or two cardboard boxes, and our trusty Kriegie stove. We brought in what little bedding we had, and now we five had a private castle away from the chaos.

Lt. Jim Keeffe cranking the handle of a Kriegie stove, and Lt. Andy Anderson outside their door tent. .
(Lt. Col. Keeffe Collection)

It was cramped with all five of us sleeping inside the tent. The blankets and doors kept the rain off, more or less, but the main thing was privacy. There was no place I could go in this camp and be alone. At least at Sagan there were individual stalls in the abort, and I could go into one of them to be by myself if I wanted to. But at VII A there was no place to go and be alone. The five of us got to a point where each of us craved being alone, being quiet and getting away from cigarette smoke and the hubbub of open-bay barracks life. This we achieved out there in our little tent.

As spring came upon us in April, so too did the breakdown of order and discipline. Fights became more prevalent. Many of the prisoners merged into gangs, some for protection, some for graft, and some just for the sake of bullying others. By the third week in April, most of the inside barbed wire fences separating the rest of the compounds and sections from each other had been torn down. Prisoners were mingling freely throughout the camp: South Africans, Yugoslavians, Italians, French, Americans, English, Poles, Russians, you name it. Officers and men of other ranks were mixing together, too. The German guards didn't do anything about it because they knew the end was coming.

I was filling up my cup from the water spigot one morning when I ran into Ray Moulton, the bombardier from my B-24 crew. Boy, what a sight for sore eyes! We shook hands and patted each other on the back and talked for quite a while. He was staying with the rest of West Compound in one of the barracks we had vacated. I told Ray about my stay in Rotterdam and about meeting Dr. Lemoine and hearing his story about treating Clyde Baker and him (Moulton) at a farm-house. Ray confirmed that that was exactly what had happened and then told me how he'd eventually wound up at Sagan in West Compound.

He and Baker had been taken to a hospital in Dordrecht where they ran into Stevens and Smith. All four of them were treated for their injuries by the German doctors. Within a couple of weeks they were transported to a German Luftwaffe hospital in Antwerp. Eventually, they were all moved to Dulag Luft. Stevens and Moulton were then sent to Stalag Luft III; Stevens was put into South Compound and Moulton was transferred into West Compound.

Lts. Bob Keller and Andy Anderson outside the door tent. (Courtesy of Stowe Keller, son of Bob Keller)

Our conversation turned to wondering about what had happened to the rest of the crew. I told him I'd seen Stevens the other day, but no one else. Ray didn't know about anyone else either, only that he and Baker had been separated at the hospital. Neither of us knew what had happened to McArthur. Later on, I found out that McArthur had been taken to Stalag Luft I, located outside a little town named Barth on the northern coast of Germany.

Moulton and I also discussed bringing charges against Stevens, but that would have been one great big administrative hassle.

"What the hell, the war's nearly over here in Europe. Let's all just go home," we finally concluded.

During the last several weeks of the war, no more German Air Force airplanes flew over the area. The Luftwaffe had been pretty much neutralized by this time. Our P-51s, P-47s, and P-38s were in the area, though, and it was a wonderful sight to see them fly over on their way to strafe targets in and around Munich. As the Allied forces came closer, the U.S. Army's little popcorn machines, the Taylor Craft and the Piper Cub artillery spotting planes, started flying around. Their job was to locate targets for the artillery and scope out enemy troop deployments and movement.

"It Ain't Gonna Be Long Now"

Somewhere around April 25th or 26th we had mixed rain and snow. It was miserable. The ground was damp, and everything was cold and soggy. A night or two later an artillery battle took place, with our camp between the two opposing forces. The battle was one-sided because the Americans had some very heavy cannon. They had the 155mm, nicknamed the Long Tom, which was an absolutely fabulous gun. They also had 155mm howitzers and other cannon of smaller calibers. All night long artillery shells were fired across our camp. The Americans were shooting at Germans who were busy destroying their bridges over the Isar River, just east of the camp and the town of Moosburg. You haven't lived until you've spent a night under an artillery barrage. A shell going across overhead sounds like a freight train roaring by a hundred feet or less away. The very air itself seemed to rip apart as those shells screamed by all night long. Add to that the deep *rumph* and crash and sudden flashes of the exploding shells, and I don't think one person slept a wink that night.

The roll call was no longer taken the last few days in camp. No more appells! I think the Germans were afraid to come into the camp. I'm sure they were beginning to experience desertions—guards throwing away their uniforms and rifles and taking off. Why the hell stick around? We knew, and the German guards knew, that it wasn't gonna be long now. Several of the younger German guards had already been taken away for the "defense of Munich," and those who were left were mostly old men or worn out soldiers.

What none of us knew at the time was that on the 26th and 27th of April, meetings were being held between representatives of the International Committee of the Red Cross and the commandant of Stalag VII A concerning the plight of the prisoners. The Germans urgently put together a proposal to declare the camp and surrounding area a neutral zone. This would have had the effect of halting the American advance toward Moosburg and would also have given the Germans a free pass to retreat across the Isar River. The German proposal was to be soundly rejected.

End Notes
The March

1. At the end of WWII, the Russians --on Stalin's orders --moved nearly 20,000 American servicemen and close to 30,000 British and Commonwealth servicemen into Russia. All of them were former POWs of the Germans who had been "liberated" by the advancing Russian army. The Russians literally kidnapped these men right from under the noses of Allied ground forces who were helpless to do anything about it, because of weak-kneed policies toward Stalin at the highest levels of both the American and British governments.

2. The towns we marched through had German names during the war. Later on, the names were changed by first the Russians, then the Poles. Below is a list of those towns with the WWII German name on the left and the post-war Polish name on the right:

   - Sagan – Zagan
   - Hammerfeld – Czerna
   - Zehrbeutel – Dolany
   - Halbau – Ilowa
   - Charlottenhof – Borowe
   - Freiwaldau – Gozdnica
   - Selingersruh – Lipna
   - Priebus – Przewoz
   - Pattag – Potok
   - Jamnitz – Jamnica
   - Lichtenberg – Letow
   - Birkfahre
   - Schrothammer – Klekot
   - Hermsdorf --Przewozniki
   - Muskau --Bad Muskau

3. We brought Popeye, Glemnitz, Simoleit, and two or three other German officers over to the United States a couple of times to our Stalag Luft III camp reunions. Some of the guys were absolutely opposed to their coming, but the sensible ones said, "Look, these people made our lives livable, and the war is over." Most of us were happy to see them. They were very decent people.

4. The terms "Non-com" or "non-commissioned officer" or "NCO," refer to enlisted ranks of authority, i.e., sergeants.

5. The Dutch named a street in Rotterdam in honor of Folkert Elsinga. It is called Folkert Elsingastraat.

6. "Oflag" is an abbreviation for *Offizierslager*, or Officer's Camp. The Germans put Allied officers in Oflags and Allied enlisted men in Stalags. Since Stalag Luft III was originally built to hold enlisted POWs, the name remained even after most of the enlisted men were moved out and it became a German POW camp for officers.

7. A Mickey ship refers to a bomber that carried a radar system that would allow for bombing in adverse weather conditions. The ball turret was removed and a retractable H2X radome system was installed in its place.

Liberation!

A Quick and Furious Fight

S aturday night, the 28th of April, things were rather quiet. Rumors were running rampant through the camp, but it was fully expected that on the next day there would be a big fight. There was no doubt what the outcome would be.

Early the next morning, I crawled out of our tent and climbed up onto the roof of the nearest barracks with some of the other fellows. A definite air of expectancy buzzed through the camp. To the west was a range of hills. At the base of these hills the Amper River flowed through the valley. This small river ran parallel to the west side of the camp about a quarter of a mile away then joined the Isar River just north of the camp. The land rose upward from the Amper toward the prison camp and the town. At this time of year the river was quite low.

I found out later that shortly before 6 a.m., one of our senior officers and a couple of the Germans had gone to the SS unit defending the area. They, along with an SS Major, all hopped into a car and drove to find U.S. Brigadier General Charles Karlstad, commander of the 14th Armored Division. Karlstad's division had halted in and around the town of Mauern just a few miles northwest of Stalag VII A. The purpose of this trip was to present, under a white flag of truce, a proposal to declare Moosburg an open city, so that there would be no fighting.

The American response was a swift and clear "No." In fact, General Karlstad demanded the unconditional surrender of all German troops and warned the SS Major. "We know the camp is there, and we know about how many prisoners are in the camp. You had better not do anything with them. Hands off!"[1]

A little later on in the morning we saw what the Germans were up to.

Previously, they'd dug a line of fox holes along the road coming from the river into town. The SS were rounding up old men and young boys and putting these poor confused civilians into those holes with *panzerfausts*, the German equivalent of our bazookas. These unfortunate people were in civilian clothes, but each one of them wore an armband on the left arm with a single word written on it—*Volksturm*—which meant "People's Storm." They had been dragooned by the SS, given ten or fifteen minutes of training on how to handle a panzerfaust, and then told to shoot at any tank that came their way.

Up on top of the barracks somebody called out. Way up on the horizon, on the ridge line across the valley, we could see tanks lining up. Around nine o'clock in the morning the tanks started firing. As they came toward us down from the ridge line, they disappeared into the trees.

We Kriegies split into three groups. One group got up on the roofs of the barracks and watched the whole battle, cheering and shouting and jumping up and down as if they were watching a football game. Another group, of which I was a part, was either up on the barracks doing the same thing or on the ground cooking up some food. We knew we were going to be liberated, so there was no sense in trying to hang onto our miserable little amounts of food. We tore a board or two off a barracks and broke it up into kindling for a fire to heat some water for tea or something else. Then we went back up onto the barracks' roof to watch the fight.

The third group were men who had decided that since they hadn't been killed yet, they weren't about to be killed now. They got into the slit trenches and the air raid shelters, and that's where they spent the morning.

We could hear the fighting down by the river. The noise from small arms and heavy machine gun fire rose to a roar. The tanks came into view again as they rumbled up from the river into the fields to the west of town, where they formed a skirmish line. Then the halftracks came along, deploying more motorized infantry that spread out in amongst and behind all the tanks.

An Allied observation airplane circled slowly overhead, probably with an artillery spotter or an officer on board to relay radio messages concerning the ground operations and situation of the enemy back to the American fighting forces. A couple of tanks began to fire at the town church in Moosburg, knocking off one of the two spires. It turned out the Germans were using it as an observation post; it was high up, and they were controlling their own forces from there.

The main part of the fight didn't last long, maybe an hour. When it was over, the SS were defeated almost to a man. Their dead lay in the trenches and foxholes where they'd made their last efforts. Unfortunately, some of the poor old men and boys, the "dreaded" *Volksturm*, who'd been too afraid to run away, were killed, too. It was criminal the way those civilians had been placed in the front lines against battle-hardened troops.

The tanks moved on toward the town with the infantry following along behind. Inside our camp, all kinds of flags appeared out of nowhere. I don't know where the guys had gotten the cloth or the materials, but there they were, American, British, and French flags hanging outside on some of the barracks. All the interior wires in the camp had been taken down by now, leaving only the formidable exterior wires.

A 14th Armored Division tank rolls toward the center of Stalag VII A. Thousands of POWs erupt in jubilation. (Courtesy of USAFA Special Collections Branch, General Clark collection)

Led by a Sherman tank, a small motorized column broke off from the main column's left flank and swung down the road past the front of the camp. The main force had already entered the town and was engaged in fighting. For some reason or other, on their way past the camp heading into town, machine gun fire from some of our tanks raked the camp. My understanding is that some Kriegies were hit and several were killed.

When the small column reached the main entrance to Stalag VII A, it swung right. The tank broke down the large wooden gates and drove right through the wires. It was under the command of a lieutenant in a jeep following right behind. Two or three halftracks filled with infantry and a couple of 6x6 canvas-covered trucks followed the jeep. The tank smashed through all the gates as it rumbled down the main street. It finally came to a stop when it reached the center of the camp.

There really is a U.S. Army Sherman tank under all those now ex-Kriegies. (Courtesy of USAFA Special Collections Branch, General Clark collection)

Stalag VII A Camp Commandant, Major Simoleit (left), Major Alton S. Kircher, Executive Officer 47th Tank Battalion (center), and Group Captain Richard Kellett, RAF, senior British officer (right). This is the moment of official surrender and Major Simoleit is establishing the time needed to get his men in from the many guard posts around the camp and disarm them. (Courtesy of USAFA Special Collections Branch, General Clark collection)

Old Glory goes up and the roar of freedom becomes deafening! (Courtesy of USAFA Special Collections Branch, General Clark collection)

It is difficult to describe the mood and the jubilant uproar of tens of thousands of caged-up men. Everybody was cheering! The day had finally come! We were liberated! We were all caught up in the moment.

Above the din, the young lieutenant standing up in the jeep shouted, "I am Lieutenant So-and-So, and I have a brother named So-and-So who is a shot-down pilot. Does anybody know where he is or what happened to him?"

As if by a miracle, the lieutenant's brother showed up at the jeep within about five minutes. The lieutenant had a case of pink champagne in the back of the jeep. He took out two bottles, broke the necks off, gave one to his brother and took one for himself. They locked arms and drank pink champagne to the cheers and shouts of wildly excited men.

I wasn't interested in champagne; I was interested in what was in those covered trucks. I walked over to one of the 6x6 trucks and lifted up the back canvas flap. Inside was a huge pile of knives, swords, and every kind of firearm you could think of, even *panzerfausts*!

"May I have a gun?" I asked the driver.

"Sure, help yourself," he said.

Several other men nearby overheard me speaking to the driver, and they started to dig through the pile. It only took about three minutes to empty the truck. There were four or five hundred shotguns, rifles, and blunderbusses. I was hoping to get a German Luger, but I didn't know what kind of holster it had. I wanted a gun with a holster and an extra clip. In the scramble with the other guys I found a pistol in a holster, and sure enough it had a spare loaded clip. The pistol turned out to be a Spanish Astra 300, a 9mm-kurz semiautomatic. This particular gun was made for Hitler's Third Reich. It had the Nazi eagle stamped on it and may have been taken off a high-ranking officer or Gestapo agent. I was certainly glad to have it.

After I retrieved the pistol, I went back to the truck driver and asked him where in the world he had gotten all the crap in the back. He told me that as the army moved through the towns and villages after securing them, they dropped off a military government detachment in each one. The first thing each detachment did was to put up a notice in German on the City Hall doors. This notice explained many things, one of which was to turn in all weapons:

> You have three hours to turn in the following: All firearms, all swords, all knives over six inches in length.

That was where the pile of arms in the back of the truck had come from.

I hurried back to our make-do tent and proceeded to examine the pistol. I had to figure out how to take it apart and reassemble it, how to cock it, and what the safeties were. Soon I'd figured out the whole gun. Inserted in the pistol was a clip with six rounds of ammunition. A full spare clip was in a container stitched to the side of the holster. When I finished, I left the tent with the holster and pistol strapped around my waist and wandered back into the jubilant mass of newly freed men.

The camp was in absolute mayhem with guys all around laughing, hugging each other, crying, and singing songs. All the different nationalities were joining in the euphoria of liberation. Many of these servicemen had been POWs since 1940—five long years!

Sporadic weapons fire came from the direction of Moosburg for a while after we were liberated, but eventually that quieted down, too. I wandered around the camp, poking my nose in everywhere, curious as usual. It was wonderful to be able to walk around and not be limited by a formidable wire fence or the threat of being shot by German guards. I made my way outside the smashed front gate to some other buildings and poked my head through the door of one of them. A few ex-Kriegies were inside rummaging through some big trunks. Wondering what they were doing, I walked in and quickly realized that they were grabbing their personnel cards out of the files.

When we bolted out of Stalag Luft III on the 27th of January, the Germans put all our records into foot lockers and trunks and had them shipped down to Stalag VII A. One of the buildings at the entrance to VII A was a headquarters for the administration of the camp, and the POW records had been stored in there.

Not only was I able to find my big personnel card in one of the trunks, but I also found my smaller locator card. It was fortunate that I arrived in the building shortly after the first fellows did because once they discovered what was in the trunks, it wasn't long before they were throwing out handfuls of paperwork looking for their own. If I'd shown up any later, I doubt I would have found my records in the mess they created. The trunks also contained many envelopes filled with things taken from the prisoners. I looked for the one that had my wristwatch and fountain pen—taken from me way back at the German police station in Antwerp—but I didn't find it.

The Aftermath of Liberation

A couple of days earlier, a message had come down from our SAO for everyone to stay put. We were one hundred percent sure a fight would erupt and that the Americans would win; there was no doubt about the outcome. When the battle was over, the senior officers wanted us to stay pretty much where we were so we could be processed as quickly as possible and flown out. We were also warned to stay put for our own safety.

"You've survived the war. Stay in the camp where you're safe. There are a lot of armed, angry German soldiers out there, and there's no sense in getting killed now," was their reasoning.

But even though the Army was told to keep us in the camp, they simply couldn't. There were too many of us, and many of the Allied POWs couldn't understand English anyway. Some of the ex-POWs cut through the peripheral wires, and we used those holes, not just the main entrance, to get out of camp. There was no way the Army could control all of this.[2]

Later on that afternoon, I found Andy and we decided to get out of camp for a while. We needed "fresh air" and just to get away from all the noise. Bob Keller joined us, and the three of us took off through one of the holes cut in the outside fence. We started walking south following a little side road to the main road. There we turned left and walked into the town of Moosburg, just a little over a mile from the prison camp.

The German civilians had white sheets and white slips hanging out of their windows. Virtually all of them were smart enough to stay indoors. The German military had already pulled out of the town to the south and the east, and they'd blown the bridge after crossing the Isar River.

We entered the town and began walking up the main street. One of the first open shops we encountered was a wine cellar. The cellar was two-thirds below grade level and one third above it. From the street level, we walked down a few steps and took a look around. It was a wine cellar with huge wooden hogsheads of wine, six feet high, sticking through the walls.

Some ex-prisoners were already in the cellar. They had gotten hold of axes or something and smashed the hogsheads, filling the floor about eight inches deep with wine. These guys, many of them Russian POWs, were sitting in the pool of wine drinking the stuff, just slurping it up. They were stone drunk. When one of them tried to stand up, he staggered and fell with a splash onto the floor. It was sickening to watch. Bob, Andy, and I looked at each other with disgust written all over our faces. Shaking our heads, we went back up the steps and out onto the street and headed farther into town.

After walking a few more blocks, we came to a "Y" in the street. Situated right in the apex of the "Y" was an office building with some gold lettering printed on the front window. One of the words was *Versicherung*, which means "insurance."

Parked outside was a U.S. Army Sherman tank with its main gun aimed through the front door of the building. We walked around the tank and went through the front door into a small office to see what the heck was going on. Against the back wall was a huge black steel wall safe about seven feet high and four feet wide. Several GI's were in the office along with the tank crew and a few ex-POWs.

"What in the world are you guys doing?" I asked one of the tankers.

"Get outta here because we're gonna blow up that safe!" he yelled. "This is a bank, and we're after the money!"

"You jerks," I said to him. "This isn't a bank, it's an insurance office! Do you see the word in the window, *Versicherung*?"

He couldn't have cared less. The tanker kept yelling for everyone to clear out. Then he climbed back into his tank, which still had its main gun pointed right inside the door.

"Everybody get out! We're gonna fire!" another GI shouted.

We all piled out of the building and "*BOOM*!!!" The tank fired a round into the mechanism of the steel door, which blew it open. The entire building shook, and dust scattered all over the place. Papers were blown everywhere. The men were practically frothing at the mouth like crazy people as they rushed greedily into the blown-open wall safe.

Sure enough, they found very little money. All they'd accomplished was to scatter insurance papers all over the place and fill the air with dust. Again, we were disgusted.

"Come on, let's get the hell out of here," I said to Bob and Andy.

So we left the building and walked down the right leg of the "Y" and on through the town.

We left what seemed to be the downtown area and came to the outskirts on the other side. GIs were in foxholes along the side of the road, which looked rather humorous to us. They had their rifles and whatever else belonged with them in the holes. As we passed by, some of them asked, "What are you guys?"

"We happen to be American officers. What the hell are you doing in that hole?"

"Well, there's a war going on, and the engineers are down there trying to rebuild the bridge across the river. You'd better get down, or you're gonna be killed," we were warned.

"We've lasted this long. We don't think we're going to be killed today," we replied.

As we walked along, our artillery was shooting across the town and the river into the German positions. I presume the Germans had light artillery on the far side of the river because their shells were going across us all the time too, but in the opposite direction.

Lt. Keeffe (center) posing with soldiers of the 68th Armored Infantry battalion. (Lt. Col. Keeffe collection)

On the right side of the road was an orchard. It was the 29th of April, and the trees had started to bloom. Several halftracks and other armored vehicles were parked in amongst the trees with GIs scattered about, resting and waiting. The three of us walked into the orchard and talked with a group of them who were lounging next to an armored troop carrier. They wanted to know who we were. We told them we were American officers just liberated from the POW camp.

The GIs introduced themselves and said they were part of the 68th Armored Infantry Battalion. They were waiting in the orchard while the engineers, half a mile down the road, established an improvised bridge over the Isar River next to the one the Germans had blown up. As soon as the engineers completed their work, the 14th Armored Division was to continue its drive deeper into Germany, pursuing and fighting the Germans. We shook hands all around, and they gave us some D-bars and asked if we wanted cigarettes.[3]

"Thanks, but no thanks. I don't smoke," I said, "But do any of you have a camera by chance that you'd be willing to give me?"

"Sure, I've got two or three of them," one GI said.

I didn't ask him where he'd "liberated" them, but he gave me a box camera and two rolls of film. This was a fine gift indeed because I was able to take some great pictures back in camp. But first, we had our pictures taken with the GIs next to their armored vehicle. The light was fading, so we decided it was time to head back. We said our good-byes to the soldiers and walked back through town. When we got back to the camp, we crawled through the hole in the fence and headed to our door tent.

The jubilation of liberation had subsided somewhat, but there was still a lot of activity. Music was playing over the loud speakers. Some of the men were doing their bartering and racketeering. The German guards had been rounded up and replaced by wonderful American GI soldiers who were trying to keep some semblance of order. It was quite late when I crawled into the sack that night, and I didn't fall asleep for a long time because my mind was filled with countless thoughts.

My First Full Day of Freedom

» Timeline «

> » April 30, 1945 – Adolf Hitler and his new wife, Eva Braun,
> kill themselves in an underground bunker in Berlin as the
> Russians advance to within a few blocks of the heart of Nazi
> Germany.

The next morning I woke up to a gray wet dawn. Andy was also awake, so we decided to go for an early walk out into the countryside. Once outside the camp, we wandered aimlessly and chanced upon a farmhouse that had been taken over by a U.S. Army artillery outfit. In the fields, they had set up their battery of 155mm "Long Toms," which were huge guns, along with their tractors and other vehicles. There was a wonderful smell of cooking emanating from the farmhouse, so we went in and found the kitchen. A group of GIs was hanging around while a couple of them stood at a stove cooking some food.

"What the hell are you two guys?" one asked, and I answered him.

"Have you had breakfast?" someone else asked.

"No, and we haven't seen ham or eggs for more than a year," said Andy. "Well, we'll take care of that right now!" said the cook.

V-Mail letter written while eating a great ham and eggs breakfast. (Lt. Col. Keeffe collection)

In no time, that cook whipped up a batch of the best eggs and ham I've ever eaten.

"How do you guys write home? Do you use letters or post cards?" I asked while sitting at the table enjoying my breakfast.

"No. We use V-Mail."

"What in the hell is V-Mail?"

"It's a single sheet of paper that you write on, fold up and give to the mail clerk. No stamps are required. Postage is free."

"Do you have any of those V-Mail forms you could give me?"

"Sure."

While stuffing myself with ham, fried eggs, and white bread, I borrowed a pencil and wrote a short note to my parents—my first letter home since December. I gave it to one of the GIs when I was finished, and he promised to drop it in the mailbag with the others.

Shortly after I'd finished the letter and the great breakfast, someone shouted, "Pack up, and move out!" Everyone kicked into gear and started to do what they needed to do to get the artillery ready to move out. We thanked the GIs, wished them well and headed back to the dreariness and misery of VII A.

In the afternoon the newly built Treadway bridge over the Isar River was completed and elements of the 14th Armored Division that had been backed up all over the area, began to stream across.

The Treadway bridge over the Isar River was constructed by the 300th Combat Engineering Battalion in less than 24 hours.
(Courtesy of Col. Riel Crandall collection)

General George S. Patton, Jr.
Commander U.S. Third Army

The next day, the 1st of May, was more of the same: cold and wet. Over the previous several days the ground had become muddier and muddier. Today was no different. In fact, it was worse.

Andy and I decided to go for a walk. As we headed down the main street toward the entrance to the camp, I looked up ahead and recognized General George S. Patton walking toward us. I immediately knew it was him from his pictures. He was accompanied by another general, a couple of colonels, and his personal GI bodyguard.

Patton had come to the camp with his own combat detachment, which he had in addition to his Headquarters' staff. Everywhere Patton went his little group went with him. A couple of the GIs with him were radiomen. On their backs they carried radios with long antennas, and they had microphones. General Patton and his people had dismounted from their vehicles at the entrance to the camp and were walking in through the mud to the cheering of hundreds of now ex-prisoners.

General George S. Patton, Jr., arrives at Stalag VII A the 1st of May.
(Courtesy of USAFA Special Collections Branch, General Clark collection)

What impressed me most about this man was that he'd gotten out of his jeep, stepped down into the mud where the rest of us lived, and walked into camp. Previously, newspaper people had come through in staff cars driven by GI soldiers. Not wanting to get dirty, they'd stayed in their cars and rolled down the windows to call out to the POWs.

"Is there anybody here from Minneapolis? Is there anybody here from Texas?"

They looked for stories from the warmth and luxury of the inside of their ve-hicles. The same was true for others. A couple of Congressmen had come in the same way; they remained in their cars, only rolling down the windows. None of them, not one, got out of their damn cars. They wouldn't demean themselves by getting out in the mud with the rest of us, but General Patton would.

As we walked toward him, Andy and I saluted and he saluted back. He continued walking into the camp, and we continued walking toward the camp's entrance. I was outside of the camp during the rest of his time there so I didn't see him again, but I heard several stories when I got back later in the afternoon.

General Patton addressing a massive crowd of ex-POWs at Stalag VII A.
(Courtesy of USAFA Special Collections Branch, General Clark collection)

General Patton continued on to the center of the camp and climbed up into a jeep to address the POWs who were crowded around. I understand there were hundreds of them, all yelling and cheering and saluting. When Patton raised his hand, the noise dropped instantly. He had already sent in a detachment of administrative people who had set up right there in the mud: shelters, portable tables, and typewriters—the whole ball of wax. My understanding is that this is some of what he said:

"I want you to gather all your camp commanders, anybody who's in charge, and bring them here."

Within minutes these people arrived. Off to the side, under U.S. Army guard, was a group of German guards who had not been taken to Munich. These poor guys were all quaking in their boots.

Patton addressed the Allied senior officers from the different nationalities.

"I want you to go in there among those guards and pull out the decent

Germans. I don't need to tell you what a decent German is."

The officers identified four or five Germans, and they were pulled out. Patton drew himself up and saluted these people.

"On behalf of the authority invested in me as 3rd Army Commander, if it is to your advantage, as of this instant you are free men. If it is to your advantage to remain in the German military, that can be accommodated. Go over to those tables with the clerks, and you will be given identity papers and passes to go home. Go home, locate your families. Those passes will get you housing, food, and a job with the American military government if you desire."

He then turned to the senior officers.

"Go in and pull out the bastards, and I don't need to tell you what a bastard is."

Among the guards at Stalag VII A, 10 to 20 percent were really decent men, and 10 percent or so had treated us badly. The rest of the guards had just done their jobs, their duty as soldiers. Many of them had lost their homes and members of their families to bombings or to the war in other ways. Patton had the bad guards marched out of the camp with a statement.

"By virtue of the authority vested in me as Commander of the 3rd Army, you are hereby summarily sentenced to death for ill-treatment of war prisoners."

He then spoke to the senior officers again.

"We promised to have you out of here in twenty-four to thirty-six hours. However, I want to beat the goddamned Russians to Vienna and to Prague. I don't need ammunition. What I need is gasoline, maps, and food. I'm using the air transport as well as the road transport to accomplish this. We made a promise, and if you insist on it, I will stop my forward movement and utilize the airplanes and the trucks to take you people out. Or, if you see fit, I would like to beat the goddamned Russians to those two capitals."

"Go to it!" the prisoners shouted, and we stayed in camp for much longer than the promised two to three days.

After passing by General Patton, Andy and I continued on and walked out of the camp through the main gate. We wandered west across the railroad tracks and headed down a dirt road past some fields. I saw some chickens in the yard of a farmhouse, just off the right side of the road, so we walked up to the front door and knocked. A timid woman opened the door a few inches and peered out at us.

"*Wir haben Hunger.*" (We are hungry.) "Would you please cook a chicken for us?"

After we spoke with her for a few moments, she invited us inside. She was happy to cook a chicken for us when she saw we weren't going to kill her, rape her, burn her house down, or kill her animals.

It turned out she lived alone. I saw a photograph of a man in a German uniform and asked if it was her husband?"

"Yes," she said.

"Where is he?" I inquired.

"I don't know." She sounded very sad. "I have not heard from him for two years now. I know he was in Russia, but I have had no information for two years."

The chicken and vegetables she cooked for us that day were wonderful, and we thanked her after we finished eating. In return, I gave her a D-bar and a bar of soap that I had with me.

Andy and I wandered back to the farmhouse where I had written the V-mail and saw that the artillery had been readied for transport to their next site. Everything was packed up, the guns were trailered and the column was just beginning to move out. Andy and I watched for a while and then continued walking around through fields and woodlands. I presume the dispossessed German family returned to their farmhouse to find only minimal or no damage.

On our way back to camp that afternoon, we crossed back over the railroad tracks. I wanted to explore some more. Andy decided to go on into camp, so he waved good-bye and turned toward the front gate. I wandered down a short railroad siding and came across a small shed right next to the tracks. It looked like a supply hut and had a small wooden porch on the front. Curious as usual, I went inside and found a bunch of boxes stacked against one wall. When I opened one up, I found it full of new red Nazi flags with the big black swastika in the center. They weren't very well made; the stitching wasn't very straight, and the cloth was of inferior quality, but they were brand new. I grabbed one of the flags along with a black German fireman's helmet that was on the floor.[4]

Back left: unknown, Lt. Jim Keeffe, unknown , Lt. Lenny Bughman. Front left: Lt. Bob Keller, unknown, Lt. Andy Anderson, unknown. The four unnamed fellows are South African ex-POWs. (Lt. Col. Keeffe collection)

"I'm Gonna Kill Me a Couple of Nazis!"

The next day found Andy and me out in the countryside again—anything to get away from the mess in camp. This time we went for a walk down toward the Amper River. It was very pleasant down there walking under the trees. It was rather chilly and overcast, but it wasn't raining or snowing. We were thoroughly enjoying the quiet solitude, the sounds of the small river and the animal and insect life that prevailed there. And as usual, I had my newly acquired Astra 9 mm pistol with me.

We ambled along the forested banks of the river on a trail barely wide enough to accommodate a small vehicle like a jeep. A smaller path wound down through the woods on the right and joined the path we were on, about forty feet in front of us. I presume this path came from the road up by the train tracks. As we drew near the side path, an American soldier came walking into view with an M1 carbine pointed at two young boys. The boys were in German army fatigue uniforms, were capless, and had their hands up over their heads. As they approached, I could see that they were crying. The GI behind the boys swung his carbine at Andy and me.

"Don't point that damned gun at me!" I shouted, as I put my hand on my pistol, ready to take it out.

The threesome continued walking down the path toward us. By now, they were only 15 or 20 feet away.

"Hold it right there!" I shouted.

The GI swung his gun at me again, and again I reached for my pistol.

"Don't point that gun at me," I repeated, "or I'll blow your damned head off!"

"What are you guys?" he asked.

Since Andy and I were still dirty and wearing a hodge-podge of clothing, the man had no idea what we were. I had on a black French beret with a tin can second lieutenant bar attached to it. I was wearing a Polish battle jacket, U.S Army GI pants, some kind of weird foot gear and a piece of white German nylon I had made into a scarf tied around my throat. Andy was wearing an Army officer's green gabardine cap with a gold eagle badge on it.

This GI was absolutely spic-and-span clean. Everything he had on was perfectly pressed. I didn't believe he was any kind of front-line soldier because firstly, he had a carbine instead of a rifle, secondly, he was a buck private, right at the bottom end of the pole and thirdly, he was completely clean. Even his boots were clean, not wet or mud-spattered.

"Who the hell are you guys?" he repeated.

"We happen to be American officers. We've just come out of the prison camp, and we're down here to get away from the noise in camp. Now I'll ask you some questions, private! What are these two boys you've got here?"

"Them are Nazis," he snarled, jabbing his carbine at them.

"Now just a minute!" I ordered.

I looked at the two boys as they stood there, shaking and quivering with their hands up and tears running down their faces.

In German I asked them, *"Wie alt bist du?"* (How old are you?)

One was thirteen and the other was fourteen years old.

"Warum bist du in Uniform?" (Why are you wearing a uniform?)

"We really don't know," one of the boys replied in German through his sniffles.

"Well, yes, but you are in a uniform. Why are you wearing a uniform?"

Then they told me their story.

They weren't brothers, nor were they related. They'd both been picked up by the German Army in the same manner. Each of them had been working on his father's farm a few days earlier, when a German army truck stopped on the road just outside where they were working. A feldwebel *(sergeant) motioned to them to come over to the fence, which they each did.*

"Get into the truck," he ordered the boys.

"No. I can't do that," each boy said. "I'm working on my father's farm."

"You will come, or we will shoot you!" the sergeant ordered.

So they got in the truck and were taken to a military caserne. *There they were told to get out of their civilian clothing, and they were given fatigue uniforms and fatigue uniform caps. They were held there for two or three days and fed. Finally, they were put back in a truck again and driven to a railroad bridge that crossed over the Isar River.*

"This railroad bridge has been armed with explosives," a German soldier told the boys, "and it is ready to be blown. Here is the control box. You will sit under the approach to the bridge by the riverside, hidden from view with a few branches as camouflage. Here is a loaf of bread, a piece of sausage, and a flask of water. You must wait until the first train comes. It will be an American train because the Amis *(German slang for American soldiers) are coming. When the train gets on the bridge, turn this handle 90 degrees and push it down. That will blow up the bridge, and then you can go home. If you leave here without doing what you're being ordered to do, you will be shot."*

The two boys waited three or four days. They heard the artillery duel one night, and they heard the shooting when the Americans came through the next day and liberated our camp. They heard additional shooting for a day or two after that, and then it became quiet. They ate their loaf of bread and piece of sausage and drank the water they had, but no train came.

(Those boys would have had a long wait for the first American train, because the Germans had blown all the bridges upstream from the one they were ordered to blow.)

After waiting three or four days, they became hungry and decided that since the shooting had stopped, they would go home. They discarded their caps, came out of their hiding place and started walking down the road toward their homes, when along came an American GI truck. The truck stopped, and our spotless buck private grabbed his carbine, jumped out of the truck, and "captured two Nazi soldiers!" as he'd proudly announced.

"How come you're so clean?" I asked the spotless, fancily-dressed American private.

"I'm a truck driver."

"Where the hell's your truck?"

"It's on the road up there," he said, pointing back along the small path they'd just walked down.

"You'll be damned lucky if it's still there when you go back. What are you going to do with these two boys?"

"Them are Nazis. I'm going to shoot 'em!"

"What have they done?"

"Well, they're German Nazis!"

"Listen, you get your ass back up to that truck and go about your business, and you leave these 'Nazis' to me. I'll take care of them, and I'll take charge right now. And don't point that bloody carbine at me anymore! Get your ass back to your truck and go do your duty. Before you leave, I want your name, your service number, your commanding officer's name, your first sergeant's name, and your organization."

He rattled them off and I could tell that he wished he was somewhere else. Then he spun around and scurried back the way he'd come.

The creep had been in the process of taking these kids down to the river, out of sight somewhere. I'm sure he planned to shoot them. He probably wouldn't have killed them outright unless he shot them in the heart. The carbine is a small caliber gun, chambered for a .30 caliber bullet, which is more like a large pistol round than a rifle round. If you know what you're doing, it is possible to kill with it. That GI truck driver probably didn't know much about his carbine, and the boys would have suffered terribly.

The two boys wiped their eyes and noses as dry as they could and tried to look brave, but their faces were still puffy from fear and crying.

"Ihr werdet mit mir kommen," (You're going to come with me.) I said to them gently. "You can put your hands down now. Go down to the river and wash the tears from your faces."

"What are you going to do with these boys, Jim?" Andy asked.

"We'll take them to the lady who cooked us up that chicken lunch yesterday."

Her farmhouse was only about a twenty-minute walk away. We turned around and headed back down the path by the river. We left the woods and crossed a field to get to her house. When we got there, I knocked on the door and the lady opened it. I told her the story the boys had told me.

"Would you please keep these boys hidden for three or four days? Then give them a piece of bread and a flask of water and let them go home."

"Jawohl," she said, "of course."

"Do you have any of your husband's clothing these boys could wear? We've got to get them out of these German uniforms."

She nodded and said she had some work clothes.

"That's good. Get the boys out of these uniforms. Burn them and don't keep anything. Burn it all. The shoes are alright though."

We left the two boys with the lady at the farmhouse. Hopefully they stayed there for a few days and then made it safely home.[5]

Russian Vengeance

Within two days of our liberation, the Russian prisoners had to be rounded up and put back in enclosed compounds. Many of them had gone about the country-side getting drunk, like the ones we saw in town in the wine cellar, and breaking into any house they could find. In some cases, they had raped and murdered women and young girls. A wire enclosure was strung up on the outside of the main wire of VII A to contain the Russian ex-POWs.

It's difficult to describe what it's like when tens of thousands of people of different nationalities and languages are suddenly set free with little or no con-trols. People were everywhere, wandering through every part of the camp. They were out in the fields, along the roads, and in town. Smart POWs slaughtered and butchered some livestock and hung the carcasses from trees: cows, sheep, and goats. Many ex-prisoners had campfires going and were trading everything they had for a piece of butchered meat to cook.

Add alcohol to the mix along with years of pent-up emotion, and you have a recipe for disaster. With the Russians, there was the added hatred they had for the Germans. We had been fighting the Germans, but we didn't have the visceral hatred for each other that the Germans and the Russians had. The atrocities the Germans and Russians had perpetrated against each other during the war were truly horrific, and revenge between the two nations was just as brutal. That's why the word had gone out through the American Army to round up the Russians and enclose them, to prevent them from further terrorizing the local German civilians.

Widow's Mill

Once when Andy and I were out on one of our wanderings, we found an old Catholic girl's school. We had walked across the bridge over the Amper River and noticed a copse of trees farther down the road, off to the left, with a school in the center. The name of the place was Wittibsmühle, which means "Widow's Mill."[6] At one time there had been a mill there, probably to grind grain. The mill itself had long ago been shut down, but the name had remained. At some point Catholic nuns had taken over the house and run a school for what the Germans called *Dienstmädchen*, "Service girls" or "Service maidens."

Lt. Keeffe (left) and Lt. Anderson standing near their door tent the day after liberation. (Lt. Col. Keeffe collection)

This particular group of buildings contained the mill where the girls had lived and a two-story building the nuns had lived in. German guards had taken over Wittibsmühle when they occupied VII A and had sent all the girls and Catholic nuns off somewhere else.

The place was now abandoned, so we decided to explore it. We went through every room of the big two story building, even up into the attic. It quickly became apparent to us that the German guards had left in a panic. The beds were unmade, drawers were pulled out, and clothes were strewn all over. Chairs and tables had been kicked around, and papers were everywhere. The place was just chaos inside.

We arranged a couple of the beds and stayed there that night. It was absolutely wonderful compared to where we'd been sleeping, on the ground in our makeshift tent.

"Let's Get the Hell out of Here"

When Andy and I returned to camp and our tent the next afternoon, we found that most of our food had been stolen. We didn't have much, but what little there was had been rifled through, and most of it was gone. Who ever stole it had also gone into our tent and rummaged through our stuff. Lenny was inside complaining that something of his had been stolen.

I was really ticked off. Over the last few days, upon returning from our wanderings, Andy and I had found that there was always something missing. It was evident that people had been poking around in our tent. This was the last straw.

Bob Keller showed up a few minutes later with our fifth tent mate (whose name I can't recall). When they found the food had been stolen, they also became quite upset. We had a conversation amongst ourselves about the latest theft, and about how long we were going to have to stay here. Right after liberation, various senior officers had drawn lots to determine the order in which the different sets of ex-POWs would be flown out. The British Indians had won first place. We Americans had wound up almost last, which meant many more days for us in this rat hole. I'd had enough.

"The hell with this," I stated. "Let's go." They all agreed.

We spent a little time gathering some of our personal things. I had swapped my long wool GI greatcoat for a short Polish battle jacket, which I was now wearing. I still had my shirt bag with the sewn-up bottom and tied sleeves. I packed a little two-can stove, my spoon, the papers I'd brought with me from Stalag Luft III, my diary, the camera, and the German flag and helmet into it. I didn't need to pack any clothes since I was wearing what little I had. Somewhere I had found an opened Red Cross parcel with some food in it and carried that with me also.

The weather was cool and overcast with no precipitation, and it was a little warmer than it had been the previous several days. Slinging my bag over my head and shoulder, I was ready to go.

The five of us took off. One last time we went through one of the holes cut in the south fence, and headed toward the Amper River. We crossed the bridge, which had not been blown, and were soon walking past Wittibsmühle as we made our way across the valley, headed in the direction from which the 14th Armored troops had come. The road, called Mauerner Strasse, ran in a northwest direction through the valley and on over the hill on the far side. It was on top of this hill that we'd first seen the tanks of the 47th Tank Battalion the morning we were liberated.

Now there was virtually no traffic on the road, except for a few U.S. Army trucks. We tried to hitchhike several times as GI trucks passed us going west, but they just roared right by. When we got to the top of the hill about three miles from camp, we stopped for a quick rest. I turned to get one last look back across the valley to Moosburg and VII A, but I couldn't see them because of the trees.

"Look, I don't think these GIs in the trucks are going to pick us up," I said. "They're probably afraid of the five of us. Let's split up into two groups."

Lenny Bughman had been getting pretty antsy and finally let us know what was on his mind.

"I really don't think it's a good idea for us to be doing this. We were ordered to stay in the camp," he said.

"Lenny, we've got to think positively about this," I said, trying to reassure him.

After a little more talk, it became clear that he wasn't going to change his mind.

"OK Lenny. If you don't want to come, why don't you just go on back?"

"Well, I wish you guys luck," he said, "but I don't care to be part of this."

We all shook hands with him, and he turned around and started back down the hill.

The rest of us picked up some twigs and used them to draw straws. Andy and I paired up, and Bob paired up with the other fellow. Then we drew straws to see who would go first. The first pair would leave now and the other pair would wait 15 or 20 minutes before following. Andy and I won the draw, so we shook hands with the other two guys and wished them luck. We took off down the backside of the hill and continued heading northwest.

A smaller road angled off to the north a couple miles farther on, but we continued on the leftward route. About a mile and a half later we walked into the town of Mauern. It wasn't a very big town, and the main road twisted and turned on its way through. In the middle of the town was a small plaza. There wasn't a soul to be seen.

Hanging out of most of the upstairs windows were white sheets, white pillowcases, ladies' white undergarments and slips. The town folks were all scared to death and stayed buttoned up in their houses. Many of the houses had shutters, and they were closed as well. It was quite eerie; here it was late afternoon with neither a sound to be heard nor a soul to be seen.

As we approached the northern outskirts of Mauern, a woman ran out of a house and came up to us. She was very distraught. Gesturing wildly, she poured out a bunch of words. Finally, I understood what she was talking about. She was telling us that there were two bad men in some kind of a garage. I had difficulty understanding some of what she said. She was afraid of them, and I'm sure she was also afraid of the Americans finding them in there. I asked her to take us to this place. She led us down the road about forty yards to a small barn-like building off on the left. It turned out to be an old converted stable.

Before reaching the door of the building, I removed my shirt bag from over my shoulder and set it on the ground so I would have full freedom of movement. Then I took out my pistol and made sure there was a round in the chamber and the safety was off. Andy opened the door to the building quietly and slowly and we went inside. The building was about the size of a large two-car garage. It had a loft used to store hay or straw. The floor was packed earth and it looked like it had been used previously for horses.

The woman stood by the door motioning with her finger to be quiet. She pointed up to the loft to indicate where the two men were. I looked around and saw two bicycles off to the left, leaning against the inside wall—beautiful bicycles with beautiful rubber tires!

Then I looked up toward the loft. I couldn't see up there because it was eight feet above us and the light was quite dim inside. The loft covered about half the area of the building, toward the rear and away from the door. I could see straw at the edge of the loft as well as a portable ladder that led from the earthen floor up to the loft. Pointing my pistol at the ground, I fired off a shot.

"Kommen Sie herunter, und mach schnell, und Hände hoch!" (Come down quickly and get your hands up!) I shouted out in my loudest German.

The shot sounded like a bloody cannon going off!

Two very well-dressed men rose up out of the straw in the loft. They both stared down at us, and I motioned for them to come down. Neither of them said a word as they climbed down the ladder. This was difficult for them to do with their hands raised in the air. Each time they tried to put their hands down, I pointed the gun at them and shouted,

"Hände hoch! Höher!" (Hands up! Higher!)

I quickly sized them up. Having lived with the number-one tailor in

Rotterdam, I was very familiar with the quality of suits now. These men were impeccably dressed in beautiful civilian suits. They had on neckties along with vests over their shirts and very expensive coats. I looked at their faces and figured that they were very important people of some sort.

"They have to be very highly-placed people. Either they're Nazis running away, trying to get home, or they're military officers who have gotten out of their uniforms into these beautiful suits," I thought to myself.

After I fired the round into the ground, several people peeked in at the doorway to see what was going on.

"Do you see those bikes over there, Andy?" I said.

"Yes, I noticed them."

"We're not walking anymore. We're riding, beginning right now."

Among the people clustered around the open door was a young man with an old rifle.

"Warum haben Sie das Gewehr?" (Why do you have that rifle?)

"Ich bin Polak." (I'm a Pole.)

"What are you doing in Germany?"

"Three years ago the Germans picked me up with a bunch of other young men. They brought us here and forced us to work on the farms. But now I am free and, therefore, I have a gun!"

"Haben Sie Kugeln?" (Do you have bullets?)

He nodded his head, yes. He was quite proud to have this gun.

"Ok," I thought, "we've got these two guys, and I don't want them. All I want are their bloody bicycles and to help the lady by getting these guys out of her bloody building."

"At the Rathaus (town hall), are there some Americans?"

"Jawohl."

"Fine. Take these two men, march them down to the Rathaus and turn them over to the American soldiers."

He was overjoyed to do this.

"You tell them to keep their hands up. And if they put their hands down, you shoot them."

He nodded he understood.

Then I turned back to our captives, who occasionally tried to put their hands down, provoking me to jab at them with my pistol.

"Hände hoch! Hoeher!" I ordered. *"Marsch! Holen Sie sich bewegen, marsch!"* (March! Get moving, march!)

They headed for their bikes.

"Nein, nein, nein. Spazieren!" (No, no, no. Walk!) I snapped.

Motioning with my pistol, I got them shuffling toward the door. The Polish kid pulled in behind them with his old rifle trained on their backs.

"If they put their hands down or try to run, shoot them!" I told the kid. "Come on Andy, we're riding."

The Kreidenweis Family

Andy and I were now mechanized. It was late in the afternoon by the time we rode our new bicycles back to the main street and headed north out of Mauern. The overcast skies darkened as evening came upon us, and I started to feel uneasy. I presumed that as the Allies roared down the roads with their tanks, they'd encounter German soldiers. Those Germans who didn't get killed or surrender would flee up into the hills on either side making the road an unsafe place to be after dark. The soldiers would be hungry and dangerous.

After riding along the road for a couple of miles, I looked over at Andy and said with concern, "We'd better get off the road, Andy."

Up ahead, we saw a farm just off the right side of the road. We rode our bikes into the packed dirt farmyard, which was surrounded by several buildings. The buildings on a German farm were usually built around an open square. This farm was no different. The house was on the left side of the square courtyard with a pig sty attached to the end of it. At a ninety-degree angle to the pig sty was a larger building for grain storage and cows. Ninety degrees to that was a building for equipment like small tractors, and ninety-degrees to that, filling out the square, was a small building for tools and other storage. We got off our bikes in front of what looked to be the farmhouse. There was no porch or covering at the front, just a couple of steps up to the front door.

On the wall by the front door was a plaque with *Ein, Doidorf* written on it. I took this to be the address #1, Doidorf. I knocked on the door and got no response. Another knock and nothing, so I banged on it. Finally, a middle-aged lady opened the door. The poor woman was shaking.

"Gnädige Frau, wir haben Hunger, und wir werden heute Abend hier schlafen" (Dear lady, we are hungry, and we will sleep here tonight), I said to her gently.

She brought us into the kitchen, which is one of the main rooms in a German farmhouse. Her husband was there, along with their little daughter.

They could see that I had a gun, and they were scared to death. I tried to reassure them. "You don't need to worry. We're not going to harm you. We just want to spend the night."

But before we went any further, I asked the man if there was somewhere we could hide the bicycles. He asked us to follow him, and we went outside to put the bikes in one of the other buildings.

When we came back into the house, the lady had already started preparing dinner. She cooked us up ham and eggs, along with some bread. All this time we still had on our muddy boots. Since the farmer hadn't taken off his boots when we came back into the house, we hadn't either. As it turned out, the custom in this farmhouse was that boots were fine in the hallway and kitchen, but not in the living room.

After we finished eating this wonderful meal the man showed us where to sleep. It was the master bedroom. The farmer indicated for us to put our muddy boots outside the door of the bedroom. I didn't really want to do this because if they made off with our boots we'd be barefooted. But I finally caved in and put them outside the door of the room.

Bavarian farmers had a strange kind of bed. It had a mattress with sheets on it and a large wedge-shaped thing that covered the top half of the bed. The Bavarians slept almost in a sitting position, halfway between lying down and sitting up, using the wedge to prop themselves up. The first thing Andy and I did was to throw the wedge thing on the floor, as neither of us wanted to sleep halfway sitting up.

That was one long night. I don't know how these people could sleep in such a bed. A down comforter that was a few inches thick and very warm covered the bed. However, it was just the size of the top of the bed. Andy and I got into the bed together and went to sleep. We woke up later in the night to find that our feet were hanging out the bottom of the comforter, and our hands were uncovered and cold. When one of us turned over it would pull the doggone comforter thing onto the floor. We spent the whole night waking up and putting that bloody thing back over us.

At first light, I tiptoed over to the door because I wanted to make sure our boots were there. I couldn't believe what I saw. Andy had regular boots with a shiny exterior, capable of being polished. Somehow I had come up with a new pair of boots in the prison camp, and these boots were made out of the new GI reversed leather. The shiny slick side of the leather was on the inside of the boot, with the rough, almost suede-like leather on the outside. The reason the boots were made this way during the war was so the soldiers wouldn't have to waste time polishing them. They just scrubbed them with a wire brush, and that was it.

The farmer and his wife must have worked for two hours on those two sets of boots; they absolutely sparkled. They shone! We put our boots on and went downstairs and thanked them for the wonderful job they'd done on our boots. The wife was cooking breakfast, and we all sat down together and ate another fine meal.

They begged us to stay because they were afraid German soldiers would come after food and cause trouble. I told them we were sorry, but we had to go. As we were departing, I asked the farmer if we could get a picture with him and his family, so we all stood in the open front doorway, and Andy, standing outside with my camera, took a picture of us.[7] Then we thanked the family for their kindness and shook hands all around. The farmer brought our bikes out to us. I slung my bag over my head and we mounted up and rode off up the road, heading north.

Lt. Keeffe with the Kreidenweis family at Ein, Doidorf 5 May, 1945 . (Lt. Col. Keeffe collection)

To France

We pedaled for several hours, stopping every once in a while to relieve our-selves and stretch our legs. Whenever a GI truck came up behind us we stuck out our thumbs, hoping to get a ride, but they just sped right on past us. Eventually one did stop. We went over to the truck to talk with the driver. After explaining who we were, we told him we wanted to go west to France and asked if we could ride with him as far as possible. He was happy to take us and told us to put the bikes in the back of the truck, which was like a dump truck. We put our bikes up in the bed and climbed into the front cab with the driver. Back on the road, the driver shifted through the gears, and we chugged along mile after pleasant mile.

An hour or two later, the truck driver told us that he had to turn off. Andy and I grabbed our bikes out of the back and continued on. Not long after a jeep pulled along side us, and we ended up riding north in it. The jeep had side curtains and a cover over the top of it, which left no room for our bicycles, so we had to leave them by the side of the road. The driver said he was going all the way to Nürnberg, which was fine with us. We figured we might be able to get on an airplane there.

Eventually we reached the beautiful medieval city of Regensburg. The jeep driver tried to cross over the Danube River, but the bridges had been blown. Hitler had sent out orders for all bridges to be blown up and all factories to be destroyed. He was crazy, but luckily some of his generals had thought of the German people and the future of Germany and had refused to carry out Hitler's "scorched earth" orders. Still, many of the bridges had been destroyed, making it difficult to find a way across. The jeep driver turned around and traveled for some distance back southwest, looking for a way across the Danube. An hour or so later we reached the town of Ingolstadt, eighty or ninety kilometers from Regensburg. There we found a treadway bridge that the GIs had put across the river, parallel to another bridge that had been blown. We drove slowly across the makeshift bridge on pontoons and headed back north. Finally we came to the city of Nürnberg.

Whereas Regensburg had escaped much war damage, Nürnberg was badly smashed up. It had been the seat of Hitler's Nazi party and had extensive rail yards, which the Allies had targeted for bombing missions. The huge Nazi parade ground was on the southeast side of Nürnberg. On the edge of this property was what had once been a camp for the Hitler Youth. This camp had eventually become Stalag XIII D, where West Compound had been sent when they were turned out of Stalag Luft III.

The driver parked in front of a building in the center of Nürnberg and told us this was as far as he was going. After thanking him and shaking hands, Andy and I walked off to find an airbase. Somewhere along the line we bumped into a military policeman.

Of course he asked us, "What the hell are you two?"

"We happen to be officers, former prisoners-of-war, and we're trying to get to an air base."

"There's an air base outside the city, north of here, called Erlangen, but you're not supposed to go there. All ex-prisoners are supposed to go to the stadium to be processed," he said and gave us directions to the stadium.

We thanked him very much and went around the corner.

"To hell with that guy," I said, "let's go find the airbase."

It was a long walk to the air base at Erlangen, maybe ten miles. By the time we got there it was after dark. At first, the military policeman at the entrance didn't want to let us come on the base. Dressed as we were, I really couldn't blame him.

"Who the hell are you two?"

"We happen to be Air Force pilots, and we're officers," I said to him very forcefully.

"Well, you don't look like officers."

"We're ex-POWs, and we're on our way to France, and by God we're coming on the base."

From right: Lt. Keeffe, jeep driver, Lt. Anderson, unknown, standing in front of the covered jeep that brought them to Nürnberg. Note Lt. Keeffe's Kriegie wings above left shirt pocket, tin can Lt. bar on beret, and Spanish Astra 9mm pistol in holster on belt. (Lt. Col. Keeffe collection)

Eventually he relented after hearing our story and let us through the gate onto the base. The Germans had smashed the whole place up, then the 8th Air Force had bombed it. Now the Americans were trying to put it back into a useful condition. There were no lights whatsoever. It was so dark I couldn't locate the BOQ (Bachelor Officer's Quarters). Nor could I locate anybody who could tell us where the Officers' Club was. We eventually walked up to what turned out to be a barracks building, opened the door and walked in on a group of NCOs. It turned out to be a GI barracks. The guys inside all turned to look at us when we came in.

"What in the hell are you two?"

And we told them.

Andy asked if they knew where the Officers' Quarters were. No one did, but they said we could stay the night there and in the morning we'd be able to find our way. There was a stack of mattresses near one wall, and the GI's pulled a couple of them off the stack onto the floor. They gave us a couple of blankets, and that's where we slept. Although my make-shift bag was full with things like my camera, my papers and the Nazi flag, I had no toothbrush, no soap, no razors, not even a comb. We were looking pretty rough.

The next morning Andy and I left the barracks. I asked the first GI we saw, "Where's the Officers' Club, the Officers' Mess?"

He pointed it out and Andy and I made our way over to it. When we entered the building, boy were we looked over by all the neat, clean officers in their nice pink and green uniforms.

A couple of them came over to us.

"Do you speak English?" one of them asked.

"I speak English as well as you do, why do you ask?" I replied.

"Possibly you're in the wrong place?"

"This is the Officers' Mess, is it not?"

"Yes, it is."

"We are ex-POWs. We've just come out of a cage, and we're here for breakfast, if you don't mind."

Andy and I were served a very nice breakfast.

Next we walked out to the airfield. The tower and the Operations building had been smashed up, but the Americans had brought in a portable Operations trailer complete with radios and parked it near the flying field.

Andy and I stepped up into the trailer and into the Operations room where we found a major. I had stubble on my face and I probably stank. I hadn't had a shower for maybe two or three months. I had on the French beret with the tin can bar shaped like a 2nd Lieutenant's bar. I also had on my set of lead Kriegie pilot's wings, which had been made back at Sagan. There we were—me with my wings and Andy with his officer's cap.

The major turned around and looked at us. I sized him up. He was a pilot because he had wings on, but he was what we called a "slick-wing pilot," a junior pilot. Additionally, he had only one ribbon, the ETO (European Theater of Operations) ribbon, which told me that he'd never flown combat. He'd probably just come over from the States.

"Major," I said, "we're two ex-POWs, and we're trying to get to either France or to England."

He went off with both barrels.

"You damned prisoners! All you do is bother me! And you steal everything! Get the hell out of here! I don't want to talk with you! You're not supposed to be out here on the flying field! You're supposed to be in town, at the stadium! I can't help you!"

"Colonel" Jimmy Blackstock

Without a word, Andy and I turned right around and went out of his trailer. Walking back from the airfield we were wondering what to do next when, out of nowhere it seemed, we ran into Jimmy Blackstock and one of his friends. I hadn't seen Jimmy since Stalag Luft III, but I still had the drawing he'd made of me free-falling to earth from my stricken B-24.(See pg. 88)

Blackstock and his friend had taken off from Moosburg a day or two after Andy and I had. Somewhere they'd wound up with a touring sedan, and they cruised up to Nürnberg in style. They were on their way out to the Operations trailer we had just left. I told them what the story was with the major.

As we were talking and catching up on all that had happened, we walked over to the PX (Post Exchange – a military store), which was close by, and picked up some candy bars. None of us had any money, but somehow Jimmy had managed to "acquire" some. Along with food and some clothing, there were uniform caps, insignia and stuff like that for sale in the PX. Suddenly, we had a bright idea.

Even though Jimmy was only a year or two older than I was, you couldn't tell if he was twenty-five or forty-five years old. We bought an Army cap, a colonel's insignia for the cap, and another set for his shoulders. Instead of a 2nd lieutenant, he was now Colonel Jimmy Blackstock!

I went to the telephone, called the base motor pool and ordered a staff car for Colonel Blackstock. A driver and an Army Plymouth showed up. We all piled in.

"Take us out to the Operations trailer," Blackstock ordered the driver.

He drove us out there, and we piled out of the car. Jimmy marched—actually he stomped—right into the building with Andy and me trailing close behind him.

"Who's in charge here!" he barked.

The major was still there. He turned around and saluted our 2nd lieutenant-turned- full-colonel, and Blackstock read him the riot act.

"I understand you don't like fellow officers who've been in prison camps, who've flown combat! And all you've done is wear that silly Spam ribbon you have on!"

"Yes, sir! Yes, sir! I'm sorry sir, but sir, we have orders..." The major whined and wrung his hands. Jimmy kept right on laying into him.

There happened to be a couple of men in flying suits inside the trailer. They were in the process of filing a flight plan prior to takeoff, and of course, they saw what was going on.

"Excuse me, Colonel," one of them said. "We've got a Gooney Bird here, and we're just about ready to take off."[8]

"Where are you going?" I asked him as Blackstock continued to chew out the major.

"We're going to Wiesbaden."

"What direction is it?" Andy asked.

"That's northwest."

"Fine, we'll go with you if that's OK?" I said.

"You're very welcome to come with us."

Blackstock wasn't quite finished with the major.

"I want your name! I want your service number! I want your CO's name! And Major, if I hear of you turning away a single ex-POW in the future, I will have your ass! Do I make myself clear!"

"Yes, sir! I'm sorry, sir!"

I was pretty impressed with "Colonel" Blackstock.

Andy, Jimmy, his friend, and I followed the two pilots out to the flight line and climbed into the waiting Gooney Bird. We all had a pretty good laugh at Jimmy's performance. He mimicked chewing out the major a couple more times, and we roared with laughter. The pilots taxied the C-47 transport out to the end of the runway, spoke to the control trailer, poured power to the engines, and we were off.

It wasn't far, maybe half an hour of flying northwest to get to Wiesbaden. After the plane taxied in and came to a halt, we got off and shook hands with the two pilots and thanked them greatly for their efforts. They were glad to have helped and wished us all the best of luck.

American forces had held Wiesbaden longer than Erlangen, giving them more time to fix things up. The Operations building was in good shape. We walked in and waited to speak with the Operations Officer.

Several military officers were inside, including two Army generals. One of the generals walked up to us and asked, "Excuse me, young fellows. What the hell are you?"

We told them we had recently come out of a prison camp and had just flown in from Erlangen, down at Nürnberg.

After taking in our interesting array of clothing and military insignia, one general asked, "Have you had lunch?"

"No, sir," we replied.

"Well, you're our guests."

The generals had a jeep waiting outside, and the driver jumped out when we approached. Andy and I and one of the generals climbed in the back. The other general got in the front next to the driver. Somehow or other, Blackstock and his friend had become separated from us in the Operations building before the two generals approached us. I didn't see Jimmy Blackstock again until long after we got back to the States.

It was quite an interesting experience riding into Wiesbaden. We were two unshaven ex-POWs in much-worn mismatched clothes, in serious need of a bath, riding with two generals who treated us as equals. The jeep driver took us into the city proper and down to the senior officers' hotel, where the generals hosted us to lunch. We were the center of attention as the other generals and colonels asked us a lot of questions.

After a great lunch, we all hopped back into the jeep, which had been waiting outside, and the two generals rode with us back out to the Operations building at the airfield.

"Put these two officers on the first airplane going west," one of the generals told the Ops officer.

There was a young lieutenant inside filing a flight plan. After saluting the generals, he said he was flying to France.

"What kind of a bird do you have, Lieutenant?" the general asked.

"Well sir, I've got a Noorduyn Norseman."

"Fine. I would greatly appreciate it if you would give these two officers a ride in your airplane as far into France as you can."

We saluted the two generals, and they both shook our hands and wished us luck. Then they left.

The young officer was ready to go, so we all walked out to his airplane and climbed in. The Noorduyn Norseman was a Canadian-built single-engine, high-wing, small passenger plane. It could hold a pilot and maybe four or five other people. Two other military fellows jumped into the airplane with us and we took off.

Once in the air, the lieutenant pointed to a case and told us to open it. It was full of pink champagne. So all the way into France, Andy and I and the other two passengers drank pink champagne. This was the first alcohol I'd had in the ten months since my fateful dinner at Big Guy's house in Antwerp.

So much had happened since that night. A lot of memories and worried thoughts about the brave folks in the Netherlands weighed heavily on my mind as we flew west over Belgium: the boys who'd rowed me up the River Noord; the lads who'd brought bicycles and led me through terribly unsafe places; the Jappe-Alberts; the Sanders; Kees van den Engel; J. J. van Dongen; the Broekhuizens; the Berlijns; the Loose family. I'd thought of all these fine people many, many times over the last months, but it wasn't until after liberation and the easing of the constant tension of being a POW that I really thought long and hard. I was very worried about the lives and wellbeing of all those who'd risked their lives for me. A knot formed in my stomach as I remembered Big Guy reading some of their names off his list.

Front left to right: Lt. Anderson, Lt. Keeffe, and pilot just before boarding the Noorduyn Norseman at Wiesbaden, bound for France. (Lt. Col. Keeffe collection)

Now we were flying over territory not that far south of where I had traveled eleven months before—first on my journey west, filled with fresh hopes of making my way back to England, and then abruptly changing direction and being moved east, ever deeper into enemy territory and an uncertain future as a prisoner of war.

Camp Lucky Strike

The pilot took us to an airfield way up in northern France. It was right on the coastline, in the middle of farm country at the west end of Normandy where the D-Day invasion had taken place. Americans were flying all ex-POWs to this base. It was where we were to be processed back to the States. We landed there on the 6th of May.

The weather was very warm. At the airfield were huge flat-bed trucks with stakes on the sides and benches in the back. Andy and I climbed up onto one of these trucks and sat on a bench with a group of other men who'd been flown in from different places. It wasn't long before the truck lurched off.

We were transported out to a huge tent camp called Camp Lucky Strike. We learned that there were actually several camps with cigarette names, and together they were called the Cigarette Camps—Camp Lucky Strike, Camp Phillip Morris, Camp Chesterfield and several others. Initially, these were camps for fresh U.S. troops who were to serve as replacements for Army combat casualties. Recently, however, Camp Lucky Strike had been turned into an out-processing camp for liberated American POWs.

The truck dropped us off outside a line of hospital tents. These were long tents that were hooked together and had wooden floors. Before entering the tents we were told to strip naked, which we did.

"Anything you want to keep," an orderly said, "put over here in a little pile. We'll take all your clothing and fumigate it, clean it and give it to the French people. You'll be getting new clothes, so don't worry about leaving your old stuff." Once again, I mouthed my two Dutch gold coins.

Camp Lucky Strike, a virtual sea of tents, in northern France. Well over 1,000,000 Allied soldiers passed through this camp on their way to join in fighting the Germans. After Germany's surrender, it processed nearly 50,000 ex-POWs before sending them back to the states. (Courtesy of USAFA Special Collections Branch, General Clark collection)

We were deloused. Standing naked outside the tents, they first squirted us with powder, then we bent over and they squirted us with both a liquid and a powder. After this, we entered the first tent, which turned out to be a shower tent. We were each handed a bar of soap and a wash cloth. There were probably 20 to 30 shower heads.

We showered and showered and showered. I'd had my last shower three months before when I was fresh out of the Snake Pit, waiting for my clothes to be gassed with cyanide. This was wonderful! And there was no hurry. We could have stayed there all day.

When we finally finished showering, we rinsed off and went to the next tent where we were handed towels. Each of us was also handed a little packet that contained a toothbrush, a bar of soap, a comb and a razor. We kept moving through the hooked-together tents. We were given shorts, undershirts and a bar-racks bag. Then I was asked what size shirt I wore.

"15 1/2," and they gave me two shirts.

"What's your waist size?"

"32," and they gave me pants.

Bing, bing, bing. By the time we got to the end of the series of tents, we each had new boots, four new pairs of socks, three sets of underwear, three handkerchiefs and a complete GI uniform—a soldier's uniform.

As we exited the last tent, we were instructed to go on over to the Admissions tent. Outside, I looked at Andy and he looked at me.

"Andy, you're beautiful!"

"Well, Jim, you're beautiful too."

"That was really nice, wasn't it?" I said.

And he replied that it was.

"Let's do it again!"

So we stripped naked, put all of our new clothes into the barracks bags they'd given us and pushed them under the wooden floor of the last tent. Then we went back to the first tent and worked our way through the whole system again. We got deloused again, went through the showers again and were given another barracks bag full of clothing.

We then went to the Admissions tent where we were checked in and assigned to our quarters, one of dozens of identical pyramid-shaped tents. The only items inside our tent were eight cots. At the Admissions tent, we were also given a list of rules that included a mimeographed sheet explaining what kinds of food we'd be eating in order to get our stomachs back into shape.

The first item on the sheet was a simple warning.

> *"Please be careful. Don't eat candy bars. Don't eat too much.*
> *We are going to feed you three times a day; any other time*
> *you can have eggnog."*

There was one tent where only eggnog was served. We could have all of that we wanted, but we could only eat three meals a day. No seconds! This was emphasized because liberated POWs had become sick and some had died because of overeating. The selling of candy bars had been stopped too, because men were gorging on them and inadvertently killing themselves.

In the Administration tent was a bulletin board that each day listed the names of the men who were to leave the following day to go to the port of Le Havre and sail for home. We were told to check this list at nine o'clock every morning and at four o'clock every afternoon.

The following day, we were scheduled for individual debriefings. I was taken into another administration tent where I was interrogated by an Army captain. He was very interested in what I had to say because I had been loose in Holland for five months. He wanted to know where I'd been, what towns and cities and so forth. He asked me to be as detailed as possible. For instance, not only did I tell him about the Jappe-Alberts, but I also told him of the five Jews the Jappe-Alberts had been hiding and of all the others I knew who had helped

Allied airmen like me. I spent quite a bit of time telling him all about my time there and my eventual capture. The captain gave me a couple of blank sheets titled "SECRET HELPERS" and asked me to write down all the names of the people who had helped me and any addresses I could remember. It was a long list.[9]

Recovered Allied Military Personnel (RAMP) Headquarters at Camp Lucky Strike.
(Courtesy of USAFA Special Collections Branch, General Clark collection)

"OK, where do you want to go? Do you want to go back to England, or do you want to go home?" he asked me when I had finished.

"No, I left nothing in England and I can go home later. I want to go to Holland. I need to find out what has happened to the people who sheltered me."

"You can't go there," he said at first.

"Young captain, sir, I've been around the block a few times since being shot down, and I'm very sorry, but I'm going to take off and make my way up there. That is, unless you lock me up, which I don't think you will."

He was a smart man. Instead of trying to pull the "tough captain" routine with me, he used psychology and began to reason with me.

"Lieutenant, number one, the people are starving up there in Holland. The Germans have been very bad to the people this past winter and were intentionally starving them. The Dutch would most certainly have to feed you, yet they can barely feed themselves and their families. Number two, the bastard Germans flooded the place, and much of the Netherlands is now under water. Transportation is almost non-existent, most of the power stations are down, and virtually nothing is operating above the Maas River. All you would do is cause trouble for yourself and for anybody else if you try to go up there."

Hearing how he described the terrible conditions in Holland made me worry even more for my friends, but I could see his points and relented.

"OK, I understand. In that case I want to go home, back to the States."

"Where are you going, Andy?" I asked later on when we were settling into our cots for the night. "Are you going back home?"

"Well Jim, I have nothing to go home to. I have only my mother, and she and I don't get along very well, so I'm going to go on back over to England and try to rejoin my outfit. I've got a girlfriend over there and I'll look her up."

How sad: "Nothing to go home to." I thought about my family, my parents and my four brothers and sisters. I thanked God for my wonderful family.

Constantly Being Hungry

Along with the euphoria of no longer being cooped up and the excitement of going home, was the ever-present thought of food and eating. We ex-POWs were always hungry and we lined up early for every meal. If lunch began at twelve o'clock, we began lining up outside the cook tent at about 11:30. Most of the cooking was being done outside because the weather was relatively decent and warm with no rain.

Ex-POWS, in their newly-issued GI fatigues, waiting in a food line at Camp Lucky Strike.
(Courtesy of USAFA Special Collections Branch, General Clark collection)

There was no place to sit and eat, but there were tents with stand-up counters. We'd get our food and drink and stand at one of these counters to eat. When we were finished eating, we'd wash our mess kits in series of drums set up specifically for that purpose.[10]

A couple of days after we arrived, we were in line waiting for lunch to begin. I was about twentieth in line, and some of us were talking with each other while waiting for the line to start moving.

Soon, a GI showed up and went to the head of the line. He just walked right on past us into the kitchen, opened up his mess kit, loaded it with food, and then left. Another GI walked by us and did the same thing. After a third one did this, we became very angry. We were officers and had been standing in line for half an hour, and these guys were just wandering into the place from wherever and cutting in front of us.

Right after this, a detachment of German prisoners was marched by. One soldier broke off from the group and did the same thing the other GIs had done. He opened up his mess kit and took out his canteen cup. We were having fried chicken, and he got his buddies in the mess cooking area to give him several pieces. They also gave him a huge scoop of mashed potatoes and a couple of thick slices of white bread, which we hadn't seen in almost a year. Then he picked up a big glob of butter that must have been at least a quarter of a pound! I really got upset when he took his canteen cup and dipped it, along with his hand, into a garbage can full of sliced peaches. When he pulled his hand and cup out of the garbage can, they were dripping peach juice. He had a full quart of peaches! With his dish heaped with food in one hand and the overflowing cup full of dripping peaches in the other, he ambled over and sat down on a box right along side us and began to eat.

We were fuming! The GI ate a few bites of chicken and only one bite of a big piece of bread. He never used the butter. Then he slurped three or four slices of peaches into his mouth, wiped his mouth off on his sleeve and headed for the trash can.

Our line had finally begun to move, and the men were getting their food. When I saw the GI heading for the garbage can, I snapped. I jumped out of line, ran over to him and got between him and the garbage can.

"Where are you going!" I demanded.

"Well, I'm goin' to the gabage can," he drawled.

"What're you going to do at the garbage can?"

"I'm gonna throw this in the gabage can."

"Oh no, you're not!"

I made him go back and sit down on the box.

"Start eating!"

The men in the line, all officer ex-POWs, started clapping. I forced the GI to eat the bread, all of the chicken, and the quarter pound of butter. By then, his eyes were about as big as golf balls. Then, I made him drink the peaches. All this time I was reading him the riot act. The fellows in the line clapped and cheered.

"We haven't seen as much food as you were going to waste, some of us for three or four years! Most of us haven't had any meat for that long, or eggs, or white bread, and here you are grabbing MORE than you can eat, and then you're going to throw it away! You don't know what hunger is!"

I said a lot more that I can't remember now, but I was really ticked off. I made him eat it all. His buddies in the cook tent were mad as hell too, but not at him. They were mad at me for "being mean."

When he'd finally crammed the rest of it down his throat, he stood, and immediately vomited it all back up. I hope he learned his lesson.

I got back in line and had my lunch.

GERMANY SIGNS
UNCONDITIONAL SURRENDER!!

Truman Proclamation of May 8, 1945

'The Allied armies, through sacrifice and devotion and with God's help, have wrung from Germany a final and unconditional surrender. The western world has been freed of the evil forces which for five years and longer have imprisoned the bodies and broken the lives of millions upon millions of free-born men. They have violated their churches, destroyed their homes, corrupted their children, and murdered their loved ones. Our Armies of Liberation have restored freedom to these suffering peoples, whose spirit and will the oppressors could never enslave...'

The 8th of May we got word that Germany had surrendered unconditionally.[11] There were celebrations everywhere. The French soldiers and American GIs were shooting their guns in the air. Guys were dancing and hollering and just letting loose everywhere. The war was officially over in the European theater, but there was already small talk and rumors of outfits being refreshed and sent over to the Pacific because the war with Japan was still in full swing.

That same day, I was called to the Administration tent and issued an identity card. Now, after fourteen months of first having a Dutch fake ID and then a German POW ID card, I was "official" again.

Two days later, my name appeared on the roster to go down to Le Havre the following day. It was time. I was finally going home! I went back to the tent and packed up my two duffel bags, even though they were mostly packed anyway. I found Andy and told him I was getting on a train for Le Havre the next day and going home. He and I had a nice talk. We wished each other the best and promised to look each other up when we were both back in the States. The next morning, May 11, I waved good-bye to Andy and was taken to the train. I didn't see him again for many, many years.

Endorsements

IDENTITY CARD

FOR

EX-PRISONER OF WAR

This Identity Card MUST be retained until collected at the Reception Camp in the United Kingdom

AGPD 2-45/225M/C546ABCD

48

Service No.
Serial No. } O-747814   Nationality   U.S.

Surname
Last Name } KEEFFE

Initials JAMES H. JR.

Rank 2ND. LT.

Regiment, Squadron, Ship
or Organization } 384TH Bomb G.(H) 566TH Bomb G.(H)

Holder's Signature   James H. Keeffe, Jr.

Signature of
P.W. Camp Contact Officer   H.W. Eden

Issued at CAMP LUCKY STRIKE on MAY 8, 1945

Ex-POW identity card issued at Camp Lucky Strike. (Lt. Col. Keeffe collection)

End Notes
Liberation

1. See Appendix C – *The Liberation of Stalag VIIA* by Jim Lankford, National Historian of the 14th Armored Division.

2. The primary reason we were ordered to stay in camp was that at the end of WWI when Germany collapsed after November 11, 1918, the Germans just walked away from their prison camps, with the result that prisoners wandered all over Germany. Unfortunately, a lot of the German soldiers came together in bands or groups, and killed many of these prisoners, who therefore never made it home. So the Allies, the British and the Americans, ordered all the POW's to stay in camp, both for control and also for protection of life.

   We were promised that we would be flown out within forty-eight hours, two days after liberation. But there were so many of us, of all different nationalities. They estimated that there were 100,000 to 110,000 prisoners, all within about a two or three mile radius of the main camp. They were not all in the camp. Many of them were just living out in the open. The Germans were marching people all over the country at the end of the war; it was absolutely crazy. They put the concentration camp people out on the roads, too. Many of them died because they were physically unable to keep moving. If they couldn't keep up, the concentration guards shot them.

3. The improvised bridge was a treadway pontoon bridge. It was built and assembled over the Isar River within 24 hours by Company C of the 300th Combat Engineering Battalion that was attached to the 14th Armored Division. Information and photos courtesy of Brad Peters and Jan Ross, creaters of the web site www.300thcombatengineersinwwii.com

4. I brought that flag and helmet home with me. In 1963 I used them in a display at the Liberty Theater in Ellensberg, Washington, to advertize the movie The Great Escape. A few years later I donated the Nazi flag and helmet to the United States Air Force WWII museum.

5. In 1995, I went back to Moosburg with a tour group I helped organize: 345 ex-POWs, their wives and families. One of the things I did was to look up this old lady at the farmhouse and ask her what happened to the two boys. Well, she was rather senile. She didn't remember me, but she did remember the two boys. She told me that she had kept them, burned the uniforms and given them her husband's clothing. She had put them on the road with a little bit to eat. That's the last she ever heard of them. My impression is that her husband never came back from the eastern front. The one thing every German soldier or German airman feared was, "Um die Ost front" (To the East Front), because going to the East Front, which meant Russia, was normally a one-way trip; very few people came back. The ones that did come back were those sufficiently wounded to warrant their being returned to Germany. I suppose, here and there, when they were able to, the Germans may have shipped a body back. But mostly they were buried there.

6. Correct translation provided by Werner Schwarz, member of the web team for www.Moosburg.org

7. In July of 1959, I went back and found the farmhouse, and I took the same picture again. In this picture are the farmer, his wife and their now grown daughter. It was on this visit that I learned their family name is Kreidenweis. The daughter's name is Katharina and her brother's name is Sebastian. I went back to Moosburg again in 1994 to set up the 1995 tour for the Stalag Luft III ex-POWs and took the same picture again, except by then the farmer and his wife were dead and Sebastian was dying of cancer.

8. "Gooney Bird" is a nickname for a C-47 airplane, which was based on the Douglas DC-3. It was a

great cargo plane and was used extensively throughout WWII.

9.   Over the next several months, the U.S. military searched for all the persons on the list. Those found to be alive were interviewed to corroborate my story and were eventually awarded citations of thanks and gratitude for helping Allied airmen. Some of the persons on the list, Marinus Veth and Samuel Esmeijer for instance, were found to have been killed.

10   In fact it was really clever. For boiling water, they had these garbage cans, which were about four feet high and two feet in diameter at the top. A gasoline stove was hung on the outside of each garbage can and had a metal tube suspended down into the water. That's how they boiled water. There were three of them for washing our mess kits when we were finished using them; we'd just start at the first can, dip the mess kit into the soapy water and then go to the next one. Those gadgets for heating the water were really tremendous.

11.   German capitulation timeline:

May 2 – German forces in Italy surrender

May 2 - Berlin falls to the Soviet Army

May 4 – German forces in North West Germany, Denmark and Holland surrender.

May 6 – German forces in Breslau surrender.

May 7 – General Alfred Jodl signs the unconditional surrender of all German forces.

May 8 – British Prime Minister Winston Churchill makes a radio broadcast at 15:00 during which he announces: "Hostilities will end officially at one minute after midnight tonight, but in the interests of saving lives the 'Cease fire' began yesterday to be sounded all along the front, and our dear Channel Islands are also to be freed today." (Wikipedia)

Going Home

"Anyone Heard of Lt. Jimmy McArthur?"

Halfway down to the port of Le Havre our train stopped. Its five or six cars were full of us ex-Kriegies being taken to the docks where ships waited to transport us back to America. Coming from the other direction, from the southwest, was another passenger train. It stopped right along side us.

It was the 11th of May and it was warm. Our windows were open, and the windows on the other train were also open. The cars were full of men. It turned out that they were American ex-POWs on their way to Camp Lucky Strike. The two trains were separated by only a few feet, so I leaned out the window and shouted to several of the men sitting directly across from me in the other train car.

"What camp were you in?"

"We were in Stalag Luft I, up at Barth," one of them shouted back. "We were liberated by the Russians, and now we're headed to some place called Camp Lucky Strike."

"Barth? Do any of you know Jimmy McArthur, Lt. Jimmy McArthur? He was the aircraft commander of my bomber."

Sure enough, somebody knew of him and shouted back. "Yeah, he's on the train here with us."

There we were—not having seen each other in more than a year, sitting a few feet from each other on two separate trains near the northern coast of France. I got off my train, Jimmy McArthur got off his train, and we met in the narrow space in between the two and shook hands and slapped each other on the back.

"My God, Keeffe, I thought you were dead!" he exclaimed. "The Germans told me you took out your pistol and got into a fight with some German Marines who shot and killed you!"

Then he told me he had written home to his mother, who in turn had written my mother that I was dead.

"Well, it's obviously not true. I never had a shootout with anybody. In fact, I hid my .45 right away after getting on the ground."

"Have you seen anyone else?" Jimmy asked.

I told him I'd seen Moulton and he'd been in our POW camp. I told him how Moulton had broken both his legs when he hit the ground after bailing out and that a Dutch doctor had patched him up. I told him about Baker, who'd been shot through both legs. I told him Stevens was in our camp, but that I didn't know where Baker or Smith or any of the others ended up.

Mac related how he had parachuted out of the B-24 after waiting several minutes for the signal from the back end that never came. He had splashed down in the water at the edge of a canal and was pulled out by the Germans and taken to a jail cell in Dordrecht. The next morning, he was put in another cell where he found Allen, Turlay, Hughes, and Hall. It was then that the Germans told him I'd been killed in a shootout, and that Moulton, Baker, Stevens and Smith had been transported to a hospital somewhere.

The steam whistle on my train shrieked out a warning blast indicating that it was ready to move.

"Come on, climb on the train with me, Jimmy. We're going down to the port. We're going home! Let's be aboard ship together!" I really wanted to get together with him again, but he shook his head.

"Well, no thanks Jim, I'm here with my friends. We've come a long way together and I think I'll stay with them."

I understood completely. We hadn't seen each other since getting shot up in our B-24 over Germany, and he'd been with the men up in Stalag Luft I for over a year. Of course he wanted to stay with them. We shook hands again and made promises to look each other up sometime down the road. He climbed back into his train and I climbed back into mine. Shortly thereafter, my train lurched forward and continued on down to the port of Le Havre.

Le Havre was a very busy port city. When our train stopped a short distance from the docks, I grabbed my duffel bags and walked with the other men a few blocks down to a long pier where several large ships were tied up. Military Policemen directed us to the gangplank of one particular ship. We walked up single file onto the ship's deck. Before it had been converted to carry passengers, this ship had carried tanks and all the equipment that goes with a tank outfit. It was a beautiful ship, the U.S.S. *Marine Panther*.

Down below its decks were large bays where vertical pipes had been welded together to form the frames for metal bunks. There were bunks everywhere, four to five high, and I was assigned to one of them. After stowing my gear on my bunk, I went back up on deck and looked out over the side at all the activity.

Lt. Keeffe boarded the Marine Panther at Le Havre on the 11th of May. In the days to come tens of thousands of ex-POWs would walk up gangplanks such as this one, and begin the final leg of their long journey back to the United States. (Courtesy of USAFA Special Collections Branch, General Clark collection)

It was a very nice day, quite different from when we left Stalag VII A only a few days earlier. Late in the afternoon, near sundown, the dockhands let loose the long mooring lines, and the *Marine Panther* pulled away from the dock. Le Havre had been pretty well smashed up during the fighting. I could see sunken ships in the harbor with only their superstructures showing above water.

Our ship moved out into the channel and formed up with a convoy of Liberty ships. We were told that even though the war in Europe had been declared over on the 8th of May, the German submarines and the German Navy had not yet surrendered.

Not long after we began our westward cruise out of the English Channel, I struck up a conversation with an officer named Olsen, which deepened the despair I had for those in Holland. I described to him my months evading in Rotterdam and told him that I stayed with a family named Jappe-Alberts. He became very animated when I mentioned Dr. Albert Jappe-Alberts, and proceeded to tell me an amazing story.

Olsen had been captured sometime in December of 1944 and had been put in the Haagse Veer, the Rotterdam jail where he met a Dr. Jappe-Alberts, also a prisoner. After getting to know each other, the doctor told Olsen all about me, and how the Gestapo had stormed into his home in early December and demanded to know where the American pilot was. The Gestapo had had a letter with them that was supposedly written by me at the interrogation camp in Oberursal, stating that I had been sheltered by the Jappe-Alberts during my period of evasion. Because of that letter, the doctor and his wife were arrested. I questioned the officer in great detail, but he didn't know anything more about Dr. Alberts, his wife, or anything that might have happened to their children.

Hearing this terrible news caused the fear and anxiety in my stomach to grow and fester. I felt sick to my stomach for the suffering those kind people were enduring because they helped me. Of course the letter was a fake. I never told the Germans anything about my time in Holland. Big Guy was the only person who ever asked, and I told him nothing. All the same, someone had betrayed the Jappe-Alberts. I prayed that nothing serious happened to them and that by now they were all safe and home again.

Two days later, well out into the Atlantic Ocean, our ship captain received word that he could break convoy, so he no longer needed to go at the slow speed of the Liberty ships. A Liberty ship's maximum speed was maybe ten knots, whereas the *Marine Panther* could get upwards of fifteen to eighteen knots. Once the captain pulled away from the convoy and increased speed, it didn't take long before we were cruising alone.

I could not believe the Atlantic Ocean could be as calm and peaceful as it was. During our entire trip across the North Atlantic, the sea was almost as smooth as glass, and the blue skies were sunny and warm. There wasn't a single woman on board the ship, so after the second day the captain announced over the loud speaker system, "We have no women aboard. You guys have horrible color. Your families are not going to like welcoming home white ghosts. So anything you want to wear, or not wear, is OK on this ship, except at mess time."

We stripped off our clothes and sunbathed all the way across the Atlantic.

Once while we were all lying naked on the deck, the captain's voice came over the speakers, "In all my life, I have never seen as many bare asses as there are aboard this ship!"

Beautiful America

Seven days after we left the convoy the eastern coast of America appeared on the horizon.

Shortly afterwards, Long Island came into view on the right side of our ship and slowly grew in size as we got closer. We passed Long Island's southern shore and finally steamed into the estuary leading into New York Harbor.

This became rather emotional for all of us. As we steamed past the Statue of Liberty, fire boats out in the harbor squirted huge streams of water in a salute to us. We continued on to dock in New Jersey. A band was playing at our pier. We all went crazy with joy, and the people on shore whooped it up along with us.

Words are not necessary to describe this photo.
(Courtesy of USAFA Special Collections Branch, General Clark collection)

It didn't take long at all for us to grab our gear and disembark. Once down on the pier, we were directed to a line of buses that took us into Camp Kilmer, New Jersey. My understanding is that Camp Kilmer was the departure place for troops heading to the European Theater of Operations—Africa and the Continent. We were treated like royalty here. I don't know how many there were of us, but we were among the first ex-prisoners to make it back to the States. We stayed at Camp Kilmer for two nights while being processed.

The first thing those in charge did was to arrange for us all to make telephone calls. I called my mom and dad, and they finally truly knew that I was OK. We then went through a session with a finance officer who arranged for us to be paid the next day. Some of us had quite a bit of money coming. I had a year-plus salary due me, but others were owed much more. We were also processed by the medics; anybody who had any medical problems whatsoever was attended to. We met a lot of beautiful nurses and WACs (Women's Army Corps) and during our two evenings at Camp Kilmer, we partied at the Officers' Club.

At Camp Kilmer, I was finally able to get rank insignia and wings. We'd all come back from the Continent looking like buck privates because we were wearing the GI uniforms issued to us at Camp Lucky Strike.

We were also given orders that put each of us on thirty days' leave. At the end of our thirty days those of us from the West Coast were to report to a series of hotels on the beach in Santa Monica, California. The men from the East Coast were to report to somewhere in Florida.

The Army had taken over hotels in these places and once we reported we would find out, or be given choices as to what we wanted to do next in our military career.

By the third day at Camp Kilmer, everything had been taken care of and we all boarded a train for home. The train cars were really neat. They had been made especially for moving troops. Each car had about four compartments with triple-decked bunks. At one end of each car was an open area called a "day room," a place where we could play cards, read magazines or write letters. There were twelve to fifteen of these troop cars hooked together. We were each assigned to a car according to our final destination. With my destination being Ft. Lewis, just south of Seattle, Washington, I was assigned to the very first car.

Late that afternoon, our train left Camp Kilmer and journeyed north through New York and into Canada. This was the quickest way to transit the country. We turned west, went through Toronto and re-entered the U.S. at Detroit. As we traveled across the country, depending on the stop, one car would be detached from our train and attached to the back end of a passenger train headed to a destination close to where the men on that car were going.

Occasionally, when our train stopped so that a troop car could be attached to another train, we'd have a pause of an hour to three hours or longer. In Detroit, there was a chain of restaurants called Harvey House. When we stopped there, several of us got off the train and went into the station to one of these restaurants. We walked in, grabbed some stools up at the counter and sat down. I ordered a chocolate sundae. The people there had difficulty figuring out what we were. We were wearing very simple GI uniforms. Some of us had rank insignia and wings pinned to us, and we were laughing and carrying on.

While I was ordering a sundae, a snotty little waitress addressed me. "What's the matter with you guys? Don't you know there's a war on?"

Instantly I jumped up, reached across the counter and grabbed her by her blouse.

" 'Don't we know there's a war on?' What the hell kind of question is that!"

Within a split second, I realized I was behaving very badly, but to have that thrown in our faces after what we'd been through! I finally relaxed my grip and let her go and spoke slowly and very clearly while looking her straight in the eyes. "We have just come out of a German prison camp. Be careful of what you say to people."

After we ate our meal, we went outside and walked around the downtown area for a while. Right away we realized that something was very strange. There were soldiers with armored vehicles and halftracks all over the downtown area.

"Why in the world are there troops here?" I asked a group of people on a street corner.

"They're here because of the riots," one of them replied.

"What riots?" I asked, and one fellow told us what had been going on for the past couple of years.

As the military conscripted people for the Army, the jobs these people left behind still needed to be done. This resulted in a flood of Negroes from the south coming up into the industrial north to fill thousands of vacant jobs. Tensions mounted over a period of time between the whites and the growing number of southern blacks migrating into the city, and riots broke out. Twenty-five blacks and nine whites had been killed, and the violence wasn't quelled until President Roosevelt dispatched Federal troops to control the area. I found it hard to believe that here in our own country we had to have the Army patrolling the streets in a major city.

The train stopped in Chicago around eleven o'clock in the morning, and we were notified it would be four or five hours before our troop cars were hooked up to the next train. By this time, we had already lost a few of the troop cars to trains in other cities. Since we had quite awhile to wait, several of us left the train and walked downtown.

A couple of gentlemen stopped us and asked us what we were. We told them and they asked us if we'd had lunch, to which we replied "no."

They took us to their club in a beautiful high-rise building right on the main boulevard paralleling Lake Michigan. They treated us royally to a wonderful luncheon and saw to it that we got back to our train on time.

One of the things that staggered me while riding the train across the country was that I never saw one single bomb crater. I didn't see a single building that had been destroyed, or hit by a bomb or artillery shell. There wasn't a single structure that had machine gun pockmarks all over it. The difference between the Continent and home was like night and day. It was as though I was in a totally different world from the one I had been living in.

Ft. Lewis—Tacoma, Washington

The rest of the trip across the country was wonderful. We traveled northwest through Minneapolis and then on through Montana, where we started the long climb up and through the Rocky Mountains. It was nighttime when we passed through Missoula and then through Idaho. For a couple of hours the next morning, we waited in Spokane, Washington, and then we began the last leg of our journey.

My heart was in my throat as the train carried us over the Cascade Mountains. What an absolutely beautiful ride! The mountain air was so clear and fresh. The forests of Douglas Fir and Western Red Cedar whooshed past the open windows and then fell behind as a new vista opened up of thickly wooded valleys surrounded by mountain ridges. Eventually, we crossed the Cascades and dropped down through the western foothills into the greater Puget Sound basin. Our train finally pulled into the outskirts of Fort Lewis, a few miles south of the city of Tacoma, on the 4th of June 1945. It was another beautiful, sunshiny day!

Lt. Keeffe, 2nd from right back row, with other ex-POWs arriving at Ft. Lewis. (Lt. Col. Keeffe collection)

By the time we arrived at Fort Lewis, ours was the only troop car left—this was the end of the line. There were about twenty of us ex-POWs and we all got off onto the wooden loading platform. I handed my camera to one of the fellows, and he took a picture of us next to the troop car. We then hopped onto a small bus that took us into the base at Fort Lewis.

We were out-processed quickly. Altogether, it took only about thirty minutes. One of the things we were each given was a bus ticket home. Arrangements had already been made for Army buses to take us from the Fort into Tacoma, a half-hour drive north. The driver took me and two or three other servicemen to the Greyhound bus station where we caught a bus north to Seattle. It was late in the afternoon when I finally arrived in my hometown.

Hometown Seattle

I stepped off the Greyhound bus at the station on Stewart Street in Seattle with my two huge barracks bags full of stuff. What a beautiful afternoon it was! My mind had been wandering all over the place on the bus trip north from Tacoma, and now, standing outside the Stewart Street station, I almost felt like a stranger. Not a stranger to Seattle, but a stranger to this life. It was so peaceful and pleasant. The people walked and talked with an air about them that was non-existent in the world I had just come from. Over there, back on the Continent, everything was drab and gray; the mood heavy and oppressive from years of war. A heightened level of anxiety and uncertainty was always present, some days more so than others, but never far from the surface. Hunger and cold, lice and fleas, the daily monotony at times so strong and never able to be alone. I could feel a strong pull on me, an urge to get back on the bus and somehow make my way back across the ocean to Holland. How were my friends over there? What was their life like now, and who was alive? Who had made it? Were the Jappe-Alberts safe?

I resolved then and there that one day, I would make my way back to Rotterdam, back to the apartments at 33a Eendrachtsweg and 60b Breitnerstraat. I would find and help my friends there in any way I could. With that settled, I stepped to the curb and hailed a cab.

"Are You My Brother Jim?"

"Where are you going?" the cabbie asked.

"Out to Hunter Boulevard in the Mount Baker district."

Two or three other people were also waiting for a taxi, and the cabbie turned to them and asked where they were going.

"We're going down to the Great Northern depot," one of them said.

"Well, get on in," he told them; and to me, "Sorry."

This happened two or three times, and finally I got the picture. The cabbies didn't want to make long runs. They only wanted to take people around the downtown area because they could do more short trips and thereby make more money.

When the next cab rolled up, I just opened the back door to the cab, threw my bags in and said, "3237 Hunter Boulevard."

"I'm sorry. I'm only making runs in the downtown area," said the driver.

"No, you're not. You're going to Hunter Boulevard. I just came out of a German prison camp, and I'm going home. You're going to have to physically throw me out of this cab."

"Is that true?" he asked quietly.

"Yes."

"Well, you just sit back, and I'll take you home."

He picked up two or three other people and dropped them off at the railroad station. Then he drove me out to Hunter Boulevard. I had him stop at the house next to my family's home because I was hoping to walk up to the porch unannounced. When I tried to pay the man, he wouldn't take any money.

Up at my parent's house, the front door opened and a young boy came out. It was my brother John. As I was getting my bags out of the taxi and talking to the cabbie, he came down to the sidewalk.

"Are you my brother Jim?" he asked.

"Yes, and I guess you're my brother, John."

At that, John turned around and ran back up onto the porch and into the house.

"Mom! Mom! Jim's home!"

It turned out that my mother was upstairs taking a bath, and I understand she got out of the bathtub pretty fast.

My other brother, Bob, was away in the South Pacific serving in the Seabees. My sister, Peggy, was a nurse and was at work, as was my dad. He came home shortly after I arrived. I had already started unloading all the stuff in my duffel bags. I had a whole case of candy bars, and I had my spoon and the little Kriegie burner I had carried all the way from Stalag VII A. Next, I pulled out the Nazi flag and the German fireman's helmet and showed them to my dad. Everyone *ooh'd* and *aah'd* when I showed them my two shiny Dutch gold coins. How I was able to hang on to those two gold coins through multiple strip searches, interrogations, and clothing exchanges is a mystery and baffles me to this day.

I had brought my dad a nice present. When I presented it to him, he couldn't understand why I'd given it to him. It was a box, a case actually, that contained a dozen boxes of razor blades! As a POW, I had become a pack rat because I never knew what the next hour or the next day would bring. Anyhow, I had this box of blades which, I guess, was enough for twenty-nine years of shaving.

We had a mighty fine reunion that evening when my other sister, Jeananne, came home from school.

When I left Moosburg in Germany, I probably weighed about 125 pounds soaking wet. Before I was shot down I was kind of lean and in good physical condition. My normal weight was about 155 pounds. Now, however, I was skinny, and hungry all the time. In fact, for the next five to six months, hunger gnawed at me constantly even though I ate very well.

Over the next few days, my dad took me to some of his clubs, the Sierra Club being one of them, and introduced me around.

"This is my son Jim, whom I'd like you to meet. He was in prison, you know."

At this, my dad's friends would look askance at me until he explained. We also went to the American Legion Lake Washington Post where my dad had recently been elected Senior Vice Commander. I had a wonderful time meeting many of the Post members and telling them my story.

June 1945 family photo in front of the home on Hunter Blvd, Seattle. Back from left: Mr. Jim Keeffe, Sr., Lt. Jim Keeffe, Jr., Mrs. Marie Keeffe, little brother John. Front left: Sisters Margarette (Peg) and Jeananne. (Lt. Col. Keeffe collection)

One evening when we were all sitting down to supper, my mother brought out all the correspondence she had kept during the war. There were letters from the War Department and telegrams from Western Union that had kept the family informed as to my status. There was a telegram describing me as MIA, and another one telling of my POW status.

Of great surprise to me, my mother showed me a couple of letters from the Netherlands and asked if I knew who the authors were and of course I did. One was from Jan Loose in Breda and the other from Anton Sanders in Rotterdam. Oddly, Sanders' letter was dated June 20th, 1945, yet it was already here when I arrived home on June 4th. The only thing I can think of is that Anton mistakenly typed June instead of May.

A. A. M. SANDERS JR.
BREITNERSTRAAT 60ᴮ
ROTTERDAM

Rotterdam, June 20th.1945.

Dear Mrs.Keeffe,

Although unknown to you we send you word that your son Jim, captain pilote, was lodging in our house during two months, viz. from May 18th.until July 15th.1944.

He was not hurt when he jumped out of his hit bomber and in good health he left Rotterdam for his journey to England. Since that time we did not hear about him and we are anxious to know whether he arrived safely home.

You will oblige my wife and me very much by sending soonest answer, now that correspondence is possible again.

We remain meanwhile, with compliments,
Yours sincerely.

Letters from Jan Loose (preceding page) and Anton Sanders. (above) (Lt. Col. Keeffe collection)

Needless to say I was ecstatic! I had been ridden with guilt and worry over what may have happened to my friends and helpers in Holland. The worst possible scenarios had been constantly going through my mind. I wrestled with thoughts of everything bad that could have befallen to them—especially the Jappe-Alberts. Now, here was proof that at least Jan Loose and family, and Anton and Cocky Sanders were alive.

The very next day I found some old letterhead and wrote a letter to Anton Sanders in which I described to him all that had happened to me after leaving Rotterdam. Over the next few days I wrote letters to everyone in Holland I could, if I had an address.

DAVIS MONTHAN FIELD
TUCSON, ARIZONA

June 10, 1945

Dear Ton and Cocky,

At long last I have arrived home, and am now able to write the full particulars of my capture, internment, etc.

After I left you I was escorted to Breda, where I stayed until the 25th of July. From there we crossed the border, and were taken into Antwerp (an

English flyer made the trip with me). On the night of the 27th we were taken to an apartment by the same girl who had been our guide to Antwerp. She fed us, and told us that we would lave that night for Lille, France, in a closed car. Later that evening the two men who were to be our escorts arrived and took us with them. We were told to be calm, etc., and not to pay any attention to any one we might pass. These men took us to a dark building about three blocks from the apartment, and showed us to a small room on about the third floor. We were told to be seated, and then they both began to laugh.

"We'll boys," said one of them, "for you the war is over. You're caught. We're members of the German Secret Police—the Gestapo, to you!!"

Never in my life have I received such a severe shock. It was impossible—I couldn't believe them. How could they, the Gestapo, be right in the organization without someone being aware of the fact??

The greatest shock was yet to come, though, for they produced files and began telling me the names of people I had probably met in Rotterdam. Many of the names were unfamiliar to me, but sad to say, some of them were known to me. They knew that I had stayed with you, and they knew the names of the people with whom I had stayed in Breda. They had Kees's name, and one or two others, but they didn't have the Jappe-Alberts, of that I am positive. After watching our reactions, and having searched our effects, they took us to the prison (in Antwerp) were we were kept until about 50 more fellows were caught. After we reached Germany, and compared notes, we found that this one organization, and those two particular men were picking up between 200 & 300 fliers a month, in the same manner in which I myself was caught.

They had many, many names, but told us that nothing would be done about it at the times because they wanted the organizations to continue sending in as many fliers as they were able to help evade. While I was in jail at Antwerp I did everything in my power to get word to you in Rotterdam of what was taking place. I sent out written and verbal notes by Dutch boys who were also prisoners, but who were allowed to have visitors from time to time. I hoped and prayed that word would reach you before the Germans tried to pick any of you up.

From Antwerp we were taken to Brussells and turned over to the Luftwaffe, and from that time on were treated just as any of the other boys who are picked up immediately after landing. We were sent to a Lager at Sagan, Silesia, and from there were taken to Moosburg, Bavaria where we were liberated on the 29th of April. When we were taken to France I asked for permission to visit you in Rotterdam, but was refused because of the unsettled conditions existing in Holland.

I arrived home last week, and was very, very happy to hear that there was a letter from you, and one from the family with whom I stayed while in Breda. You'll never know how happy and relieved I was to hear that you were all right.

However, I fear for the Jappe-Alberts. I met an officer on the boat while coming home who had met Dr. Alberts in the jail at Rotterdam on Christmas day. Dr. Alberts told this officer all about me, and told him that in November the police had come to his home with a letter which I was supposed to have written that I had been sheltered by the Alberts during my period of evasion. Consequently he and his wife were arrested, but this officer did not know what had become of their children or of the other people who were in the house.

Of course the paper was a forgery and a lie. I never told the Germans anything of my whereabouts or actions during my evasion. In fact, they never asked me--I suppose because the Gestapo seemed to know all about me anyhow.

I was deeply grieved to learn that these people had suffered because of me, and pray that nothing more was done to them. Please let me know any particulars regarding their capture and the whereabouts of them and their children. Also let me know if Kees is safe.

Well Ton, although this letter should be filled with joy and thanksgiving, I'm afraid it must be one of deepest anxiety for their associations with me. Please let me know about all the people who befriended me during those months.

I'll write again in the very near future, and

will try to be a little more comprehensive about
things. Just now I have so very many people to whom
I must write immediately trying to find out whether
they're all O'K.

   Well Ton and Cocky, I'll never be able to
adequately express exactly how grateful I am to you
both for having sheltered me for those long months.
If there is ever anything I can do to better express
my appreciation, I hope that you will not hesitate
to write me.

   Until I hear from you then, I remain,

                 Very sincerely yours,

                 Jim

A week after I got home, a telegram from the War Department arrived at our house telling my mother the great news that her son had "Returned to Military Control."

Final telegram from the War Department. (Lt. Col. Keeffe collection)

   Shortly afterward, several articles appeared in the local paper, the *Seattle Times*, about my coming home. It seems there was a reporter at one of the talks

I gave as my Dad took me to various places around town.

Time Out For A "Hail Mary" Saved Him Says Pilot

Lieut. James Keefe, took time out for a "Hail Mary" before bailing out of his helpless plane 5,000 feet above a flaming German city. The prayer and the time it took to say it saved his life, the Lieutenant told the Seattle Serra Club here, Friday. Had he jumped a few seconds before he would have chuted through heavy flak into hostile hands. As it was he landed in the city suburbs and was sheltered for a while by underground forces. Later, he was captured and felt the rigors of German prison camp.

Lieut. Keefe is a son of Mr. and Mrs. James H. Keefe of Seattle.

Seattle Times article. (Lt. Col. Keeffe collection)

Well, the reporter got it mostly right, though the "flaming city," (Berlin) was miles away from where we finally ditched the airplane. I vividly remember pausing at the open camera hatch in the tail of the airplane, on my knees preparing myself to tip forward and fall head first through the opening. Right then it seemed the most natural thing to do was to say a short prayer. I did….then out I went.

Letters From Holland

Over the next weeks and months I began to receive replies to many of the letters I had mailed to people in Holland. The first one to arrive was from Anton Sanders, followed within a few days by one from Mrs. Jappe-Alberts. The fog of uncertainty slowly cleared as their stories unfolded through their letters, and I learned what happened to these fine people. Their suffering and loss was terrible. Although I was truly happy that many of my helpers and friends survived, my heart broke for those that didn't and for the survivors' anguish and bitterness. The cost they paid for resisting the iron fist of their Nazi occupiers, and for opening their homes to shelter and care for me and hundreds of other downed Allied airmen, was tremendous. I'll let their letters speak for themselves.

(Author's note: The first letters from Anton Sanders and Mrs. Jappe-Alberts appear below. You will find the rest of the letters from Mrs. Jappe-Alberts, Kees van den Engel, Mr. van Dongen and others from Holland and Belgium in Appendix F. Please read those letters to find out first-hand what life was like for them during the last few months of the war and immediately afterward.)

Anton Sanders' letter

Rotterdam, July 25th 1945.

Dear Jim,

Most heartily we congratulate you with your liberation and your return home. It must have been quite a joyday for your parents. We are terribly rejoiced to learn from your letter of June the 10th, which we just received!!, that you are quite all right. We hope you have received many Red Cross packets in Moosburg.

Here are the particulars about your friends in Rotterdam. Kees is safe. Shortly after you had gone, he was caught (not for your sake) and taken to Vught. He saw there Jo Berlijn for the last time. Jo has been executed and so has Uncle Bertus. You and we expected that. Broekhuizen's wife is also dead.

From Vught Kees was sent to Oranienburg and liberated by the Russians. He is now growing fat again and together with his girl Marijke who is liberated too.

Sad to say, Dr. Jappe Alberts has been shot on Feb. 18th. After being captured the whole family, except Opa, and the Jews on Dec. 5th., Mr. J.A. and Mrs. J.A. were taken to Scheveningen and Ger and Aut were left in jail at Rotterdam. The Jews were sent to a "Lager" at Westerbork.

I never heard about a letter from you in November. That must be a mistake of the officer you met. Do you know his name for Mrs. J.A.?

Your written and verbal notes from Antwerp never reached us.

Mr. J.A. was afterwards taken to Heinenoord together with 9 other men and shot there for "reprisals." Mrs. J.A., Ger and Aut are quite healthy again. Ger wants to go to the Dutch Indies.

As the 10 Gestapo men were at Albert's about 2 o'clock, it must have been 3 when they came in the Breitnerstraat. Not finding me seven of them went to the business. They learned the address from a letter in our cabinet. Thanks to your prayers I just returned from buying something for Cocky's Santa Claus when the S.D. was standing before the door. I walked round the corner and looked at the business from behind the fence. By the Doctor's balcony they passed through my very window and I saw then walking with their pistols. They picked my radio, which was not hidden, all my gin and cognac etc., about 36 bottles, cigars and what was worse Cocky's and my fleeing baggage, mainly undies, shirts, pajamas, gowns and socks. Further clothing materials. Incomprehensibly they picked neither Cocky nor my brother. They did not even put our home under seal, as they did at Alberts'.

Next day Cocky "dived" together with me and we have done well through the hunger times. Only the 10th of May we were liberated by the coming of Canadians. We have no damage.

Now have you any idea who was the betrayer? De Groot, not the gin-man, but you met him at v.Dongen's, has already been shot by our boys; he was a traitor. I did not know him. The boy who was your guide to Breda was safe. Probably the family in Breda have had no trouble because they were liberated much earlier than we were.

Father Hanckx, Curate Haanen, Ubink and Sissing have had no trouble. Sissing asked your address yesterday, to make inquiries about you. The boy said he sheltered and helped you one month! Is he trustworthy? You had to leave there so at once. What do you think of Prisre (Piercelear) and Miss Wilhon - Mathenesserlaan?

Curate Haanen cycled to Breda with your grey socks and undies and sweets from Cocky, but you were just gone.

Well Jim, I'm afraid that you are going to the Pacific in short time and you well be training again when you receive this letter. Perhaps for you it has been not so bad after all that the Huns left you in

Bavaria. Send us please a nice photo and not such a small one. By the way, a swell newspaper article! Are you Captain now?

Cocky is learning English very seriously and she can write you in due time.

Father Hanckx asks to write his best wishes.

Curate Haanen is Chaplain now.

Will you please greet your mother from Cocky and me; we know so much about her though unknown. Also best wishes to your father and what about Pat?

We hope you have now all particulars of your relations here in Rotterdam.

Awaiting a faster and more comprehensive letter from you we wish you all the best and good luck.

Your friends,
Cocky & Ton

1st letter from Mrs. Jappe-Alberts

31st July 1945

My Dear Jim.

Ever since you left us, have I been thinking about the letter I was going to write to your mother one day -- when it was all over, but little did I dream, that it would be to your good self. I was going to write so soon, This letter shows you that I am still in the land of the living, so are Ans and Ger. Wished I could tell you we had all been happily re-united, but so far my good man has not come home yet. In fact — every body except myself believes he has been shot on the 10th of February this year. I have recognized his clothes, but a famous trick of the Huns at Scheveningen was, to make prisoners put on each others clothes, so make sure of a proper chaos when the graves were opened. One of his colleagues has seen his teeth though and said they were my husband's for certain. And still I am not convinced. It's not obstinacy, but just intuition. I can wait because there are still some 50,000 Hollanders to come home, who are at present too ill to be removed from German hospitals. A special

mission has set out to collect them and possibly
bring these men and women back to Holland. So why
should my husband not be one of them.

Of course I have seen your letter to Ton (Kees
will also get a copy of it) and I do think it's an
almost unbelievable coincidence, that you should
meet Olsen, who could inform you of what had
happened to us. We are absolutely certain now, that
de Groot has betrayed us, although we never met
him. You will never know how awfully pleased I was
to read your report about your capture and what
passed there. Most people believed the story which
the German investigator tried to stuff me with,
that you had betrayed us and many others with us!
My face went the color of beetroot—and if looks
could kill—he would have been a dead body. Never in
this world would I believe such a thing—unless I
heard it from your own lips. Even if you had been
tortured, I still could swear that you never would
tell the tale. Quite a number of people did believe
it, but then, they didn't know you as well as I do,
do they? Here is the story in a few words. We were
caught on Dec 5th about 2 o'clock. Of course Eust
and Lies were hanging over the banister to hear what
was going on down stairs, with the result that they
hadn't enough time to get into the shelter and were
promptly brought down. There were 7 of the Green
Police, and after they put us in the waiting room,
they did not search the house--they just stuffed
their pockets and every bag and basket they could
find with articles of their fancy. It was sheer
robbery. We went all to the Haagshe Veer—except my
father—they left him in the house right till the
beginning of February when some Germans went to
live in it themselves with their Dutch lady lovers.
Then the proper cleaning out began. All my husbands
instruments and inventory have gone—even the plugs
from the walls. We are lucky to have a few chairs
and tables left, but not one bed or blanket and you
know, we had quite a few.

However, all that I only found out when I was
released from Scheveningen on May 6th where they had
taken me with the Bakkers and Aat and Niesje. They
were sent on to Westerbork, the Jewish camp on Febr.
2nd and were liberated some weeks before us. Ans and

Ger stayed at the H.V. right till the end. I've had no idea what had happened to my husband. I went all over in search of him, without any success. Early July a large grave was opened and then bodies were discovered. By sheer accident another dentist was asked to look for a patient of his—but all he was able to discover were what he thought the remains of my husband. Those 10 men had been fetched from Scheveningen and been brought to a small country place near Rotterdam called Heynenoord, where a Nazi farmer had been killed by the "underground". The death of the 10 men was a reprisal, and executed on the same spot as the farmer was found. They had been killing people in batches, 10 and 20 at the time, and they were left lying in the street for 24 hours before being taken away. On the Coolsingel this has happened several times. Sometimes I am not sorry I was not at home this last winter. People did really drop dead in the streets with hunger, and my little party at home took some feeding, as you have seen.

My husband was taken to Scheveningen, 12 days after me, but I never knew he was there until I came back to Rotterdam. I didn't want to make things awkward by refusing to believe what the colleague said, so agreed to a quiet funeral at the tiny village cemetery, where they had first brought the bodies. Only Ans and Ger went with me. You know how he liked things plain and simple and hated show, so I am sure this way of burying him would meet his last wish if he had known. But you'll get a wire if he really is one of the 50,000!! Meanwhile life goes on and a new Doctor has taken over the practice, but does not live in the house. This address will find me for some time to come. My plans are very vague. Ger is trying to go to the Dutch East Indies with the flying forces and Ans wants to go also with some women's corps if possible. My own son is being trained as a Naval officer and hopes to finish his course in a few weeks time. Then he will come over to Holland on three weeks leave before going to the Far East! What mother will do is still a big question mark. A very wonderful chapter of my life will close—if I am to remain by myself; as you know we were very happy together. That reminds me of the first words my husband spoke after the front door closed behind you: "Why didn't you give the boy one big hug before he sets out on this perilous trip?" I really don't know why I didn't.

That's an awful lot about ourselves. Sorry, but I thought I might as well give you details as you are sure to be asking for them. Life at the H.V. was not bad at all. Ans and I were together with a number of other women in one room. Later at Scheveningen I was in a cell, and those German girls in grey costumes were the wardresses and they loved to give you ☐cold meals☐ as punishment, which meant no food! They have never touched us, neither my husband, I am glad to see. There would have been murder if they had. I got ☐cold meals☐ several times, usually two days running because I could not bring myself to smile at those loathsome females. You see Jim, we do hate the Germans—and now more than ever, if possible. Ans is simply eaten up by hatred for them and I cannot stop her. She works hard, bringing the NSB members to light and in prison, together with Riet Haagendorp. The girl with the glasses who used to come to Saunders. She lives with us, also Aat and Niesje and two of their small brothers 11 and 13 yrs of age—they haven't been given a house so far and their father who is a well known Rotterdam Doctor needs a big one for his family of eight. Except one sister who died at Theresiensbad—they have all returned safely.

I suppose your mother will read this letter too, but as soon as I have a quiet hour to myself—I will still write her the letter I have had in mind. I had some letters from people who have been friends with Malcolm during the last five years, and it's nice to hear what other people think of your Son!!

All I want is a nice long letter from you, telling us about your people and Pat!. I wonder if we will ever meet again but if you let me have that studio photo taken in uniform as you promised, you won't be very far away from us!

Kindest regards to your family
and lots more to yourself
Yours   Jackie Jappe Alberts

The Navy Again

Thirty days flew by. They were full of meeting up with old friends, spending time sailing (and almost drowning!) on Lake Washington, going here and there and trying to soak it all in. I wrote letters to all the people I had addresses for in Holland, settled some of my affairs here at home, and then it was time for me to go down to Santa Monica.

Before I left, I took my footlocker to the Railway Express office at the train station to ship it to Santa Monica. It was packed full of new uniforms and other things. The building had an elevated loading dock where trucks could back up and unload directly onto the platform.

I parked the car, man-handled my trunk up onto the platform and hauled it inside. A number of sailors were all lined up to ship their stuff home by Railway Express also. Dressed in civilian clothes, I got in line behind them. As we worked our way up to the counter, a bus drove up with more sailors. They were all happy because they were going home.

It was finally my turn. The guy working behind the counter looked at me. "Where are your tags?"

"What tags?" I asked.

"You have to go get tags, and you have to weigh your trunk back there on the scales."

I pulled out of line, dragged my trunk back to the scales and weighed it, made out the tags, and then went back to the end of the line. There was a sailor near the end of the line who was sick with a cold or something else, and he wasn't looking or feeling well at all.

"Young man, you know you really should be in a hospital or something," I told him.

"Oh no, sir. I'm headed home. I'm going home."

I worked my way up in the line again. Another bus pulled up, and another pile of sailors got in line. These guys were chatting and happy. They were going home on leave, too. Even though the war in Europe was over, the war with Japan was still going on. I was sure a lot of these sailors were due to ship out eventually to somewhere in the Pacific Theater.

All of a sudden every sailor became quiet.

"I wonder what's happened? What's caused everyone to stop?" I thought.

The doors leading out onto the loading platform were open, so I was able to see what was going on. A Navy staff car had pulled up. It was a war-time black Chevrolet.

A Navy commander and a lieutenant commander stepped out of the staff car. Then their driver got out. (A Navy Commander and Lieutenant Commander are equivalent to an Air Force Lieutenant Colonel and Major respectively.) The driver opened the trunk and started hauling baggage out. Both of these nattily-dressed Navy officers had golf bags, suitcases, barracks bags, you name it. The poor driver heaved their stuff up onto the platform. While the driver was huffing and puffing away, the two officers talked quietly to each other while looking over at us. They walked down to the end of the building and came up the stairs onto the platform. Then they walked into the shipping area. There was dead silence from all the sailors. The two Navy officers whispered some more to each other.

By now, I was only a few places back from the front of the counter. I knew what those two characters were going to do. Sure enough, they headed for the front of the line. I bolted out of line and stopped in front of the commander.

With my feet planted apart and my hands on my hips, I said to him, "Where the hell do you think you're going?"

He looked a little taken aback.

"I'm going to the counter," he answered.

"The end of the line is back there," I said firmly, pointing back down the line.

"But, we happen to be officers!"

"You are not officers. You're disgusting. You're on the beach, and you're no different than these men. The end of the line is back there!"

He looked at me, and I looked at him. I was on fire.

Everything had stopped. The clerks behind the counter had stopped what they were doing, and all the sailors had stopped. If the commander had moved, I would have knocked him flat and I think he could sense this.

He turned to his buddy, the lieutenant commander.

"Come on, let's go. We'll come back later."

By this time, their driver had finished heaving all their things onto the platform. The two Navy officers went back outside, climbed into the back seat of their staff car and closed the doors. The poor driver loaded all their crap back into the car. Then they drove away.

When the black car pulled away from the platform, the sailors burst out cheering and clapping.

The clerk behind the counter commented, "Boy, you've got a lot of guts. That happens in here ten times a day, and we don't like it. You bring your trunk on up here now, and I'll take care of you. I'm sorry I spoke sharply to you."

"No, these guys are all trying to get home. Besides, I'm almost back up to you again anyway."

A few minutes later, I got up to the counter.

"That really took guts," the clerk said again to me. "I want to thank you."

"Well, I just came out of a German prison camp and I don't take that kind of bull from anybody." Once again, I didn't like the way Navy officers treated the sailors.

After finally checking in my footlocker, I took the sick kid home with me and Mother made him some chicken soup. The next day, I took him back down to the train station, and he went home.

Finally! To Become a Fighter Pilot!

When my thirty days leave was over, I said goodbye to my family once again and took a train down to southern California. I had orders to report to Santa Monica. When I arrived I checked into one of the hotels on the beach the Army had taken over for rest and recuperation of personnel returning from overseas. A couple of days later I was called in for an interview and one of the questions had to do with what I wanted to do next.

"What do you want to do? Do you want to continue flying or stop flying?"

"I want to keep flying."

"What do you want to fly? I see you're a B-24 pilot."

"Well, I've had a belly full of B-24s. I want to fly P-51s."

"Fine. We'll cut you some orders and send you off to become a fighter pilot."

That was shortly after the 4th of July. On the 6th of August, the "Enola Gay," a B-29 Superfortress assigned to the 393rd Bombardment Squadron of the 509th Composite Group, dropped an atomic bomb on the Japanese city of Hiroshima. On the 9th of August, another atomic bomb was dropped on the city of Nagasaki. That was enough to convince the Japanese Emperor to surrender, which he officially did on the 15th of August, 1945.

I boarded a train the next day to Luke Field, just west of Phoenix, Arizona where I started P-51 training. I actually flew about three flights in the T-6 when, from one day to the next, all American flying of, and training in, the P-51 Mustangs was stopped. That was it. No more flying—period. The war was over and to save fuel and money, all non-essential flying was terminated. My career as a fighter pilot was over before it even began.

This essentially ended my career in the United States Army Air Forces. I was given the chance to stay in if I wanted to, but not as a fighter pilot. I declined. In October I was given orders to report to Army Detachment in Portland for out-processing. I elected to stay on in the reserves, but essentially was transferred out into civilian life. While in Portland I filled out some forms for the FAA, Federal Aviation Administration. As a result of my flying experience during the war, I was given a civilian pilot's license. Then I headed back home to Seattle.

I actually had one more chance to fly P-51s. The reserves in Seattle met at Boeing Field and lo and behold there were some P-51s there. I immediately signed up for ground school and was learning the P-51 fuel and hydraulic systems when the program was cancelled and the P-51s were taken away.

Flying for United Air Lines

I spent the next few months settling into civilian life and travelling a bit. I also filled out a lot of applications. One was for a regular commission in the Army. Others were to United Airlines and the Dutch airlines, KLM. I even filled out an application for the Flying Tiger Line, formed by ex-Flying Tiger pilots who had come back from fighting the Japanese in Burma and China.

In the spring of 1946 I received a call from the United Airlines office in downtown Seattle. I was told to go to Boeing Field for an interview with the Chief Pilot of the Western Division of United Airlines, Bill Groen.

The interview was quite interesting. When I arrived at the Boeing Field Administration Building, I was directed to a room where four or five fellows were being interviewed. I introduced myself and the interviewer told me to take a chair. He had a little pile of folders on his desk and he'd pick one up and talk to one of the guys.

One of the files had printed on it "B-29, so many hours, Instructor Pilot."

"Just what we're looking for," he told the guy whose file it was. "Take this down to Colorado and go to school."

The next file had "P-47" on it.

"Do you have any multi-engine experience?" he asked another fellow.

"No. I was a fighter pilot."

"Well we're not looking for fighter pilots. We're looking for multi-engine pilots."

As the interviews progressed I got a picture of what he was after. He was looking for high time, four-engine experience. I knew I was going to be turned down because I didn't have much flying time.

My turn came and he said while looking at my folder, "Well, you did well on our three tests downtown. *Hmmm, ah ah!* B-24: four engine. What's this? Five hundred ninety-two hours, is that all the time you have?"

"Yes, sir. There was no flying in the POW camp I was in."

He closed the file. "I'm sorry Mr. Keeffe. As you've heard here I'm looking for people with over one thousand hours in four-engine equipment."

I was pretty ticked off. "You know Mr. Groen, my mother was taught how to drive by my dad in 1922. I don't know how many hours driving my mother has, but I can tell you something. My mother still can't drive a car with all the years of driving behind her. I wouldn't have bothered you if I didn't think I was certainly average, or better than average, as a pilot."

"Well I'm sorry, those are the rules," whereupon we both stood up and shook hands and I left.

Two weeks later I got a phone call from the downtown United Airlines office. "Mr. Keeffe, Mr. Groen is down at Boeing Field and he would like to talk with you."

"I saw him two weeks ago."

"I know that, but for some reason or other he wants to talk with you."

I borrowed a car from Dad and drove down to Boeing Field to the same little office. But this time Groen was the only one in there. I stood before his door and knocked.

"Come in Mr. Keeffe and have a chair. I'll be finished in just a couple of minutes."

When Mr. Groen finished reading through some material in a file, he closed it and looked up at me. "You know, two weeks ago when you were here and told me the story about your mom, I went home and told my wife that story and we had a good laugh. I did some thinking. I'm going to take a chance and send you down to Denver and we'll see whether the system is correct, or whether what you said was correct."

He took a pen, and with a wink, placed a "2" in front of my total pilot time, thus changing it to 2,592 hours. He then signed the order for me to go down to Seattle to get money for a ticket to go to Denver, where I went through United Airline pilot's training school. When I finished up I was assigned back to Seattle, which I had requested, and started flying in December of 1946.

Back in the Military

A lot of things happened during the summer of 1947 that set the stage for another career change for me. Due to several circumstances, one being the introduction of larger four-engine passenger planes, we junior pilots got the word that there was going to be a "technological unemployment period" coming soon. As soon as the larger planes started arriving, pilots began to be laid off. I knew that my time at United was to be short.

Around the same time, I received a telegram in response to my application for a regular commission in the Army. On the world scene, the "Iron Curtain" had come down in the middle of 1946. By 1947 the threat and spread of Communism was real. Many people were concerned about war again, but this time with Russia.

I guess you could say I "heard the call" to fight Communism. After the telegram from the Army arrived, I went down to Ft. Lewis where I was interviewed and approved for a regular commission as a 1st. Lieutenant. I was given a military furlough from United Airlines and orders from the Army to report to Fairchild Air Force Base near Spokane. When I arrived there in September of 1947, the U.S. Army Air Forces had a new name, the United States Air Force.

My career in the Air Force spanned twenty-two years and concluded when I retired in 1966 as a Lieutenant Colonel at Castle Air Force Base, just outside of Atwater, California. During that time I married my beautiful wife, Sandy, and we had six children; Kerry, Jim III, Kevin, Leslie, Brian and Tina. We spent time in quite a few places—Japan, Alabama, England, Germany and California. When I finally retired I moved my family back up to Washington State to a home in Bellevue, just east of Seattle, where we've been ever since.

When I look back over the years to my time during WWII, my fondest memories are always of the nearly five months I spent in Rotterdam with the amazing Dutch Underground people. I have always considered my experiences and adventures there more defining and instructive than any master's or doctorate degree I could ever have achieved in a university.

I remember vividly the times when it seemed that Lady Luck was the unseen force tipping the scales in my favor: the Green Policeman missing me in Korteland's rabbit shed, even though he was only two feet from me; having virtually unlimited freedom of movement as a deaf and dumb basketmaker; passing safely by the SD agent walking down the steps at Anton Sanders' place; being asked for my PB only once, and that by a good decent Dutch policeman; even to being captured by the German Abwehr instead of any of the other more sinister and deadly Nazi services.

I think back to the hectic moments just before bailout when I knelt down at the edge of the open camera hatch. I could have dropped through that hatch at any time. Nothing was holding me back. In fact every normal instinct was firing off loud and clear to go, now! But a quiet voice inside, calmly and clearly, told me there was time to say a prayer. I took a few precious moments and said a prayer.

Hummmm…maybe it wasn't Lady Luck after all.

Epilogue

The Germans captured Cornelius (Kees) Hendrik van den Engel in Rotterdam on the 25th of August, 1944. He was first taken to the Bunker at the Vught concentration camp. The torture he endured was not caused by physical beatings—he would have preferred that—but by the mental games the SD subjected him to during his interrogations. They pulled the Russian Roulette routine on him many times. They also put his name on lists to be shot, only to tell him "not today" after he had agonized during the moments leading up to his supposed execution; moments where the SD actually put a pistol to his head before standing down. The SD did this many times.

When the Canadian military began sweeping into South Holland, the Germans quickly evacuated the Vught concentration camp on the 5th of September, 1944. The prisoners, including Kees, were transported to Sachsenhausen concentration camp outside the town of Oranienburg near Berlin. Luckily for Kees, in the near-panic of the evacuation the Germans lost most of their paperwork, including the orders of execution for one Kees van den Engel. Therefore, when he wound up at Sachsenhausen, the administration staff did not know that he was marked for death.

Kees made anti aircraft shells at one of the work camps for about a month. Then he was taken to another sub-camp at Rathenau where he was put to work in the Heinkel airplane factory until he was liberated on the 27th of April 1945 by the advancing Russians.

The first time Kees and the other prisoners were out of their compound, he and a few others went to the commandant's house and down into his basement. Some ex-prisoners had been there before, ransacked the place, and found some sugar. Those inmates had taken all the food and had torn open these sacks of sugar; Kees gorged on the sugar, which in a way rejuvenated him, but also made him very ill.

Kees ran into some American soldiers and they asked him who he was. He was near to starving and must have looked terrible—just one more of thousands of displaced persons wandering around. Kees told the soldiers who he was and that he had been in the concentration camp, but that he had also helped American pilots. This caught the soldiers' attention and they wanted to know where he was from. Kees told then that he was a Dutchman and his home was Rotterdam. One of the soldiers took Kees to an American officer and told him Kees' story.

After questioning Kees a little more the officer told him, "Well, son, you're on your way back home." He gave Kees a pass stating, "Every consideration and assistance will be rendered this young man who has helped downed Allied airmen." With that pass in hand, Kees began his journey home.

The End

Afterword

The Death of Dr. Albert Jappe-Alberts

Many thousands of Dutch civilians were murdered by the Germans in reprisal shootings, with the number escalating during the last few months of the war. Today, at the site of each reprisal killing stands a monument; some small and simple, others large and bold. Many of them are plain white concrete crosses, about two and a half feet high, with the words *Voor Hen Die Vielen,* "For Those Who Fell," written across the arms of the cross. At the base of many monuments is a large bowl.

Every year at 8pm on the 4th of May, all of Holland honors the victims of World War II, both civilian and military, in a nation-wide remembrance ceremony called Dodenherdenking, "Remembrance of the Dead." Flags fly at half-mast, all traffic stops, and a couple of moments of silence are observed. At the monuments erected for those murdered in reprisal shootings, oil is poured into the bowls at the bases and lit. People come in silence, place flowers and wreaths, bow their heads—and remember.

A few miles south of Rotterdam on the south shore of the Oude Maas, is the small town of Heinenoord. On the side of a small country road called Provincialeweg N217 stands a monument topped by a bronze statue of a young boy crying out, "Mother." It is a monument dedicated to Dutch civilians killed in reprisal by the Germans. One of the men shot on the side of Provincialeweg was Dr. Albert Jappe-Alberts.

When the SD hit the home of Dr. Jappe-Alberts, the doctor, his wife and their children were separated and taken to the Scheveningen prison in The Hague. Mrs. Jappe-Alberts had no idea what happened to her husband. Only after the war ended did she find out that her husband had been taken out of the Scheveningen prison with nine other men and murdered in cold blood on a lonely road near Heinenoord. He was the victim of a reprisal killing.

On the right side of the monument are ten names, and at the top of the list is Dr. Albert Jappe-Alberts. The front reads:

MOTHER

For Those Who Fell

For and Because of the Resistance

1940 – 1945

How Could People Ever Annul

The Wish to Live?

Here Sounded the Cry of One

Who Spoke for Ten Comrades

The monument near the town of Heinenoord dedicated, in part, to the men who were murdered Feb. 18, 1945, by the Germans in reprisal for the killing of a Dutch Nazi. (Lt. Col. Keeffe collection)

Retracing My Steps

Two of the places where I was stationed early in my Air Force career were Burtonwood, near Warrington, England, and then USAFE Headquarters, Wiesbaden, Germany. While at both of these airbases, I made several trips back to Holland and visited many of my Dutch friends. During the first trip, in the late 1950s, I rented a car and Kees van den Engel and I drove around and visited many of the places I had been during the war. One of the first stops was Noordhoek, Papendrecht. After some detective work, we found the dike road and Korteland's home. In 1953 there had been a tremendously destructive flood and the Noord River had torn through the dike and laid waste to many of the homes on the other side. Korteland's home was spared, but enough damage to the area remained so that it was difficult to get my bearings.

It was during that visit that I met the man in the fedora hat again and learned his name, Adriaan van Wijngaarden. He was a painter who worked at the boat yard across the dike road—the same boat yard where I hopped aboard the row boat on my journey up the dark river fourteen years earlier. I also met Johannes Verdoorn and his wife, and his brother, Willem—the big man who Dr. Reitvelt sent to look for the .45 semi-automatic I had hidden behind the rabbit hutch.

Adriaan van Wijngaarden – The man with the fedora hat. (Photo supplied by his son, Pieter van Wijngaarden)

I learned many things on that trip, especially what had happened to most everyone I knew in Holland. Their earlier letters had provided me with some of the details, but having the time to sit down and visit with them—Kees and Marijke van den Engel (yes they got married), Anton Sanders, Albert Broekhuizen, Johannes Verdoorn—and others, provided me with so much more.

In 1959, when I was stationed at Wiesbaden, I took my two children, Kerry and Jimmy, on a road trip to Moosburg and found the farm family Andy Anderson and I had stayed with the first night after we took off from Stalag VII A. They were the Kreidenweis family. The little girl, Katharina, who was probably six years old when I first met her, was now grown up. Before I left to go back to Wiesbaden, we all stood in their front doorway and Katharina's brother, Sebastian, took our picture.

Years later, in 1994, I was back in Moosburg helping to plan for the 50th anniversary of the liberation of Stalag VII A. I again visited the Kreidenweis family and we had our photo taken in their front doorway. By this time, both Katharina's parents had died and her brother, Sebastian, was dying of cancer.

Left: 1959 photo of Kreidenweis doorway. L to R: Mr. Kreidenweis, Katharina, Mrs. Kreidenweis with Jim Keeffe behind. Right: 1994 photo of same doorway. L to R: Sebastian, Jim Keeffe, Katharina. (Lt. Col. Keeffe collection)

Miss Mae Arduini

One of the people I wrote to when I came home from the war in July of 1945 was Miss Mae Arduini of Rural Valley, Pennsylvania. I never forgot the name tag that I found in the sleeve of that wonderful wool sweater back at Dulag Luft. A little while later she wrote back to me the following:

```
I have to confess that I did not knit that sweater,
my mother did. The reason we did it was because
```

the War Department and the Red Cross asked people
to do things to aid the war effort. In our area,
they asked the women who knew how to knit, to knit
sweaters. They furnished the wool and the mothers
who could knit came together, and they chatted
together while they knitted. Finally, after knitting
one or two sweaters, most of the women quit because
they said, "This is all make-do work. They're just
trying to keep us busy, and nobody is going to see
these sweaters."

When the Arduinis received my letter, they were able to go to the Casandras and tell them they were wrong. Some of their neighbors had scoffed at their sweater knitting, making comments like, "You're just wasting your time. No one will ever see those sweaters." In my letter I told them how that sweater had kept me warm during the horrible winter of '44– '45, during the long march, and that I had kept it with me until I arrived in France the following spring, when I finally gave it to a Frenchman.

Later, in 1968 when I was working at Boeing in Seattle, I went to Pittsburg. I wrote the Arduinis before going there, telling them I was going to be in Pittsburg and would like to visit them. I took my scrap book and all my pictures, letters, and telegrams with me. I rented a car and drove out to a little town, Rural Valley, Pennsylvania, which is outside of Pittsburg. The Arduinis were a nice Italian family. By now, poor old mama Arduini was in a bed in the living room and being cared for by her daughters. Almost the entire town came to see this former pilot who had received a sweater from one of them.

My Dear Friend Kees van den Engel

Kees became a life-long dear friend of mine. He and Marijke married a couple years after the war and had three sons— Cees, Hans, and Frank.

For quite some time after the war, Kees advocated for and helped many Dutch men and women, including Albert Broekhuizen, apply for and receive distinguished honors from the Dutch government for their exceptional courage and risk-taking in the Dutch Resistance—especially regarding their activities in hiding and helping downed Allied airmen, like myself. As the years went by, the number of petitions for these awards, including the highly honored *Verzetskruis*, the Resistance Cross, dwindled. Eventually the Dutch government put a hard cut-off date, after which no more petitions would be reviewed. Unfortunately, no one helped or championed the cause for Kees to receive recognition by his government, and he was too humble to submit a petition himself.

The wedding of Kees and Marijke van den Engel. (Photo supplied by Kees' son Frank)

In 1995, during one of my trips to Holland, I visited Hendrik-Ido-Ambacht, the place where my B-24 came to rest in a field, and met with the mayor of the city. Kees came with me, and during our time there, I convinced him to write a petition for recognition, which the mayor of Hendrik-Ido-Ambacht agreed to send through the governmental channels. But the cut-off date for petitions had long since come and gone. Even with the Mayor's help, Kees' petition went nowhere.

However, to the credit of the United States and Britain, Kees did receive recognition from both nations, grateful to him for his help in aiding Allied airmen. After the war my family and I were vacationing at Diano Marina on the Italian Riviera. Kees came with us, and one night he and I were lying out under the stars, just being quiet and enjoying the night in each other's company. He finally said to me, "Do you mind if I ask you a question?"

I said, "Of course not, Kees, go ahead."

"Well, there's one thing I've been pondering all these years, and that is how you and I can be such good friends."

I was rather taken aback and said, "That's a remarkable statement. Why in the world should we not be friends?"

He replied, "Well, the fact that I am Dutch Reform and you are Roman Catholic."

"What's that got to do with the price of hay? I don't care what your religion is."

"This is what I have been pondering all these years" he said. "Apparently, in your country it doesn't make much difference, but Jim, I can tell you, in my country it makes all the difference in the world. If you and I were working in an office somewhere, we would work together while keeping each other, more or less, at arm's length and staying away from the subject of religion, per se. But out on the streets and after hours, we would never socialize. You would go your way, and I would go my way. If we passed each other on the street, either alone or with our families, we would greet each other, but that's all."

This certificate is awarded to

Cornelis van den Engel

as a token of gratitude for and appreciation of the help given to the Sailors, Soldiers and Airmen of the British Commonwealth of Nations, which enabled them to escape from, or evade capture by the enemy.

Air Chief Marshal,
Deputy Supreme Commander,
Allied Expeditionary Force

1939-1945

"Well done Kees, and our deepest thanks!" Signed by Air Chief Marshal, Sir Arthur William Tedder.
(Lt. Col. Keeffe collection)

"Well, Kees, don't you think that is pretty stupid?" I said.

"Yes, I do. But that's the way it is in Holland. During the war much of this was set aside. The different religions worked rather well together because their common enemies were the German occupation, the Nazi aspects of the occupation and our own Dutch Nazis, the NSBers."

Kees van den Engel and I remained steadfast friends until his death on May 9, 2004.

Left: Kees van den Engel and Jim Keeffe in Rotterdam, 1978. (Lt. Col. Keeffe collection)

Appendix A

Night and Fog Decree

On December 7, 1941, Hitler issued *Nacht und Nebel Erlass*, the Night and Fog Decree.

This decree replaced the unsuccessful Nazi policy of taking hostages to undermine underground activities. Suspected underground agents and others would now vanish without a trace into the night and fog.

SS Reichsführer Himmler issued the following instructions to the Gestapo.

"After lengthy consideration, it is the will of the Führer that the measures taken against those who are guilty of offenses against the Reich or against the occupation forces in occupied areas should be altered. The Führer is of the opinion that in such cases penal servitude or even a hard labor sentence for life will be regarded as a sign of weakness. An effective and lasting deterrent can be achieved only by the death penalty or by taking measures which will leave the family and the population uncertain as to the fate of the offender. Deportation to Germany serves this purpose."

Field Marshall Keitel issued a letter stating:

"Efficient and enduring intimidation can only be achieved either by capital punishment or by measures by which the relatives of the criminals do not know the fate of the criminal. The prisoners are, in future, to be transported to Germany secretly, and further treatment of the offenders will take place here;

these measures will have a deterrent effect because - A. The prisoners will vanish without a trace. B. No information may be given as to their whereabouts or their fate."

The victims were mostly from France, Belgium and Holland. They were usually arrested in the middle of the night and quickly taken to prisons hundreds of miles away for questioning and torture, eventually arriving at the concentration camps of Natzweiler or Gross-Rosen, if they survived.

Night and Fog Decree

GEHEIM (SECRET)

Directives for the prosecution of offences committed within the occupied territories against the German State or the occupying power, of December 7th, 1941.

Within the occupied territories, communistic elements and other circles hostile to Germany have increased their efforts against the German State and the occupying powers since the Russian campaign started. The amount and the danger of these machinations oblige us to take severe measures as a detriment. First of all the following directives are to be applied:

I. Within the occupied territories, the adequate punishment for offences committed against the German State or the occupying power which endanger their security or a state of readiness is on principle the death penalty.

II. The offences listed in paragraph I as a rule are to be dealt with in the occupied countries only if it is probable that sentence of death will be passed upon the offender, at least the principal offender, and if the trial and the execution can be completed in a very short time. Otherwise the offenders, at least the principal offenders, are to be taken to Germany.

III. Prisoners taken to Germany are subjected to military procedure only if particular military interests require this. In case German or foreign authorities inquire about such prisoners, they are to be told that they were arrested, but that the proceedings do not allow any further information.

IV. The Commanders in the occupied territories and the Court authorities within the framework of their jurisdiction, are personally responsible for the observance of this decree.

V. The Chief of the High Command of the Armed Forces determines in which occupied territories this decree is to be applied. He is authorized to explain and to issue executive orders and supplements. The Reich Minister of Justice will issue executive orders within his own jurisdiction.

Source: Nazi Conspiracy and Aggression Volume 7 Document No. L-90. The document was retrieved from the archives of the Avalon Project at the Yale Law School.

Appendix B

The Notorious False Escape Route Known as the KLM Line

Little did Lt. Keeffe know when he reached the Dutch/Belgian border in July of 1944, that once he stepped across into Belgium, he would be in the clutches of a well-oiled false escape line run by Belgian and Dutch traitors working for the Germans.

Outwardly nothing had changed. A young girl in her early 20s introduced herself as Anna and escorted Lt. Keeffe and Jenkins, the Englishman, to Antwerp. To Lt. Keeffe, Anna was another brave girl working for the resistance, risking her life to help downed Allied airmen like himself. In fact, the ruse was so well played that all the characters he met in Antwerp showed no sign that they were anything other than dedicated civilian men and women doing their best to aid the cause of their countries in the fight against the tyranny of their occupiers. Yet everyone of them, with the exception of Mrs. Rommens, was either a German agent or a traitor working for the Germans.

There were several legitimate escape lines operating between Belgium, France and Spain; the Comet Line (Le Réseau Comète) being one of the more famous. The Germans were constantly trying to infiltrate and break these lines.

The Abwehr, a German military intelligence gathering agency, had a department, AST III/f. The primary objectives of AST III/f were counter espionage and infiltrating organized resistance. A couple of the top dogs in the department were two Germans named Piepe and Kramer. One of the deputies was Karl Helmer (alias Stahl). Helmer had several men operating under him, one of whom was Karl Ulrich. Among those working for Ulrich were the following:

Rene van Muylem (alias Robert, Donald, and several more); Pauline Vlaming (alias Pam); and Maria Verhulst-Oomes (alias Anna). Van Muylem and Oomes were Belgians and Vlaming was Dutch. All were traitors. In addition to these upper echelon people were webs of innocent helpers, guides and safe houses, such as the Rommens. Yes indeed, it was well-organized—and expanding, in scope as well as penetration.

Helmer, Ulrich and van Muylem wanted to do more than collect information concerning espionage and resistance groups, so they developed a plan they called the "Airmen's Sluice." They were rebuffed by Piepe because the plan was beyond III/f's purpose. So Helmer went to the main Belgium AST in Brussels and got permission and funding from a German named Moehring to operate as AST III/c2.

With official approval and backing, Van Muylem ingratiated himself with the heads of several local Antwerp resistance groups. He brought money, supplied munitions and offered hope of a safe passage out of Belgium. Thus was the corruption of legitimate operations undertaken and made complete. The team Rene van Muylem managed to insert was small but decisive. So effective were they that it was not till well after liberation that anyone had an inkling something was amiss.

Left: Karl Helmer, alias 'Stahl,' whom Lt. Keeffe dubbed 'Big Guy.' He was indeed a large man as he towers over the other men in the photo. Right: Luftwaffe Oberleutnant, Dr. Werner, whom Lt. Keeffe called 'Little Guy.' (Courtesy of Michael LeBlanc collection)

The Belgium chain of command appears to have been: Moehring, Piepe, Kramer, Ulrich and Helmer, and van Muylem. Helmer seems to have been rather a free agent and the operational chief of the "Airmen's Sluice". He had a driver called Janko, with a petrol powered car, and frequently involved Luftwaffe Oberleutnant Dr. Werner of Deurne airport in the questioning of airmen. In addition Helmer dealt with the S.D., the G.F.P, the Green Police and the Heer

(German Army) operators of the Begijnenstraat Gefangnis.

Several of above characters who inserted themselves into Lt. Keeffe's journey now become evident. They were:

Karl Helmer—Big Guy
Rene van Muylem—Big Boss
Dr. Werner—Little Guy
Pauline Vlaming—Pam
Maria Verhulst-Oomes—Anna

By the time Anna brought Keeffe and Jenkins to see the Big Boss at Van Eycklei 17, the "Airmen's Sluice" was a well established and efficient operation. The apartment belonged to Pam (Pauline) who pretended to be the girlfriend of the Big Boss (van Muylem). In actuality she was one of Karl Helmer's girlfriends. Helmer (Big Guy) had his office on the top floor of Van Eycklei.

The KLM Line ceased to exist operationally when the Canadian military advanced through and liberated Belgium during the first couple of weeks of September, 1944. But by then, the Airmen's Sluice had netted and captured 235 Allied airmen, and Lt. Keeffe was one of them.

The Allies' advance eastward pushed the Germans ahead of them, through Belgium and South Holland. Thousands grabbed what they had and fled toward Germany. In Holland, the 5th of September is known as Dolle Dinsdag (Mad Tuesday). Rumors of liberation spread like wild fire with the result that thousands and tens of thousands of Dutch were out en masse that Tuesday with banners and flags, wildly celebrating the imminent arrival of the liberators. The German occupation forces and Dutch Nazis flew into a panic and many fled to Germany.

In the ensuing chaos, word went out from German authorities to hunt down and kill all the Dutch and Belgium people they knew who were involved in the resistance; those they had previously left alone in order that they would continue to feed airmen unawares into their clutches.

Many helpers were killed during those hectic days; for example, the two uniformed Dutch Marechaussee, Adrianus van Gestel and Gradus Gerritsen, who brought John Jenkins to join Lt. Keeffe at the border, and who saved Keeffe's life there by convincing him to burn the map he had made and brought with him of German fortifications in Rotterdam. The "dive" location of these two was betrayed to Helmer by Pauline Vlaming and Marie Verhulst-Oomes on 7 September. The two Marechaussee were picked up on the 9th along with Mrs. Maria Josepha Verhoeven-Cornelissen (alias Miet Pauw), a mother of seven who was sheltering them. Gestel, Gerritsen and Mrs. Verhoeven were brutally interrogated and tortured. All three were executed on the 10th in the woods near

Breda. Hundreds more would soon have been killed had the situation remained more stable. Needless to say, Lt. Keeffe was a very lucky fellow. And so were people like the Rommens in Antwerp, and the Looses in Breda.

BID VOOR DE ZIEL VAN ZALIGER
GRADUS ANTONIUS GERRITSEN
Wachtmeester der Marechaussee
geboren te Arnhem, 19 Juli 1917 en
gefusilleerd voor het vaderland op de Schietbei
te Breda, 10 September 1944.

BID VOOR DE ZIEL VAN ZALIGER
MARIA JOSEPHA VERHOEVEN
echtgenoote van
HUGO CORNELISSEN
Lid van den Bond van het H. Hart
geboren te Hoogstraten, 30 November 1898
en gefusilleerd voor het vaderland op de Schietbei
te Breda, 10 September 1944.

BID VOOR DE ZIEL VAN ZALIGER
Adrianus Theodorus Joannes van Gestel
Wachtmeester der Marechaussee
echtgenoot van
Petronella Boerenkamp
geboren te Eindhoven, 18 Januari 1916 en
gefusilleerd voor het vaderland op de Schietbei
te Breda, 10 September 1944.

Memorial notices for the three Dutch Resistance members who were betrayed by Pauline Vlaming and shot on the 10th of September 1944. (Lt. Col. Keeffe collection)

After the liberation of Belgium in September of '44, the search for German agents and Belgian and Dutch traitors began in earnest. Pauline Vlaming was arrested in November, 1944, but denied her role as an agent of the Abwehr. She fled from prison in June 1945, but was arrested again in April 1946. In October 1947 she fled for the second time and made her way across the Dutch border. In July 1948, she was sentenced to death by default by a Belgian high court. In the Netherlands she was safe from the Belgian authorities. The betrayal of the airmen had only taken place in Belgium and the Dutch could not convict her for those crimes. But, she was eventually sentenced in a Dutch court to fifteen years for her involvement in the arrest and execution of resistance workers, including Gestel, Gerritsen, and Mrs. Verhoeven, in and around Breda.

Pauline Vlaming's helper, Maria Verhulst-Oomes, was arrested in 1945 and committed suicide in prison. Rene van Muylem was executed in 1948 by the Belgians. His discovery and captured were an ironic twist of fate.

Pauline 'Pam' Vlaming's mug shot when she finally went to prison for her crimes. Notice how she's aged compared to her NSB photo on page 172. (Courtesy of Michael LeBlanc collection)

Maria Verhulst-Ommes, alias 'Anna'. This photo shows her sitting in a prison interrogation room an hour before she committed suicide. Photo in insert shows Maria in happier times. (Courtesy of Michael LeBlanc collection)

As the Germans were fleeing the advancing Allies, van Muylem disappeared into the throng going into Germany where he flitted around from one place to another. Immediately after the war, he wandered over to France looking for work. He landed a job as a bartender in a club at—of all places—Camp Luck Strike. Of course the camp had been turned into a repatriation center for American ex-POWs. Unfortunately for Rene, one of the men he served at the club was none other than one of the American airmen he had betrayed and had sent to a POW camp, Lt. Robert Hoke of the 388 Bomb Group.

Rene van Muylem was sent back to Belgium and thoroughly debriefed. He was very candid in his interrogation, which had a wealth of information about his activities and particularly about the character of his resistance colleagues. He had great respect for the genuine patriots he came into contact with and disdained those he considered involved in resistance work only for mercenary reasons.

Eventually, he faced a trial and was executed in 1947. Despite his betrayal of many Belgians saboteurs and allied airmen, even his prosecutor admitted he had always behaved as a gentleman and had protected most of his 'duped' safe-house keepers from arrest by the Germans. Standing before the firing post, he asked the firing squad to hurry up and get it over with.

A bronze monument created in 1949 to honor Maria Josepha Verhoeven and the two Dutch Marechaussee, Gerritsen and Gestel who were murdered the 10th of September 1944 by the Germans. Crouching on Maria's right is an Allied airman with goggles. Maria's position highlights her bravery in protecting not only evading Allied airmen, but also those in the Resistance who needed shelter. (Courtesy of www.verzet.org)

(Author's note: Most of the information in Appendix B concerning the organization of, and people in, the KLM Line—the "Airmen's Sluice"—was meticulously gathered over years of research by Michael Moores LeBlanc. A special thanks to Mr. LeBlanc for his detective work in piecing together literally thousands of clues found in moldy faded letters, old archive lists, interviews, and decades-old trial papers. Through his careful cross referencing, double and triple checking of sources and data, and his dedication to uncovering and exposing the truth, Michael has shined a light on a fascinating chapter in the murky and deadly underworld of escape and betrayal.

Appendix C

LIBERATORS

THE LIBERATION OF STALAG VIIA
by Jim Lankford, National Historian

On 30 April, 1945 the *New York Times* reported; 'Huge Prison Camp Liberated...27,000 American and British prisoners of war at a large camp at Moosburg.' The report was correct, the camp was huge, but it was also wrong. The following day, the *Times* printed a correction; 'The Fourteenth Armored Division liberated 110,000 Allied prisoners of war at Stalag 7A at Moosburg, instead of the 27,000 prisoners previously reported. This was Germany's largest prisoner of war camp.'[1]

On 28 April the 14th Armored Division crossed the Danube River at Ingolstadt, and passed through the 86th Infantry Division, which had established the bridgehead on the previous day, with the mission of securing crossings of the Isar River at Moosburg and Landshut. Combat Command A (CCA) was on the right of the division's line of advance, Combat Command R (CCR) was on the left, and Combat Command B (CCB) was in reserve.

Large numbers of German troops were falling back on Moosburg to cross the river. Among them were the remnants of the 17th SS Panzer Grenadier and

719th Infantry Divisions. [2] It was, as it had been for much of the way across France and Germany, a race to capture a crucial bridge before retreating German units got safely to the other side, and blew it up in the faces of the oncoming Americans.

Under its commanding officer, Brig. Gen. C.H. Karlstad, CCA moved quickly toward Moosburg. The order of battle consisted of the 47th Tank Bn., the 500th Armored Field Artillery Bn., D Troop, 94th Cavalry Squadron, C Company, 125th Armored Engineers Bn., B Company, 68th Armored Infantry Bn, and B Battery, 398th Antiaircraft Bn.[3] Total strength of the command was about 1,750 men, including support units.[4] With only one company of infantry at its disposal, the combat command was significantly under strength in infantry.

Brig. Gen. Charles H. Karlstad

Photo: "History of the 14th Armored Division"

The combat command advanced nearly 50 miles on the 28th, against sporadic resistance. CCA Headquarters settled in for the night at Puttenhausen at 2300 hours. The main force, including the 47th Tank Bn. and the infantry of B-68, was eight miles to the southeast at Mauern. They were only four miles from Moosburg.[5] The entry into Mauern had not been an easy one. Not long before midnight, the infantry went in ahead of the tanks to clear the town, and were ambushed by SS soldiers using machineguns and automatic antiaircraft guns. The enemy resistance was eliminated in a short, but intense firefight. B-68 lost several men before the town was finally secured.[6]

During the early morning hours of the 29th, a car approached a roadblock on the southeast side of Mauern from the direction of Moosburg. The car was not fired on as it was seen to be flying a white flag. In the car were four men who asked to speak with a senior officer. They were escorted to Lt. Col. James

W. Lann, the commanding officer of the 47th Tank Bn.[7]

The party included a representative of the Swiss Red Cross, a major in the SS, Col. Paul S. Goode (U.S. Army), and Group Captain Willets (RAF).[8] The latter two were the senior American and British officers from Stalag VIIA, a prisoner of war camp near Moosburg. The SS major carried a written proposal from the area commander, which he was to present to the commanding officer of the American force. After a brief discussion, Lt. Col. Lann escorted the group to Puttenhausen to meet with Gen. Karlstad.

Dispositions of Combat Command A, 0600 Hours 29 April 1945

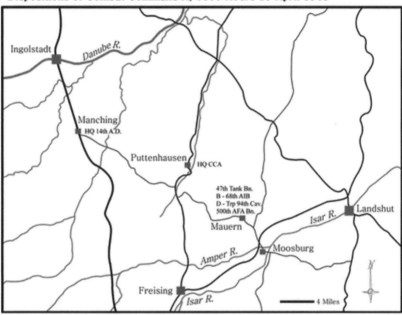

Map by Jim and Mariko Lankford

The combat command's intelligence officer (S-2), Major Daniel Gentry, was on duty in CCA headquarters when Lt. Col. Lann arrived. Lt. Col. Lann went in, leaving the delegates to wait outside. He told Major Gentry about the delegation, and asked if Gen. Karlstad was available. Major Gentry told him that the general had just awakened, and would be in the command post shortly. Gen. Karlstad walked in a few minutes later, and heard Lt. Col. Lann's report before the delegation was brought in.

The delegation entered the command post just before 0600. Col. Goode and Gen. Karlstad immediately recognized each other. They were old friends, and greeted each other warmly by their first names. Major Gentry was somewhat dismayed at Col. Goode's appearance. His jacket was not the right color, and was made of a coarse, poor quality wool. The rest of his uniform was badly worn, and in generally poor condition. Col. Goode was wearing a single insignia of rank which was pinned to his jacket collar. It was crude, and appeared to have been cut from a piece of tin. In contrast, Group Captain Willets' uniform was in excellent condition. He was even carrying an officer's swagger stick.

After the introductions, the Red Cross representative and the SS major discussed the German proposal with Gen. Karlstad. Col. Goode and Group Captain Willets did not take part in the discussion, and for the most part, spent their time talking with various officers in the command post. At some point during the discussions, Col. Goode left the room to get something to eat. Since it was actively engaged in combat operations, and far ahead of Division Trains, the combat command was on C Rations. Learning that Col. Goode was a prisoner of war, some of the men, who had acquired a few fresh eggs for their personal use, cooked him a breakfast of fried eggs, bacon, and toast.

The German proposal was written in English. It called for an armistice in the area around Moosburg, using as a reason, the presence of a large prisoner of war camp. It also called "...for the creation of a neutral zone surrounding Moosburg, all movement of allied troops in the general vicinity of Moosburg to stop while representatives of the Allied and German governments conferred on the disposition of the Allied prisoners of war in that vicinity." Prior to this, no one in the division had even known there was a prison camp at Moosburg, much less how large it was.[9]

On learning the details of the German proposal, Gen. Karlstad sent a radio message to division headquarters at Manching, asking the division commander, Maj. Gen. Albert C. Smith for instructions. It was clear that if accepted, the proposal would prevent CCA from capturing the bridge across the Isar River, as it was located within the proposed "neutral zone." It would also give the retreating Germans more time to withdraw across the river, and provided them with the opportunity to move at least some of the Allied prisoners with them. Gen. Smith rejected the proposal, and added a demand for the unconditional surrender of all German troops at Moosburg. Gen. Karlstad relayed Gen. Smith's response to the SS major. He did not issue a deadline by which the German commander must respond or make any allowances that might further delay the combat command in the fulfillment of its mission. After the delegation left the command post to return to Moosburg, Gen. Karlstad issued orders for the attack on Moosburg to proceed.

In his message, Gen. Smith had ordered Gen. Karlstad to: "Lead your troops into Moosburg." The order was unusual, and not in keeping with the way Gen. Smith typically worded orders to his officers. As a result, there was some discussion in the command post regarding Gen. Smith's meaning. Gen. Karlstad decided that it was his superior's intention that he was to actually lead the attack. He subsequently climbed into his peep (jeep), along with his aide, 2nd Lt. William J. Hodges, and accompanied by Lt. John Sawyer of D Troop, drove to the 47th Tank Bn. headquarters at Mauren.[10] There he joined Lt. Col. Lann, and with him, moved with the tank battalion in its attack on Moosburg.

There was no further discussion regarding the prison camp or its capture. The combat command was to continue with its primary mission of seizing a useable bridge across the Isar River.[11] Regardless, the liberation and security of the Allied prisoners of war was clearly of great importance, and the combat command would take the necessary steps to ensure this was accomplished. The men of the division had done this sort of thing before. Three weeks earlier, they had fought their way into Hammelburg to liberate Stalag XIIIC and Oflag XIIIB.[12]

As soon as its units were in position, CCA attacked down the main road between Mauern and Moosburg. The infantry platoons of B-68 were attached to the tank companies. The tanks of C-47, along with the 2nd platoon of B-68, were in the lead. They were followed by the tanks of B-47, with A-47 in support. Simultaneously, a platoon of tanks from C-47, and a platoon of infantry executed a flanking maneuver on the right of the main line of attack. Lt. Col. Lann took command of the main force, and Major Alton S. Kircher, the 47th's Operations Officer (S-3), led the flanking force.[13] Since there were so many Allied prisoners of war in the area, the risk of casualties due to "friendly fire" was high. As a result, the attack was made without the powerful guns of the 500th Armored Field Artillery Bn.[14]

The main force advanced without meeting any resistance to a point about 1 mile west of Moosburg, where the road crossed the Amper River. It was there, on the east bank of the stream, that the SS decided to make their stand.[15] The first tank to move across the bridge came under intense small arms fire from SS troops located on the far side of the stream. The infantry quickly took cover behind the tank, while the rest of the tanks and infantry took up positions along the bank of the river, and opened fire on the enemy positions. Several infantrymen on the bridge were wounded by the first bursts of enemy fire. After they were evacuated from the bridge, the American tanks and infantry moved forward into the fight.[16]

The SS fought from dug-in positions in the fields leading to the town, and from positions behind a railroad embankment on the Americans' left flank. The embankment was about 500 yards from the bridge, and lay on a direct line between it and the prison camp.[17] Resistance was stiff, even fanatic, but short lived. The SS had no tanks or antitank guns, and were armed only with small arms, machineguns, mortars, and panzerfausts. The battle-hardened Americans fought their way through the SS positions in the fields with relative ease, while returning the fire coming from the railroad embankment. The Germans surrendered when the Americans reached the edge of Moosburg, and by 1030, "... the SS were lying dead in their foxholes or going to the rear a prisoner...."[18]

The tanks of C-47, and their supporting infantry, moved out at once to seize the bridge across the Isar. They raced through the streets at 20 miles an hour without meeting any resistance. On arriving at the bridge, the force came under small arms and machinegun fire from the far side of the river. The infantry dismounted from the tanks, and returned fire while the lead tank rolled out onto the bridge. Just as the tank got fully onto the bridge, the Germans set off the demolition charge, and the center of the bridge disappeared in a massive explosion. The section of the span under the tank began tilting precariously down, towards the water. The driver brought his 32 ton vehicle to a halt, and slammed its transmission into reverse. With the tank's treads spinning, he skillfully backed the tank off the tilting portion of the bridge, and onto firm ground, before it slid into the river.[19]

Attack on Moosburg 0930 Hours 29 April 1945

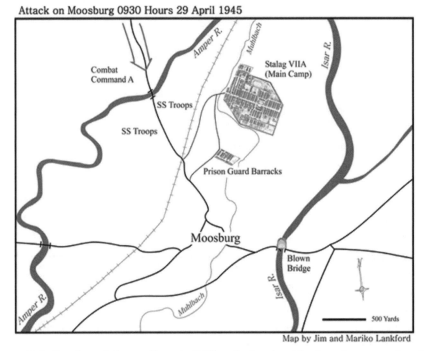

Map by Jim and Mariko Lankford

Col. Goode and Group Captain Willets had arrived back at the camp shortly before the engagement at the Amper River bridge. They told their fellow prisoners that an armored unit was coming to free them, and while the German resistance was expected to be light, they should keep their heads down. The prisoners and guards watched as the SS took up defensive positions in the area. It was not long before the sounds of battle came from the distance. The fight for Moosburg was underway. Fire from the American tanks and infantry, aimed at the SS who were firing from behind the railroad embankment, came into the camp. Prisoners and guards alike hurriedly sought cover in ditches, under buildings, and behind brick walls[20]. Adding to the commotion was the sound of the demolition charges exploding as the Germans destroyed the bridge across the Isar. As soon as it had started, it was over. The firing ceased except for the occasional sounds of small arms and machinegun fire from the direction of the bridge.

While the effort to capture the bridge was underway, Gen. Karlstad went into Moosburg with the main body of his force. "Large numbers of German prisoners were being rounded up by Lann's tank and infantry platoons, including one large group that stated it was the guard of the prison camp." Gen. Karlstad and his staff questioned some of the German officers regarding the prison camp, "... and selected a German captain to act as his guide to the prison camp."[21]

Gen. Karlstad ...

With 1st Lieutenant Joseph P. Luby of the 68th Armored Infantry Battalion and 2nd Lieutenant William J. Hodges, and their 3 "Peep Drivers", this party started out across town, guided by the German captain. As this little convoy, carrying one mounted .30 caliber machine-gun, approached the camp gate, the alarming sight of a large number of armed "Heinies" in the outer yard of the great camp was noted, but Lt. Luby took exactly the right action. Without slackening his speed but with both hands on the business end of his machine-gun he rolled into the middle of the German formation, brought his peep to a sudden halt and called "Actung." [sic] The German guard of 240 men was ordered to line up and to drop their weapons in front of them. The two young officers and 3 drivers went rapidly down the line receiving the pistol belts from officers and making a quick search of arms in the pockets of the guards.[22]

Moments later, a battle-scarred medium tank joined them at the main gate. Still others, carrying infantrymen on their backs, took up positions outside the camp.

Gen. Karlstad called for the German Camp commander Col. Otto Burger and received an unconditional surrender of the German garrison and the camp. The first allied prisoners to present themselves were Group Captain Willets and Colonel Goode, ... In a few moments an enterprising American produced a United States Flag -- from where, perhaps only he knew -- and amid thunderous cheers from the prisoners, ran it to the top of the camp flag pole. It was a dramatic moment."[23]

The liberators had arrived, and the prisoners were now, finally safe. As the realization of this sank in:

Scenes of the wildest rejoicing accompanied the tanks as they crashed through the double 10-foot wire fences of the prison camps. There were Norwegians, Brazilians, French, Poles, Dutch, Greeks, Rumanians, Bulgars. There were Americans, Russians, Serbs, Italians, New Zealanders, South Africans, Australians, British, Canadians—men from every nation fighting the Nazis. There were officers and men. Twenty-seven Russian Generals, sons of four American Generals. There were men and women in the prison camps. ... There were men of every rank and every branch of service, there were war correspondents and radio men.[24]

They rushed to greet their liberators. So many flowed around and over the tanks, peeps, and half-tracks, that even the huge Sherman tanks completely disappeared beneath a mass of jubilating humanity.

"You damned bloody Yanks, I love you!" shouted a six-foot four Australian and threw his arms around a peep driver.

A weary bearded American paratrooper climbed onto a tank and kissed the tank commander. Tears streamed from his cheeks.

Italians and Serbs, tired and drawn, jammed around the vehicles, eagerly thrusting out their hands to touch their liberators, weeping.

An American Air Corps lieutenant kissed a tank. "God damn, do I love the ground forces," he said.

"This is the happiest day of my life!"

"You were a long time coming, but now you are here!"

"Endlich frei, endlich frei,"[25]

> Here the division found many of its own soldiers, some of whom had been listed as Missing in Action since mid-November when the division first went into combat. The tankers of C Company were thrilled to see eight of their comrades who had been captured the previous January. Tech 5 Floyd G. Mahoney, also of C Company, "... was particularly overjoyed upon finding that his son, an air corps lieutenant, was a prisoner there."[26]

Most of the American soldiers who fought at Moosburg never actually saw the prison camp. They did not have much time to join in the celebrations or even to reflect on what they had accomplished. That would come later. That afternoon the infantry of B-68 crossed the Isar on a footbridge built by the engineers, and began patrolling the far side of the river. They took some more casualties when they came under sporadic fire from small arms, mortars, self-propelled guns, and artillery.[27] The rest of the combat command set up a defensive perimeter around Moosburg, and began patrolling the west bank of the Isar. Virtually everyone became involved in the task of rounding up the thousands of German soldiers who had been trapped in the area when the bridge was destroyed. Even Gen. Smith brought in a prisoner. Early in the afternoon he arrived at the CCA command post in Moosburg with an SS major riding on the hood of his peep. In one of those strange coincidences of war, it was the same SS major who had led the delegation to CCA headquarters early that morning.[28]

CCA failed in its mission to capture a bridge across the Isar, but this was soon overshadowed by the magnitude of the liberation of Stalag VIIA. It did not hold 27,000 prisoners of war, as was originally reported, but 110,000.[29] Among them were 30,000 American soldiers, sailors, and airmen![30] Word of the massive liberation spread quickly, and even General Patton visited the prison camp with an entourage of high ranking officers.[31]

Combat Command B closed in on Moosburg that afternoon, along with elements of the 395th Regiment. The following night they crossed the Isar River on a bridge which had been built by C-125th Armored Engineers Bn. and the 998th Treadway Bridge Company. "... tanks and endless lines of silent infantrymen, ... faces set and hardly seeing the weaving scene about them, eyes straight ahead ..." moved forward, across the Isar River, and deeper into Germany.[32] Behind them the war was over, but ahead, although it was entering its final days, the war was still very much alive. For the soldiers of the 14th Armored Division, there was a little more fighting and liberating, and some dying, left to be done.[33]

Postscript

In its advance across Germany, the 14th Armored Division liberated approximately 200,000 Allied prisoners of war from German captivity. Among them were more than 30,000 Americans or about forty percent of the total number held in Germany.[34] The division also liberated some 250,000 "displaced persons," as well as the large Dachau sub-camp at Ampfing. Shortly after the end of the war, the nickname "LIBERATORS" was suggested for the division in an article which appeared in *Army Times*.[35] Understandably, the nickname stuck, and "LIBERATORS" became the division's official nickname.[36]

Jim Lankford's Comments

The author wishes to thank James F. Kneeland, Ray F. Lohof, Samuel R. Glenn, Robert A. Allwein, John Sawyer, Charles Franklin, and Col. Bob E. Edwards, former commanding officer of the 68th Armored Infantry Battalion, for sharing their experiences, and expanding on their personal memories and observations during interviews. Daniel R. Gentry deserves special recognition for sharing with the author, his clear, unvarnished recollections and observations of the events which occurred at the Combat Command A command post on 29 April, 1945. A special debt is owed to Col. George England Jr., former commanding officer of the 94th Cavalry Reconnaissance Squadron, who so generously shared with the author his vast knowledge of the 14th Armored Division's combat history and its personnel, and for guiding the author to those veterans who could best relate the events surrounding the liberation of Stalag VIIA. The author also wishes to thank Lt. Gen. Arthur P. Clark for his time and patience in answering the author's questions about his experiences "inside the wire" at Stalag VIIA. Any errors contained in this article are the sole responsibility of the author.

End Notes
Appendix C

1. *The New York Times*, 30 April, 1945, Section A, p. 3 and 1 May, 1945, Section A, p. 4.

2. 12th Army Group; Situation Maps, 28 and 29 April, 1945.

3. Historical Report, 47th Tank Bn., April 1945.; Historical Report: 94th Cavalry Squadron (Mechanized), April 1945.; *History: 125th Armored Engineers Bn.*, p.89; *History of the 68th Armored Infantry Bn.*, p.32.; *Combat Command A: History; European Operations,* p.17. The 68th AIB was attached to CCA when it crossed the Danube River, but late on 28 April the battalion, minus C Company, was attached to CCR in preparation for an attack on the city of Landshut.

4. The strength estimate is based on data from, Stanton, Shelby L. *World War II Order of Battle,* (Galahad Books, New York) 1984. p. 18.

5. *Combat Command A: History,* p. 17.; *Highly Mobile "A": The Combat History of Headquarters and Headquarters Company, Combat Command "A",* p. 6.

6. Interview with author: James F. Kneeland, 20 June, 2005. Mr. Kneeland was a squad leader in the 2nd Platoon, B-68.

7. Ibid. Mr. Kneeland recalls that the units at the roadblock had been warned to expect a vehicle flying a white flag, and not to fire on it.; *Combat Command A: History,* p. 21.

8. Interviews with author: Lt. Gen. Albert P. Clark, 16 June and 8 July, 2005. Gen. Clark, was a Lt. Col. during WWII. He was the second most senior American officer at Luft III, and later at Stalag VIIA. Gen. Clark served as the Intelligence/Security officer in both camps. According to Gen. Clark, Group Captain Willets is sometimes confused with a Group Captain Kellet, who was also a prisoner at Stalag VIIA.; Interviews with author: Daniel R. Gentry, 20 June and 7 July, 2005. At the time in question, Mr. Gentry held the rank of Major, and was the Intelligence Officer (S-2) of Combat Command A. Due to an unusual set of circumstances, he also functioned as the Operations Officer (S-3). Mr. Gentry was present in the CCA command post during the entire time that the delegation was there, and was involved in the later discussions regarding Gen. Smith's orders and the impending attack on Moosburg. According to Mr. Gentry, Willets was the Group Captain who traveled to CCA Headquarters with the delegation.; *Combat Command A: History,* pp. 21-22.

9. *Combat Command A: History,* p. 21.; Interview with author: Daniel R. Gentry, 20 June and 7 July, 2005. Mr. Gentry recalls that this sort of intelligence often did not reach the division level, and its lack contributed to the frequent "surprises" experienced by the advancing units.

10. "Peep" was used by the U.S. Armored Forces instead of the more common term, "jeep."

11. Interviews with author: Daniel R. Gentry, 20 June and 7 July, 2005.

12. MacDonald, Charles B., *The Last Offensive,* (GPO, Washington), 1972, pp. 418-19.

13. *47th Tank Battalion: History from New York o/Hudson to Muhldorf o/Inn.,* (Druck von Geiger, Muhldorf) 1945, p. 35.

14. Interview with author: Charles A. Franklin, 2 July, 2005.; Mr. Franklin served in C Battery, 500th AFA.

15. Interview with author: James F. Kneeland, 20 June, 2005.

16.   *Ibid.; 47th Tank Battalion History,* p. 37.

17.   Durand, Arthur A., *Stalag Luft III: The Secret Story,* (Touchstone, New York) 1989., p. 353.; Clark, Albert
      P., 33 *Months as a POW in Stalag Luft III,* (Fulcrum, Golden, CO) 2005., p. 173.; Interview with author:
      James F. Kneeland, 20 June, 2005. Prior to crossing the bridge over the Amper River, Mr. Kneeland
      recalls being cautioned by a superior not to fire to the left because stray rounds might go into the
      prison camp. Evidently, the admonition was promptly forgotten when the SS troops opened fire
      from behind the railroad embankment.

18.   Carter, *History of the 14th Armored Division.; 47th Tank Battalion: History,* p. 37. The size of the SS force
      which defended the town is unknown, but 6,000 German soldiers, including many SS, were taken
      prisoner at Moosburg.

19.   Interview with author: James F. Kneeland, 20 June, 2005.; Interview with author: Robert A. Allwein,
      11 June, 2005. At Moosburg, Mr. Allwein was the Asst. Driver of the tank which nearly slid off the
      bridge into the Isar River.

20.   Durand, *Stalag Luft III: The Secret Story,* p. 353.

21.   *Combat Command A: History,* pp. 22.

22.   *Ibid.,* p. 22.; Major Gustov Simoleit, the Assistant Commandant of the camp, presided over the sur-
      render of the prison guards.

23.   *Ibid.,* p. 22.

24.   *Ibid.,* p. 22.; *History of the 14th Armored Division.* Both sources state that there were 27 Russian gener-
      als at Stalag VIIA. In his book, Lt. Gen. Clark gives the number as "about ten," and includes a photo of
      ten Russian generals taken after the liberation. (pp. 178-179.)

25.   Carter, *History of the 14th Armored Division.*

26.   *47th Tank Battalion: History,* p. 37.

27.   *Combat Command A: Historical Report,* April 1945, p. 8.

28.   Interviews with author: Daniel R. Gentry, 20 June and 7 July, 2005.

29.   *Combat Command A: History,* p.22. This source states that according to "German estimates" the
      number of Allied POWs was 110,000.; Interviews with author: Lt. Gen. Albert P. Clark, 16 June and 8
      July, 2005. Only about 30,000 POWs were held in the main camp *(stammlager).* The majority, who
      were enlisted men and NCOs, were held in temporary camps in the immediate area of Moosburg,
      and were used as workers on farms, factories, and construction projects in the area between
      Landshut and Munich.

30.   *U.S. Air Force Oral History Interview;* Lt. Gen. Albert P. Clark, 20-21 June, 1979. Albert F. Simpson
      Historical Research Center, Office of Air Force History, Headquarter USAF, Washington, p.127..;
      Interview with author: Lt. Gen. Albert P. Clark, 16 June and 8 July, 2005. Gen. Clark believes that it is
      impossible to know the exact number of American POWs at Moosburg, but he thinks 30,000, "is a
      good number."; Carter, History of the 14th Armored Division .

31.   *Combat Command A: History,* p.21;

32.   Carter, *History of the 14th Armored Division.*

33.   *Ibid.* The 14th Armored Division moved quickly forward, and established two bridgeheads across

the Inn River before the end of the war.

34. The total number of American prisoners of war officially reported in enemy hands at the end of the war was 75,034. (Statistical Review, World War II: A Summary of ASF Activities, Headquarters, Army Service Forces, Washington, 1945, p. 157.)

35. *Army Times, Vol. 6, No. 8*, 29 September, 1945, p.15.

36. The list of Army units with officially authorized Special Designations (nicknames) can be seen at: http://www.army.mil/CMH-PG/lineage/SpcDes-123.htm. The 14th Armored Division is also recognized as a "Liberation Unit" by the U.S. Memorial Holocaust Museum.

Author's note: Jim Lankford kindly gave permission to reprint the Liberation of Stalag VII A. Some of the photos from the original article have been deleted because they appear elsewhere in the story. The web site for the 14th Armored Division is www.14tharmoreddivision.org.

Appendix D

A Missing Air Crew Report (MACR) was submitted to U.S. Army Air Forces Headquarters within 48 hours after an aircraft or crew failed to return from a combat mission. Over time an individual MACR file could grow to include many pages as more information was gathered from various sources, including eye-witness accounts and Casualty Questionnaires. The Germans also kept a file for each Allied airplane that was shot down. Information in that file included identification of captured or dead aircrew, status of their wounds and transportation documents to hospitals, jails or interrogation camps.

Lt. Keeffe's MACR number is 2959, and the matching German file number is KU 1171. MACR 2959 includes nearly 50 documents. See the following pages for a few of the MACR documents relating to missing aircraft B-24J, serial number 42-100375.

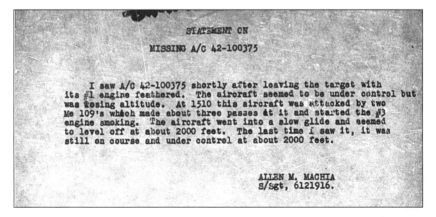

STATEMENT ON

MISSING A/C 42-100375

I saw A/C 42-100375 shortly after leaving the target with its #1 engine feathered. The aircraft seemed to be under control but was losing altitude. At 1510 this aircraft was attacked by two Me 109's which made about three passes at it and started the #3 engine smoking. The aircraft went into a slow glide and seemed to level off at about 2000 feet. The last time I saw it, it was still on course and under control at about 2000 feet.

ALLEN M. MACHIA
S/Sgt, 6121916.

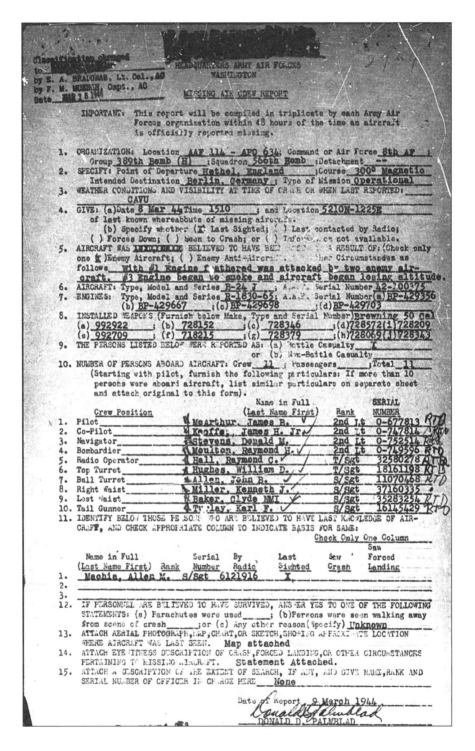

HEADQUARTERS ARMY AIR FORCES
WASHINGTON

MISSING AIR CREW REPORT

IMPORTANT: This report will be compiled in triplicate by each Army Air
Forces organization within 48 hours of the time an aircraft
is officially reported missing.

1. ORGANIZATION: Location AAF 114 - APO 634; Command or Air Force 8th AF ;
   Group 389th Bomb (H) ; Squadron 566th Bomb ; Detachment --

2. SPECIFY: Point of Departure Hethel, England ; Course 300° Magnetic
   Intended Destination Berlin, Germany ; Type of Mission Operational

3. WEATHER CONDITIONS AND VISIBILITY AT TIME OF CRASH OR WHEN LAST REPORTED:
   CAVU

4. GIVE: (a) Date 8 Mar 44 Time 1510 ; and Location 5210N-1225E
   of last known whereabouts of missing aircraft.
   (b) Specify whether (X) Last Sighted; ( ) Last contacted by Radio;
   ( ) Forces Down; ( ) Seen to Crash; or ( ) Information not available.

5. AIRCRAFT WAS ████████ BELIEVED TO HAVE BEEN LOST AS A RESULT OF: (Check only
   one (X) Enemy Aircraft; ( ) Enemy Anti-Aircraft; ( ) Other Circumstances as
   follows With #1 Engine feathered was attacked by two enemy aircraft. #3 Engine began to smoke and aircraft began losing altitude.

6. AIRCRAFT: Type, Model and Series B-24 J ; A.A.F. Serial Number 42-100375

7. ENGINES: Type, Model and Series R-1830-65; A.A.F. Serial Number (a) BP-429356
   (b) BP-429667 ; (c) BP-429698 ; (d) BP-429703

8. INSTALLED WEAPONS (Furnish below Make, Type and Serial Number) Browning 50 cal)
   (a) 992922 ; (b) 728152 ; (c) 728346 ; (d) 728572 (1) 728209
   (e) 992709 ; (f) 718215 ; (g) 728379 ; (h) 728069 (1) 728343

9. THE PERSONS LISTED BELOW WERE REPORTED AS: (a) Battle Casualty X
   or (b) Non-Battle Casualty

10. NUMBER OF PERSONS ABOARD AIRCRAFT: Crew 11 ; Passengers ; Total 11
    (Starting with pilot, furnish the following particulars: If more than 10
    persons were aboard aircraft, list similar particulars on separate sheet
    and attach original to this form).

Crew Position	Name in Full (Last Name First)	Rank	SERIAL NUMBER
1. Pilot	McArthur, James R.	2nd Lt	O-677813
2. Co-Pilot	Knoffe, James H. Jr	2nd Lt	O-747814
3. Navigator	Stevens, Donald M.	2nd Lt	O-752514
4. Bombardier	Moulton, Raymond H.	2nd Lt	O-749596
5. Radio Operator	Hall, Raymond C.	T/Sgt	32580278
6. Top Turret	Hughes, William D.	T/Sgt	18161198
7. Ball Turret	Allen, John B.	S/Sgt	11070468
8. Right Waist	Miller, Kenneth J.	S/Sgt	37160335
9. Left Waist	Baker, Clyde NMI	S/Sgt	35283254
10. Tail Gunner	Trolay, Karl F.	S/Sgt	16145429

11. IDENTIFY BELOW THOSE PERSONS WHO ARE BELIEVED TO HAVE LAST KNOWLEDGE OF AIR-
    CRAFT, AND CHECK APPROPRIATE COLUMN TO INDICATE BASIS FOR SAME:

	Name in Full (Last Name First)	Rank	Serial Number	By Radio	Last Sighted	Saw Crash	Saw Forced Landing
1.	Machia, Allen M.	S/Sgt	6121916		X		
2.							
3.							

12. IF PERSONNEL ARE BELIEVED TO HAVE SURVIVED, ANSWER YES TO ONE OF THE FOLLOWING
    STATEMENTS: (a) Parachutes were used____ ; (b) Persons were seen walking away
    from scene of crash____ ;or (c) Any other reason (Specify) Unknown

13. ATTACH AERIAL PHOTOGRAPH, MAP, CHART, OR SKETCH, SHOWING APPROXIMATE LOCATION
    WHERE AIRCRAFT WAS LAST SEEN. Map attached

14. ATTACH EYE WITNESS DESCRIPTION OF CRASH, FORCED LANDING, OR OTHER CIRCUMSTANCES
    PERTAINING TO MISSING AIRCRAFT. Statement Attached.

15. ATTACH A DESCRIPTION OF THE EXTENT OF SEARCH, IF ANY, AND GIVE NAME, RANK AND
    SERIAL NUMBER OF OFFICER IN CHARGE HERE None

Date of Report 9 March 1944

DONALD D. PALMBLAD

AFHPA-12

CASUALTY QUESTIONNAIRE

1. Your name James H. KEEFFE, Jr.   Rank 1st Lt. Serial No. O-747814

2. Organization 389 HBGp Commander M.W.Arnold Rank Col. Sqn. CO T.C.Conroy Rank Lt. Col.
                     (full name)   (full name)

3. What year 1944   month March   day 8 did you go down?

4. What was the mission, my 4th mission, target, Berlin   , target
time, 1330 (I think) , altitude, 21,000   route scheduled, Amsterdam,
Hanover, Berlin , route flown the same.

5. Where were you when you left formation? The formation was East of Dummer Lake
on the return trip from the target. --- I was in the Pilot's seat.

6. Did you bail out? Yes.

7. Did other members of crew bail out? All excepting Kenneth Miller, who was mor-
tally wounded, and who subsequently died as a result of fighter attacks.

8. Tell all you know about when, where, how each person in your aircraft for whom no
individual questionnaire is attached bailed out. A crew list is attached. Please
give facts. If you don't know, say: "No Knowledge". The tail-gunner, ball-turret
gunner, the wounded left waist-gunner and I bailed out from the camera
hatch upon my orders. The bombardier, navigator, radio-operator, top-
turret gunner, nose turret gunner, and pilot bailed out from the
bomb-bay in more or less the sequence related above.

9. Where did your aircraft strike the ground? Near H. I. Ambacht, Holland.

10. What members of your crew were in the aircraft when it struck the ground? (Should
cross check with 8 above and individual questionnaires) Only Kenneth Miller,
who had died at least 45 minutes to an hour before the rest of the
crew abandoned the ship.

11. Where was he in aircraft? In the waist.

12. What was his condition? He was dead.

13. When, where, and in what condition did you last see any members not already described above? All crew members are mentioned in the above narration.

14. Please give any similar information on personnel of any other crew of which you
have knowledge. Indicate source of information. In Rotterdam, Holland, while
with the Dutch underground, I met Lt. Jack Bennett (Navigator), Dick
Dabney, Sgt. (Radio-operator gunner), -- both of whom were crew members on
a B-17-- and Sgt. Charles Zesch (Gunner, B-17), These men were shot down
in November of 1943, as I recall. They left Rotterdam in April or May of
'44, determined to make their way to France and Spain, as the Organization handling them was unable to find a means for their return to UK.
In June or July I met a Lt. Brown, and several of his crew members (he
was the Pilot) who were shot down on a night pamphlet mission (B-17) over
            (Any additional information may be written on the back)
Holland, and whose ship crashed near Scheveningen, Holland, As I left
Holland before these men, I'm not aware of their fate.
                                         6-3862, AF

Item 10. Additional information.

Position	Name	Rank	ASN
Nose Gunner	Smith, Hugh W.	S/Sgt	34163042

APPA-11   2957

INDIVIDUAL CASUALTY QUESTIONNAIRE

Name of crew member: **K I S L E R, Kenneth J.**
Rank: **S/Sgt.**
Serial number:
Position: Crew (Bomber) XX Crew (Fighter)

Right Waist Gunner

Did he bail out? No. He was dead when the rest of the crew abandoned ship.

Where? _____

If not, why not? He was dead when the rest of the crew abandoned ship.

Last contact or conversation just prior to or at time of loss of plane: The gunners in

the waist were reporting fighters -- then the interphone was shot out.

Was he injured? His right hand and fore-arm were severed about 5 inches below
the wrist. Too, he had sustained 20mm fragments in the face, neck, and body.
Where was he when last seen? He was lying dead in the waist when I bailed out
from the camera hatch.
Any hearsay information: None. I went to the waist three times prior to
                           abandoning ship, in the course of 2½ hours.

Source: _____

Any explanation of his fate based in part or wholly on supposition: None. All

              knowlege is factual.

Total number of missions of above crew member: 4 or 5.

Dates and destinations if possible: My four were: Diepholz -- 21 Feb. 1944.
                                                  Gotha ------24 Feb. 1944.
                                                  Landes de Bussac
                                                           -- 5 March 1944.
                                                  Berlin --- 8 March 1944.

                                                              6-3861, AF

CONFIDENTIAL

CASUALTY INTERROGATION FORM
THE ADJUTANT GENERAL'S OFFICE

THE FAMILIES OF MANY OF YOUR COMRADES HAVE NOT BEEN AS FORTUNATE AS YOURS.
THEIR SONS AND HUSBANDS HAVE BEEN REPORTED MISSING IN ACTION AND THEY ARE ANXIOUSLY
WAITING TO LEARN THEIR FATE. YOU MAY BE ABLE TO SUPPLY THE INFORMATION WHICH WILL
HELP TO TERMINATE THE SUSPENSE AND ANXIETY THEY ARE SUFFERING.

IF YOU HAVE INFORMATION CONCERNING THE DEATH IN ACTION OR DURING IMPRISONMENT
OF ANY MEMBER OF THE ARMED FORCES YOU ARE REQUESTED TO FURNISH THE FOLLOWING INFORMA-
TION ABOUT THE DECEASED:

FULL NAME OF DECEASED   Kenneth Miller   Waist Gunner   B-24

HOME TOWN OR STATE   Unknown

GRADE OR RANK   S/Sgt

ORGANIZATION   566 Bomb Sq   389 Bomb Gp   8th AF
                        March 8/44   Berlin
DATE AND PLACE OF DEATH Plane hit by flak and attacked by fighters. S/Sgt Clyde
                        Baker, Waist Gunner, told me that Miller was hit by a 20MM shell.
                        He died within 20 seconds.

PLACE OF BURIAL   Not known.

WERE YOU AN EYEWITNESS TO HIS DEATH   No.

NAMES OF PERSONS BELIEVED TO HAVE WITNESSED
    HIS DEATH   S/Sgt Clyde Baker   2nd Lt. James Keeffe, CoPilot
                       Palmyra Rd, Warren, Ohio   Seattle, Washington

IF YOUR INFORMATION IS HEARSAY
    GIVE NAME AND ADDRESS OF YOUR
    INFORMANT   S/Sgt Clyde Baker   2nd Lt. James Keeffe,

3 Aug 45

                                        SIGN HERE _Raymond H. Moulton_____
                                        Name and Serial Number
                                        RAYMOND H. MOULTON 0749596
                                        172 Charlton St., Southbridge, Mass
                                        Your home address

NOTE: THIS FORM IS FOR USE BY CASUALTY BRANCH, THE ADJUTANT GENERAL'S OFFICE,
        WASHINGTON 25, D.C. ADDITIONAL COPIES OF THE FORM ARE AVAILABLE TO YOU.
        PLEASE FILL ONE OUT FOR EACH MEMBER OF THE ARMED FORCES WHOM YOU KNOW OR
        BELIEVE TO BE DEAD.

KU 117.

RM 1A

<u>REPORT ON CAPTURE OF MEMBERS OF ENEMY AIR FORCES</u>

PLACE: Airfield H.Q. (A) 201 / FL. Gilze Rijen.

DATE: 10 March 1944

NAME AND FIRST NAME OF PRISONER: Baker Clyde.

YEAR OF BIRTH: 2. February 1920

RANK: Pfc.   Refused to make any statment.

PLACE AND DATE OF CAPTURE: Near Dortrecht (HOlland) Hendric Idoembach on 8 March 1944

PARTICULARS CONCERNING CAPTURE:-
(CRASHED?   EMERGENCY LANDING?   SHOT DOWN?)   Bailed.

TYPE OF CRAFT   Liberator.

REMARKS: Identification tag No 35 283 254 T 42.
          Wounded in the Field Hospital Dortrecht

In addition:
          2nd LT. Mc Arthur J.B.
          T/Srgt. Hall C.H.
          "   Hughes W.D.
          S/Sgt   Turlay K.F.
          Sgt.   Allen B. J.

                    Signed: Schaischmidt.
                    Captain and officer for special disposition.

                    Page 52.

                                        6-3224.AF(2)

Appendix E

War Department Letters

WAR DEPARTMENT

THE ADJUTANT GENERAL'S OFFICE   mf

WASHINGTON

IN REPLY
REFER TO

AG 201 Keeffe, James H., Jr.
  PC-N ET0013

29 March 1944.

     Mrs. Marie W. Keeffe,
        3237 Hunter Boulevard,
        Seattle, Washington.

Dear Mrs. Keeffe:

     This letter is to confirm my recent telegram in which you were regretfully informed that your son, Second Lieutenant James H. Keeffe, Jr., O-747,814, Air Corps, has been reported missing in action over Germany since 8 March 1944.

     I know that added distress is caused by failure to receive more information or details. Therefore, I wish to assure you that at any time additional information is received it will be transmitted to you without delay, and, if in the meantime no additional information is received, I will again communicate with you at the expiration of three months. Also, it is the policy of the Commanding General of the Army Air Forces upon receipt of the "Missing Air Crew Report" to convey to you any details that might be contained in that report.

     The term "missing in action" is used only to indicate that the whereabouts or status of an individual is not immediately known. It is not intended to convey the impression that the case is closed. I wish to emphasize that every effort is exerted continuously to clear up the status of our personnel. Under war conditions this is a difficult task as you must readily realize. Experience has shown that many persons reported missing in action are subsequently reported as being prisoners of war. However, since we are entirely dependent upon governments with which we are at war to forward this information, the War Department is helpless to expedite these reports.

     In order to relieve financial worry on the part of the dependents of military personnel being carried in a missing status, Congress enacted legislation which continues the pay, allowances and allotments of such persons until their status is definitely established.

     Permit me to extend to you my heartfelt sympathy during this period of uncertainty.

               Sincerely yours,

                    J. A. ULIO
                    Major General,
               The Adjutant General.

ve

WAR DEPARTMENT

THE ADJUTANT GENERAL'S OFFICE

WASHINGTON 25, D. C.

IN REPLY REFER TO:

Keeffe, James H., Jr.
PC-N ET0013

3 July 1944

Mrs. Marie W. Keeffe
3237 Hunter Boulevard
Seattle, Washington

Dear Mrs. Keeffe:

As promised you, I am writing again regarding your son, Second Lieutenant James H. Keeffe, Jr.

It has been my fervent hope that favorable information would be forthcoming and that you might be relieved from the great anxiety which you have borne during these months. It is therefore with deep regret that I must state that no further report in his case has been forwarded to the War Department.

I want to again emphasize the fact that the Commanding Generals in all our theaters of operations are making a continuous effort to establish the actual status of personnel who have been reported as missing, or missing in action. In many instances the War Department must rely upon the reports by a belligerent government through the International Red Cross for information.

You may be certain that when any information is received, it will be promptly transmitted to you. In the event no additional information is received within the next three months, I will again communicate with you.

Sincerely yours,

J. A. ULIO
Major General,
The Adjutant General.

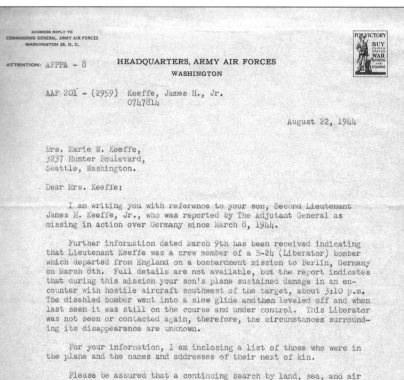

ADDRESS REPLY TO
COMMANDING GENERAL ARMY AIR FORCES
WASHINGTON 25, D. C.

ATTENTION: AFPPA - 8   HEADQUARTERS, ARMY AIR FORCES
WASHINGTON

AAF 201 - (2959)   Keeffe, James H., Jr.
0747814

August 22, 1944

Mrs. Marie W. Keeffe,
3237 Hunter Boulevard,
Seattle, Washington.

Dear Mrs. Keeffe:

     I am writing you with reference to your son, Second Lieutenant
James H. Keeffe, Jr., who was reported by The Adjutant General as
missing in action over Germany since March 8, 1944.

     Further information dated March 9th has been received indicating
that Lieutenant Keeffe was a crew member of a B-24 (Liberator) bomber
which departed from England on a bombardment mission to Berlin, Germany
on March 8th. Full details are not available, but the report indicates
that during this mission your son's plane sustained damage in an encounter with hostile aircraft southwest of the target, about 3:10 p.m.
The disabled bomber went into a slow glide and then leveled off and when
last seen it was still on the course and under control. This Liberator
was not seen or contacted again, therefore, the circumstances surrounding its disappearance are unknown.

     For your information, I am inclosing a list of those who were in
the plane and the names and addresses of their next of kin.

     Please be assured that a continuing search by land, sea, and air
is being made to discover the whereabouts of our missing personnel.
As our armies advance over enemy occupied territory, special troops
are assigned to this task, and all agencies of the government in every
country are constantly sending in details which aid us in bringing
additional information to you.

Very sincerely,

E. A. Bradunas

E. A. BRADUNAS,
Major, A. G. D.,
Chief, Notification Branch,
Personal Affairs Division,
Assistant Chief of Air Staff, Personnel.

1 Incl

Appendix F

Foreign Correspondence

2nd letter from Mrs. Jappe-Alberts

7th October 1945

My Grand 1st Lt!

Congratulations and a big hug! (never mind what the Army will say). How immensely glad I was to get your letter of the 24th September! I was just going to reply to your first one of Aug. 22 when the second one came along. The blue envelop is all in rags—because so many of our mutual pals wanted to read your letter, Kees, Piet, Boy, Ton—they all took their turn and from this you know at once that they're sound and well. I'll say more about them later. In a way, I am glad my letter was sent off before yours arrived—I told you all I had to say on the subject and from that you could see, that we never regretted what we did. Read Ans's letter carefully and you'll understand even better what I mean. She is a plucky kid—to say the least! We still don't believe that our capture had anything to do with you being taken prisoner—we are following another, most unexpected, trail of which you'll hear more as soon as it develops into something substantive. Bad as it was for you to be caught—once you were in a camp, you were amongst your own countrymen. I remember you saying that you preferred that to being locked in all day, never thinking it would actually come to pass. Shall we put a big "full stop" behind the "war" talk and continue on new lines? The way my husband and Olsen met in prison was like a storie from a book—but even stranger things happen in real life. That's why I keep on hoping for his return. The house is ready for him, all he needs is to walk straight in. About the watch my husband gave you. It was his own—not Malcolm's and I'd like you to keep it—if it still keeps time, wear it, and have "Rotterdam March-July 1944 A.JA" engraved in it for me.

Here's to answer your letters properly. The Bakkers or rather Cohens, as their real name was, with Aat and Niesji were sent on to Westerbork after a few weeks at Schevenigen. They were liberated before the 6th of May and are back in their own home—Aat and Niesje have gone back to their parents. They come almost every day and had Niesje been left to the choice she would have remained with me.

Kees came back from Oranienburg like a ghost. Very weak and unable to follow any conversation for more than a few minutes. He came to see me after he had been home only a few days. His girl friend is also back looking her old self again—but poor Mrs. Broekhausen died in a prison camp in Germany. Jo Berlijn, or as he was then called Fransen, was shot at Vught on Aug. 30th 1944. His wife never got to know until after the capitulation. Piet comes quite often, first time, I was only home 3 days. He arrived in uniform of the Irene Brigade— Dutch forces. He looked splendid, life in the Army in England since November '44 had done him a lot of good. He nor I even knew we would be so happy to find we had both come through. He brought me a little wireless set the other day. Between his coming and going to England (he is still with the forces) he always pops in for a chat and a smoke. "Boy" looks every so much more respectable, always clean shaven and he has lost that funny look in his eyes. His father came home last month, but he lost a foot when his ship was torpedoed, so he can't go back to sea. Jannie—or Tilly as she was called later I haven't seen yet. Ted—the dark girl with the black curls, went to a German camp from Vught, was liberated and sent to Sweden to recuperate. She is back in Rotterdam, fatter than ever! The girl you met at Cockie's house, "Riet," was caught the same day as we were and stayed at the Haagsche Veer for nearly three weeks. She proved a great friend and is living with me at present—although Ans has gone to the University at Leiden. Well I think that's all I can tell you about our friends. No, I am forgetting one of your oldest friends and my greatest help—Veenstra—at whose wedding you were invited. He was betrayed by one of his own men, found in a house and was shot while hiding in a cupboard. The traitor is standing his trial this week and will in all probability, be shot too. Veenstra's wife had a baby in January and Bertus's wife had one after Xmas I believe. Rumors about Bertus will have it that he is still alive, but other information says he was also shot at Vught with Jo Berlijn. When you add up all the good men who have fallen to the Huns, it's very difficult to be tolerant with the way they are being tried at various courts. There's one big difference to be considered—a victorious German, as you have met and we have known for 5 years—barks and snarls—a beaten German crawls in the dust! And that's the type the Allies meet. They have never seen them in their true form. And how can you make them understand anyhow!!

How many people have been in my house and carried things away I don't know—but a very small portion I got back from the homes of the girlfriends of the Germans. Of all the material things we have lost including practically all our clothes—I really regret the loss of my stamp collection. Putting all these silly tiny bits of paper together, you can almost say you love a hobby like that. It was one of the first questions Malcolm asked in his letters, "Have you still got our stamps and our South African photos?" Yes, I have still got them, being of no sales value.

Ever since you left us I have been thinking about the letter I was going to write to your mother one day and she is still going to get it—perhaps not quite as I hoped it would be—but I am not so pessimistic as she is. The world is really such a small place and Seattle is on the map so why should we not meet one day. I may find some work for the next 10 years (I prefer working for a living—no sitting at home and moaning for me) and after that I am going to follow my life's ambition and travel—TRAVEL—right round the world!

Yes, Jim dear—you'll have a portrait of all of us as soon as they can be made. Photographers don't take orders at present having no material, only for very special occasions. I had a very fine enlargement made of a P.B. photo of my husband—I am going to send you one too. Thank you for the snaps you sent of yourself, they are very good - but you have lost that lovely touch of naughtiness, what made your bonnie face so attractive. Just peeping round the corner and saying "-----?" I wish you were saying it just now. If you have talked to your mother about us for hours—I have done no less. It has been a good time darling—(I don't care if you snigger) and it has been my happiest time in those long 5 years of uphill fighting.

I will never get this letter finished—I can chatter on for hours and still not tell you all you want to know. Ans has gone to live in Leiden. She only comes home for weekends—we are great pals, have both gone through the same ordeal and come out the better for it. Sorry I cannot say the same about Ger. He has gone to the Hague where he was at school and lives with his prospective parents-in-laws. I have never heard from them or met them. Malcolm was home for 9 days, a very short time after 5 1/2 years of absence. But we can write letters and he writes food ones, (so do you—I hugged your last one—it made me really happy to get it). His hobby is music—he plays very well, and what he doesn't play himself, he buys on records. I do hope you two will meet one day. In Dec. he hopes to get his Officer's rank and with a bit of luck he may get billeted in Holland as liaison officer. In the meantime he had to sign for two years—so I really don't know when he'll be a naval architect. When do you expect to continue your studies? If you are going to be a K.L.M. pilot I'll have to go and live in Amsterdam, near the aerodrome! Just think of it.

Yes—an American officer called some weeks ago. He wouldn't say how he got our address. Now I know, but I'd like to see your face when you hear he's called Nathan! Because of the Jewish people we harbored he came and brought me a No.10 prisoners of war parcel. "It's a real BEAUTY madam" he said. And so it was. There was a tiny tin of coffee in it too and only this morning I treated myself to a cup of it. Opa and I are alone this weekend and he enjoyed it too. What else Mr. Nathan is going to do I don't know, but he insisted on "doing something" for me. All I wanted or want is a visum to go to England on short notice and not having to wait for months like so many people.

Jim dear, I must stop or the post won't take my letter for the Air Mail. You'll hear from me again soon. Kindest regards to your good people. All the very best to yourself - Your Jackie

---

A letter from Ans Jappe-Alberts

R'dam 5 Oct. 1945

Dear Jim

Only a few words from me, now you can't tell we forget you. We received your second letter just a week after the day you wrote it. I'm very pleased you were more joyful in your last one. I only want to say to "Cheer up". We do so too. The worst has come to the worst and we had to go over it.

I myself was never sorry and I know sure Father wasn't for what he and mams did. He liked you very much and I know you liked him. Don't make it difficult for yourself.

Malcolm has been home a week. Probably in December he will return again for a week or 10 days. Ger is in the Hague at school. I'm now at the University in Leiden and enjoy it very much. My study will last about six years.

I'm intended to complete it in England or in the U.S. if that is possible. Nice plans aren't they. The weekends I'm at home, mams and I are going to some concerts this winter. It is more difficult to finish a letter, than to begin. I once said "Good Luck", but now repeat it again "Good luck to you Jim!".

Ans

Two letters from Kees van den Engel

Rotterdam, 17 October 1945.

REF. C.H. v.d. Engel,
Breeplein 3a.

By Air Mail.

Lt. James H. Keeffe Jr.
3237 Hunter Blvd.
Seattle 44 Wash.
U.S.A.

Halloh Jim,

I was very glad to hear that you are safe and well at your base again. And I feel sorry about your capture by the S.D. in Antwerp.

Oh boy what a time was that crossing Rotterdam by cycle, streetcar and on foot. I preferred that time of fighting against the S.D.. and that helping of all kind of people, above this after-war-time. I am sorry to say, but there is something rotten here at the moment. The leaders of piece-time, who were afraid to fight and speak in war-time, are back again and with very great mouths. And the men of the onderground had to disappear [out] of the theatre as soon as possible. As you will understand we don't like that. I prefer to leave my county and look out for a job elsewhere.

As you has already heard of Ton, I was picked up by the S.D. on August the 25th. at Rotterdam. The boys who tried to liberate me from the police-office were 5 minutes too late. Very sorry indeed. I was arrested with a lot of P.B.'s and other papers and the S.D. expected that the "Knock Ploeg" would try to liberate me and therefore they immediately brought me to the Concentraciencamp Vught. They forgot to shot me, I stood on a list of people who were shot and they transported me with the other boys and girls of this camp on the 6th of September, as the allied forces came in Holland to an concentraciencamp in Germany called Oraniënburg-Sachsenhausen and there I was liberated by the

Russian Forces. They brought us to the Elbe-river and I was handed over to the American Forces. Oh boy, I was so glad to see your boys and to speak your language again and to see your very fine equipment. It was a bad time there boy, but I was still in live and that was the main thing. And now I am back in Holland, healthy but weak and completely undernourished. Don't mentioned boy, my parents will fatten up me again. And also my girlfriend Rie did. Hey boy, what about your girl-friend! I hope she is still in live too.

As you have probably heard of Ton, our battle against the "Moffen" has also in our organization in Rotterdam cost some victims e.o. Uncle Berlijn, Mr. Jappe-Alberts, Bertus, Folkert Elsinga (the son of the big boss) and Mrs. Broekhuizen.

I heard from Ton the members of the Gestapo in Antwerp knew my Christian name. Do you perhaps know how that in the world is possible?

I hope to receive a letter from you soon an until then, Jim, best   s.o.s
BEST greetings and so long.

> I hope to see you later.
> Kees vd Engel

> Rotterdam, 30 November 1945.

Dear Jim,

So sorry that I didn't write you back immediately after receiving your letter, but as you has probably seen I am engaged with Marijke (Rie) and the preparations costed me a lot of time, next time better, George.

I've been anxiously awaiting a letter from you. I thought that you still knew my address until Mrs. Jappe Alberts told me you asked her my address and at last I received your letter. So many thanks for the letter and photo's.

You didn't write if you still enjoy the Army Air Forces or not. Or what you gonna do in the last case, to study or to work.

For the matter of looking into the possibility of coming to the States I can assure you if there is a possibility to find a good job for me in your country, I come immediately. As you already know it's my heart's desire.

I asked the big boss (Theo) /best wishes from him/ for a P.B. for you and he promised me to send me one as soon as possible. So I shall prepare that P.B. as I once made you, the same name and so on and enclose it in the next letter.

To eat up again I took a holiday of about 2 months. 1 month of that holiday I was sailing with Marijke and my friend Bram and his girlfriend on the "Brasemermeet" near Leiden. The weather was very fine for sailing, sunny and windy. As you perhaps on the enclosed photo's will see we had a very fine boat. We in Holland call it a "Pampus" and 18 m2 sailing-yacht. A typical Dutch water landscape, with these clouds and that windmill, isn't it? It was wonderfull.

You wrote about your bombers, how majestically beautifull they looked as they came over to bomb. I saw them often when they came over and bombed Berlin about 40 miles of our camp. It was beautifull indeed and I shall not forget it my whole live either. But when I think of these bombardments, I think of that time the German fighters intercepted the last formation of about 14 planes and shot down 12 of them. It was a terrible view and I could cry of fury. I thought of that time you were over Germany, and your formation was intercept by the German fighters too and several of your friends were shot down.

After the war I flew from Halle-Leipzig to Eindhoven in an D.C. 3, transport-plane. I saw a lot of destroyed towns e.o. Duisburg and Keulen.

What I think of the Russian troops I encountered?

Individual most of the Russian soldiers are good people, but not so very clever. As an army however they are wild, disordered and without discipline. When I was liberated I spook to an American soldier, who was flighted off a camp of prisoners of war. He said I cannot rather imagine that these undisciplinable forces have booked such successes. Of course I cannot compare them to the American forces or it must be of their equipment but that's American material too.

We, in Holland, are under the jurisdiction of the Canadian Forces and what I think of them? That's easy to say. I am fond of the Americans and I don't like the Englishmen and the Canadians are between them.

If you has a pair of shoes that fits me, it will be very fine. We, in Holland, cannot buy shoes and clothing. And as a matter of fact, after my prison-time, (the S.D. stole the whole business) I have no more.

The Dutch size of my shoes is 43 that's, I mean the American size 9 1/2. As I have breath foot I suppose it's your size 9 1/2 C. (s.o.s)

Give my heartiest regards to your entire family, Jim, and please write me often and send me a lot of photo's of yourself, your plane, motorcar, motorcycle, sailing yacht e.o., e.o. I am sorry I havnt a photo of myself.

Until next time, then, so long and I hope to see you later.

Kees.

————

From Mrs. Jappe-Alberts

12th Dec. 1945

My Dearest Jim!

What am I to say to you about the wonderful gifts we received all within 10 days! I have just finished my letter to your mother—trying to make her understand how touched we were, when opening the parcel and Christmas hose—but I am afraid I have made a very poor job of it. When I got word from the Holland America Line about the case I still didn't think it came from you-but having to pass through the customs I was handed the list of articles and then saw the name of the sender. Well, I got a lump in my throat and did not care whether anyone saw me bring out my hankie or not. Thank you Jim darling! And how to thank you for the beautiful photograph!

It's the very smile I used to look for when I answered your ring at the door, looking up from downstairs before you dashed up. It brings back lots of happy moments, as I am sure you felt often, while you were with us and could banish your worries for a while. The first snapshots you sent were very good indeed—but my first remark was—he looks a lot older. Since I have seen the prison camp snaps it is quite easy to understand what made you look so serious. If some of the people who lead the proceedings at Neurenberg had gone through a similar ordeal, they wouldn't waste so much time on talking. Did the "huns" talk when they caught our men? I don't think you will ever forget your close contact with German methods, will you! And that brings me to your letter of 5 November. It's lovely to have letters reach their destination in about 10 days. It does bring the farthest friends so near. I did as you told me to—cut off the few bottom lines. Not that there is any chance of Ton and Cocky seeing the letter. I hate to say it, but we are not very friendly, especially with Ton. It sounds like old women's gossip, but I asked him to reconsider his price, when he charged me 125 guilders just to make a coat for Ans—it was my own material and lining. All he had to say was—I could pay by installments if that suited me better! I was raving mad! Telling me to pay by installments is nothing short of an insult. The order was placed before 5th Dec, at a time when we could reckon on a certain income, but considering the lucky escape he had, he might have modified his price. He dodges me—that's why I do not see him.

About answering letters promptly—you are a splendid correspondent. But writing has to be a pleasure not a duty—so any time you take a little while before answering will not be misunderstood—and I hope you will apply the same rule to my writing.

Riet is the girl who was going to take you to Linburg. She remembers you quite well. Kapelaan Haanen has been transferred to Amsterdam—and is quite well.

Last week I went to see "dude" and his wife and Heleendje. They couldn't make me stay for even one night because I don't fancy their company for any length of time. They are going to Palestine as soon as possible, and I wish them luck!

The two airplane drawings were taken down after you left. The police never saw them. The maps I had taken to the safe - nobody even looked there. Don't get all sorts of ideas into your head dear. I am looking in an entirely different direction. It is almost certain that a de Groot has opened his mouth. He knew a lot of pilots, because he paid the landlords or host and where there was nothing for him to be made out of you—he demanded a lump sum, sheer blackmail. He was put out of the way by the underground before May. Did you have a pair of compasses? The SD put in on the table when I was interrogated the first time - but I took no notice.

I am wearing the wings as I suppose you wanted me to. When turning the cute little bussom bag out, the first thing I spotted was the "bar" and wings. I am awfully pleased with both. One cannot help being a bit pessimistic about the next war. No nation starts again in the very near future, but we are almost certain to be in the thick of it within the next ten years. Are you going back to the University? Has aviation lost some of its glory or will you consider a pilot job with one of the Trans Atlantic Line Co.? In your next letter tell me something about Pat—She does look very young—we all like the tiny photo best. She will be happy to have you safely home again. Have your brothers come through alright?

And to finish something about stamps. I am enclosing a complete set of Child Welfare stamps, and the set on the envelop you should keep too. Maybe there is one amongst you friends who'd like to have them and care to part with some American stamps. You know they have taken my whole collection but for Malcolm's sake I'll start again. He passed his officers exam and will probably get indefinite leave. He will be home any day after Sunday. That's all for today. The very best for 1946. May all your wishes come true.

Always yours — Jackie

Letter from Kees van den Engel

Rotterdam, 30 November 1946.

Dear Jim,

As I didn't hear anything from you the last monthes, I supposed that my letter of the 4th of May had gone lost. In that letter I enclosed viz. a P.B. and I thought that could be the reason you didn't receive it.

Now I heard from Mrs. Jappe Alberts that you indeed didn't receive my letter. Well, boy, that's a pity. First you didn't know if I had received your very fine parcel and second your P.B. has gone lost and I think it better not to try it again just now.

In your last letter you wrote that you should send a parcel. But I was very surprised to receive such a big and fine parcel. Well George, I thank you from the bottom of my heart too from Maryke and my parents. The foodstuff was delicious and the shoes fit me excellent, so that I can assure you, you become a famous engineer.

My congratulations!!

In my above mentioned letter I wrote you what I found out for you by K.L.M. As I heard from Mrs. Jappe Alberts she informed you about this matter, I can drop this point of your questions. There is only one thing in this connection I wish to draw your attention to viz. the words of the sub-manager when I told him that there was an American pilot who wants to join the K.L.M.. He said: "That's fine, we like to fly with American pilots, they are, except the Dutch, the best in the world." Hé boy, what do you think about that. Ha-ha-ha!!! What about "God's own Country" C'est toujours la même chanson, n'cest-ce pas.

For some weeks I was at Mrs. Van Rhijn (my landlady). You know perhaps I brought you there one sunny Sunday morning when American fighters came over on their way to Germany. It was my dive-address in a beautiful house with garden in the Eastern part of our town. She gave me enclosed pictures to send to you with her best greetings. Her husband was a prisoner of war, as you perhaps know. He returned from Germany, went to the States for military re-training and now joins the Dutch Army again in our India as colonel of the Mariniers (sea-soldiers). I must say Halloh to you from "the big boss" and his family (with his other son and daughter all is o.k.)

I must say halloh too from Mr. Broekhuizen (as you already know his wife died in a concentration-camp). He would be pleased to receive a letter from you. His address is again Mr. A. Broekhuizen, Oostzeedijk 130, Rotterdam.

The box of things you mentioned in your letter has been found by the S.D. at the house of Mr. Elsinga (the big boss). The events leading to that fact are, that in the house there was an operating secret sender. The Germans sounded that sender and at last found the whole stuff. You may say that it was very dangerous a P.B.-Section and an operating sender in the same house and which house. Indeed that was dangerous but don't forget that the Germans had to do a lot of things these last monthes and could impossible look for all the houses of undergrounders and moreover the people in generally was very afraid after all the executions of the past monthes so that it was rather difficult to find a house for such dangerous purposes. By this opportunity Folkert Elsinga was picked up and a few weeks later executed. So you see the box of things finally fell into the hands of the S.D. but not accordingly to my arrest.

I have been picked up on the street by members of the S.D., when I came, by cycle, from a meeting. They wanted to bring me to the police-office but as I had many dangerous papers in my pockets, (I got at the meeting a lot of P.B.'s, Ausweisen etc.) I didn't like to go with these jokers. So when we were on half the distance to that office I gave the fellow who cycled beside me a kick against his fore-wheel so that he fell on the ground and started to cycle for my life. The two fellows who cycled behind me began to shoot with their pistols and the bullets flow to every direction except in my body. After a few minutes there was a distance between us of about 50 m. so that they could no longer hit me. There is no doubt my escape-attempt would be succeeded if not a baker, who became nervous of the noice of the shooting, drove his car just for my cycle. That was the end. I fell on the ground and before I was on my feet again that jokers were too close to me to escape again.

Well I'm not yet married boy : Here in Holland it's a custom to engage first and after some time (some months, 1 or 2 year) to marry. So I like to marry next year. But I don't know if it is possible, for it's hardly impossible to get a house and I don't like to live with my parents-in-law or my own parents. (this is done aften at the moment). It's also very difficult to dress a house for carpets, curtains and all that stuff is not to obtain or so abnormal expensive that I don't wish to buy it for it.

Indeed I've a private job at a large warehouse - coldstorage - and forward-ing company with branch offices all over the world a.o. at New-York. It's a very interesting job. I often come on board of large cargo-vessels for the transship-ment or loading of the cargo, special grain, for I'm a grain-assistant.

Well George, I think I must close this letter for otherwise it becomes a book.

So until next time, best greeting from

Your pal,

Kees

Boy! Is there a garden at your house? Do you like tulipbulbs or something like that. Please tell me in your next letter and I shall ship you a lot of them.

K.

Kees refers to K.L.M. a couple of times, which is the Royal Dutch Airlines—Koninklijke Luchtvaart Maatschappij.

A letter from Cor Veth, sister of Marinus Veth (who helped row Lt. Keeffe to Dordrecht)

78 Noordhoek
Popendrecht, 4 April 1948.

Dear James.

I received your letter in a very good soundness and was very glad to heard what from you.

I translated your letter in the Dutch language what was he write in very good English or Americans so my parents also can read him. Also have I been by the man in whose rabbit hutch you had that first afternoon. He cannot understood that you was in live.

James that boy who was your gunner and killed in the airplane while you were over Germany, was that K. J. Miller Army-number 37160335? He is buried in Margraten (Limburg - Holland) now. Can you call his adress of his parents? so that I also can write to her, and when they will have a photo of his graf so can I made him.

When you willing shall I made also a photo from the place were has fallen your airplane.

I have been on that place on the 2nd Taasday next.

You asked me also about Dr. Lemoine and the advocate in Dordrecht. They are very well. The adress of Dr. Lemoine is Cortgene Alblasserdam and that from the advocate is E. A. Gomm, notaries, Varkenmarkt te Dordrecht.

The Air Force ring have we still and I also - a wool tee from one of the boys who are helped by my sisters in Voud Alblas. James may we hold the ring, he was from Marinus and therefore have they much more worth for us.

Can you understand my letter, I learned English from September 1947 and before that time I have nothing heard then speak from the Canadians.

And now what from Marinus. We have still nothing heard from him. We must now think that he is killed by the Germans. But then has he fallen in the fight for his country as like as Miller one of your gunners.

And now James go we in the fight too the Soviets too – it communism and even much bitterness as against the Germans in the years 1940-45. Here in Holland all the communisters have shut out of the town-councils have you read it the news-papers?

What have you much must endure after your time in Rotterdam what was that mankind yet bad, can you understand me?

James here in Holland where there also from that who colluded with the Germans and that was in every country we seen it now also with the communisters but I and many no most shall go in the fight against here.

Now I go end but write you me quick back! and give you answer on the questions?

"Look not to the wrongs."
It is write by a Dutch
boy, and not by an   Sincerely yours.
Englishman.   Cor Veth

A letter from J.J. van Dongen

Rotterdam, May 25th 1948

Dear James,

We were very pleasantly surprised this morning when we received your letter of the 21st inst. So you are back in the Ball club and besides on such a congenial task as recruiting greenhorns and travel around all over the West to that purpose. I had read about the seventy groups in the newspapers, which, though limited in size, give all world news very accurately. We can only appreciate the way in which Uncle Sam is again building up strength, for this is the only thing by which certain countries can be impressed. A further step will probably be a guarantee for the five Western Powers by the U.S.A. Nevertheless I don't believe in an imminent war as we must not forget that Russia was completely destroyed from the German frontier up to Moscou and there is every indication that reconstruction in that country is not progressing very rapidly. I must however admit that there are others of different opinion and should they prove right you might well have to make the same investigations on our part as you did in the case of Bennett, Dabney and Zesch.

We were indeed very pleased to learn that these airmen are still alive, which is a great satisfaction for us as we believed them dead long since. We are however completely at a loss to see that they never wrote a word about their experiences and have never replied to my letters. We wonder what may be the reason for this strange behaviour. Both my wife and I would be only too glad to hear that they are well and came through safely. So give them a firm kick in the pants when you locate them. And a bad mark for conduct.

After all your job won't be finished by recruiting airmen but you will have to look around for suitable airbases on this side of the Continent. So I am rather certain to see you here sooner or later. Peacetime-conditions in this country have much improved though practically everything, except shoes, is still on coupons especially meat, butter, sugar, cheese and clothing. Cigarets 60 a week and part of them are poor quality. The black-market value of the $ is about guilders 5 up to 7. I just paid Fl. 300,- for a new suit, which works out at about $115,- at the official rate of exchange. Everything costs about 2 or 3 times the pre-war price. Only the rent is unchanged and that is the source from which I derive my income. Since the liberation I have been working very hard for that life-assurance co. of which I am a manager and I daresay not without results. Taxes however are extravagant and pick the last flesh off our bones. Income-tax alone amounts to about one quarter of my income. So there is nor much left for pleasure or saving not to speak of travels to Switzerland and other countries.

This is election-year in Holland and the issue a modification in the constitution in order to make possible a so-called "Union" with Indonesia. Many people are very dissatisfied with the lack of strength demonstrated by the Government in handling that matter. As a whole I expect a slight turn to the right as the parties in Office (R.C. and social-democrats) are not strong enough by themselves to form the necessary two-third majority, and a decrease of the communist party who got 10% of the votes after the liberation from disgruntled citizens who could only express their anger in that way without being a member of that party. Polls will probably be by July 7th and the jubilee of queen Wilhelmina on August 31st, on which occasion she will resume her duties during one week. Her decision is a wise one as the pending issues will probably take years to be solved. My wife's youngest brother, a doctor, is still in Java together with an army of over 100,000 excellent men who hate to be idle and see the population in part of that island left to the mercy of hooligans paid by a bad republic.

Hope to hear—and see—more of you. So long !

sincerely, jj van Dongen

J.J. van DONGEN
Graaf Florisstraat 105
ROTTERDAM

Lt. Colonel James H. Keeffe, Jr. holding a model of a B-24 bomber painted with 389th Bomb Group colors. This photo was taken in 1962 when Lt. Col. Keeffe was teaching ROTC at Central Washington State College in Ellensburg, Wash. (Lt. Col. Keeffe collection)

Acknowledgments

When I first began this project to put my father's World War II story down on paper, I had no idea of what I was getting myself into. Nor did I have a clue as to the places I would go, the people I would meet, the friends I would make and the stories I would uncover. I wish to thank and express my utmost gratitude to everyone who has helped make this book a success.

First and foremost, I thank my father. His nearly total recall was the fertile ground from which sprang countless vivid details of people, places, dates, and circumstances. And his patience over the years answering the countless questions I'd come up with at all hours of the day, never faltered. Thank you Dad!

Research into and uncovering the behind-the-scenes facts and histories of the multitude of characters, organizations, situations, and locations became a labor that propelled me onto many cold trails. Without the help, enthusiastically given at every turn, of so many selfless individuals, much of my research would have fallen well short. I want to express my eternal gratitude to the following people:

From the Netherlands: Alexander Tuinhout—for your amazing help with digging into Dutch and Belgium archives, for translating Dutch and German, and for your research into so many topics. Mark Lubbers—to think that a young brave Dutch Resistance boy named Folkert Elsinga would bring us together half way around the world and sixty-five years after his murder by the Germans. Thank you for explaining the Dutch Resistance organizations so well and for photos of various resistance members. Honors to your grandfather who was in the Resistance. For other invaluable research, information and/or translations, and photos, thank you Rene van Heijningen, Co Maarschalkerweerd, Hans Budde,

Ben van Drogenbroek, Iris Lamers-Hoogeweegen, Eduard Hoogeweegen, Ron Raajmakers, Hanneke Hollander-Doyle, Pieter van Wijngaarden, Frank van den Engel, Cees van den Engel, Hans van den Engel, Ellen Brok, Els van der Meer, and Jasper and Eveline of Delfshaven.

From Belgium: Eduard Reniere.

From Germany: Werner Schwarz and Claudio Becker.

From Canada: A special thank you to Michael Moores Leblanc, a research-er who laboriously pieced together the workings of the notorious KLM Line.

From the USA: Marilyn Jeffers Walton—what would I have done without you! From your first e-mail saying "Hi," to your wonderful friendship, to the time we shared in Poland and Germany walking the route our fathers took so many years before, to your great editing skills and advice with grammar and punctuation. You were the first to attack and hack your way through my mess and wore out numerous comma keys on your keyboard. Without your help, I never would have been able to turn a massive written interview into anything resembling a readable story. Your energy, encouragements, and crack-up humor shored up many weary hours I spent stuck in one hole after another.

The next person I wish to thank, who poured soul and spirit into editing, is my sister Kerry Radley. Bless you for working your way through the manuscript time after time. Next, I wish to thank Ruth Cook. Ruth, your great editing and advice on foreshadowing and grammar really helped to clear up the confusion I found myself in many times. More editors and proofers followed Ruth, each one adding their skills in fine tuning and uncovering the elusive mistakes that never seem to completely go away. Thanks to Sheryl Stebbins, my brother Kevin, Mississippi John Lewis, Dave Hodel, and Sherrill Carlson. Any and all goofs that are still in the final product, I take full responsibility for. (I wish there was no such thing as a comma!)

A special thank you to all those who shared information about members of their own families who served in WWII, many of whom were POWs in the same camps as my dad: Stowe Keller, Patricia Moulton, Val Burgess, Jim Lankford, Lezlie Burda Beach, Ray Sisson, and Jim Reeves..

To all who gave me permission to use material from their books and websites, especially photos, thank you very much!: Mark Copeland, Mark Brotherton, Brian Wickham, Jon Moran, Paul Wilson, Brad Peters and Jan Ross, and Arthur Durand.

To those who helped organize my labor, the layout and design of the book, and getting it to press and beyond: Jennifer McCord, Jeanie James—who had the difficult job of laying everything out, Kent Sturgis, and Robert Cronan. Wonderful job y'all. My deepest gratitude.

Much thanks and appreciation to Kelsey McMillan, the awesome official historian for the 389th Bomb Group. Kelsey, your efforts and dedication to the 389th are forever appreciated.

And finally, I want to express my most heart-felt gratitude to **my wife, Paula, and daughter, Reilly.** You put up with days, weeks, months, and years of, "Well, I'm heading back upstairs now to the keyboard. See you later— I've got lots to do." You put up with a lot of missing time together, yet you were always gracious about it. Paula, even though you were joking around when you said, "I need to find a 12-step program for wives of writers," I knew you were telling me the truth. Thank you for allowing me to do what I needed to do.

I know that I have missed some fine people who gave their time and memories to this project. I thank you in my heart and apologize if I forgot to mention you personally. You know who you are and I want you to know that I am grateful for your help.

Index

Page numbers for photographs are in **bold**

—A—

—B—

—C—

—G—

—H—

—J—

—L—

—M—

—W—

—Y—

—Z—

About the Authors

James H. Keeffe III, (left) eldest son of James H. Keeffe Jr., spent his early years traveling the world with his military family. He has been working in IT data networking for the last eighteen years for Group Health Cooperative. He resides in Fall City, Washington, with his wife Paula and his daughter Reilly.

James H. Keeffe Jr., a WWII and Korean War veteran, received his degree in Meteorology at UCLA. During his twenty-two years in the Air Force, he was a pilot, weatherman, and instructor. He lives in Bellevue, Washington, with his wife Sandy. They have six children and many grandchildren.